kwayask ê-kî-pê-kiskinowâpahtihicik
Their Example Showed Me the Way

Emma and Joseph Minde, c.1927

kwayask
ê-kî-pê-kiskinowâpahtihicik

Their Example
Showed Me the Way

A Cree Woman's Life Shaped by Two Cultures

Told by Emma Minde

Edited, translated and with a glossary by
Freda Ahenakew & H.C. Wolfart

 The University of Alberta Press

Published by
The University of Alberta Press
Ring House 2
Edmonton, Alberta, Canada T6G 2E1

Copyright © The University of Alberta Press 1997
5 4 3 2
ISBN 0–88864–291–1

Canadian Cataloguing in Publication Data
Minde, Emma, 1907–
  Kwayask ê-kî-pê-kiskinowâpahtihicik = Their example showed
  me the way

  Includes bibliographical references.
  Text in Cree and English.
  ISBN 0–88864–291–1

  1. Minde, Emma, 1907– 2. Cree women—Alberta—Hobbema—
Biography. 3. Minde family. 4. Hobbema (Alta.)—Biography.
I. Ahenakew, Freda, 1932– II. Wolfart, H. Christoph, 1943–
III. Title. IV. Title: Their example showed me the way.
E99.C88M56 1997   971.23'3   C97–911013–0

**All royalties from the sale of this book revert to the publication fund
of the Algonquian Text Society**

∞ Printed on acid-free paper.

Printed and bound in Canada by Friesens, Altona, Manitoba.

Contents

Preface

The personal reminiscences which Emma Minde recorded for Freda Ahenakew in June 1988 offer rare insights into a life history guided by two powerful forces: the traditional world of the Plains Cree and the Catholic missions with their boarding-schools, designed to re-make their charges entirely.

Rarely has the interplay of these two world views — often in conflict, but often also, it seems, very much in harmony with one another —been sketched so eloquently as in Emma Minde's autobiography.

Thanks are due above all to Mrs. Emma Minde, who gave this *âcimowin* to Freda Ahenakew to publish, and also to Mrs. Theresa Wildcat, her daughter, who helped with all the practical arrangements and approvals and, especially, provided the family photographs which illustrate this book.

The text is presented in its original Cree form, with a translation into English on facing pages. For technical advice and support we are, as always, indebted to our colleagues in the Cree Language Project at the University of Manitoba, especially Arden Ogg. Without the travel and infrastructure support provided at various times by the Social Sciences and Humanities Research Council of Canada, the University of Manitoba Research Board and the Faculty of Arts at the University of Manitoba, the laborious task of transcribing, analysing and editing the audio recordings and preparing the translation and the glossaries would have taken even longer.

The publication of this book is made possible by subsidies from the Miyo-Wâhkôhtowin Community Education Authority at Hobbema and the Multiculturalism Program of the Department of Canadian Heritage, which are hereby gratefully acknowledged.

FA & HCW

The Education of a Cree Woman

H.C. Wolfart

Emma Minde's portraits of the family into which she was given in marriage sixty years earlier are instructive and touching at once. They show
us a young woman obediently but tearfully leaving her home at Saddle
Lake to join a new and, to her, completely strange household at
Hobbema — comprising not only a young husband she has yet to meet,
but also four powerful adults who will henceforth shape her life: her
husband's parents, Mary-Jane and Dan Minde, and Dan Minde's
younger brother Sam and his wife Mary.

While the Minde brothers are well-known figures in the history of
Alberta during the mid-twentieth century — having been among the
founders in 1944 of the Indian Association of Alberta — the reminiscences of Emma Minde throw fresh light on an aspect of their political
lives that is often neglected: the fact that their public work was heavily
dependent on the active support of their strong-willed wives.

The education which the newly arrived wife of Joseph Minde
received in the households of her mother-in-law and Mary Minde was
built on obedience, hard work and a firmly-held set of beliefs. Seen as
essential preparation for a life of uncertainty and rapid change, hard-
ship and constant struggle, these are the virtues that pervade the text.
Some of the specific life skills, both ancient and modern, are also
sketched from the perspective of a woman's primary responsibilities,
which focus on the integrity of the family and the importance of planning ahead.

Mrs. Emma Minde, c.1988

The reminiscences of Emma Minde are at their most poignant when
she describes the arranged marriage into which she was given — and
then repeats much the same account for Mary-Jane Minde and
Mary Minde, evidently her most important teachers in what it took to
become a resourceful and self-reliant woman.

IF THERE IS A SINGLE FEATURE that defines Emma Minde's autobiography, it is her relationship with her two 'mothers-in-law' — her husband's mother and his aunt, the wife of her husband's father's brother.

The relationship between the young wife and these two older women lies at the heart of the book. No terminological distinction is made between the two models, who are treated as equal in status and importance. They are both called *nisikos* 'my father's sister, my mother's brother's wife; my mother-in-law, my father-in-law's brother's wife', and this lack of differentiation further appears to be reflected in the indiscriminate use, in English, of the term *Mrs. Minde*.

Her mother-in-law may well be the most important person in a young woman's life — at least as important, from the day of marriage onward, as her own mother. At the time, of course, she may seem even more important if the bride joins her husband in a faraway place, where she finds herself among strangers.

The teaching rôle of the mother-in-law covers the entire range of human life; as is so movingly recalled by Glecia Bear (in her chapter on 'A Woman's Life' in *kôhkominawak otâcimowiniwâwa / Our Grandmothers' Lives, As Told in Their Own Words*, told by Glecia Bear *et al.*, edited and translated by Freda Ahenakew & H.C. Wolfart, Saskatoon, 1992), the purview of the young wife's dependence may even include instruction about the basic facts of human biology.

The relationship between sisters-in-law (who under cross-cousin marriage were, of course, also the daughters of siblings) is of similar importance, and the narrative offers eloquent testimony of this. But the dominant figures in Emma Minde's life were clearly her seniors, Mary-Jane and Mary Minde.

Filial piety apart, the bond between these three women, as illustrated in the Minde reminiscences, will stand as a lasting monument to female solidarity.

Two Worlds, One Life

On the North Saskatchewan, the world into which Emma Minde had been born in 1907 differed fundamentally from that of the late twentieth century. The contrast between the teams of horses or oxen of that day and the air-conditioned, digitally-audioed farm machinery of the present is deceptive — when Emma Minde was a child, her extended family still included old men who had themselves hunted buffalo or crossed the prairies on foot, seeking fame and horses in warfare with

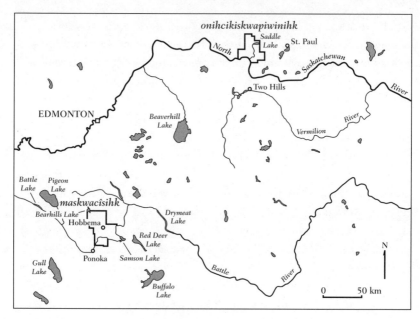

The North Saskatchewan and Battle River region

the Blackfoot. At the same time, the early twentieth century was marked by intense missionary activities by Catholics and others who entertained little doubt that their efforts were noble and wholly in the interest of those they sought to convert and educate in the new way of life.

Emma Minde (née Memnook) was born at *onihcikiskwapiwinihk*, also known as *Saddle Lake*, a large reserve on the north bank of the North Saskatchewan River (roughly 200 km downstream of Edmonton, due north of the settlement of Brosseau, formerly St-Paul-des-Cris, and the small town of Two Hills).

She left her own family behind in 1927, when the parents of Joseph Minde, her future husband, came to fetch her and took her back to *maskwacîsihk*, sometimes translated as 'Bear Hills' (or also 'Bear's Hill') but commonly referred to as *Hobbema* (ca. 80 km south of Edmonton). There, in an area generally to the northwest of Samson Lake, the four reserves located largely on the north bank of the Battle River faithfully reflect the competitive history of Christian missions on the northern plains. The efforts of the early Methodists (most prominently R.T. Rundle, who by 1850 had established a mission at Pigeon Lake, not far upstream) are still measurable on Samson and Montana Reserves (where in 1939 Catholics reportedly accounted for 441 and 49, or 70% and 61%, in a total population of 633 and 81, respectively); conversely, Ermineskin and Louis Bull Reserves (with populations of 331 and 148 in 1939) are reported to have been almost exclusively Roman Catholic.

The establishment of a permanent Roman Catholic mission at *maskwacîsihk* came relatively late (with Hippolyte Beillevaire, a secular priest, arriving in 1881 but soon moving downstream to the Laboucane Métis settlement and returning only for occasional visits); but once the Oblates had taken over (in 1884, with P. Constantine Scollon staying only a few months but, crucially, P. Victorin Gabillon remaining *in situ* for more than a decade), they soon began a day school (1887), which by 1897 had become a boarding-school run by the Soeurs de l'Assomption de la Sainte-Vièrge of Nicolet, Québec.

Once institutionalised, the Roman Catholic presence became firmly entrenched at Hobbema — the published record mentions, for example, a pilgrimage to Cap-de-la-Madeleine, Québec in 1954, with the party including Mrs. Dan Minde, Mrs. Joseph Minde, Mrs. Sam Minde and Miss Theresa Minde. But the spoken narrative of Emma Minde (even though it does not include an account of this journey) still provides the strongest evidence throughout of the Catholic fact.

THE ELDER MINDES who had such a profound influence on the young woman brought to Ermineskin's reserve to marry their son and nephew are presented in loving detail (as, of course, is her husband, Joseph Minde).

In full accordance with Cree tradition, Emma Minde and her husband began their married life in the household of his parents. By the same general pattern, Mary Minde and her husband Sam had also at first lived at his older brother's house.

The elder of the two was Daniel Minde, usually called Dan Minde, whose Cree name was *kâ-mahihkani-pimohtêw*. Mary-Jane (née *onâcowêsis*) was his second wife — his first, Celina, had died when their son Joseph was three years old — and Emma Minde never tires of singing the virtues of this step-mother and her infinite kindness towards her step-son. (Many years later, as Emma Minde told Freda Ahenakew on another occasion, Mary-Jane and Dan Minde were to

The family of Mary-Jane and Dan Minde
left to right, sitting: Daniel Minde, Joseph (son), Justine (daughter), Mary-Jane Minde
(second wife); standing: Sophie (daughter), Julie (daughter)

play a similarly decisive rôle in the upbringing of their youngest daughter's son, Wilton Littlechild M.P.) Mary-Jane Minde was younger than her sister-in-law, Mary Minde.

The Cree name of Sam Minde was *okikocêsîs*. His widow, Mary Minde, died in April 1988, not long before this text was recorded, at the age of ninety-five.

The Cree names of Mary-Jane and Mary Minde are not given in the narrative; instead, both are frequently referred to, with obvious deference, as *Mrs. Minde*. Neither is there any mention of the Minde brothers' mother (whose Cree name was *mâmitonêyihcikan*). Dan and Sam also had an older brother, *kayâsiyâkan*; their sister, the eldest, was called *wâpanohtêw*.

The focus of this text is clearly on the Mindes of *maskwacîsihk*. The narrator tells us nothing about her own parents, about her brothers and sisters or about her childhood and youth. The only thing she reveals about her mother is that she had come from Onion Lake and that she, too, had been given away into an arranged marriage.

IN TENOR AND PERSPECTIVE, the narrative of Emma Minde is above all autobiographical; to a lesser extent it is also historical. It is further interspersed throughout with expository stretches attending to traditional matters and with didactic passages which occasionally border on the homiletic.

Emma Minde's reminiscences are classical in form; within the overall genre of the *âcimowin*, the factual account, she alternates between the autobiographical text or *âcimisowin* and the counselling text or *kakêskihkêmowin* (*cf.* Wolfart & Carroll 1982, Ahenakew & Wolfart 1987).

In all of this, the degree to which traditional Cree beliefs and the teachings of the Roman Catholic church seem to have become integrated one into the other seems extraordinary.

To Watch and to Listen

Emma Minde's reminiscences are permeated by the paramount importance of teaching the young, expressed in a profusion of terms for advice and counsel, for teaching and parental control:

kakêskim– VTA 'counsel s.o., preach at s.o.'
kakêskimiso– VAI 'counsel oneself'
kakêskihkêmo– VAI 'counsel people, preach at people'
miyo-kakêskihkêmowin– NI 'good counselling, good preaching'

sîhkim– VTA 'urge s.o. by speech'
sîhkiskaw– VTA 'urge s.o. bodily'

kitahamaw– VTA 'advise s.o. against (it/him)'

kîhkâm– VTA 'scold s.o.'

itâspinêm– VTA 'call s.o. thus in anger, angrily call s.o. such a name, thus scold s.o. in anger'

kiskinohamaw– VTA 'teach s.o., teach (it) to s.o.'
kiskinohamâkê– VAI 'teach things'
kiskinohamâso– VAI 'teach oneself'
kiskinohamâto– VAI 'teach one another'

kiskinowâpam– VTA 'watch s.o.'s example'
kiskinowâpahtih– VTA 'teach s.o. by example'
kiskinowâpahtihiwê– VAI 'teach people by example'

Despite the obvious importance of learning by example, these terms of counsel and instruction, which seem equally common in traditional and Christian discourse, indicate that a great deal of teaching takes the form of urging and lecturing, warning and scolding.

THE VALUES BEING TAUGHT prominently include respect for the aged and charity towards those who cannot help themselves. Leadership is characterised further by the willingness to intercede on behalf of one's people.

Emma Minde is firmly committed to the values of Roman Catholic education, and she expresses nothing but praise for the accomplishments of Roman Catholic boarding-schools. No mention is made of any of the problems that appear to have been a systemic trait of residential schools for much of the twentieth century; instead, her narrative is explicitly laudatory and expansive about those aspects of Roman Catholic education which are seen as positive. Deference and obedience, hard work and devotion to duty are essential features of a value system, typically acquired at boarding-school, which she regards as the foundation of a proper life.

IN EMMA MINDE'S WORLD VIEW and, presumably, in her life experience, transcendental values are tightly linked to practical competence. In discussing the division of labour between men and women and the traditional skills that have been disappearing more and more rapidly, she stresses the virtue of self-reliance, of being in control to the extent that natural circumstances permit and, in particular, the crucial importance of planning ahead, each year, for the severe winter.

Industry and cleanliness around the house are taken for granted as an integral part of a woman's duties as taught in a Catholic boarding-school. A wide range of household practices are surveyed, from sewing techniques and beadwork design to culinary specialties, but rarely discussed in detail.

Doing the laundry at the slough is one activity which Emma Minde treats less cursorily, and her tale is a welcome complement to Rosa Longneck's account (in chapter 9 of Bear *et al.* 1992) of soap-making — a commonplace task, to be sure, but transcended by an extraordinarily lively and well-presented narrative of how it is done and how she herself used to do it.

The most remarkable report, ironically of a wholly innovative technology, is Emma Minde's description of how the girls of a Roman Catholic boarding-school in the 1920s would produce woollen stockings, first knitting them by hand and then mass-producing them by a combination of simple machinery and handiwork.

Throughout, wifely loyalty ranks high among the virtues extolled in this text; it is memorably illustrated in the vignette of Dan Minde being taught to read, as an adult and a chief, by his second wife.

RESPECT FOR ONE'S ELDERS is a dominant theme in Cree education, and Emma Minde relies on a rich choice of terms for its expression, *e.g.*,

kihcêyim– VTA 'think highly of s.o.'
ayiwâkêyim– VTA 'think more of s.o., regard s.o. more highly'

manâcim– VTA 'speak to s.o. with respect, speak of s.o. with respect'
manâcih– VTA 'treat s.o. with respect'

She employs three pairs of stems to speak about the care and love with which people should treat one another:

kitimâkêyim– VTA 'feel pity towards s.o., be kind to s.o., love s.o.'
kitimâkinaw– VTA 'take pity upon s.o., lovingly tend s.o.'

kanawêyim– VTA 'look after s.o., take care of s.o.'
kanawâpam– VTA 'look at s.o.; look after s.o.'

pamih– VTA 'tend to s.o., look after s.o.'
pamin– VTA 'tend to s.o., look after s.o. (with one's hands)'

Ranging from character and attitude to the purely practical, these six are in turn embedded in sets of closely related terms, *e.g.*,

pamih– VTA 'tend to s.o., look after s.o.'
  pamihiso– VAI 'tend oneself, look after oneself'
  pamihtamaw– VTA 'tend to (it/him) for s.o., look after (it/him)
    for s.o.'
  pamihtamâso– VAI 'tend to (it/him) for or by oneself, look after
    (it/him) for or by oneself'.

Mere lists of abstract stems, however, pale beside the complex inter-play of actual, inflected verb forms in their text sequence. In relating the marriage of Mary-Jane Minde, for example, Emma Minde begins with a set of four verbs in which two instances of the stem *pamih–* constitute an outer layer enclosing an inner pair of instances of the stem *kitimâkêyim–* :

STEM			SUBJECT
A	*ka-miyo-pamihikot* 'that he would provide well for her'	A
B	*ka-kitimâkêyimik* 'he will care for you'	A
B	*ê-kî-kitimâkêyimât* 'she loved him'	B
A	*kwayask ê-kî-pamihât* 'she looked after him properly'	B

While the choice of stems exhibits one pattern (represented schemati-cally by ABBA), the agentive subjects alternate in another (schematically AABB), with the prospective husband given grammatical prominence in the first two verb forms, and the prospective wife in the last two; the two patterns crosscut each other.

Elaborate figures of repetition and variation of terms for care and love are conspicuous throughout this passage (in chapter v, section 43), which ends with eloquent praise for Emma Minde's sister-in-law Sophie and her devoted care for Chief Ermineskin's widow:

> . . . , *ayiwâk êwako ê-kî-kitimâkêyimit,*
> . . . , *ê-kî-kitimâkêyimât ayisiyiniwa,*
> *ê-kî-kitimâkêyimât kêhtê-aya;*
> *pêyak mâna nôtokwêsiwa mîn ê-kî-kanawêyimât*
>   *ê-kî-kitimâkêyimât.* (EM43)
> ' . . . , she especially used to love me,
>   . . . , she loved people,
>   she loved old people;
>   she also used to keep one old lady,
>   lovingly.'

RELIANCE ON INTERCESSION is another central domain where it would be forbiddingly difficult to disentangle the pre-Christian and Catholic strands.

The rôle of advocacy in a Cree context is beautifully laid out in the story which Emma Minde (who by her marriage herself became a member of the Ermineskin band) relates of the making of a chief. As Dan Minde is trained for his future rôle as a leader, he is taught one obligation above all others: to take up for his people, to intercede for them with the outside authorities, to serve as their advocate.

The Cree terms which have come into use as translations of English legal terms, especially in the field of criminal justice, guilt and innocence, differ dramatically from their English models in that most of them include a presupposition of guilt; they have a built-in sense, which may well reflect the realities of a small-scale, band-level society, that to be accused is to be guilty.

In one of the highlights of the text (in chapter v, section 44), Emma Minde reports the counselling which Dan Minde, while still a young man, received from the old chief *k-ôsihkosiwayâniw*, more widely known as *Ermineskin* — an account further confirmed and authenticated by reference to *oscikwânis*, Ermineskin's widow, who was personally known to the narrator since she had been kept in her old age by Emma Minde's sister-in-law.

We are told of the old chief's prophesy that Dan Minde, too, would some day become chief and we are then given his instructions about the foremost duty of a chief: "to take up for his people" (with the term *otiyinîma* 'his people' here referring to the people in his charge). The injunction is illustrated in the context of the Anglo-Canadian legal system, which is seen from a perspective not of right or wrong, guilt or innocence, but of the need for intercession and grace.

This fundamental lack of agreement between the adversary system of Anglo-Saxon justice and the Cree system, where the accused begs for mercy (and which shows remarkable similarities to the theology of the New Testament), results in a monumental lack of understanding — and rarely has the Cree system of suing for leniency been put more clearly and more eloquently than in Emma Minde's account of how Dan Minde was instructed in his chiefly duties by Ermineskin.

New Terms, Old Form

While Emma Minde's autobiographical narrative is heavily Catholic in inspiration, its literary form belongs to a genre of *âcimowin*-texts in which narrative stretches are interspersed with didactic or homiletic passages.

Throughout her text, Emma Minde relies on subtle variations in the formation of verb stems to create the dense texture typical of literary texts in Cree. The stem *wîkim–*, for instance, together with other stems derived from it, constitutes a simple etymological set:

wîkim– VTA 'live with s.o.; be married to s.o.'
 kihci-wîkim– VTA 'be formally married to s.o.'
wîkihto– VAI 'live with one another, be married to one another'
 kihci-wîkihto– VAI 'be formally married to one another'.

In establishing such a set and then varying the elements and adding to them (the preverb *kihci*, for instance, with its overtones of ritual sanction), storytellers employ one of the most common figures of Cree rhetoric.

In Emma Minde's discourse, the set of textually linked stems, in fact, extends far beyond the four examples above. In terms of etymologically related elements alone we also find verb stems like

wîki– VAI 'live there, have one's home there'
    kihci-wîki– VAI 'live formally; live in residence'

and nouns like

wîkihtowin– NI 'living together, matrimony'
    kihci-wîkihtowin– NI 'formal marriage, Holy Matrimony'.

The semantic field further includes many stems which overlap with the above but also cover additional ranges of meaning, *e.g.,*

wîcêw– VTA 'accompany s.o., live with s.o.'
wîcêhto– VAI 'live with one another'

wîtokwêm– VTA 'share a dwelling with s.o., live with so.'

ayâ– VAI 'be there, live there'
wîc-âyâm– VTA 'live with s.o.'

Whether by accident or as a consequence of the perspective from which she tells her story, Emma Minde further uses the term *onâpêmi–* VAI 'have a husband, be married (as a woman)' while omitting the corresponding *wîwi–* VAI 'have a wife, be married (as a man)'.

In all the above examples, the use of the preverb particle *kihci* 'grand, formal; holy' is an overt sign of a Christian term; in others, the influence of English-language patterns, both linguistic and cultural, may be less obvious, as for instance in *otinito–* VAI 'take one another; marry each other'. There are certain subject areas in which Emma Minde seems to show a distinct preference for abstract nouns, *e.g.,*

kihci-wîkihtowin– NI 'formal marriage, Holy Matrimony'
iyisâhowin– NI 'resisting temptation'.

She also uses various turns of phrase which appear to be based on English models, such as the indirect question *tânitê k-êsi-kwêskîcik* 'where to turn' and the object-and-verb phrase *miyawâtamowin ê-nitonahkik* 'seeking fun' in

> . . . , *namôy kiskêyihtamwak tânitê k-êsi-kwêskîcik anima miyawâtamowin ê-nitonahkik.* (EM9)
> ' . . . , they don't know where to turn next in their search for amusement.'

or the metaphor suggesting that days might be 'lost' in

> *namôy ôhci-nakîw ka-mâh-minihkwêt, kîsikâwa ka-wanihtât,* . . . (EM28)
> 'He did not stop [in his work] to go drinking around, to lose whole days, . . . '

Despite the occasional loan translation, the phraseology of these remi-niscences is clearly traditional, and terms with an obvious Catholic overburden (though typically on a Cree base) such as *iyisâhowin–* NI 'resisting temptation' occur side by side with ordinary Cree expressions such as *êkâ kwayask ê-itâtisit* (EM65) 'because his character is evil'.

The established norms of Cree literary style prevail even where the subject matter may be thought of as purely Catholic. In the following example, both verb stems are marked (by the stem-final derivational suffix *-hto-*, which precedes the inflectional suffix *-t*) as reciprocal:

> . . . , *ayisiyiniw aya, kâ-kitimâkêyihtot kwayask kâ-wîkihtot.* (EM7)
> ' . . . , when people love one another and when they are properly married.'

While the rules of English grammar restrict reciprocal verbs to the plural form (*they love each other*, never *she loves each other* — which is why the translation of the above sentence into English has to be fairly free), the use of reciprocal verb stems in the singular form is a tell-tale sign of high rhetoric in Cree.

THE DEVOUTLY CATHOLIC content of this text is reflected in an exceptionally rich set of terms dealing with matters of doctrine and conduct. The interplay between the Cree virtue of hard work with the Catholic doctrine of good works is a fundamental part of Emma Minde's story.

A truly noteworthy pattern is the re-use of ordinary and traditional terms in specifically Christian senses, *e.g.*,

> *pihkoho–* VAI 'free oneself, escape; be saved'
> *patinikê–* VAI 'make a mistake, take a wrong step, transgress; sin'

In some cases, such semantic extensions are triggered by the introduction of new objects or practices, *e.g.*,

> *minihkwê–* VAI 'drink; use alcohol, abuse alcohol'
> *pîhtwâwin–* NI 'smoking; smoking cannabis, cannabis abuse'

In the same fashion, some of these re-used terms reflect the shift from one moral and religious system to another, *e.g.*,

> *pawâmiwin–* NI 'spirit power; witchcraft'
> *pâstâho–* VAI 'have one's transgressions fall upon oneself and one's children; sin, be a sinner'

Words which retain both their basic and their extended meanings are common, with all their ambiguities and tensions, in technical contexts — whether theological or commercial:

> . . . , *nikî-wâpahtên kisê-manitow ê-tipêyimikoyahk ê-kî-awihit êkoni anih âya, awâsisa kâw ê-kî-otinât.* (EM4)
> '. . . , I saw that God in His power over us had given us this child on loan and that He had taken her back again.'

> *âtiht nêhiyawa, âtiht môniyâwa kî-awihêw.* (EM58)
> 'Some [fields] he had rented out to Crees, some to White people.'

Similarly:

> *. . . kî-wawêyîstam ka-nakatahk askiy . . .* (EM4)
> '. . . she was prepared to leave this world behind . . .'

> *nikî-miyâwak anih âya askiya nôsisimak; pêyak iskwêw, êkwa nîso*
> *nâpêwak, nôsisimak nikî-miyâwak.* (EM58)
> 'I gave the land [lit., these pieces of land] to my grandchildren; to
> one granddaughter and to two grandsons I gave it.'

The context may be commercial, the lexical meaning may be extended
well beyond its traditional realm to include divisible real estate, but in
this last example the construction displays the classical form of a chias-
tic reversal of word order.

NEW TERMS AND INNOVATIVE USES of age-old terms are readily integrated, as the above examples illustrate, into a discourse which, despite
its Roman Catholic content and flavour, exhibits the established features of Cree literary form.

Among the more striking aspects of Emma Minde's text are the long
sequences of parallel clauses, *e.g.,*

> *. . . êkwa môy ê-kiskêyihtahkik ê-tôtahkik êtok ôm âya,*
>   *kâ-tôtâsocik,*
>   *kâ-misiwanâcihisocik,*
>   *kâ-nipahisocik.* (EM36)
> '. . . and they presumably do not know what they are doing
>   when they do this to themselves,
>   when they destroy themselves,
>   when they kill themselves.'

> *kîspin kâ-kisiwâhikoyahkik,*
>   *ka-pônêyihtamawâyahkik,*
>   *namôya ka-~, namôya ka-kisîstawâyahkik ayisiyiniwak,*
>   *namôy mîna ka-~ kîmôc ka-nôtinâyahkik,*
>   *môy k-âh-âyimômâyahkik.* (EM34)

'if they have angered us,
　　for us to forgive them,
　　not to —~, not to stay angry with people,
　　not to fight them behind their backs,
　　not to spread gossip about them.'

Parallelism is a fundamental feature of Cree rhetoric; when taken to
the lengths illustrated here and used repeatedly, it imparts a special
force to the homiletic tone of the text.

In referring to the two women who exercised such a profound influence on her life, Emma Minde goes back and forth between kin terms
such as *nisikos* 'my father's sister, my mother's brother's wife; my
mother-in-law, my father-in-law's brother's wife' and English appella-
tions such as *Mrs. Minde*; one reason for this usage may well be that
these are public figures whose names are widely recognised in central
Alberta. (In most traditional texts, the use of personal names for
deceased members of the family is avoided and kin terms appear either
with the absentative suffix *-pan*, e.g., *nôhkomipan* 'my late grandmother', or in periphrastic constructions; *cf.* Wolfart 1992: 405–6.)

At the same time, the narrator studiously comments on the anachronistic use of ordinary kin terms, as when she refers to her future husband as *niwîkimâkan* 'my spouse' even though she reports from the perspective of the bride-to-be, and also when she uses the same term for
him retrospectively even though he is no longer alive:

> . . . , *niwîkimâkan êkwa — nik-êtâhkômâw, âsay êkwa*
> *ê-kî-nakasit —* (EM41)
> ' . . . , and my husband — I will call him by that kin term even
> though he has already left me behind —'

She similarly employs a distancing comment on the one occasion
where her discourse might be misunderstood as implying self-
aggrandisement, a serious violation of Cree social norms:

> *namôya ninôhtê-mâh-mamihcimon pimâtisiwin ohci, mâka* . . . (EM5)
> 'I do not want to brag about the life I lead, but . . .'

Finally, she opens the chapters of her narrative with a self-effacing comment designed to stress that she only speaks about her life in response to repeated requests:

awa kâ-kakwêcimit iskwêw aw ôta kâ-pîkiskwêhit; (EM7)
'This woman [Freda Ahenakew] asked me, when she made me speak in here [the tape-recorder];'

. . . , êwakw âw âya, iskwêw awa k-âcimôhit aya, êkosi
ê-isi-nitawêyihtahk k-âcimostawak, . . . (EM11)
' . . . , it is this woman [Freda Ahenakew] who is making me tell about it, that is what she wants me to tell her about, . . .'

êkonik ôk âya, ê-nitawêyimit aw âya Mrs. Ahenakew *k-âcimakik aya,*
nisis êkwa aya nisikos, . . . (EM43)
'It is these Mrs. Ahenakew wants me to tell about, my father-in-law and my mother-in-law, . . .'

êkwa ôk âya iskwêwak kâ-nitawêyimikawiyân aya kik-âcimakik aya,
ôta maskwacîsihk, . . . (EM50)
'And it is these women I am expected to tell about, here at
maskwacîsihk, . . .'

These formal opening passages illustrate another characteristic feature of Cree literary form.

Bearing the hallmarks of classical style and form, the reminiscences of Emma Minde are an eloquent testimony of the remarkable education which turned the shy, even morose girl she insists she once was into an old woman of resounding rhetorical gifts.

Arranged Marriages

Emma Minde outlines the married lives of three women: her own and that of two older women, the wives of her father-in-law and his brother, whose teachings shaped her life as a married woman. In effect, then, we are told much the same tale three times over — and the repetition makes it all the more impressive.

The decision for a young woman to be married is made, at least formally, by her father. When she first introduces the topic of her arranged marriage, Emma Minde speaks only of her parents, *e.g.*,

mâka ninîkihikwak ê-wî-nanahihtawakik ê-sîhkimicik, . . . (EM3)
'But I was going to obey my parents since they urged me, . . .'

Her narrative tells us nothing of the consultations and negotiations which may have been part of the arrangements between the two sets of parents. She merely reports that her parents would habitually stop and stay with her future husband's parents when travelling in the region.

In the event, the young man's parents come to Saddle Lake to ask for the young woman, and they proceed to take her home with them. Emma Minde uses the plural form for the first two verbs in the following sentence to suggest that the discussions included both fathers and mothers:

*. . . , kâ-kî-pê-nitawâpamâ**cik** aya ninîkihikwa, ê-pê-mâmiskôtamawâ**cik** ôm âya, **o**kosisa êyâpic ê-môsâpêwiyit, ê-kî-nitawêyim**it o**kosisa ka-wîcêwimak.* (EM39)
' . . . , that is when **they** came to see my parents, **they** came and discussed with them the fact that **his** son was still a bachelor and that **he** wanted me to marry **his** son.'

In the second half of the sentence, however, she chooses the singular for the main verb, and also the singular possessor for the two instances of the possessed noun *okosisa*, to indicate that the key phrases were spoken by the (previously mentioned) groom's father.

It is the bride's father, too, who finally puts the question to her:

"kiwî-wîcêwâw cî aw ôskinîkiw?" ê-itikawiyân; (EM40)
'"Are you going to marry this young man?" was said to me;'

(even though the quotative verb form which follows does not specify the speaker). When she remains silent, she is scolded — she still remembers the very words her father spoke — and only then she acquiesces, hesitantly and with filial deference:

"wiy ê-sîhkimiyan, 'êhâ' nik-êtwân êtokwê." (EM40)
'"Since you urge me, I will presumably say yes."'

THE CRITERIA AND ARGUMENTS which a young woman's father
would have weighed in agreeing to give her away are implicitly recited
in the same passage:

> . . . , *wiyawâw êwako ê-kî-wiyasiwâtahkik ôm âya, ê-kî-kakâyawisît
> awa, . . . , ê-kî-nanahihtawât ôhtâwiya.* (EM40)
> ' . . . but they [the parents] made the decision, and he [her future
> husband] was a good worker . . . , and he obeyed his father.'

In the opening summary, her parents' thoughts are represented as
follows:

> *ê-itêyihtahkik êkoni kwayask, ka-kî-pamihit kihci-wîkimak[i] êwakw
> âna nâpêw, . . .* (EM3)
> 'they [my parents] thought that he would [do] the right thing, that
> this man would be able to provide for me if I married him . . . '

The narrative goes on to impute a motive to the other side as well:

> *ê-kî-êtokwê-nisis-kakwê-miskamawât iskwêwa aya, tânih êkoni
> ka-kitimâkêyimikot, . . .* (EM40)
> 'My father-in-law must have tried to find a wife for him, one who
> would love him, . . . ';

but then the narrator, ever sensitive to reproach (for self-righteous-
ness), immediately distances herself by a self-deprecatory remark.
     When Mary-Jane Minde was given to Dan Minde, it was her older
brother who arranged the marriage:

> . . . , *êkon ês ê-kî-aya-sîhkimikot* . . . (EM43)
> ' . . . , that one had urged her . . . '

In this case, the narrative reports an explicit argument in favour of the
particular suitor: that he would be a good provider and that he was
already accustomed to a life with children.

For Mary Minde, finally, the *de facto* guardians who took charge and acted *in loco parentis* were the nuns running the boarding-school:

> . . . , *êkâ ê-nitawêyimiht ka-kîwêtotawât osâm aya,* . . . (EM65)
> ' . . . , for they did not want her to go back to her grandfather, . . . ';

(they thoroughly disapproved of his conjuring). Explicitly declaring their intention,

> *"ka-miskamâtinân awiyak ka-wîcêwat."* (EM65)
> '"We will find you someone to marry."',

they chose in Sam Minde a young man who had worked at the school:

> . . . , *ê-kî-itikot êkoni ka-kihci-wîkimât,* . . . (EM65)
> ' . . . , they had told her to marry that one, . . . '

—and in her case there is none of the normal lament, for we are told that she knew him.

BOTH THE RITUALS of marriage and the values for which they stand offer wide scope for conflict between traditional Cree practices and the doctrines enforced from time to time by the Roman Catholic Church.

The conflict of values is most obvious with respect to cross-cousin marriage. Under this ancient principle, cohesion between families is maintained from generation to generation; but to a Roman Catholic priest, the very notion of a woman marrying the son of her father's sister or of her mother's brother (one of her *cross*-cousins) is repugnant — and it seems to matter little that, conversely, the sons of her father's brother or of her mother's sister (her *parallel* cousins) are classified as her brothers and subject to the strictest taboo.

When the young woman to whose reminiscences we are listening was taken from her childhood home at Saddle Lake to be married at Hobbema to a man she had never seen before, she did not, as she puts it, know any of her future family. Her father-in-law, Dan Minde, had in fact accompanied her parents when they went to visit her in hospital at Ponoka (not far from Hobbema), where she had spent several months having "lost her voice" (EM39). A mere two weeks after her release from hospital, Dan Minde had come to arrange her marriage to his son and to take her away.

There is no indication in the narrative of the relationship, genealogical or conventional, between the two families which in traditional Cree society determines the eligibility of marriage partners, and the absence of any such cross-cousin relationship has since been explicitly confirmed (to Freda Ahenakew) by the narrator; but this, of course, is an aspect of Cree culture which the missionaries had been especially anxious to modify. For the present case, the Roman Catholic influence is reflected in the fact that the term *nisis* 'my mother's brother, my father's sister's husband; my father-in-law, my father-in-law's brother', which in the proper genealogical context would have been appropriate for a potential or future father-in-law as well as for an actual one and thus might have been used from the outset, does not appear until after the marriage.

The motive Emma Minde attributes to her parents sixty years later recalls the common pattern of folk etymologies:

> *êwak ôhc êtokwê kâ-kî-nawasônamawicik nâpêwa ka-wîcêwimak, . . . ,*
> *êkâ ê-ohci-nisitawêyimakik ayisiyiniwak.* (EM8)
> 'That must have been the reason why they chose a man for me to marry, . . . , because I did not know people.'

It certainly need not be taken literally.

It is noteworthy that Emma Minde seems so thoroughly steeped in Roman Catholic doctrine that the institution of cross-cousin marriage does not even rate a mention in her narrative — or should the implicit excoriation of this mortal sin be part of the constant emphasis on proper marriage? Instances are plentiful, and some stand out by their rhythmic style:

> *êkos ânim ê-kî-isi-miyo-pimâtisicik,*
>   *wîkiwin ê-kî-miyâcik aya otawâsimisiwâwa aya,*
> *kâh-kihci-wîkimâtwâw[i] âwiya.* (EM34)
> 'In this way they have led a good life,
>   they have given their children a home,
> after getting properly married to someone.'

ahpô wiya cêsos ôhtâwîhkâwina, 'kihcihtwâwi-côsap' kâ-kî-isiyîhkâsot,
êkwa okâwiya, kihcihtwâwi-mariy, ê-kî-kihci-wîkihtoyit,
cîsas wîst âya, ê-kî-ayât anim âya wîkiwin, ita ê-kî-kitimâkêyimikot,
ôhtâwiya nik-êtwân êkwa okâwiya; (EM42)
'Even in the case of Jésus, his step-father, St. Joseph as he is called,
and his mother, Ste-Marie, had been properly married,
and Jesus, too, had a home where they loved him,
his father (I will say) and his mother;'

tânitahtwâw nipêhtên ôtê nâway,
êkonik anohc kâ-kîsikâk kwayask ê-pimâtisicik,
    kâ-kihci-wîkihtocik,
kwayask ê-paminâcik otawâsimisiwâwa,
êkoni ôhi ê-pê-pêhtamân nîst âya pîkiskwêwina. (EM5)
'Many times I have heard in the past
that those live right to this day
    who were properly married to each other,
that they look after their children properly,
these words I have been hearing myself.'

êyâpic kiwâpamâwâwak âtiht ayisiyiniwak,
    kâh-otinitotwâwi
    kâh-kihci-wîkihtotwâwi,
êyâpic ê-wîcêhtocik,
êyâpic ê-kitimâkêyihtocik,
êyâpic wîkiwin ê-miyâcik aya otawâsimisiwâwa. (EM34)
'Some people you still see,
    if they have made a commitment to each other
    and were properly married to each other,
still staying married to each other,
still loving each other,
still giving their children a home.'

Overtly, the above examples simply extol the virtues of a life-long commitment, of a stable home for the children, and of a formal act accompanied by high ritual.

Beside those areas where Cree and Roman Catholic traditions are most sharply in conflict, there are many others where they are fully in concord: the need to provide for one's children, above all, but also for the orphans; the virtue of providence and hard work; charity towards the old and the poor; etc. In the absence of conflict, however, such topics tend to receive very little attention from missionaries, historians, ethnologists and those who themselves live at the intersection of these two worlds.

Paradoxical as it may seem, scholarly neglect of how closely structural configurations may be matched across cultures even extends to topics which are otherwise of perennial interest. In the case of the arranged marriages related in this text, the most striking pattern illustrated is that of patriarchal control, with the key rôle readily passing from Cree fathers (or older brothers) to Roman Catholic priests.

THE WOMEN whose life histories we have been recording agree to a remarkable extent in the sentiments to which they give voice. There is no overt expression of resentment or of objections to their powerless state; if such exist, they are coded in other terms.

The explicit remark of Rosa Longneck (in chapter 9 of Bear *et al.* 1992; *cf.* also the discussion in Wolfart 1992: 393–96) is all the more noteworthy:

> *awas, ê-kî-mêkihk anima niya, môy ânima ê-ohci-pakitinisoyân, êkota.* (RL9-8)
> 'Go on, the fact is that I was given away, the fact is that I did not have a choice in the matter.'

Obviously, the absence of overt statements cannot by itself be construed to prove absence of the underlying emotions.

The only emotion which is openly discussed is the overwhelming horror of a husband and a family the young woman has not even met.

This is a recurrent theme. In Emma Minde's narrative, it almost sounds like a refrain, first invoked at the very beginning:

> *kî-âyiman . . . , êkâ ê-nisitawêyimakik ayisiyiniwak.* (EM3)
> 'It was difficult . . . , since I did not know the people.'

mâk âyiwâk kî-âyiman . . . , môy âhpô cêskwa ê-nisitawêyimak. (EM3)
'But it was worse . . . , I did not even know him yet [the young man whom I was to marry].'

kî-âyiman pimâtisiwin osâm; namôy âya, môy sêmâk ayisiyiniw ati-nakayâskawâw êkâ kâ-nisitawêyimiht, . . . (EM3)
'Life was difficult, and you don't get used to a person right away when you haven't known him before, . . .'

She then repeats the lament at the close of her own story, albeit with a slight variation:

. . . , môya wîst ê-ohci-nisitawêyimit, êkwa môy nîst ê-ohci-nisitawêyimak. (EM40)
'. . . , he did not know me, and I did not know him.'

. . . , osâm êkâ cêskw âhpô ohkwâkan ê-wâpahtamwak, . . . (EM40)
'. . . , for I had not yet even seen his face, . . .'

kî-âyiman . . . ; nikî-miskamâkawin niya nâpêw ka-wîcêwak, êkosi môy ê-ohci-nisitawêyimak, . . . (EM40)
'It was hard . . . ; a man had been found for me to marry, and I did not know him, . . .'

It is striking that Glecia Bear uses almost the same words (in her chapter on 'A Woman's Life' in Bear *et al.* 1992):

môy ôm âhpô ê-nisitawêyimak awa nâpêw, kâ-wîkihtahikawiyân. (GB8-10)
'I did not even know the man whom it was arranged that I would marry.'

. . . , êkâ ê-nisitawêyimak aw âwiyak kâ-miyiht niya, ka-wîkimak. (GB8-10)
'. . . , since I did not even know this person to whom I had been given, for me to be married to him.'

The parallels range from the overall sentiment all the way to the choice of words and, indeed, of the grammatical constructions with their preference for indefinite agent forms.

For Mary-Jane Minde, too, the salient point which is being repeated is that she did not know the man she was to marry:

> *wîsta namôy ê-ohci-nakayâskawât ôhi nâpêwa, . . .* (EM43)
> 'she, too, had not been familiar with that man, . . .'

In Emma Minde's own story, the whole issue of being married to a stranger culminates in the dramatic scene of her arrival: at midnight, coming into a strange house, to have her sleeping husband pointed out to her by an eleven-year-old sister-in-law:

> *"aw îta . . . !"* (EM41)
> '"There he is . . . !"'

Given Emma Minde's rhetorical exuberance on many other occasions, it is remarkable that she treats this crucial scene with climactic understatement.

The anguish which even after a lifetime permeates these narratives is almost palpable. In listening to them on the eve of the millennium, we may find a measure of relief in the more joyous emotions which, in retrospect at least, were also part of Emma Minde's new life:

> *pêyakwan mistah âya nikî-miyawâtên, nikî-miywêyihtên —~* (EM42)
> 'All the same I had lots of fun and I was happy —~'

This remark concludes the report of the church wedding, attended only by the couple, two witnesses and the priest.

STATEMENTS OF EMOTION or evaluations from a personal point of view are rare in Cree texts, but in a woman's life history — as illustrated by Glecia Bear and Emma Minde alike — the experience of being given away in marriage is evidently the most dramatic:

. . . , iyikohk ê-pakwâtamân ê-mâtoyân, . . . (GB8-11)
'. . . , I hated it so much and I was crying, . . .'

ê-kî-mâtoyâhk anima nikâwiy aya, . . . (EM41)
'We did cry, my mother and I, . . .'

Even when recalled from the philosophical perspective of old age, the young brides' distress reverberates still in the old wives' lament.

Editorial Notes

The text here presented was recorded in two sessions, the first on 15 June 1988 (the introduction and chapters II and III) and the second, larger part (chapters IV-VIII) on 22 June 1988.

Presentation of the Text

The editorial conventions in general follow the practice of other recent text editions (Vandall and Douquette 1987, Bear *et al.* 1992, Whitecalf 1993). In preserving the variation between the full form of words and preverbs and their reduced variants (with word-final vowels elided), we specifically adopt the conventions of Bear *et al.* 1992; *cf.* Wolfart 1992: 32–37, 351–56.

THE CRITICAL EDITION is an attempt to transfer as much as possible of the spoken performance onto the printed page; while some normalisation is inevitable, there is a conscious effort to keep it to a minimum.

The distinction between the text itself and the editorial apparatus needs to be maintained at all times. All queries and comments (and any other editorial matter not relegated to the *Notes to the Text*) are marked typographically, either by means of special symbols or by being enclosed in square brackets.

The only exceptions to this rule are the chapter and section numbers and the chapter titles and section headings (printed as part of the English translation), all of which are editorial additions.

When the spoken text includes occasional words or brief stretches in English, these are printed *in italics*; the same rule applies to English proper names. (In the translation, conversely, proper names or technical terms which retain their original Cree form are also printed in italics.) Terms being cited or defined, including proper names, are enclosed in single quotation marks.

The text here printed is much closer to normal conversation in every aspect of its style than the prose to which most readers are accustomed. We have also refrained from re-arranging sections within the text even though one and the same topic may come up in a number of different contexts and prose of considerable substance or power may alternate with more mundane passages. The printed text reflects the spoken text as recorded.

THE SPOKEN PERFORMANCE represented by the printed text is transcribed as fully as possible from audio-tape; but the extraneous sounds which are recorded along with it are documented only if they directly affect the discourse. When the speaker interrupts herself and the recorder is turned off and on, this is documented in the printed text by the symbol ≈≈≈ , while the symbol ≈/≈ marks the involuntary interruption at the end of the tape. In all such cases, the recording may stop while the speaker is still in mid-sentence (or start after she has already begun to speak); as a result, the record often shows a fragmentary sentence.

Fragmentary words are mainly due to the speaker interrupting herself while searching for the right word, or catching herself in a slip of the tongue. In normal speech, however, not all slips of the tongue are corrected, and audio-recordings in any language include sentences which an author might well rewrite in revising a written text for publication; such sentences have not been modified in this edition but left as originally spoken.

All external breaks and ellipses are fully marked, including the recording faults (signalled by the symbol ⚡⚡⚡ printed centred on a separate line) and minor technical flaws (with the symbol ⚡ embedded in the running text) found with increasing frequency in the later third of the text.

THE MANUAL AND FACIAL GESTURES which are part of most narrative events are documented only at a minimal level. Where their linguistic and pragmatic traces can be recovered in the text as recorded, they are identified by the standard notation [*gesture*] and, occasionally, some further detail.

Amongst other nonlinguistic features, only those audible responses which can be subsumed under the category of laughter have been included. While the notations [*ê-pâhpit*] and [*laughs*] refer to the speaker, [*ê-pâhpihk*] and [*laughter*] mark the response of the audience (but may, of course, also include the speaker).

In the introductory essay and in the editorial notes, passages cited from the text are identified by the two-letter code EM followed by a section number; citations from Bear *et al.* 1992 are similarly identified by chapter-and-section number and the codes GB for Glecia Bear and RL for Rosa Longneck. In both the text and the translation, centred queries, comments or asides are individually identified as spoken by Freda Ahenakew [FA] or Emma Minde [EM].

TYPOGRAPHICAL CONVENTIONS, SPECIAL SYMBOLS
AND ABBREVIATIONS:

---

xxxx   [text in roman type]
        primary language (Cree in the text, English in the translation)

xxxx   [text in italic type]
        secondary language (English in the text, Cree in the translation)

"xxxx"   [double quotation marks]
        quoted speech

'xxxx'   [single quotation marks]
        [1] quoted speech (if embedded within quoted speech)
        [2] cited word

—   [em-dash]
        syntactic or rhetorical break (usually sharper than those marked by comma or semicolon) within a sentence

( )   [parentheses]
      parenthetical insertion (usually spoken at lower pitch
      or volume)

-~-   [wave-hyphen within the word]
      fragmentary word, resumed

-~   [wave-hyphen at the end of the word]
      fragmentary word

—~   [wave-hyphen following the word]
      fragmentary sentence

≈≈≈   [three doubled wave-hyphens]
      external break

≈/≈   [two doubled wave-hyphens separated by a slash]
      external break: change of tape

≉≉≉   [three doubled wave-hyphens, slashed]
      recording fault

≉   [doubled wave-hyphen, slashed]
      minor recording flaw

---

[a]   [roman type enclosed in square brackets]
         editorially supplied word-final vowel (elided under the rules
         of vowel combination and restored on the basis of vocalic,
         prosodic or syntactic evidence)

[*xxxx*] [italic type enclosed in square brackets]
         editorial comment (including such standard comments as
         [*ê-pâhpit*], [*laughs*], [*gesture*], etc.)

[*sic*] ['indeed']

confirmation that the preceding word is correctly printed (usually in the case of an uncommon or otherwise remarkable form, *e.g.,* minor idiosyncracies, dialect discrepancies, slips of the tongue)

[*i.e.*] ['that is']

proposed emendation or completion of a fragment; explication or elaboration (used in the English translation instead of the more technical *sc.,* which is restricted to the *Notes to the Text*)

[*?sic*] ['really?']

caution that the identification of the preceding word remains in doubt

---

Translation

Although no effort has been spared to keep the translation faithful to the original text, there are all too many occasions where a literal translation would mislead rather than illuminate the meaning it attempts to express in another language.

By retaining Cree names in the English translation (even where widely known English equivalents exist), we preserve the distinction made by the narrator, who in certain contexts may have a preference for one term or the other and sometimes goes back and forth between them.

Proper names, moreover, are notoriously difficult to translate. Popular practice notwithstanding, many names resist morphological analysis and etymological interpretation, and even the pragmatic identification of persons and places is often difficult.

Both in the translation of the text and in the introductory essay, we follow Emma Minde's own usage (EM33) in choosing the somewhat archaic term 'boarding-school' (where the context indicates that this is the reference of the unmarked term *kiskinohamâtowikamikw–* 'school,

school-house') in preference to the more recent term 'residential school', which might be anachronistic.

Note that the translations presented in the introductory essay are occasionally more literal than those given in the text edition itself.

In the glossary, entries which have both a general and an ecclesiastical meaning include an explicit notation:

pihkoho– VAI 'free oneself, escape; [*Christian:*] be saved'.

Terms which are invariably Christian in reference, like *ayamihâ–* VAI 'pray, say prayers; participate in a religious observance', are not specially flagged.

IN THE TRANSLATION of the Cree text into English, ethnological and genealogical accuracy have on occasion had to be sacrified to the requirements of fluency. In particular, we have chosen to translate *nisikos* as 'my mother-in-law' when it refers to Mary-Jane Minde, the mother (in fact, step-mother) of Emma Minde's husband, but as 'my aunt' when it refers to Jane Minde, the wife of her husband's paternal uncle.

The problem is acute when the term appears in the plural, as in

. . . *ôki nisikosak nîs ôki kâ-mâmiskômakik.* (EM68)
' . . . these two *nisikosak* about whom I am speaking.'

A literal translation, 'these two mothers-in-law', would be confusing; the only practical solution is to use a conjunction in English and refer to the two individuals who are combinable in Cree but not in English as 'both my mother-in-law and the wife of my father-in-law's brother'.

In the parallel case of the term *nisis* 'my mother's brother, my father's sister's husband; my father-in-law, my father-in-law's brother', the text provides an instance of both the noun (*nisisak*, literally 'my fathers-in-law') and the verb (*kî-nîsiwak* 'they were two') appearing in the plural — and the verb stem itself expressing a specific number:

kî-nîsiwak ôki nisisak, . . . (EM45)
'These *nisisak* were two in number, . . .'

Since a direct translation of these Cree plurals into English plurals would be unacceptable (and an insensitive translation might even give offence), a fairly free rendition is called for (and, in the event, less awkward than in the previous case): 'My father-in-law was one of two brothers, . . . '.

REFERENCES

The recent history of the Crees at *maskwacîsihk* is sketched in various works, but rarely documented; MacGregor's popular history (1976) of the Battle River region stands out. For the early Methodist activities, the best survey is still Hutchinson 1977. The statistical summary of denominational affiliation is based on Breton and Drouin 1968.

For additional comments on the form and etymology of the place name *onihcikaskwapiwinihk* we are indebted to Emily Hunter.

Ahenakew, Freda
    1987   *Cree Languages Structures: A Cree Approach*. Winnipeg: Pemmican Publications.

Ahenakew, Freda, and H.C. Wolfart
    1987   'The Story-tellers and Their Stories.' Freda Ahenakew, ed., *wâskahikaniwiyiniw-âcimowina / Stories of the House People*, Told by Peter Vandall and Joe Douquette, pp. x–xiv. Winnipeg: University of Manitoba Press.

Bear, Glecia, *et al.*
    1992   *kôhkominawak otâcimowiniwâwa / Our Grandmothers' Lives, As Told in Their Own Words*, Told by Glecia Bear *et al.* Edited and translated by Freda Ahenakew and H.C. Wolfart. Saskatoon: Fifth House Publishers.

Breton, P.-E., and E.O. Drouin
    1968   *Hobbema: Ongoing Mission of Central Alberta*. Translated, completed and updated [on the basis of P. Breton's original edition of 1962] by E.O. Drouin. [Cardston, Alberta: the author.]

Hutchinson, Gerald M.
    1977   'Introduction.' Hugh A. Dempsey, ed., *The Rundle Journals, 1840–1848*, pp. ix–lxiv. Historical Society of Alberta, 1. [Calgary:] Alberta Records Publication Board / Historical Society of Alberta & Glenbow-Alberta Institute.

MacGregor, J.G.

1976   *The Battle River Valley.* Saskatoon: Western Producer Prairie Books.

Vandall, Peter, and Joe Douquette

1987   *wâskahikaniwiyiniw-âcimowina / Stories of the House People.* Told by Peter Vandall and Joe Douquette. Edited, translated and with a glossary by Freda Ahenakew. Publications of the Algonquian Text Society. Winnipeg: University of Manitoba Press.

Whitecalf, Sarah

1993   *kinêhiyâwiwininaw nêhiyawêwin / The Cree Language Is Our Identity: The La Ronge Lectures of Sarah Whitecalf.* Edited, translated and with a glossary by H.C. Wolfart and Freda Ahenakew. Publications of the Algonquian Text Society. Winnipeg: University of Manitoba Press.

Wolfart, H.C.

1992   'Introduction to the Texts; Notes.' Freda Ahenakew and H.C. Wolfart, eds., *kôhkominawak otâcimowiniwâwa / Our Grandmothers' Lives, As Told in Their Own Words,* Told by Glecia Bear *et al.,* pp. 17–37; 351–408, Saskatoon: Fifth House Publishers.

1996   'Sketch of Cree, an Algonquian Language.' Ives Goddard, ed., *Languages,* pp. 390–439. William C. Sturtevant, gen. ed., *Handbook of North American Indians,* vol. 17. Washington, D.C.: Smithsonian Institution.

Wolfart, H.C., and Freda Ahenakew

1987   'Notes on the Orthography and the Glossary.' Freda Ahenakew, ed., *wâskahikaniwiyiniw-âcimowina / Stories of the House People,* Told by Peter Vandall and Joe Douquette, pp. 113–26. Winnipeg: University of Manitoba Press.

Wolfart, H.C., and Janet F. Carroll

1981   *Meet Cree: A Guide to the Cree Language.* Second edition. Edmonton: University of Alberta Press.

kwayask ê-kî-pê-kiskinowâpahtihicik

Their Example Showed Me the Way

[FA:]　âsay? êskwa.　êkw êkwayâc êkwa mâcipayin.

　　　　Mrs. Minde awa kâ-wî-âcimostâkoyahk anohc, *Hobbema*
ohci, maskwacîsihk ohc êtikwê.　êkosi, kiya sôskwâc âcimo!

I

[1]　　　niya *Emma Minde*, maskwacîsihk ohci, pêyak niy âya,
kêhtê-ayak anik âya k-êtihcik, ayinânêwimitanaw ayiwâk pêyak
ê-itahtopiponwêyân; môy kayâs, ayîki-pîsim, êkota ê-kî-otihtamân.

[2]　　mâk âya, namôy âyi nitayiwêpin, k-âyiwêpicik mân âya
kêhtê-ayak, môy　—~ môy âya êwako nipimitisahên, êyâpic aya
niwîcihtâson mâna ê-isko-kaskihtâyân pikw îta; ita
kâ-mamisîtotâkawiyân.　mâcik âya, ê-kî-mamisîtotawit
ayamihêwiyiniw ka-wîcihak ôta, ayamihâwin ohci.　nik-~ aya,
nikiyokawâwak mân âya otâhkosiwak, ninitawi-wîc-âyamihâmâwak.
êkwa kihc-âyamihêwiyiniw mîn ê-kî-sawêyimit aya,
ayamihêwi-saskamon ka-miyakik otâhkosiwak, êwako atoskêwin
nitôtên; êkwa kâ-nîpêpihk, êkota mîna mân âyamihêwiyiniw êkw
âyamihêwiskwêw niwîcêwâwak, ê-nitaw-âyamihêstamawâyâhkik,
ayisiyiniwak kâ-nakatask-~ ayi, kâ-nakataskêcik.

[3]　　êkwa at-~, ôta ê-kî-pê-wîcihiwêyân ôta maskwacîsihk,
onihcikiskwapiwinihk ohci, êkotê niy ê-ohcîyân, *'Saddle Lake'*
k-êsiyîhkâtêk.　kayâs êwako, môy âhpô ka-~ nika-kî-têpakihtên,
tahtw-âskiy ôta kâ-pê-wîcihiwêyân.　kî-âyiman ôtê
ka-pê-wîcihiwêyân maskwacîsihk, êkâ ê-nisitawêyimakik
ayisiyiniwak.　mâk âyiwâk kî-âyiman an[a] â-~, an[a] âw ôskinîkiw
kâ-wî-wîcêwak, *'Joe Minde'* ê-isiyîhkâsot, môy âhpô cêskwa
ê-nisitawêyimak.　mâka ninîkihikwak ê-wî-nanahihtawakik
ê-sîhkimicik, wiyawâw ê-kî-nisitawêyimâcik ê-kî-miskawâcik;

[FA:] Ready? Wait. It only just started now.

It is Mrs. Minde who is about to tell us stories today, from Hobbema, from *maskwacîsihk*, I guess. Now it is your turn, go on and tell!

I
....

Emma Minde's Life

[1] I am Emma Minde, from *maskwacîsihk*, and I am one of those Elders, as they are called, I am eighty-one years old; I reached that age in April, not long ago.

[2] But I am not retired the way old people retire, I do not follow that way of life, I still help everywhere as much as I can; where people rely on me. The priest, for instance, has relied upon me to help him with the church work here. I usually visit the sick, I go and pray with them. And now the Bishop has blessed me so that I give Holy Communion to the sick, that is the work I do now; and at wakes, at that time, too, I usually go along with the priest and the sister, when we go to pray for the people who have departed this world.

[3] I had come from *onihcikiskwapiwinihk* to live here at *maskwacîsihk*, for I, I am from Saddle Lake as it is called. That was long ago, I cannot even count how many years I have been living here. It was difficult to come and live here at *maskwacîsihk* as I did not know the people. But it was worse for I did not even know the young man yet, his name was Joe Minde, whom I was to marry. But I was going to obey my parents when they urged me, they knew him and they had found him; they thought that this man

ê-itêyihtahkik êkoni kwayask, ka-kî-pamihit kihci-wîkimak[i] êwakw
âna nâpêw, êkwa nikî-kihci-wîkimâw. kî-âyiman pimâtisiwin osâm;
namôy âya, môy sêmâk ayisiyiniw ati-nakayâskawâw êkâ
kâ-nisitawêyimiht, mâk ê-isko-kaskihtâyân, nikî-wî-kakwê-sâkihâw
ana nâpêw kâ-kî-kihci-wîkimak.

[4] êkwa awâsisak nikî-ayâwânânak, nisto, iskwêsisak piko
kâ-kî-ayâwâyâhkik. êwakw âna nitânis anohc êkw-~ êkwa mân âya,
kâ-kiskinohamâkêt nêhiyawêwin, 'Theresa Wildcat' isiyîhkâsow,
êwako nitânis, êkwa kotak mîna nitânis ê-wîcihtâsot mân âya
kiskinohamâtowikamikohk, ê-kî-kakêskimât mâna
kiskinohamawâkana ôh âya, kâ-nôhtê-sâ-sipwêhtêyit. mâka kotak
atoskêwin kî-miyâw, mâk êyâpic mân âya kiyokawêw aya,
kiskinohamawâkana kiskinohamâtowikamikohk. êkonik ôki nîso
nitânisak ê-pimâtisicik, an[a] ôsîmimâw, 'Clara' kî-isiyîhkâsow,
êwakw âya, têpakohposâp ê-itahtopiponwêt nikî-nakatikonân. mâka
n-~, ât[a] ê-kî-âyimahk ê-wanihak nitawâsimis, nikî-wâpahtên
kisê-manitow ê-tipêyimikoyahk, ê-kî-awihit êkoni anih âya, awâsisa
kâw ê-kî-otinât. êkwa nimiywêyihtên anohc êkosi kik-êtwêyân,
ê-kî-miyo-nakataskêt nitânis. nîsw-âskiy ê-kî-âhkosit, êkwa
kî-wawêyîstam ka-nakatahk askiy êkwa nikî-kâh-kakêskimikonân,
nikî-kakêskimik mâna. êkos ânim êtokw ê-itastêk kipimâtisiwininaw,
môy ê-tipêyihtamahk. mîna namôy ê-tipêyimâyahkik awâsisak ôki,
ê-awihikoyahk kimanitôminaw, êkwa iyikohk ê-kaskihtâyahk piko
ka-kakwê-wîcihâyahkik ôk âwâsisak, ka-miy-ôhpikihâyahkik. êwako
niya, êkos ê-itastêk aya nimâmitonêyihcikan, êwako ê-~
ê-tâpwêwakêyihtamân. awâsis kâ-miy-ôhpikihiht, namôy wîhkâc
sasîhciwihêw onîkihikwa, kâ-kîs-ôhpikit. êkos ânima
ê-kî-pê-is-ôhpikihikawiyân niya, ê-kî-pê-is-ôhpikihikawiyâhk; kotakak
nîtisânak mîn êkosi ê-kî-pê-is-ôhpikihihcik, ka-manâcihâyâhkik
ayisiyiniwak, ka-kihcêyimâyâhkik, âsônê kêhtê-ayak. mîna
ayamihâwinihk ê-kî-ohpikihikawiyâhk, tahtw-âyamihêwi-kîsikâw
ê-kî-nitaw-âyamihâhtahikawiyâhk. êkwa mîna ê-kî-pakitinikawiyâhk
kiskinohamâtowikamik (anima, itowahk mâna kâ-kî-kanawêyimihcik
aya kiskinohamawâkanak, êkotowihk ê-kî-pakitinikawiyâhk); êwak

would be able to provide well for me if I married him, and I married him. Life was difficult because you do not get used to a person right away when you do not know him, but I tried as much as I could to love the man I had married.

[4]   And we had three children, we only had daughters. That was my daughter, today, the one who teaches Cree, her name is Theresa Wildcat, that is my daughter; and my other daughter helps at the school, she used to counsel the students who want to drop out. She has been given another job, but she still visits the students at the school. These are two of my daughters that are alive, the youngest one, Clara had been her name, she had left us behind when she was seventeen years old. But although it had been difficult to lose my child, I saw that God has power over us, that He had given us this child on loan, and that He had taken her back. And I am glad to say today that my daughter departed this world peacefully. She had been sick for two years, she was prepared to leave the world behind, she used to counsel all of us, and she used to counsel me. That is how it is with our life, I guess, we have no power over it. We also do not have power over these children, our God lends them to us and we must try to help them as much as we can, we must raise these children well. That is me, that is how my thinking runs, that I believe. Children who are raised well will never put their parents to shame when they are grown up. That is how I myself was raised, how we were raised; that is how my other brothers and sisters, too, were raised, to treat people with respect, to think highly of them, especially the old people. We were also raised in the faith, we were taken to Mass every Sunday. And we were also sent to school (we were sent to the kind where the students used to be boarded); that is the reason, I guess, why we have

ôhc êtokwê anohc kâ-kîsikâk nowâhc[1] ê-kî-pê-tôtamâhk, osâm
misakâmê kîkway ê-kî-pê-wîhtamâkawiyâhk, kîkwây anim
ê-wî-tâwinamâhk ôtê nîkân, êkosi mân ê-kî-isi-kakêskimikawiyâhk.

[5]   êkwa mêkwâc ôma kâ-pê-pimâtisiyân, pêyakwan êkosi
nikî-wî-kakwê-tôtên. nitawâsimisak aya, nikî-~ nikî-kakêskimâwak
mân êkwa môy nôh-kostên ka-kakêskimakik, osâm
ê-kî-kitimâkêyimakik ê-itêyihtamân, êwak ôhci kâ-kî-kakêskimakik.
êkwa mîna mâna ayamihâwinihk ê-kî-wî-kakwê-ohpikihakik,
ê-kî-itohtahakik ayamihêwikamikohk. ât[a] êkâ anohc
ê-pimitisahahkik, anima kâ-kî-is-ôhpikihakik, âtiht —~ nîso piko
nitayâwâwak, mâka —~, pêyak kâkikê aya pê-wîcihiwêw
ayamihêwikamikohk ê-pê-itohtêt, pêyak namôy êkwayikohk — mâka
namôy nika-kî-wîhâwak. mâk âhci pikw âya, kwayask
nikitâpamâwak nitawâsimisak aya, kisêwâtisiwinihk kâkikê ohci
niwî-kakwê-aya-kitotâwak, êkwa mîn âya niwî-kakwê-kiskisomâwak[2]
kwayask ka-tôtahkik, otawâsimisiwâwa mîna ka-kakêskimâcik.
âskaw ahpô ninitotamâkwak ka-kakêskimimak otawâsimisiwâwa.
tâpwê êtokwê mân âskaw nipîkiskwâtâwak nôsisimak, mâka namôy
êkwayikohk nikakêskimâwak, "misawâc," ê-itêyihtamân, "ayisiyiniw
anima k-êsi-pimâtisit aya, kwayask kâ-kakwê-tôtahk, kisê-manitowa
kâ-manâcihât mîn âya wîcayisiyiniwa kâ-kakwê-kitimâkêyimât, anim
ôpimâtisiwinihk, êkota ohci kakêskihkêmow," ê-itwêhk mâna,
"k-êsi-pimâtisiyan, êkota ohc âyihk kik-~ kikakêskimâw ayisiyiniw;"
êkosi miyâ-~, mîn ây-~, ê-itikawiyâhk mân ê-kakêskimikawiyâhk.
wiya kâkikê ê-pîhtokwêyân ayamihêwikamikohk, môy niwanikiskisin
tânisi k-êsi-kakêskihkêmot ayamihêwiyiniw. ât[a] ân[a]
ê-wî-kakwê-aya-miyo-tôtâkoyahk ayamihêwiyiniw,
ê-wî-kakwê-miyohtahikoyahk ana kihci-kîsikohk, namôya
ka-pakwâtâyahk ayamihêwiyiniw, mîna ayamihêwiskwêwak. mîn ôm
âyamihâwin, namôy ka-pakwâtamahk, kisê-manitow an[a]
ê-kî-miyikoyahk, ê-kî-kitimâkêyimikoyahk ayamihâwin
kâ-kî-miyikoyahk, êkota ohci kwayask ka-pimâtisiyahk. pikw âwiyak
kiskêyihtam, kîkway ê-miywâsik mîna kîkway ê-mâyâtahk, êkota ohc
âyisiyiniw kâh-kî-kakêskimisow, opimâtisiwinihk, tânit-~ tânim

been doing the decent thing to this day, because we had been told all along what we would come up against in the future, that is how we had been counselled.

[5]   And I have been trying to do the same throughout my own life. I have always counselled my children and I was not afraid to counsel them for I think I counselled them because I loved them. And I have also been trying to raise them in the faith, I used to take them to church. Although today some of them do not follow the way in which I had raised them —~, I only have two, one always joins in and comes to church, and one not so much — but I cannot mention them by name. Nevertheless, I look on my children with favour, I always try to speak to them with kindness, and I also try to remind them to do the right thing and also to counsel their children. Sometimes they even ask me to counsel their children. It is true, I guess, I sometimes speak to my grandchildren but I do not counsel them enough; "Anyway," I think, "the way people live, when they try to do the right thing and treat God with respect and also try to love their neighbour, then they preach by the example of their life," they say, "you counsel people by the way you live;" that is what is said to us in counselling. For I always go to church and I do not forget what the priest preaches. The priest, let it be said, is trying to do us good, he is trying to guide us to heaven, we should not hate the priest and the nuns. Nor should we hate religion either, God gave it to us because he loved us, that is why he gave us the faith with which to live right. Everyone knows what is good and what is evil, and with that people could counsel themselves in their life, what to choose, how to live their life. Many of the people here at *maskwacîsihk* know me, they probably know me from when I go to wakes and I also meet them at church and when they

êwako ka-nawasônahk, ka-pimâtisîtotahk. mihcêt ôta,
maskwacîsihk, ayisiyiniwak ninisitawêyimikwak, ita ohc êtokwê
ka-nisitawêyimicik anima, kâ-nîpêpihk mân îtê k-êtohtêyân, êkwa
ôta mîna mân âyamihêwikamikohk kâ-nakiskawakik, êkwa ôta nîkihk
kâ-pê-kiyokawicik. namôya ninôhtê-mâh-mamihcimon
nipimâtisiwin ohci, mâka âtiht mân âya, iskwêwak —~

≈ / ≈

[FA:]   ka-wîhtamâtin ispî. êkw ân[i] êkwa!

ayisiyiniwak mân ê-pê-nâtâmototawicik ôta nîkihk,
wêwânêyihtahkwâwi tânisi ka-tôtahkik. êkwa, ê-itêyihtahkik êtokwê,
ka-kî-wîcihakik ohc âya, nimiyo-kakêskihkêmowin tânis
ê-isi-kiskêyihtamân nipimâtisiwin ohci. tânitahto aya, nikiskêyihtên
ê-atamihakik ayisiyiniwak, kîkway kâ-wîhtamawakik tânis
ê-kî-pê-isi-wîhtamawicik nîst âya, ninîkihikwak, tânim êwako
k-âpacihikoyân kâ-kî-wîhtamawicik. tânitaht ôta iskwêwak aya, ahpô
âskaw nipâwak nîkihk, ê-miywêyihtahkik anim âya, ê-pêhtahkik
kîkway kâ-wîhtamawakik, ayamihâwin ohci; môy êtokwê ôk âya
ayisiyiniwak aya, âtiht ê-kiskêyihtahkik, tânisi ka-tôtahkik
wêwânêyihtahkwâwi, êkây êkwayikohk ê-kiskêyihtahkik ayamihâwin,
anima manitow-~ kisê-manitowi-pîkiskwêwin anim âya,
kâ-pê-kiskinohamâkawiyâhk niyanân mihcêt ôk âya, kayâs
kâ-kî-ayâcik kiskinohamâtowikamikohk, ayamihêwiskwêwa
kâ-kî-paminikocik; êkwa ayamihêwiyiniwa mîna kâ-kî-kakêskimikocik,
kiskinohamâtowikamikohk ê-ayâcik. nawac êkonik nikiskêyihtên
ê-pê-aya-~, kwayask ê-pê-itâcihocik, kwayask ê-pê-pimâtisicik mîn
ê-~ ê-atoskêcik, aniki kâ-kî-ayâcik kiskinohamâtowikamikohk; kayâs
kâ-kî-ihtakoki ita ê-kanawêyimihcik aya kiskinohamawâkanak.
tânitahtwâw nipêhtên ôtê nâway, êkonik anohc kâ-kîsikâk kwayask
ê-pimâtisicik, kâ-kihci-wîkihtocik, kwayask ê-paminâcik
otawâsimisiwâwa, êkoni ôhi ê-pê-pêhtamân nîst âya pîkiskwêwina.

visit me here at my house. I do not want to brag about my life, but some women —~

≈ / ≈

[FA:]   I will tell you, when. It is ready now!

People come to me for help here at my home when they are troubled as to what to do. And perhaps they think I can help them because I counsel good things, as I know them through my life. I know I have made many people grateful, telling them something of what my parents had told me, too, what they had told me would help me. Many women even sleep over at my house sometimes, they like to hear what I tell them about the faith; perhaps some of these people do not know what to do when they are troubled, they do not know enough of the faith, the word of God, which many of us were taught while we were students at boarding-school long ago, with nuns looking after us; and also with priests preaching to us while we were in boarding-school. I know that they have been leading better lives, they have been living right and they have been working, these who used to be in boarding-school; the schools that used to exist long ago, where the students were boarded. Many times I have heard it, in the past, that they live right today, having been married in church, that they look after their children properly, I myself have been hearing these accounts.

[6]   misakâmê ayisk ôma, kâ-mêkwâ-pimâtisiyahk,
kitâcimostâtonânaw mâna tânis ê-ispayik aya, ôm âya, m-~
pimâtisiwin ôma kâ-pimâtisîtotamahk mêkwâc. pêci-nâway ôtê
nawac ayisiyiniwak (tânitahto nipêhtawâwak) ê-kî-pê-miyawâtahkik,
nawac ahpô, ê-itwêcik, ê-mêkwâ-kitimâkisicik, nawac
ê-kî-miyawâtahkik, osâm ê-kî-sâkihitocik, nanâtohk is
ê-kî-aya-wîcihitocik mîn âya, ê-kî-kiyokâtocik,
miyêkwâ-wâskamisîtwâwi; êkosi mân îtwêwak; êkwa wêtinahk
ê-kî-âcimostâtocik, ê-miywâsik kîkway
ê-kî-mâmiton-~-mâmiskôtahkik.

[6]   For all along, throughout our life, we tell one another about what is happening, about this life we are in the midst of living. In the past, people had been happier (I have heard many say that), they had been happier even when they were poor, because they used to love one another, they used to help one another in various ways, and they also visited one another when they were settled down; that is what they say; and they used to take time to tell stories to one another and to talk about good things.

II

[7]   awa kâ-kakwêcimit iskwêw aw ôta kâ-pîkiskwêhit, namôy
nipê-nisitawêyimâwak —~ ninîkihikwak, ayisk aya (namôy cêskwa
nitâcimostawâw aya), wîhcêkaskosîwi-sâkahikanihk nikâwiy
ê-kî-oht-~ ê-kî-ohtohtêt; wîsta ê-kî-pê-aya-kihci-wîkihtot aya
onihcikiskwapiwinihk, êkwa môy —~ môya kêhcinâ
nôh-nisitawêyimâwak nimosôm êkwa aya nôhkom, têpiyâhk mâna
ê-kî-pê-kiyôtêcik, êkota mâna piko ê-kî-wâpamakik. mâka
nikî-kiskêyihtên, ê-kî-~ mistah ê-kî-miyohtwât nimosôm, tahtwâw
wiyâpamak[i] îyikohk ê-kî-kisêwâtisit. nôhkom mîn âya, nawac piko
kî-âhkwâtisiw nôhkom, nikî-itikawin mâna [ê-pâhpit]. mâka
kwayask kî-pimâtisiw nôhkom, misakâmê kî-wîcêwêw nimosôma,
iskw ê-~ iskw ê-nakataskêyit. êwakw ânim êtokwê kêhcinâ
k-âkihtêk, ayisiyiniw aya, kâ-kitimâkêyihtot kwayask kâ-wîkihtot.
nikî-pâhpinân mâna, ê-kî-nihtâ-naniwêyatwêt nôhkom, êkosi
nikî-isi-nisitawêyimâw nôhkom. êkwa, namôy kîkway aya
ê-mâyâtahk nika-sîhkimikonân nôhkom, êkosi
nikî-isi-nisitawêyimâw. êkwayikohk piko ê-kî-nisitawêyimakik,
nimosôm êkwa nôhkom.

[8]   êkwa, kâw êkwa aya, nika-mâmiskôtên ôm âya, maskwacîsihk
ôma kâ-wîcihiwêyân; kinwês âsay ôta kâ-wîcihiwêyân, mitoni kêkâc
êtokwê nikotwâsomitanaw-askiy ôta ê-wîcihiwêyân. mistahi mâna
nistam ôta kâ-pê-wîcihiwêyân, mîna maywês ôtê kâ-pê-ayâyân,
mistahi nikî-nêpêwisin mân âya, ayisiyiniwak ka-pîkiskwâtakik;
itowahk kâ-nêpêwisicik, êkotowahk ê-~, êkos ê-kî-pê-is-âyâyan niya

II

Family Background

[7]   This woman [Freda Ahenakew] asked me [about my grandparents], when she made me speak in here [the tape-recorder]; but I did not know them well, for my parents (I have not yet told her about them), my mother had come from *wîhcêkaskosîwi-sâkahikanihk*; she, too, had come from there [away from home] to get married, at *onihcikiskwapiwinihk*, and I never really knew my grandfather and my grandmother, just barely, when they had come to visit, only then would I see them. But I knew that my grandfather was very good-natured, each time I saw him he was so kind. And also about my grandmother, my grandmother was fairly severe, I used to be told [*laughs*]. But my grandmother used to live right, she had lived with my grandfather all along, until he departed this world. That, I guess, is what really counts, when people love one another and when they are properly married. We used to laugh, my grandmother was a great one for joking, that is how I used to know my grandmother. And she would never have encouraged us to do anything bad, that is how I used to know her. That is as much as I knew of my grandfather and my grandmother.

[8]   And now I will go back and talk about when I came to live at *maskwacîsihk*; I have been living here a long time already, it must be almost sixty years that I have been living here. When I had first come to live here, and even before I came to stay over here, I used to be very shy when it came to speaking to people; the kind that is shy,

nipimâtisiwinihk, êkwa ahpô êtokwê mâna nikî-pômêhâwak âskaw
ninîkihikwak, êkâ —~ êkâ tâpwê ayisiyiniwak
ê-ohc-âya-pîkiskwâtakik, êkâ ê-ohc-ôtôtêmiyân, môy ât[a]
ê-ohci-pakwâtakik. misakâmê âta nikî-pê-aya-ayamihân, êkwa môy
nôh-pakwâtâwak ayisiyiniwak. êwak ôhc êtokwê
kâ-kî-nawasônamawicik nâpêwa ka-wîcêwimak,[3] osâm ôm ôhc
ê-kî-is-âyâyân, êka-~, êkâ ê-ohci-nisitawêyimakik ayisiyiniwak.
mîna môy pikw îta ê-kî-itohtahikawiyâhk niyanân, ahpô
nîmihitowinihk môy mistahi nôh-itohtahikawinân, ê-kî-kostamihk
êtokwê êkâ kwayask ka-tôtamâhk, mistahi itahkamikisiyâhki
nîmihitowinihk. êkos ânima ninîkihikonânak wiy
ê-kî-pê-is-ôhpikihikoyâhkik. mâka, niya wiya môy nôh-pakwâtên
anima kâ-kî-pê-is-ôhpikihikawiyâhk, nikî-miywêyihtên mistahi.

[9]   wânaskêwinihk ayâw ayisiyiniw, mâskôc êkâ nanâtohk
k-êtahkamikisit ayisiyiniw, êkosi mâna nititêyihtên. mîna
nipêhtamowinihk ohci (ôk âyahk nêhiyawak kâ-kakêskihkêmocik
nipêhtawâwak) ayisiyiniw êkâ nanâtohk kâ-tôtahk, êkâ
kâ-mâyi-tôtawât wîcayisiyiniwa, wânaskêwinihk pimâtisiw. êkosi
môy âyiwâk êtokwê kîkway ka-nitawêyihtamahk, kîspin aya
kimiyo-wîcêwânawak ayisiyiniwak. anohc kâ-kîsikâk ayisk ôk âya
osk-âyak, namôy kiskêyihtamwak tânitê k-êsi-kwêskîcik anima
miyawâtamowin ê-nitonahkik. êwakw êtokwê ohc âya, osâm êkâ
ê-kiskêyihtahkik (êkâ êkwayikohk ê-wîhtamâhcik,
ê-isi-wâh-wîkicik), onîkihikomâwak, êkâ êkwayikohk ê-kaskihtâcik,
ahpô êtokwê wîstawâw môy ê-kiskêyihtahkik, tânisi
k-êsi-kakêskimâcik otawâsimisiwâwa, k-êsi-nisitawêyimâyit
kisê-manitowa. kipêhtâtinâwâw mihcêtwâw ê-pêyakot
kisê-manitow ê-mamisîyêk; mistah ân[a] ê-kisêwâtisit kisê-manitow
aya, êwakw âwa mâna kâ-mâmiskômâyâhk. ahpô kiyawâw
kipêhtâtinâwâw, 'mâmaw-ôhtâwîmâw' kitisiyîhkâtâwâw
kisê-manitow — pêyakwâw nikî-waniw-~-wanwêhkâkawin, awîn
ân[a] êwako, mâmaw-ôhtâwîmâw. êkwa pêyak iskwêw
nikî-wîhtamâk piyisk aya, êkotê ohci wîhcêkaskosîwi-sâkahikanihk
ê-ohtohtêt ê-pê-kiyokawit ôta, kêhtêskwêw, "awîn ân[a] êwako,"

of that kind I have been all my life, and I must even have disappointed my parents sometimes by not talking to people at all, by not being friendly to them, although I did not mind them. I always did pray, and I did not mind people. That must have been the reason why they chose a man for me to marry, because of the way I was, because I did not know people. And we also were not taken everywhere, we were not even taken to dances much; they must have been afraid that we might not behave properly, that we might seriously misbehave at the dance. That is the way our parents had raised us. But I did not mind the way in which we were raised, I was very happy with it.

[9]   People are at peace with themselves when they do not do all kinds of crazy things, that is what I think. Also, according to what I hear (I listen to these Indians preach), people are at peace with themselves when they do not do all kinds of things, when they do not harm their fellow-man. In this way we should probably not want anything more if only we live in harmony with people. For today the young people do not know where to turn next in their search for amusement. The reason must be that the parents do not know (because they [themselves] are not told enough, each in their own home), they are not competent enough, they themselves do not even know how to counsel their children, for them to know God. Many times I have heard you [the Elders] say that there is only one God on whom you rely; God is indeed merciful, the one we talk about. I have even heard you call God the 'Father of All' — at one time I had been confused as to who is this 'Father of All'. Then finally one woman told me, she came from *wîhcêkaskosîwi-sâkahikanihk* over there and she had come to visit me here, an elderly woman, "Who is that one," I said to her, " 'Father of All'?" I

k-êtak, "mâmaw-ôhtâwîmâw?" ê-itak; "kisê-manitow ana, kâ-itak,"
ê-kî-isit. êkota ohc êkwa mâna kinisitohtâtinâwâw,
'mâmaw-ôhtâwîmâw' k-êtwêyâhk —~, k-êtwêyêk. mâka niya nawac
ê-miyohtamân aya, 'kisê-manitow' k-êtwêyahk, miyâmiskômâyahki
kisê-manitow. tânêhk ânim ânima, 'kisê-manitow' k-êsiyîhkâsot,
môy piko 'manitow' ê-itwêhk, osâm an[a] ê-kisêwâtisit, êwak ôhc
âna 'kisê-manitow' k-ôh-isiyîhkâsot: kahkiyaw ôta askîhk
ê-kitimâkêyimikoyahk kisê-manitow. êwako niya
nitâpwêwakêyihtên, kiyâm âta kâ-pâstâhoyahk, kiyâm âta
kâ-maci-pimâtisiyahk, môy kitasênikonaw awa kisê-manitow,
'kôhtâwînaw' k-êtâyahk. kâkikê kitasawâpamikonaw, kwayask
ka-tôtamahk ka-kîwêtotawâyahk.

[10]   êwakw ânima kitimâkêyihtowin, ka-wîhtamâtoyahk kîkway
ê-miywâsik, ka-nisitawêyimâyahk kisê-manitow, wâwîs cî ôk âya
osk-âyak, ayiwâk mâna niya êkonik nikitimâkêyimâwak. nama
wîhkâc nipôn-âyamihêstamawâwak, êkwa pî-~ piyîkiskwâtakwâw[i]
âya, mitoni kwayask kisêwâtisiwinihk ohc âya, nipîkiskwâtâwak,
mâskôc nawac ê-itêyihtamân —~

≈ / ≈

said to her; "That is the Merciful God, that is what I call him," she said to me. Now, with that I understand you when we —~ when you say 'Father of All'. But as for me, I prefer to hear us say 'Merciful God' when we talk about God. The reason why he is called 'Merciful God' and you do not simply say 'God' is that He is merciful, that is why he is called the 'Merciful God:' the Merciful God loves all of us here on earth. I believe that, even though we sin, even though we live a wicked life, the Merciful God does not reject us, 'Our Father' as we call him. He is always watching over us, for us to do the right thing and to go back to him.

[10]   That is what it means to love one another, to tell one another what is good, so that we may know God, especially these young people, I love them especially. I never cease praying for them, and even when I speak to them, I speak to them in kindness, I think it would be better —~

≈ / ≈

[FA:]   —~ êskwa; ka-wîhtamâtin. êkwa, êkwa!

III

[11]   nik-âtotên êkwa, nitawâsisîwiwin ohc âya, iyikohk
kaskihtâyân⁴ ê-isi-kiskisiyân, êwakw âw âya, iskwêw awa k-âcimôhit
aya, êkos ê-isi-nitawêyihtahk k-âcimostawak, tânis
ê-kî-pê-is-ôhp-~,⁵ ê-kî-pê-ispayik nitawâsisîwiwinihk.

[12]   ê-pê-kiskisiyân aya, aspin ohc âya kâ-awâsisîwiyân, ê-kî-wâpamakik
aya, ninîkihikwak êkwa kotakak ayisiyiniwak, kotakak
onîkihikomâwak, iyikohk ê-kî-atoskêcik, ê-wî-pimâcihocik. êkoni ôhi
ê-kî-tôtahkik, ê-kî-mâcîcik mâna wiyâs kik-âyâcik, êkwa mîn âya
ê-kî-nôcihcikêcik, wat-~ wacaskwa osâm piko kâ-kî-nôcihâcik êkospî,
môy êkwayikohk amiskwa. êkwa mîn ê-kî-nôcikinosêwêcik mâna.
kâkikê kî-wawêyîstamwak aya kâ-wî-pipok aya, mîciwin mân
ê-kî-astamâsocik; ê-kî-sipwêpicicik mân ê-nitawi-wîkicik êkotê,
ê-minahocik, môswa osâm piko, êkwa apisimôsosa, êkwa mîn âya;
môy êkwayikohk wiya kâ-takwâkik wacaskwa, ayisk mêyoskamiki
mâna kâ-kî-nôcihcikêhk. êkota mîna mâna kî-nitawi-wîkiwak,
miyoskamiki mân ê-kî-nitaw-âya-wanihikêcik mâna âh-~, wacaskwa
mân ê-kî-tasôhâcik. êwakw ânim êkos ê-kî-isi-pimâcihocik kayâs
ayisiyiniwak.

[13]   êkwa mîna kâ-takwâkik, kâ-miskahkik mînisa, êkotê ê-~,
nôcihcikêwaskîhk mînisa kâ-miskahkik, êkoni mîna kî-mawisowak.
iyinimina kî-ihtakonwa êkwa aya, 'wîsakîmina' ê-kî-isiyîhkâtêki
êkoni mînisa, êkotê ê-kî-ayâki, êkwa nik-~ nikikomina mîna.
nanâtohk isi iskwêwak mîna kî-kakwê-isi-pimâcihowak,
otawâsimisiwâwa aya ê-kakwê-pimâcihâcik, êkwa onâpêmiwâwa
mîna ê-kî-wîcihâcik aya, tânisi k-êsi-pimâcihocik.

[FA:]   —~ wait; I will tell you. Now, now!

III

....

Childhood Memories

[11]   Now I will tell about my childhood, as much as I am able to remember, it is this woman [Freda Ahenakew] who is making me tell about it, that is what she wants me to tell her about, how I was —~ how things used to be in my childhood.

[12]   From the time I was a child, I still remember, I saw my parents and other people, other parents, work so hard at making a living. These are things they used to do: they used to hunt so they had meat, and they also used to trap, at that time they mostly used to trap for muskrat, not so much for beaver. And they also used to fish. All the time they used to prepare for the next winter, storing up food for themselves; they would move their camps out and go to live out there [on the trapline], killing game, mostly moose and deer, and also muskrats; but not as many in the fall, for they used to trap for them in the spring. And then they used to go to live out there, in the spring they used to go to set traps and they used to trap muskrats. That is how the people made a living long ago.

[13]   And in the fall, when they found berries, when they found berries out there on the trapline, they also used to pick berries. There were blueberries and cranberries, as these berries were called, they grew over there, and also wild black-currants. The women also had various ways of trying to make a living, trying to make a living for their children, and they also used to help their husbands in making a living.

[14]   kotak kîkway mîn ê-kiskisiyân, iyikohk mâna mistah âya, mihta
ê-pâstêyiki ê-kî-~ ê-kî-kwayâtastamâsocik, êkâ ka-nôhtêpayicik aya,
kisiniyiki kâ-pipok. mistahi mâna kwayask
ê-kî-mâmitonêyihtêstamâsocik, ê-itêyihtamân kayâs, kêhtê-ayak,
tânis âya, kik-ês-âya-~, êkâ êkwayikohk ka-wawânêyihtahkik ôma
kâ-kisik kâ-pipok; kahkiyaw kîkway ê-kî-kwayâtastamâsocik, mistahi
mân ê-kî-ispastâcik mihta. êkwa âtiht ê-kwayâc-âya-kîskipotâcik
ahpô ê-nikohtêcik, ê-kwayâtastamawâcik aya owîkimâkaniwâwa
sêpwêhtêtwâwi, sêpwêhtêtwâwi k-âpacihtâyit.

[15]   êkwa kî-miywâsinwa êkospî aya, ascikêwikamikwa ê-kî-ayâcik
ayisiyiniwak, ita wiyâs ê-kanawêyihtahkik kâ-pipok, asiskiy ohci
ê-kî-apahkwâtahkik anih âya, wâ-~ wâskahikanisa,
'ascikêwikamikwa' kî-isiyîhkâtêwa, ê-kî-sisoskiwakinikâtêki mân
âsiskiy ohc êkwa, asiskiy mîn ê-~ ê-apahkwâtêki ohci. êkwa k-~
kâ-nîpik mîna mitoni kî-tahkâwa êkoni wâskahikanisa.
[16]   ê-pê-kiskisiyân tânis ê-kî-isi-paminikoyâhk nikâwînân;
ê-kî-yîkinikêt mâna, ê-miyosiyit mâna mostoswa ê-kî-ayâwât,
yîkinikana. mistahi mân âya, tôhtôsâpoy nikî-ohci-pimâcihikonân
êkwa aya, manahikan êkwa ascascwâs, mîna mân ê-kî-~,
ê-kî-kîsisahk mâna ê-pakâhtât, ascascwâs anim ê-kîsisahk, môy
miton ê-pakâhtât mâk ê-kî-kîsisahk, êwako ê-kî-asamikoyâhk;
manahikan ê-astât.
[17]   kiyâm âta kâ-pipok, âhci piko mân ê-kî-yîkinikêt nikâwînân.
êkwa mistahi mân âya, ê-kî-papâmohtêyâhk, ê-wîcêwâyâhk âskaw
ê-~ ê-papâmi-mawisot, êkwa ê-kî-nayahtahk mâna mînisa aya,
ê-pê-kîwêhtatât êkwa ê-kî-pâsahk misâskwatômina. êkwa mîna
takwahiminâna mân ê-kî-takwahahk, ê-pâsahk êkoni; kâ-pipok
êkoni ê-mîciyâhk. sôskwâc mistahi kîkway kî-kaskihtâwak kayâs
kêhtê-ayak ê-~ ê-kwayâtastamâsocik mîciwin, êkâ
ka-wawânêyihtahkik; êkwa mîn ôtawâsimisiwâwa êkâ ka-waw-~
ka-nôhtêhkatêyit. wâwâc mân ânim âya, kotak kîkway aya, pikw
âwiyak miywêyihtam êkoni, kâhkêwakwa mîna mân ê-kî-osîhtâcik,

[14]   And another thing I remember is how much dry firewood they used to pile up, getting it ready for themselves so that they would not run short if it was cold during the winter. The old people used to plan things well for themselves long ago, I think, how not to have to worry so much when it was cold, in winter; they used to get everything ready for themselves, they used to build up big piles of firewood. And some they used to have sawn ready into stove-lengths or even split, getting it ready for their wives for the time when they themselves would leave, for their wives to use when they [the men] would leave.

[15]   And people had good storage shacks then, where they kept the meat during winter, they used to roof the little shacks with sod, they used to be called storage shacks, they used to mud them, roofing them with sod. And in the summer these shacks used to be cool.

[16]   I still remember how our mother used to take care of us; she used to milk cows, she used to have good cows, milk cows. She used to have lots of milk on which to sustain us, and cream, and curds and whey, and she would also cook this, boiling it, cooking it to make cottage cheese, she did not quite boil it but she used to cook it, and this she fed us; putting cream on it.

[17]   Even during the winter our mother would still milk the cows. And we used to go around a lot, sometimes going along with her as she went about berry-picking, and she used to carry the berries on her back and bring them back home, and she used to dry saskatoons. And she also used to pound chokecherries and dry them; these we ate during the winter. The old people long ago surely used to accomplish a great deal, getting food ready for themselves so that they would not have to worry about it; and so that their children would not have to go hungry. There were even those other

kâ-nîpik mân âya ê-kî-pâsahkik êkwa ê-kaskâpasahkik. êkwa mîna
mân ê-pahkêkinoh-~, ê-kî-pahkêkinohkêcik, pahkêkinwa
ê-kî-osîhtâcik; êwakw ânim îskwêwak otatoskêwiniwâw. âta wiy
êtokwê mâ-~, ita k-âyimaniyik, nâpêwak mîna mâna kî-wîcihêwak
wîwiwâwa, ita aya, ita k-âyimaniyik aya, pahkêkin ohc ânim âhpô
piko kâ-sînamihk ê-kî-âyimahk aya, mistikwa ê-kî-âpacihtâhk, anihi
m-~ anihi pahkêkinwa ê-sînâskwahamihk mistikwa ohci.

[18]   nîsta mân ê-awâsisîwiyân ê-kiskisiyân, nikâwiy ê-kî-wîcihak mân
âya, kâ-misipocikêt, kâ-misipotât aya pahkêkin, ka-yôskâyik,
kî-âyiman êwakw âtoskêwin. pîwâpisk mân ê-kî-tahkopitahkik
ê-napakâyik êkwa êkota aya, pahkêkin aya, ê-misipotâhk, ê-apihk
ê-~ âh-âyîtaw ohc ê-itinamihk ê-~, ê-~ ê-yôskipotâhk êwakw ânima
pahkêkin. nikî-nâh-nôhtêsinin mâna [ê-pâhpit], ê-awâsisîwiyân;
êwako mân ê-kî-wîcihak nikâwiy. kahkiyaw kîkway kî-tôtam
nikâwiy, mîna mostoswayâna mîna mân ê-kî-osîhât.

[19]   sôskwâc aya, kahkiyaw kîkway nikiskisin, nikâwînân
ê-kî-kiskinohamâkoyâhk atoskêwin mîn ôhc ôm âya, tâpiskôc
ê-awâsisîwiyân ohci nikî-kiskinohamâk ka-kisêpêkinamân wiyâkana,
êkwa ka-nahastâyân, êkwa ka-wêpahikêyân. môy ê-misikitiyân ohc
êwakw ânima ê-kî-aya-itôtamôhit nikâwiy, êkwa êkâ —~ êkâ
wâh-tôtamân[i] âya, kâ-nitawi-kâsoyân ahpô kâ-nitawi-mêtawêyân
kâ-wayawîpahtâyân, êkâ kâ-wî-kâsîyâkanêyân, ê-kî-pê-wayawît mâna
nikâwiy aya, nîpisîs[a] ê-pê-tahkonahk ê-wî-~ ê-wî-pasastêhot
ka-nitawi-kâsîyâkanêyân. mâka namôy wîhkâc nôh-pasastêhok,
nikî-têtipêwêyâmon mân ê-nitawi-pîhtokwêyâmoyân
ê-nitawi-kâsîyâkanêyân, êkosi môy ôhc-âpacihtâw anima nîpisîs
[ê-pâhpit]. êwak ôhc ânohc kâ-kîsikâk mîna kayâhtê kâ-pê-wîcêwak
ispî niwîkimâkan, nikî-kaskihtân êkoni ê-tôtamân, ê-kâsîyâkanêyân
êkwa ê-~, êkw ê-wêpahikêyân; ê-wî-kakwê-kanâcihtâyân wâskahikan
ayisk, nikâwiy êwako ê-kî-kiskinohamawit. êkwa namôy wîhkâc
nôh-kisiwâhik aya nikâwiy aya, êwak ôma kâ-kî-pê-is-ôhpikihit.
misakâmê nipê-nanâskomâw ê-kî-miy-ôhpikihit nikâwiy, ahpô âskaw

things, everybody likes them, they also used to make dried meat, they used to dry and smoke it during the summer. And they also used to make leather, they used to tan the hides; that was women's work. Where it was hard, though, I guess the men used to help their wives, where it was hard, especially when it came to wringing out the hide, this was hard work, they used to employ rails, wringing the hides out with the help of wooden rails.

[18]   I, too, as a child, I remember, used to help my mother, when she did the rolling, when she rolled the hide over a blade so that it would be soft, that was hard work. They used to tie fast a steel blade, and then you would run the hide over it, sitting on either side and holding on to the hide and softening it [by running it back and forth across the blade]. More than once did I get played out [*laughs*], as a child; I used to help my mother with that. My mother used to do everything, she also tanned cow hides.

[19]   I remember that our mother used to teach us everything about work, from childhood on, for instance, she used to teach me to wash the dishes and to put them away, and to do the sweeping. From the time when I was small my mother used to make me do that, and any time I would not do it, when I went to hide or went to play, when I ran outside, when I would not wash the dishes, my mother used to come outside carrying a willow-switch and ready to whip me so I would go and wash the dishes. But she never did whip me, I would run in a circle and then inside and go to wash the dishes, and so she never used that willow-switch [*laughs*]. That is the reason why today and earlier on, at the time I came to marry my husband, I was able to do these things, to wash the dishes and to do the sweeping; for my mother had taught me to try and keep the house clean. And my mother never made me angry at her, at the way she raised me. All along I have

kâ-pasastêhot, kâ-kaskihtamâsoyân, namôy wîhkâc aya
nôh-kisîstawâw nikâwiy, âhci piko nikî-sâkihâw; mâka kahkiyaw
pâh-pîtos kitis-âyânânaw [ê-pâhpit]. ka-kî-sâkihâyahkik
kikâwînawak, ayisk aya mistahi pê-kakwâtakihtâwak, ê-aya-~
ê-wî-ohpikihikoyahkik. môy kikiskêyihtê-~ [6]

≈ / ≈

[FA:]   êkwa!

[20]   êkwa ôm âya, mîna nik-âtotên nikâwiy aya, maskisina
ê-kî-nihtâ-kaskikwâtahk, ê-kî-âpacihtât mân ânim âya, 'astinwân'
k-êsiyîhkâtêk, ê-kî-osîhtamâsot mîn êwakw ânim âya, pahkêkin
kâ-osîhtâci, kahkiyaw ê-kî-osîhtamâkoyâhk mân âya,
'napakaskisina' mân îsiyîhkâtêwa, êkotowahk miton ê-kî-kaskihtât.
êkwa, anihi mîna mâna kotaka kî-osîhtâw, 'ocîhkwêhikana'
kî-isiyîhkâtêwa, êkoni mîna kî-kaskihtâw ê-osîhtât nikâwiy.
misatimow-~ misatimwâyowa mâna· kî-~ kî-atisamwak aya,
ê-titipikwanahahkik êkoni anih âya, ocîhkwêhikana,
ka-miyonâkwaniyiki ê-kî-isîhtâcik mâna. miton âpisis kî-kaskihtâw
nikâwiy mîkisihkahcikêwin, mâka wiy êwak ôma mitoni
kî-kaskihtâw aya, maskisina ê-osîhtât êkwa ocîhkwêhikana mîn
ê-osîhtât. êkwayikohk kî-nihtâw-~ kî-nihtâwisîhcikêw nikâwiy,
maskisina kî-nihtâ-osîhtâw.

[21]   êkwa mîn âya, nitayiwinisinâna mîn âya kî-kaskikwâtam,
nikî-postayiwinisahikonân wiy ê-wiyisahk ayiwinisa êkwa
ê-kaskikwâtamâkoyâhk. kayâs mâna mistahi mîna kî-moscikwâsowak
iskwêwak.· mâka piyisk aya, nikâwiy kî-ayâw aya, 'kaskikwâswâkan'
mân ôhi k-êsiyîhkâtamahk aya, mêkwâc k-âpatahki,
kâ-kaskikwâsopayihcikâkêhk, êkotowahk kî-ayâw mâka mân
ê-kî-mosci-wâskânahk ê-kî-papâmohtatât mân âya, êkoni anih âya
kayâs kî-ihtakonwa (âtiht êyâpic êtokwê ihtakonwa
ê-mosci-wâskânamihk aya, kaskikwâsopayihcikanisa), êkotowahk
mân ê-kî-ayât nikâwiy, nîstanân mâna nikî-âpacihtânân, ispî

been grateful to my mother that she raised me well, even when she whipped me sometimes when I deserved it, I never stayed angry at my mother and I still loved her; but we are all different. We should love our mothers for they have suffered greatly in raising us. We do not know —~

≈ / ≈

[FA:]   Now!

[20]   And now I will also tell about the fact that my mother was good at sewing moccasins, that she used to use sinew as it is called, that she used to prepare that for herself, too, when she had tanned the leather, she used to make moccasins for all of us, they are called flat moccasins, she was good at making that kind. And she also used to make the other kind, they were called gathered, my mother used to be able to make those, too. They used to dye horse-hair, sewing it around the vamp of the gathered moccasins so as to make them look nice. My mother used to know a little bit of beadwork, but she used to know a lot about making moccasins, and about making gathered moccasins. My mother was quite versatile in making things, she was good at sewing moccasins.

[21]   She also used to sew our clothes, she used to clothe us, cutting the pieces out herself and sewing the clothes for us. The women used to sew a lot by hand long ago. But finally my mother had a sewing-machine, as we call these things now, the kind used today, the ones you use to machine-sew, she had that kind and she used to turn the wheel by hand, she used to take it with her, those are the ones that existed here long ago (some of these little sewing-machines must still be around), my mother had that kind, and we used it, too, when we learnt to sew for

ê-kaskihtâyâhk ka-kaskikwâtisoyâhk, nîstanân nikî-âpacihtânân aya,
kiskinohamâtowikamikohk ê-kî-kiskinohamâkawiyâhk, tânisi
k-êsi-kaskikwâsoyâhk, êkwa mîna tânisi k-ês-âpihkêyâhk; êwako
kiskinohamâtowikamikohk nikî-kiskinohamâkawinân, êkwa
nikî-kaskihtânân aya, k-ôsîhtamâsoyâhk miskotâkaya, êkwa
aspastâkana, êkwa itâmihk mîn ôh âyiwinisa mâna
kî-osîhtamâsonâniwiw kayâs, ê-kî-kitimâkisihk aya, maskimotêkinwa
mâna kâ-wâpiskâki, 'pahkwêsikaniwata' kî-isiyîhkâtêwa, êkotowahk
mân âya, ê-kî-~ itâmihk ayiwinisa kâ-kikiskamihk ê-kî-ohc-ôsîhtâhk.
kahkiyaw kîkway ayisiyiniwak aya êkospî, môy ôhc-âtawêyihtamwak,
têpiyâhk kwayask ka-postayiwinisêcik, êwako ê-kî-kitâpahtahkik.
ahpô âtiht mân êkoni ôhi maskimotêkinwa, ê-kî-mân-âya-atisahkik,
kotak kîkway ê-osîhtâcik, miskotâkaya ahpô aspastâkana
ê-kî-osîhtamâsocik aya, kâh-atisahkwâw[i], âhpô papakiwayâna,
nâpêwak mâna ê-kî-kikiskahkik. miton âya, kahkiyaw kîkway aya,
namôy ôhc-âtâwêwak kîkway ayisiyiniwak aya mistah âya,
ka-mêstinikêcik ka-postayiwinisahisocik. êkwa mîn êwakw ânima
ê-kî-kaskihtâcik mân ôki kiskinohamawâkanak kâ-wayawîcik aya,
ê-kî-apihkât-~ ê-kî-apihkâtâcik mân âsikana, nâpêwasikana mân
ê-kî-osîhâcik; onâpêmiwâwa mân ê-kî-osîhtamawâcik asikana.

[22]   anohc êkwa êkoni, mistahi mâna kwîtawêyihcikâtêwa[7] aya;
ê-kî-wanihtâhk mistah âya, ayisiyiniw anima
kâ-kî-isi-miyo-waskawîstamâsot, êkây êkwa êwakw ânim âya
ê-ispayik. nayêstaw piko atâwêwikamikohk ê-itohtêhk, nayêstaw
kîkway ê-wî-kakwê-atâwêhk. êwak ôhc ôm ôm âya, âcimowin ôma
k-o-~ k-ôh-nitotamâkawiyân k-âtotamân, ka-kiskêyihtahkik osk-âyak,
tânis âya, nâway ôtê kêhtê-aya, tânis ê-kî-pê-is-âya-paminamiyit aya,
opimâtisiwiniyiw êkwa mîna, anim âya, tânis
ê-kî-pê-isi-postayiwinisahisocik ayisiyiniwak. kahkiyaw âyimanohk
ohci kîkway ê-kî-kâhcitinahkik mâk âya, namôya wiya wiyawâw ohc
âya ohc-âyimaniyiw, ayisk kî-nakayâskamwak. kî-miywêyihtamwak
êkoni ôhi ê-tôtahkik, ê-papâmi-mâcîcik, ê-papâmipicicik. êkwa mîna
mâna kâ-nîpik ê-kî-nôcihâcik sîsîpa; êkoni mîna ê-kî-mowâcik mân

ourselves, we used it, too, we were taught sewing at school and also knitting; we were taught that at school, and we were able to sew dresses for ourselves, and aprons, and people made undergarments for themselves long ago, for they were poor, white sack-cloth, flour-bags they were called, people used to wear undergarments made from that kind. The people did not reject anything in those days so long as they were dressed properly, that is what they looked at. Some even used to dye this sack-cloth to make other things, making dresses or aprons for themselves once they had dyed it, or the shirts men used to wear. They really made everything, the people did not buy very much, spending money to buy clothes for themselves. And also, when the students came out of school, they were able to knit socks, they used to make men's socks; they used to make socks for their husbands.

[22]   And today these skills are greatly missed; people have largely lost how well they used to shift for themselves, now there is none of that taking place. You just go to the store now, you just go and try to buy something. This is why it is that I am asked to tell about it, so that the young people would know how the old people back then used to run their lives, and also how the people used to clothe themselves. Everything used to be hard to obtain, but for them it was not hard because they were used to it. They were happy to do these things, hunting here and there, moving their camps about. And also, in the summer, they used to hunt ducks; these, too, they used to eat when they went duck-hunting. They even used to search for eggs,

âya, ê-nôcisipêcik. wâwâc mân ê-kî-nitawâwêcik, ê-kî-kitimahâcik
mâna sîsîpa aya, owâwiyiwa mân ê-kî-otinamwâcik, êkoni ê-mîcicik.
[23]   sôskwâc kî-miywâsin kayâs pimâcihowin, mâk ânohc êtokwê
êkwa, namôy êkosi mistahi ka-kî-isi-pimâcihonâniwiw, osâm mistah
êkwa misiwanâcihtâniwiw askiy, iyikohk ê-pîkopitamihk misiw îtê.
ahpô piko, pihêwa mîn ê-kî-ohtâcihocik ayisiyiniwak, ê-namatêcik
êkwa osâm êkâ nânitaw ê-kî-owâwicik, misiw îtê ê-pîkopicikâtêk.
âta wiya êyâpic êtokwê ihtakowak aya, sakâwi-pihêwak
paspaskiwak, âtiht êtokwê êyâpic âta wiy êkotowahk aya, ohcâ-~
ohtâcihowak, êkwa wâposwa mîna kî-ohtâcihowak.

[24]   kiwanihtânânaw êkwa êwakw ânima pimâcihowin aya, ayisk aya,
kahkiyaw kîkway aya, pîtos êkwa ê-itâcihohk ôk âya, môniyâwak
kâ-pê-kiskinohamâkoyahkik ôma, pîtos itâcihowin, mihcêt kîkway
êkoni ôh âya ê-misiwanâcihtâcik. nipiya mîn ôh âya ê-pisc-~
ê-piscipohtâcik; âtiht mân âya, kinos-~ kinosêwak ê-itwêhk
ê-piscipocik anim âya, mihcêt kîkway anim êkwa ê-wêpinahkik
êtokwê ôk âya, atoskêwin ohci kâ-tôtahkik aya. pimiy êtokwê
kêhcinâ mân ânima kâ-piscipôskâcik kinosêwak, êkwa sîsîpak
mîna. êwako wiy êkwa ânohc[8] kâ-pêhtâkwahk, êkos ê-ispayik. môy
kêhcinâ êtokwê aya, ka-kî-kîwêtotênânaw ôm êwako pimâtisiwin,
iyikohk kayâs kâ-kî-miywâsik, mâka ê-isko-kaskihtâyahk ôm îyikohk
kâ-kiskinohamâkoyahkik ôk âya ('kiciwâminawak' isiyîhkâtêwak mân
âya, nêhiyawak aya, 'môniyâw' k-êsiyîhkâtâyahk),
ê-wî-kakwê-wîcihikoyahk ât[a] êtokwê, nanâtohk isi kîstanaw
k-êsi-pimâtisiyahk —~ k-êsi-pimâcihoyahk.
[25]   mâk âya, namôya ka-nôtinamahk êwakw ânim âya, kîspin
kiwî-wîcihikawinânaw tânisi k-êsi-pimâcihoyahk,
ka-kî-anima-wîcêhtamahk, ka-kî-anima-kiskinohamâkosiyahk, tânisi
kwayask k-êsi-pimâcihoyahk. môy nayêstaw ka-nawaswâtamahk aya
(âtiht ayisiyiniwak môy miywêyihtamwak anima pinkow, osâm
mistahi nawaswâtamwak ayisiyiniwak); ê-itwêcik mâna, osâm
mistahi nawaswâtêwak sôniyâwa aya, nêhiyawak anohc kâ-kîsikâk;
"kêtahtawê nôt-~ nôhtêhkatêhki, namôy ka-kî-mowêwak sôniyâwa."

they were mean to the ducks, they used to take their eggs
and eat them.

[23]   The life of long ago certainly was good, but you
probably could not really live like that today, for there is
too much damage to the earth, there is so much
cultivation all over. For example, the people used to live
on prairie-chickens, they are gone now because they have
no place where they might lay their eggs, the land is
cultivated all over. Although there must still be some
wood-chickens, partridges, some people must still live on
that kind, and they also used to live on rabbits.

[24]   We have lost that way of making a living, for in
everything there is now a different way of making a living,
the Whites have come to teach us a different way of life
and they have destroyed many of these things. They have
also poisoned the water; some fish are poisoned, too, it is
said, they must be dumping lots of things from what they
do in their factories. Surely it has to be the oil that has
poisoned the fish, and the ducks, too. And that is what
one hears is going on today. Surely we could not go back
to that life which used to be so good, but should follow as
best we can what they teach us (the Crees often call them
'our brothers', the 'Whites' as we call them), for they are
trying to help us, I guess, for us, too, to live in a different
way, to follow a different lifestyle.

[25]   But we should not fight that, if we are going to be
helped with a different lifestyle, we should cooperate
with that, we should be educated in how to live in that
lifestyle. We should not only chase after bingo (some
people do not like it because the people chase after it too
much); as they say, the Crees chase after money too
much nowadays; "Someday when there is hunger, they
will not be able to eat money." That is what the people

êkosi mân ê-ititocik ayisiyiniwak anohc kâ-kîsikâk, namôy kahkiyaw
ayisiyiniw kâ-miywêyihtahk anima pinkow, osâm aya, awâsisak
mistahi ê-nakatihcik ê-kitimahihcik. mâskôt nawac aya, pîtos is
ôma êyâpic mistahi kikiskêyihtênânaw, pîtos isi
k-ês-âya-pahpakwacihoyahk ôma, ahpô piko ka-kaskikwâsoyahk,
êkwa âtiht kaskihtâwak aya, ta-mîkisihkahcikêcik. mistahi pikw
âwiyak miywêyihtam mîkisihkahcikêwin, ka-kî-~ êwakw âna —~
anima ohci-pimâcihonâniwiw, mihcêt êtokwê ôtê kîwêtinohk,
êwakw ânim ê-ohci-pimâcihocik aya, mîkisihkahcikêwin anima,
êkwa aya maskisina, astisak, êkwa aya miskotâkaya anihi
ê-osîhtâcik; êyâpic ôma mihcêt ayisiyiniwak ôtê kîwêtinohk,
iskwêwak mîna mistah ê-atoskêcik, ka-kakwê-pimâcihocik. êkwa
aya, êkwa mîciwin mîn êtokwê mistahi kîkway aya
kaskihtamâsowak, osîhtamâsowak aya, ê-nôcikinosêwêcik êkwa
ê-pâswâ-~ ê-pâswâcik mîn âya (tânisi mân âniki kâ-kaskâpasohcik
kinosêwak), êkonik ê-wawêyîstahkik mîn ôpimâcihowiniwâw —~

≈ / ≈

say to one another today, not everybody likes that bingo because the children are often left alone and neglected. It would perhaps be better for us, for we know lots of other kinds of entertainment, to entertain ourselves differently, for instance to sew, and some know how to bead. Everybody really likes beaded things, and people could make a living with that, a lot of people up North must be living on that, on beadwork, and they also make moccasins, mittens and coats; there are still many people in the North, women also work in order to try and make a living. And they must also earn a lot of food for themselves, they also make it for themselves, they catch fish and then dry them (what is it again when the fish are smoked?), they also prepare these for their livelihood —~

≈ / ≈

[EM:] —~ ê-nitotamawiyan, —

[FA:] êha.

[EM:] — ê-mâc-âcimostâtân ê-kî-miywêyihtamân, *oxen* mân
ê-kî-~ ê-kî-âpacihât aya, *thirteen* pikw ê-itahtopiponwêt ês
ê-kî-mâcatoskêt[9] —~

[FA:] âsay anima mâcipayin êkwa.

[EM:] ôh.

....

[FA:] *Emma Minde* awa ê-wî-âcimostâkoyahk, *Hobbema* ohci,
kîhtwâm ê-wî-âcimostâkoyahk, âsay nîswâw êtikwê *tapes*
anihi kikîsîhtânaw.

[EM:] êha.

[FA:] êkosi, kiya, âcimo!

IV

[26] anohc êkwa ôm âya, ê-wî-âcimostawak aw âya, *Freda
Ahenakew*, niwîkimâkana aya ê-kî-mâc-âcimostawak, tânis
ê-kî-is-âya-mâc-ôkistikêwiyinîwit niwîkimâkan aya, *'Joe Minde'*
kâ-kî-isiyîhkâsot (*'Joseph Minde'* ê-kî-isiyîhkâsot, mâka kâkikê *'Joe
Minde'* kî-~ kî-isi-wîhâw mâna); êwakw âwa niwîkimâkan
ê-kî-âcimostawit wiya, êwak ôma kâ-wî-âtotamân.

[27] pêyakwâw ê-âcimostawit, nistosâp ê-itahtopiponwêt,
kâ-kî-mâc-âtoskêt kistikânihk; ôhtâwiya ê-âhkosiyit ê-kî-wîcihât.
êkwa miton âya ê-kî-miywêyihtamân ê-itâcimostawit osâm aya, môy
âyiwâk kîkway êkwa êkos îsi ê-wâpahtamihk. ayêhkwêwa mân ê-~,
nîsw ê-kî-nîswahpisoyit, ê-kî-pîkopicikêt ê-mostohtêt, nîsw

[EM:]	—~ you asked me for it, —
[FA:]	Yes.
[EM:]	— I began to tell you that I was happy [when I heard] that he had used oxen and that he had begun to work when he was only thirteen years old —~
[FA:]	It [the tape] has already started to run.
[EM:]	Oh.

....

[FA:]	It is Emma Minde who is going to tell us stories, from Hobbema; she is going to tell us stories again, and we have already finished recording two tapes, I guess.
[EM:]	Yes.
[FA:]	That's it, your turn, do tell!

IV

Emma Minde's Marriage

Joe Minde

[26]   Today now I am going to tell Freda Ahenakew about my husband, I had begun to tell her about how my husband, whose name was Joe Minde, had started to farm (Joseph Minde had been his name but he always used to be called Joe Minde); and it was my husband himself who told me the story I am about to tell.

[27]   Once he told me the story of when he had begun, at the age of thirteen, to work in the fields; his father was ill and he was helping him. And I was very happy about what he told me because you do not see anything like that any more. He had harnessed two oxen together and

âyêhkwêwa ê-pîkopicikêhât. miton êtokwê kî-âm-~-âyimaniyiw
niwîkimâkan opimâtisiwin, ê-awâsisîwit itêyihtâkwan
ê-kî-mâc-âya-okistikêwiyinîwit. êkwa tânisi
ê-kî-is-âya-nisitawêyimak niwîkimâkan, kî-pakwâtam wiy âya,
nâh-nîkân kâ-nôkosit, môy ôhci-miywêyihtam wiy âya,
ka-pêhtâkwaniyik owîhowin. kî-otinâw pêyakwâw ê-~ ê-nakat-~,
mwêstas ê-kî-nakataskêyit aya ôhtâwiya, mâmawi-ayisiyiniwa
kî-otinik, ka-tâpapîstamawât ôhtâwiya k-ôkimâhkâniwit; miton
êwakw ânima namôy ôhci-miywêyihtam. kî-wîhtamawêw êsa
ayisiyiniwa, "sôskwâc nama kîkway êwakw ânima ninitawêyihtên niy
âya, k-âtoskâtamân, niwî-ôm-âya-~ niwî-tôtên ôma,
niwî-okistikêwiyinîwin, êkos êwako niwi-~ niwî-kisâtên, osâm
mistahi nika-wanihtân nitatoskêwin, ôma okimâhkâniwiyâni,"
ê-kî-itwêt, nîsta nikî-pêhtawâw êkos ê-itwêt. ahpô ôm âya, tâpiskôc
ôma mêkwâc kâ-tôtamân, ê-wî-âcimôhiht, namôya mîn êwak
ôhci-nitawêyihtam, môy ôhci-nôhtê-tôtam, mîna namôy ôhc-~
ohci-nitawêyihtam wîhkâc omasinipayiwina nânitaw
ka-wâpamimiht kik-âcim-~ kik-âcimiht [ê-pâhpit].

[28]   êkos ê-~, ê-kî-nakatahk êkwa askiy, ayis môy êkwa kiskêyihtam
niwîkimâkan, nik-âcimâw êkwa; wîsta miton âya, pâh-pahk[i] îta
ê-kî-aya-pahkisihk, tâpiskôc aya k-âyisiyinîwiyahk ôm âya,
kahkiyaw kîkway ê-miywâsik kitayânânaw ê-is-âyisiyinîwiyahk,
mîna kîkway ê-mâyâtahk. kîkwây ê-kî-kitimahikot niwîkimâkan,
ê-kî-minihkwêskit; êwakw ânim ê-wi-~ ê-wî-wîhtamân anohc,
mâka ayiwâk kîkway ê-miywâsik êkota aya kik-ôhcipayin,
kik-âcimak ohci niwîkimâkan. ât[a] ê-kî-minihkwêt niwîkimâkan,
âhci piko ê-kî-kaskihtât ê-atoskêt. namôy ôhci-nakîw
ka-mâh-minihkwêt, kîsikâwa ka-wanihtât, atoskêwin aya, anima
ka-~ k-âyât okistikêwiyinîwiwin, môy ôhci-nakatam otatoskêwin;
âhci piko mâna kâ-mâh-minihkwêci êkwa kâ-ayiwêpici kâ-nipâci,
kî-wayawîw mân ê-nitaw-âtoskêt kistikânihk. môy
ôhc-âya-âtawêyihtam niwîkimâkan (mwêhc ânohc ôm
ê-wâpamak), môy ôhci-âtawêyihtam kik-âsiskîwihkwêt, kik-âtoskêt
kistikânihk. ê-kî-pîwêyimot êtokwê mâna, nikî-itêyihtên aya,

had ploughed, walking behind them, driving a team of two oxen to plough the land. My husband's life must have been difficult, he was no more than a child, you might think, when he began to farm. And as I knew my husband, he disliked being in the limelight, he did not like for his name to be heard. He had been chosen once, after the death of his father, he had been chosen by the assembled people to take his father's place as chief; he really had not liked that at all. He had told the people, "I simply do not want that kind of work at all; I am going to do this, I am going to farm, and so I am going to stay with it, because I will lose too much of my working time if I am a chief," he had said, and I myself had heard him say that. Even what I am doing right now, when he was asked to tell a story, he did not want that either, he did not want to do that, and he never wanted his pictures to be seen so that his story would be told [*laughs*].

[28]   And so, now that he has departed this world, I will tell about my husband, for now he will not know about it; he, too, used to have a few real weaknesses here and there, just like other people, all of us who are human have good traits and bad traits. What used to give my husband trouble was that he used to drink; today I am going to speak about that, but something good will come of it, of what I will tell about my husband. Although he used to drink, my husband still used to be able to work. He did not use to stop in order to go drinking around, to lose days of work from his farming, he did not use to leave his work; when he had been drinking, then when he had rested and slept, he would still go out to go and work in the fields. My husband did not think anything (it is as if I saw him today), he did not think anything of getting dirt on his face, of working in the fields. He must have been truly

niwîkimâkan aya, êkâ ê-ohc-âtawêyihtahk ê-âyimaniyik atoskêwin.
ahpô mâna nikî-koskohik nistam kâ-wîcêwak, âta kâ-kimiwahk,
kâ-kîsowê-~-postayiwinisêci kâ-kimiwaniyik, âhci piko mân
ê-kî-pîkopicikêt, ahpô ê-sikwahcisikêt. môy ôhci-kostam
atoskêwin, tâpiskôc anima êkâ k-ôhci-kostahk minihkwêwin,
mâk ânima mîna atoskêwin sôskwâc namôy ôhci-kostam, môy
ôhc-âsênam. nikah-miywêyihtên[10] êwak ôm âya, mihcêt
oskinîkiwak êkwa nâpêwak ka-pêhtahkik, tânisi pêyak ayisiyiniw
ê-nêhiyâwit ê-kî-p-~ ê-kî-pê-is-âya-ayisiyinîwit. tâpwê ê-kî-~
kî-sâkôcihik minihkwêwin, mâka namôya wiy ôhc âya nîhcipitik
aya owaskawîwinihk isi, âhci piko kî-atoskêw. êwakw ânima
kêhcinâ aya ê-kî-miywêyihtamân, ê-kî-oh-~ aya ê-kî-isi-wâpamak
niwîkimâkan ôtê kâ-pê-wîcêwak, ê-~ ê-oskinîkit êkospî
niwîkimâkan kâ-pê-wîcêwak, êkwa nîst ê-~
ê-kî-oskinîkiskwêwiyân, pêyakwan ê-kî-itahtopiponwêyâhk kêswân
awa kâ-kî-wîcêwak nâpêw.

[29]   êkwa ê-wî-wîhtamân ôta, âskaw mâna nikî-nêpêwihik, iyikohk
ê-kî-miyohtwât niwîkimâkan, ê-kî-miyo-tôtawât wîcayisiyiniwa.
mihcêt ayisiyiniwa ê-kî-pê-nitâhtâmikot aya sôniyâwa, êkos
ê-kî-is-âyâwahkahoht niwîkimâkan, namôy wîhkâc
ê-ohci-tipahamâkot. mâka ê-itêyihtamân, nitawâsimisak mân êkosi
ê-kî-itakik êkwa ê-ati-kîs-ôhpikicik (ê-kî-mâna-pakwâtahkik iyikohk
ê-kitimahimiht ôhtâwîwâwa, sôniyâwa ê-~ ê-nitâhtâmimiht, êkwa
êkâ wîhkâc kâw âtiht ê-miyâcik), ômisi mâna nikî-itâwak
nitawâsimisak: "êkây nânitaw itwêk! êkos ân[a] ê-wî-isi-pihkohot
kôhtâwîwâw, êkos ân[a] ê-wî-isi-kâsînamâsot, ka-pihkohow ôma
kâ-tôtahk, ê-kitimâkêyimât wîcayisiyiniwa;" êkosi mân ê-kî-itakik
nitânisak. ayisk iskwêwak piko ê-kî-ayâwâyâhkik nisto, môy wîhkâc
aya nâpêsisak nôh-ayâwânânak, êkosi nîst êtokwê
ê-kî-isi-miyikowisiyân. êwak ôhc âya kâ-kî-kakêskimakik mâna
nitawâsimisak, êkâ nânitaw kik-êtêyihtahkik ôhtâwîwâwa
ê-kî-kitimahimiht, mâka môy —~ môy ê-kitimahiht ayisiyiniw,
nititêyihtên aya, êk-~ êkosi —~ êkosi k-êsi-miyo-tôtahk êkwa
ayisiyiniwa êkâ kâ-nanâskomikot; ahpô wiya kimanitôminaw môy

humble, I used to think, not to have thought anything of hard work. He even used to surprise me when I was first married to him, even when it was raining he would still dress and do his ploughing or harrowing. He was not afraid of work, just as he was not afraid of drinking, but he also was not at all afraid of work, he did not shirk it. I would be happy for many teenagers and men to hear this, how this human being, a Cree, had come to live. True, drink did get the better of him, but it did not drag him down in his activities, he still did his work. I certainly used to be happy that I could see my husband in this light when I came over here to be married to him, he was a young man when I came to be married to him, and I was a young woman, too, it just happened that we were the same age, I and the man to whom I was married.

[29]   And I am going to speak about it here, my husband used to put me to shame at times because he was so good-natured and treated his fellow-man so well. Many people used to come to borrow money from my husband, and he was buried without ever having been paid back by them. That is what I think and what I used to tell my children as they came to be adults (they used to hate the way people took advantage of their father by borrowing money from him and in some cases never giving it back), I used to tell my children as follows: "Don't say anything! That is how your father will get saved, that is how his sins will be wiped off, he will get saved by what he did, his love for his fellow-man;" that is what I used to tell my daughters. For we only had three girls, we never had boys, that is what I was given, I guess. That is why I counselled my children not to mind it that people took advantage of their father, on the contrary, a person suffers no harm, I think, when he does good works in this way and earns no thanks from people,

wîhkâc ohci-nanâskomik awiya ê-kî-~ ê-kî-miyo-tôtawât, êkosi mîna
mâna nikî-isi-mâmitonêyihtên.

[30]   êkwa ôhtâwiya êkwa anih âya, kâ-kî-wîcêwâyit aya, okâwîsa, môy
wîhkâc 'nikâwiy' ohc-îtêw, 'nikâwîs' kî-itêw mâna, mâka kwayask
kî-pamihikwak aya, kwayask kî-pamihik, kwayask kî-kitâpamik.
mâka môy wîhkâc ohci-kaskihtâw 'nikâwiy' kik-êtât. mâka wiya
kî-manâcihêw; kîkway wiyîhtamâkoci, kî-tâpwêhtawêw. ôhtâwiya
mîna, kîkway kâ-wîhtamâkot, kiyâm âta kâ-kisîkitotikot,
kî-manâcihêw ôhtâwiya, kî-tâpwêhtawêw. mîna mân âstamispî
ât[a] ê-kihci-wîkihtot, kî-atoskawêw mâna kistikânihk;
ê-kî-atoskêstamawât ôhtâwiya. êkos ânim âya, êkoni kêhcinâ ôh âya
kâ-nitawêyihtamân aya, oskayisiyiniwak nâpêwak ka-pêhtahkik,
wîstawâw ka-kitimâkêyimâcik aya ôhtâwîwâwa, mîn ôkâwîwâwa
ka-nanahihtawâcik, kîkway kâ-miyo-sîhkimikocik,
ka-tâpwêhtawâcik mîn âya atoskêwinihk isi, namôy ânim ânima
ka-pakwâtahkik atoskêwin, ka-kî-anim-âya-~ kahkiyaw (iskwêwak
mîna kâ-itakik, môy katâc piko nâpêwak êkosi kit-êtakik), kahkiyaw
anima ê-kî-pakitinikowisiyahk ôta waskitaskamik aya,
kik-âtoskêyahk êkwa kik-âpwêsiyahk, ka-kîspinatamahk kîkway aya
k-ôhci-pimâcihoyahk. êkosi, môy âyiwâk ka-kî-pîkiskwâtitinâwâw,
misawâc ê-kiskêyihtamêk ôma kîkway kâ-wîhtamâtakok, têpiyâhk
ê-~ ê-kiskisômitakok.

≈≈≈

[FA:]   êkwa!

[31]   nisis êkwa aya, nimanâcimâkan aya, *Daniel Minde*
ê-kî-isiyîhkâsot aya, niwîkimâkan ôhtâwiya, êwakw êkwa, nîsw

even our God himself never got any thanks when he would do a good deed to someone, and that is how I used to think about it.

[30]   And he never used to call her 'mother', the one his father was married to, his step-mother, he used to call her 'step-mother', but she used to treat them properly, she treated him properly, she accepted him properly. He never was able, however, to call her 'mother'. But he used to respect her; whatever she told him, he would obey her. Also, anything his father told him, even when he spoke to him in anger, he used to respect his father and he used to obey him. And later, too, even when he was married, he would work for his father in the fields; he used to do his work for him. And so I definitely want these young people and men to hear this, for them, too, to love their fathers and to listen to their mothers, to obey them in the good things in which they encourage them, in work, it is not right that they should dislike work, they should all (and I am talking to the women too, it does not only have to be men to whom I say this), we have all of us been placed upon this earth so that we should work in sweat, so that we should earn our livelihood. That is it, I will not be able to speak to you any more, in any case you know what I am telling you, I am merely reminding you.

≈≈≈

[FA:]   Now!

Joe Minde's Family

[31]   Now it is my father-in-law, my parent-in-law, Daniel Minde was his name, my husband's father, now it is

ê-wî-âcimakik aya, êwakw âw âya, nimanâcimâkan kâ-kî-wîcêwât
aya, êkoni aya, âstamispî iskwêwa ê-kî-aya-wîcêwât; niwîkimâkan
okâwiya ê-pôni-pimâtisiyit, kotaka iskwêwa ê-kî-wîcêwât aya;
ê-osk-âyiwiyit nawac iyikohk aya, iyikohk wiya. 'Mary-Jane
onâcowêsis' êwako ê-kî-isiyîhkâsot, êkoni niw-~ niwîkimâkan aya
ê-kî-~ ê-kî-ohpikihikot, okâwîsa. ê-nistopiponwêt êsa kâ-kîwâtisit
niwîkimâkan, êkwa êkoni ôh âya ê-kî-ohpikihikot ok-~ okâwîsa.
êwakw ânima aya, anohc k-âtotamân, namôy wîhkâc 'nikâwiy'
ê-ohc-îtât aya niwîkimâkan, 'nikâwîs' mân ê-kî-itâhkômât aya.
pêyak kî-osîmisiw aya êkota ohc îskwêwa, êkwa pêyak nâpêwa êsa
mîna kî-osîmisiw. mâk ês âna wiya nâpêsis ana nistam
kâ-kî-nihtâwikit, êkw êsa ê-kî-pôni-pimâtisit; 'Paul' ês êwako
ê-kî-isiyîhkâsot. êkwa kîhtwâm awa ('nisikos' nikî-itâhkômâw mân
âya, Mary-Jane Minde), kotak[a] êkwa kî-otânisiw, 'Justine' (mêkwâc
anohc ôma nika-wîhâw ê-isiyîhkâsot, 'Justine Littlechild', êkos
ê-isiyîhkâsot awa nicâhkos); êkoni kotaka osîma niwîkimâkan,
okâwîsa ohc ânih âya ê-otânisiyit; êkwa kotaka mîna
ê-kî-aya-owîtisânit, mâka wiy êkonik anik âya, môy kêhcinâ kîkway
ê-kiskêyihtamân, môy nika-kî-mâmiskômâwak — aniki pikw âya,
nistam anih ô-~ aya, owîkimâkana anihi nistam aya,
nimanâcimâkan awa Dan Minde, 'Celina' ês ê-kî-isiyîhkâsoyit,
êkoni aya niwîkimâkan okâwiya. êkwa kî-omisiw, 'Sophie'
ê-isiyîhkâsoyit; êkwa kotaka mîna kî-omisiw, 'Julie' êwako
ê-kî-isiyîhkâsot; êkonik ôki nîso aya, niwîkimâkan êkoni nistam
okâwiya —~ okâwîwâwa aya ohc âya, êkota êkonik ê-kî-nisticik;
êkwa êkonik anik âya, âsay môy pimâtisiwak êkonik nicâhkosak.
êwakw âna Sophie, 'Sophie Wolfe' kî-isiyîhkâsow, 'Pete Wolfe'
ê-kî-isiyîhkâsoyit owîkimâkana, êkwa ana nit-~ kotak nicâhkos,
êwako ê-kî-osk-~, iyaskohc, 'Julie Headman' êwako ê-kî-isiyîhkâsot,
anihi kâ-kî-~ kâ-kî-kâh-kihci-wîkimâcik nâpêwa; êwakw âw
ônâpêma kî-isiyîhkâsoyiwa aya, 'Jimmy Headman'. mâka kahkiyaw
êkwa ôk âya ayisiyiniwak kâ-wîhakik, môy pimâtisiwak êkonik.
mâka wiy âw âya, Justine Littlechild, êyâpic pimâtisiw; êkwa anihi
kâ-kî-wîcêwât aya nâpêwa, ê-kî-nitaw-~ ê-kî-nitawi-nôtinikêyit

this one, I am going to tell about the two of them, this one, my father-in-law, and the one he was married to, he had married this woman later in life; my husband's mother had died and he had married another woman; she was younger than he was. She was called Mary-Jane *onâcowêsis*, she had raised my husband, his step-mother. My husband was orphaned at the age of three, and it was this one, his step-mother, who raised him. That I have just told about, that my husband never used to call her 'mother', that his kinship term for her was 'step-mother'. He had one younger sister from this [second] marriage, and also one younger brother. But the first-born boy, that one had died; Paul had been his name. And then again, she (my kinship term for Mary-Jane Minde used to be 'mother-in-law'), she had another daughter, Justine (I will give her full name as it is today, Justine Littlechild, that is my sister-in-law's name); she was another younger sister of my husband's, she was from his step-mother, she was her daughter; and he also had other siblings, but as for those, I do not really know anything for certain, I will not be able to talk about them — except for these, my father-in-law Dan Minde's first wife, Celina was her name, she was my husband's mother. And he [my husband] had an older sister, Sophie was her name; and he also had another older sister, Julie was that one's name; these two were from my husband's first mother [*sic*] —~ their mother, they were three children of hers; and these, these sisters-in-law of mine, have already died. It was that one, her name was Sophie Wolfe, her husband's name was Pete Wolfe, and my other sister-in-law, next in line, her name was Julie Headman, they had married these men in church; and that one's husband was called Jimmy Headman. But the people whom I have named, they are all dead. But this one, Justine Littlechild, she is still alive; and the man she was married to had gone ê-kî-simâkanisihkâniwiyit, êkwa aya nîso kî-owîhowiniw, 'Joseph-Smith' kî-isiyîhkâsow êwakw ân[a] âya, 'nitawêmâw' mâna nikî-itâhkômâw.

[32]   êwako mîna nâpêw aya, niya wiy ôhci nikî-itêyihtên, ê-kî-iyinîsit mân êwakw âna nâpêw, piyêhtawaki mân âya, ê-kî-~ ê-kî-pêhtawak niya tipiyaw, ê-kî-kakêskimât mân ôtawâsimisa, êkos êkota ohci miton âya, niya wiy êkota nikî-ohtinên ê-kî-kîhkâtêyimak aw âya, 'Smith Littlechild' kâ-kî-isiyîhkâsot; ê-k-~ ê-kî-pêhtawak otânisa ê-kâh-kakêskimât, êkwa mîn ê-miyo-sîhkimât. pêyak êwakw ân[a] âya, 'Agnes' isiyîhkâsow, ê-kî-âcimostawit, "kâkikê awa nôhtâwiy ê-sîhkimikoyâhk, 'atoskêk! êkây konit ây-ayâk!' ê-kî-itikoyâhk mâna nôhtâwiy," — ôma mân âya, ê-kî-~ êkây ôki k-âtoskêcik, êkâ kâ-masinahikêhihcik nânitaw kik-ôh-pimâcihocik ka-k-~, êkota ohci kik-ôh-pimâcihocik, sôniyâw ohci tipahamâhtwâwi, êwakw ânim ôhci kâ-kî-sîhkiskâkocik mân ôhtâwîwâwa. êkwa mîna mân ê-~ ê-kî-sîhkiskâkocik mîna mâna ka-kiskinohamâkosicik ayiwâk, ka-kiskêyihtamâcik ayiwâk. êkonik ôk âyisiyiniwak êkâ wîhkâc êtokw ê-âcimihcik aya, ôtê nâway omiyo-tôtamowiniwâw, êkonik ôk âya k-âcimakik niya. nîst ôm ê-isi-pêyakoyân, êkosi mân ê-kî-isi-miyo-kiskinowâpahtihicik ôk âyisiyiniwak aya, tânis ê-isi-pîkiskwêcik, mîna tânis ê-~ ê-itâcihocik; ê-kî-miywêyihtahkik k-âtoskêcik. pêyakwâw ê-kî-pê-wîkimikoyâhkik êwak ôhci kâ-kî-pêhtawak anim âya, êwakw âwa Smith Littlechild, ê-kakêskimât otânisa êkwa mîn âya ê-kâh-kiskinohamawât anim âya, kiskinohamâkosiwin aya, kâ-pêtâcik mân âwâsisak aya, wîkiwâhk k-âtoskâtahkik okiskinohamâkosiwiniwâw. ê-kî-wâh-wîcihikocik ôhtâwîwâwa êwakw ânim âya, tânisi kik-êsi-masinahahkik anim âya (môy nika-kî-âkayâsîmon aya), atoskêwin mâna kâ-miyihcik

to be in the war, he was a soldier, and he had two names, Joseph-Smith that one was called, and my kinship term for him used to be 'brother'.

Counselling

[32]   And that man, too, so far as I was concerned, I thought that man was clever, and each time I heard him, and I did hear him myself, he used to counsel his children, and it was because of that that I formed a high opinion of him, of the one who was called Smith Littlechild; I used to hear him counsel his daughters and encourage them in the right way. The one was called Agnes, and she used to tell me, "My father is forever urging us, 'Work, you all! Don't just hang around!' my father used to tell us," — there are those, after all, who do not work, whom no one will hire so that they might earn a living, so that they might live on it when they are paid wages, that is why their father used to urge them on. And he also used to urge them to go to school more, so that they would have more knowledge. Since these are the people that no one ever tells about, their good works back then, these are the ones about whom I tell. I, too, am now widowed, and this is how these people had shown me by their fine example, how they spoke and also how they made a living; they liked to work. At one time they had come to live with us, and that was the occasion when I had heard him, it was Smith Littlechild counselling his daughters and also teaching them about that, the schoolwork which children bring home, to work at their schoolwork at home. Their father would help them with writing that (I must not say it in English), the work which

kiskinohamâtowin ohci. êkwa mân ê-masinahahkik aya, wîkiwâhk
ê-atoskâtahkik êkwa, kiskinohamâtowikamikohk êkwa mân
êtohtatâtwâw[i] ânima kîkway kâ-masinahahkik, okiskinohamâkêwa
mân ê-miyâcik, mahti kwayask kik-êtastâcik êwakw ânima.

[33]   miton ôm âya, ê-isko-kaskihtâyân, pikw êkâ k-âkayâsîmoyân ôm
âya, kiskinohamâtowin ôm ê-âyimahk aya, kwayask ka-wîhtamihk
tânis âya k-êsi-kiskiwêhamihk mân ânihi tahto-aya,[11] mêkwâc anohc
kâ-kiskinohamâkosicik osk-âyak; môy niy êwako nôh-tâwinên.
mâka pêyak kîkway mân ê-itwêyân (itê kâ-kî-kiskinohamâkosiyân
aya, têpakohp-askiy nikî-ayân aya, kiskinohamâtowikamikohk aya),
ôhi mâna kâ-kihci-wîkicik kiskinohamawâkanak ita,
kâ-kiskinohamâkosicik; êkota ê-nipâcik êkwa êkota ohci mîn
ê-kiskinohamâkosicik, êkota aya, êkotowihk
ê-kî-kiskinohamâkosiyâhk; *excuse me,* nik-êtwân, *'boarding-school'*
kî-isiyîhkâtêwa — môy niwî-nêhiyawâh,[12] mâka pikw êkwa
ka-nêhiyawêyân,[13] ka-nisitohtâkawiyân kîkway kâ-mâmiskôtamân
[*ê-pâhpit*]. êkoni anih âya, mistah ê-kî-miywâsiki kâ-k-~
kâ-kî-ihtakoki aya, ayamihêwiskwêwak mân ê-kî-kanawêyimâcik aya
awâsisa êkospî, nâpêsisa êkwa iskwêsisa. êkwa mitoni mân âya
ayamihêwiskwêwak kwayask ê-kî-paminikoyâhkik, kwayask mîn
ê-kî-kakêskimikoyâhkik.

[34]   êwak ôhc êkospî, anik âstamispî aya wêyawîtwâwi
kiskinohamâtowikamikohk ohci, kâh-kihci-wîkihtotwâwi, nâpêw
êkwa iskwêw ahpô oskinîkiw êkwa oskinîkiskwêw, kwayask anima
kî-is-âyâwak êkonik anik âya ayisiyiniwak. wîkiwin kî-miyêwak
otawâsimisiwâwa, êkwa kî-kaskihtâwak mîn âya, otatoskêwiniwâw
ohc ê-pamihâcik otaw-~ otawâsimisiwâwa. môy âwiya aya
ohci-miyikwak aya, kihci-m-~ kihc-ôkimânâhk ohc âya ta-miyikocik
k-ôh-pamihâcik otawâsimisiwâwa; wiyawâw otatoskêwiniwâw ohci
kâ-kî-pamihâcik otawâsimisiwâwa. êkwa mîn âya, iskwêwak
ê-kî-kisâtahkik aya, ê-isi-wâh-wîkicik otawâsimisiwâwa
ê-kî-pamihtamâsocik. êkwa mîn âya, ê-kî-nôhâcik mân
ôtawâsimisiwâwa, iyikohk ê-kitimâkêyimâcik, êkwa namôy mistah
ôhpimê ê-ohc-âya-kanawêyihtamôhâcik otawâsimisiwâwa; êkosi

they are given by the school. And they write it, working on it at home, and when they take back to school what they have written, they give it to the teacher to see if they have done it correctly.

[33]   This is as much as I am able to do, I must not use English to speak about education, it is hard to speak properly in rendering these various terms having to do with when the young people go to school; I have never come across that [a Cree term for 'homework']. But one thing I usually say, where I used to go to school (I had been there for seven years, at that school), these schools where the students lived in residence when they went to school; they slept there and went to school from there, there, in that kind we used to go to school; excuse me, I will use the word, they are called boarding-school — I was not going to speak Cree [*i.e.*, English], but I have to speak Cree [*i.e.*, English] now so I will be understood in what I am talking about [*laughs*]. These [schools] used to be very good when they existed, the nuns used to keep the children in those days, the boys and the girls. And the nuns really used to take proper care of us and they also counselled us properly.

[34]   And because of that, in those days, when they would later go out from the school, when they got formally married, men and women or young men and young women, these people used to behave properly. They used to give their children a home, and they were also able to provide for their children by means of their work. No one used to give them anything, there was no welfare for them from the government with which to provide for their children; it was with their own work that they used to provide for their children. And the women also stayed at home with their children and looked after them for themselves. And they also breast-fed their children, they loved them so much, and they did not leave their children

ê-pê-isi-kiskêyihtamân niy âya, taht ôki kâ-pê-wîc-ôhpikîmakik aya,
oskinîkiskwêwak êkwa mîn ôskinîkiwak
kâ-kî-wîci-kiskinohamâkosîmakik; êkos ânim
ê-kî-isi-miyo-pimâtisicik, wîkiwin ê-kî-miyâcik aya otawâsimisiwâwa
aya, kâh-kihci-wîkimâtwâw[i] âwiya. namôy ôhci-paskêwihitowak,
môy ôhci-wêpinêwak otawâsimisiwâwa. kêyâpic[14] mân ânohc,
kêhtê-ayak êwako mistahi k-âkâwâtahkik, ka-kî-~ osk-âyak mîn
êwakw ânima ka-kî-âsawinamâhcik mâk ânohc êtokwê êkwa, mistah
êtokwê ê-âyimahk êkwa êwakw ânim âya, nêhiyawak
k-êsi-wâh-wîkicik, ka-wîhtamawâcik aya osk-âya, osâm êkâ
ê-wî-nitohtâkocik. mâka mîn êtokwê aya, namôy mitoni nipîmakan
êwak ôma kâ-mâmiskôtamân. êyâpic kiwâpamâwâwak âtiht
ayisiyiniwak, kâh-otinitotwâwi kâh-kihci-wîkihtotwâwi, êyâpic
ê-wîcêhtocik, êyâpic ê-kitimâkêyihtocik, êyâpic wîkiwin ê-miyâcik aya
otawâsimisiwâwa. ê-miy-~ ê-miywâ-~ ê-miywâpisinihk anim êwakw
ânima kâ-wâpahtamihk, ayisiyiniwak kâ-wâp-~ kâ-wâpamihcik aya,
ê-kisâtahkik wîkiwâwa, wîkiwin ê-miyâcik otawâsimisiwâwa. êkwa
âtiht êtokwê êyâpic kisê-manitowa sawêyimikwak aya,
ê-wî-kakwê-miy-ôhpikihâcik otawâsimisiwâwa êkwa ê-kakêskimâcik.
môya wiya mitoni ta-pômêhk ôma, ayisiyiniwak âtiht anik âya,
ê-iskonikowisicik, nititwân mâna, kwayask ê-wî-kakwê-pimâtisicik
wîkiwâhk, iyisâhowin ê-ayâcik. êwakw ânima kâ-pêhtamân,
ayisiyiniwak êkwa êkâ ê-nisitohtahkik êwako pîkiskwêwin,
iyisâhowin. ayisiyiniw ohcitaw waskitaskamik anim âya, ê-nêsowisit
ayisiyiniw, kahkiyaw ê-ihtasiyahk anima, ê-nêsowisiyahk anima
ê-pâstâhoyahk, ê-patinikêyahk. mâka osâm mistahi
kiwâhkêyêyihtênânaw êkwa aya, êkâ ayahk, ê-wî-kâsînamawâyahkik
ayisiyiniwak kîkway, kîspin kîkway k-ôhci-kisiwâhikoyahkik; êkota
anim êkwa, pîkiskwêwin anim ê-âpatahk, 'iyisâhowin' anima ka-~
kâ-itamihk aya; ayisiyiniw aya, kîspin ayâw êwakw ânima 'iyisâhowin'
k-êsiyîhkâtêk, êkâ ka-tôtahk kîkway niyôhtê-mâyi-tôtahki. tâpiskôc
ayisiyiniw awiya kâ-kisiwâhikot, namôya ka-kisîstawât, namôya ki-~
ka-mac-âyimômât, namôya kika-nitawi-nôtinât ka-pakamahwât,
kik-êyisâhot êkâ ka-tôtahk êwakw ânima. êkwa ka-kitâpamât

to be kept somewhere else; that is what I myself have come to know about all those with whom I have grown up, the young women and also the young men with whom I have gone to school; that is how they have led a good life, giving their children a home, after getting properly married to someone. They did not separate, they did not abandon their children. Still today the elders very much wish for that, that this be passed on to the young people, but today that is very difficult, I guess, given how the Crees are living, to tell the young ones, because they are not going to listen to them. But what I am talking about cannot be completely dead. You still see some people, when they have chosen one another and have gotten married to one another, still staying married, still loving one another, still giving their children a home. It is good to see that, when you do see it, when one sees people staying with their homes, giving their children a home. And some, I guess, still have the blessing of God, because they try to raise their children well and counsel them. One should not give up, there are still some people left by divine grace, I always say, who are trying to live properly in their homes, who are able to resist temptation. I hear that people do not understand that word, to resist temptation. It is natural for people on this earth to be weak, all of us, we are all weak in our sins and transgressions. But now we are too weak in our spirits, so that we are not going to wipe the slate clean for people if they have in some way angered us; that is where this word is used, 'resisting temptation' as they call it, if people have that, 'resisting temptation' as it is called, to hold back when they want to do something bad. When someone angers them, for instance, for them not to stay angry at that person, not to gossip about him, not to go fight him and hit him, but to resist temptation and hold back in that. And to look at

wîcayisiyiniwa, "wîst âwa ê-sâkihikot kisê-manitowa," kik-êtêyimât,
ka-kâsînamawât, ka-pônêyihtamawât anima, kîkway ohci
kâ-kî-paci-tôtâkot, kâ-kî-paciyawêhikot; êwakw ânima kahkiyaw
ê-manêsiyahk kipimâcihowininâhk. mâka ayiwâk ayisiyiniwak
ka-kî-ihtakocik, êwako ka-wîhtamâkoyahkik, kitêhinawa
k-âpacihtâyahk, môy piko kimâmitonêyihcikaninaw, kitêhinawa k-â-~
kik-âpacihtâyahk ka-kitimâkêyimâyahkik ayisiyiniwak,
ka-kitimâkinawâyahkik ayisiyiniwak; kîspin kâ-kisiwâhikoyahkik,
ka-pônêyihtamawâyahkik, namôya ka-~, namôya ka-kisîstawâyahkik
ayisiyiniwak, namôy mîna ka-~ kîmôc ka-nôtinâyahkik, môy
k-âh-âyimômâyahkik. êwakw ânima iyisâhowin aya, êkâ tôtamahki,
êkâ ka-mâyi-tôtawâyahk kîcayisiyinînaw.

[35]   anohc ayamihêwiyiniw, kâ-nahiniht an[a] ôskinîkiw
ê-kî-misiwanâcihisot, anohc ayamihêwiyiniw, êkos
ê-isi-kakêsk-~-kakêskimikoyâhk. "sâkihitok!" ê-itikoyâhk,
"kâsînamâtok kîkway kâ-tôtamêk! pônêyihtamâtok! kitimâkêyihtok!"
êwakw ânima kitimâkêyihtowin aya, ka-kâsînamâtoyahk. mîna kotak
kîkway ê-kiskisômât ayisiyiniwa, "kakwê-sâkihihk kisê-manitow!
kwayask kakwê-tôtamok! êkwa aniki kiwîcêwâkaniwâwak,
wîsâmihkok, kîspin kimiskawâwâwak ayisiyiniwak
k-ôwîcêwâkaniyêk! itohtahihkok kisê-manitowa ka-sâkihâcik!
kiskinohamâhkok tânisi k-êsi-sâkihâcik kisê-manitowa!" êkos ân[a]
ê-itikoyâhk anohc, ayamihêwiyiniw ôta anohc, k-âyamihêstamâht
an[a] ôskinîkiw kâ-misiwanâcihisot ana; iyikohk mân ê-~
ê-wîsakitêhêyahk, oskayisiyiniwak kâ-misiwanâcihisocik, oskinîkiwak
êkwa oskinîkiskwêwak. "hêy, kîh-kitimâkêyimak êsa,"
kititêyihtênânaw, awiyak wiyâpamâyahk[i] âya, oskayisiyiniw kâ-m-~
kâ-misiwanâcihisot. môy pikw êkosi k-êsi-mâmitonêyihtamahk,
ka-tôtamahk anima, ka-wâpahtihâyahkik aniki ê-sâkihâyahkik ôk âya,
osk-âyak, oskayisiyiniwak. ka-p-~ ka-pâhpiyahk ka-pîkiskwâtâyahkik,
ka-wâpahtihâyahkik ê-kitimâkêyimâyahkik. êwakw ânim
ê-manêsicik, êwako ~ êwak ôhc êtok ôm âhpô aya, "môy nânitaw
itâpatan ôta ka-pimâtisiyân askîhk, môy âwiyak nikitimâkêyimik;"
âskaw anik êtokw êkos ê-isi-mâmitonêyihtahkik, êwak ôhc êtokw
âniki kâ-mâh-misiwanâcihisocik osk-âyak.

their fellow-man and think, "He too is loved by God," to wipe the slate clean for him and to forgive him for whatever wrong he had done to them, for having grievously angered them; that is what we all lack in our lives. But there should be more people to tell us this, for us to use our hearts and not only our minds, for us to use our hearts and to love people, to care for people; if they have angered us, for us to forgive them, not to —~ not to stay angry with people, not to fight them behind their backs, not to keep gossiping about them. That is the meaning of 'resisting temptation' if we do not do this, for us not to harm our fellow-man.

[35]   The priest today, at the burial of the young man who had killed himself, the priest today counselled us like that. "Love one another!" he said to us, "wipe the slate clean for one another for what you have done! Forgive one another! Love one another!" That is the meaning of loving one another, for us to wipe the slate clean for one another. He also reminded people about another thing, "Try to love God! Try to do right! And ask your friends along, if you find people to have as your friends! Take them along for them to love God! Teach them how to love God!" That is what the priest told us today, at the prayers for that young man who killed himself; we have such heavy hearts when young people kill themselves, young men and young women. "Oh, if only I had loved him," we think when we see a young person who has killed himself. We should not only think that way, we should do it, we should show these young ones, these young people, that we love them. We should laugh and speak to these young people, we should show them that we care for them. That is what they lack, that is probably why they sometimes think, "There is no use living on this earth for me, nobody cares for me;" and that is probably the reason why these young people kill themselves.

[36]   êk ôm ânohc piyisk aya, nitat-âtotên ôm ânohc tânis ê-ispayik,
osâm mistah ê-môsihtâyân aya, ê-kitimâkinawakik mâna
onîkihikomâwak; iyikohk ê-mâtocik, ê-sisikotêyihtahkik
otawâsimisiwâwa kâ-pimâcihiso-~ kâ-~ kâ-aya-misiwanâcihisoyit,
kâ-nipahisoyit. mâmitonêyihcikan ê-nôhtê-astâyân aya,
omâmitonêyihcikaniwâhk êkonik ôki kâ-mâtocik, pêhtahkwâw[i]
ôm âya, kisê-manitowa aya ka-nitotamawâcik, kwayask
k-ôtinikowisiyit ôh ôtawâsimisiwâwa kâ-nakatikocik. môy ânik
ê-mac-âyiwicik osk-âyak ôma kâ-tôtahkik, mâka êtokwê mân âya,
mistahi piyisk mâmitonêyihcikan ê-ayâcik êkwa môy
ê-kiskêyihtahkik ê-tôtahkik êtok ôm âya, kâ-tôtâsocik,
kâ-misiwanâcihisocik, kâ-nipahisocik. môy ânima êtokwê
omâmitonêyihcikaniwâw ê-kikiskâkocik; ê-wanêyihtahkik anim âya,
âskaw ohci minihkwêwin, âskaw ohci pîhtwâwin ôma kâ-tôtahkik,
iyâyaw mân êkosi niya nitisi-mâmitonêyihtên aya, osk-âyak
kâ-misiwanâcihisocik.

[37]   mâka pêyak kîkway mîna, kotak kîkway ka-kî-tôtamahk,
ka-nitohtâkowisinânaw anima, k-âhkam-âyamihêstamawâyahkik ôk
ôsk-âyak. môy pik ôsk-âyak, kêhtê-ayak mîna
k-âyamihêstamawâyahkik, ê-nêsowâtisicik kêhtê-ayak. kêhtê-ayak ôki
mîna ka-kî-kitimâkêyimâyahkik, osâm ê-~ ê-kêhtê-ayiwicik êkwa
ê-âhkosicik, êkwa êkonik ôk âya, kitawâsimisinawak mîna
kôsisiminawak, nik-êtwân, ka-kî-kiskinohamawâyahkik anima tânisi
k-ês-âya-sâkihâcik kêhtê-aya, tânisi k-êsi-manâcihâcik. kiyânaw anim
êwako kitatoskêwininaw, âta wiya nîsta pêyak ôma aya, kêhtê-aya aya,
ka-~ kâ-tipahamâhcik mân ôki kêhtê-ayak, nî-~ nîst ôma pêyak êwak
ôma k-êsi-pîkiskwêyân, mâk êyâpic aya, nitân-~ nôsisimak êkwa —~,
nitawâsimisak êkwa nôsisimak iyikohk ê-kitimâkêyimakik; kiyâm ât[a]
âya, kâ-wîsakitêhêyân aya, "nika-kisîmâwak," k-êtêyihtamân, âhci piko
mân âya, ê-kakêskimakik; âhci piko mân ê-wî-kakwê-ma-mînomakik,
osâm —~, môya kâkikê misawâc nika-kî-kisîmâwak, mwêstas
ka-mâmitonêyihtamwak anima kîkway, ê-miywâsik kâ-wîhtamawakik;
êkos ânim ê-ispayik. kâ-kêhtê-ayiwiyahk tahto, môy ânima
ka-kostamahk ka-kakêskimâyahkik kitawâsimisinawak; môy mîna

[36]   And finally, in telling what is going on today, I feel it so much, I feel sympathy for the parents; they cry so much and they are so shocked when their children commit suicide, when they kill themselves. I want this thought to take hold in the thoughts of those who are crying, if they hear this, that they will ask God that these their children who have left them behind be nevertheless admitted through His grace. These young people are not bad when they do this, but they must get to a point where they have a great deal on their minds and do not know what they are doing when they do this to themselves, when they commit suicide, when they kill themselves. They must be out of their minds; their minds are blurred when they do that, sometimes from drinking, sometimes from smoking that stuff, that is usually the first thing that comes to my mind when young people kill themselves.

[37]   But there is one thing also, another thing we should do, and God will hear us, to persist in praying for the young people. Not only for the young people, to pray also for the old people, because the old people are frail. We should also care for the old people because they are old and sick, and also for these, our children and our grandchildren, I will say, we should show them how to love the old people, how to respect them. For us, that is our responsibility, although I am one of the old people myself, the ones who get old-age pensions, I am one of them and I am talking this way, but I still —~ I love my grandchildren, my children and my grandchildren so much; and even though I have a heavy heart and think, "I will anger them with what I say," I still counsel them; I still try to straighten them out by what I say because I will not anger them forever in any case, later they will think about the good things which I told them; that is what happens. As many of us as are old, we should not

ka-kostamahk, kôsisiminawak ka-kakêskimâyahkik. miton ânik âskaw
ê-miywêyihtahkik, ka-pêhtahkik kîkway, ka-wîhtamawâyahkik, êkâ
ê-kiskêyihtahkik wiyawâw, mâka kiyânaw ê-kiskêyihtamahk,
ta-kî-âsawinamawâyahkik anima, kîkway ê-miywâsik
ê-kiskêyihtamahk, êkos êwakw ânima kâkikê ka-pimipayin,
ay-âsawi-kakêskimâyahkwâwi kitawâsimisinawak êkwa kôsisiminawak,
wîstawâw êkosi ka-tôtamwak aya, otawâsimisiwâwa êkosi k-~
kik-êsi-paminêwak aya, môy ka-kostamwak ka-kakêskimâcik. êwakw
ânim ânohc kâ-mâmiskôtahk ayamihêwiyiniw, pik ôma
ka-mâmawôhkamâtoyahk, kwayask ka-kakwê-isi-pimâtisiyahk,
nowâhc[15] ka-kakwê-isi-pimâtisiyahk; êkosi piko
k-ês-âya-miyawâtênânaw, pikw âwiyak nawaswâtam miyawâtamowin;
êkos âyisk ê-kî-isîhikoyahk kisê-manitow, êkosi mîna mân âya
kititikawinânaw kâ-kakêskimikawiyahk, ayamihêwiyiniwak kêhcinâ
êkw âyamihêwiskwêwak kâ-pêhtawakik, êkosi ê-isi-kakêskihkêmocik:
"kisê-manitow ôm ê-kî-osîhât ayisiyiniwa, ka-miyawâtamiyit, namôy
âya ka-kakwâtakêyihtamiyit;" êkosi mân ê-itwêcik. êkos ôma
ê-kî-isi-pakitinaw-~-pakitinât ayisiyiniwa ka-miyawâtamiyit, namôy
ôhci-pakitinêw ayisiyiniwa ka-kakwâtakihtâyit mîna
ka-kakwâtakêyihtamiyit, êkosi mân ê-itwêcik, mâka
manitowi-masinahikanihk, kisê-manitowi-pîkiskwêwin, êkota êtokwê
êwako mîn ôm ê-~ ê-astêk ôma kâ-kî-wâh-wîhtamâkawiyâhk niyanân.
mâk êyâpic misiwê aya kâ-miywâsiki ayamihcikêwina, êkota astêwa ôh
âya kâ-wîhtamân; âtiht ôhi ê-ayamihtâyân ôta kâ-wîhtamâtakok.

[38]   êkwa mân âya pêyak kîkway, kâkikê ê-ispayik ôta waskitaskamik,
ayisiyiniw kâ-wâpamiht, k-âyamihêwâtisit, pi-~ kwayask
kâ-kakwê-tôtahk, ayisiyiniwak ê-yîkatêstawâcik êkoni ayisiyiniwa;
ê-yîkatêhtêcik, môy ê-nôhtê-pîkiskwâtâcik, ê-kostâcik, nik-êtwân.
tânêhk ânim êwako k-êspayik, tânêhk ânima ka-kostiht ayisiyiniw
aya, kâ-wâpamiht kisê-manitowa ê-manâcihât. ahpô êtokwê mâna
(niy ê-itêyihtamân, môy cêskw âwiyak nôh-kakwêcimâw), "êwakw
âw âyisiyiniw aya nitaw-îsîhkawaki, nitawi-pîkiskwâtaki,
kik-âtawêyihtam nipimâtisiwin, wiya kwayask ê-kakwê-pimâtisit;"
ahpô êtokwê mân êkos ê-itêyihtahkik ayisiyiniwak. mâka niya wiy

be afraid to counsel our children; we also should not be afraid to counsel our grandchildren. Sometimes they are really happy to hear something, for us to tell them something, for they themselves do not know but we, we know, and we should pass on to them the good things we know, and in this way these things will live on forever, if we pass our counselling on to our children and grandchildren, they in turn will do the same, they will treat their children the same, they will not be afraid to counsel them. That is what the priest talked about today, we must work together to try to lead a good life, to try to lead a better life; that is the only way we will be happy, and everyone chases after happiness; for that is how God has made us, and that is what we are told when we are counselled, that is certainly the counsel of the priests and nuns whom I hear: "God has created man to be happy, not to live in torment;" that is what they say. In that way He has put man on earth to be happy, He did not put man here to suffer, and not to live in torment, that is what they say, but God's word is written in the Bible, and that is in there, too, what we have been told about over and over. And these good verses are still in there, the things which I am telling about; I read some of these things which I am telling you about.

[38]   And now one other thing: it always happens on the face of this earth, when a person is seen as being religious and tries to do right, people stay away from that person; they walk away, they do not want to talk to that person, they are afraid, I will say. Why does that happen, why is a person feared when she is seen to respect God. Maybe it is (this is what I think, I have not asked anyone yet), perhaps people think, "This person, if I go and bother her, if I go and talk to her, she will disapprove of my way of life, for she is trying to live righteously." I, however, I

ê-itêyihtamân aya — niy êwako nimâmitonêyihcikan, mâk âhpô
êtokwê ê-miyikowisiyân êkosi k-êsi-mâmitonêyihtamân. ayisiyiniw
kâ-kakwê-miyo-pimâtisit, mistah ân[a] ê-manâcihât wîcayisiyiniwa;
mistah ân[a] ê-manâcimât. namôy ânim êkos ê-isi-kitâpamât,
anima k-êsi-kostikot kîkwây k-êsi-mâmitonêyimât; kisê-manitow
k-êsi-kitâpamikoyahk, êkos ânim ê-isi-kitâpamât; kahkiyaw ê-~
ê-kitimâkêyimikoyahk, êk ômis ânim ê-isi-kitâpamikoyahk. namôy
âya kitâpahtam kimâyinikêwiniwâ-~ kimâyinikêwininaw[a], ânihi
piko kâ-miyo-tôtamahk; kâ-kakwê-sâkihâyahk, êwakw ânim âyiwâk
ê-kitâpahtahk kimanitôminaw; otayamihâw mîn êkos
ê-isi-mâmitonêyihtahk, ê-kakwê-kitimâkêyimât wîcayisiyiniwa.
êwako niya nimâmitonêyihcikan ê-âsawinamâtakok.

[39]   êkwa ôk âya, pîtos êkwa ôma n-~, aya (kâwi nêma
kâ-pê-mâci-mâmiskômâ-~-mâmiskôtamân, nisis êkwa nisikos,
kâ-wî-âcimâcik —~ kâ-wî-âcimo-~-âcimakik; êkw êkwa kâw âya
nika-kîwêtotên k-âtot-~ k-âtotamân), êkonik ôk âyisiyiniwak aya,
niwîkimâkan onîkihikwa, nik-êtwân, miton ôta kâ-pê-ayâyân, aya,
maskwacîsihk (môy kinwês nôh-wîcêwâwak aya,
nîsw-âyamihêwi-kîsikâw aya), ê-kî-~ ê-kî-nâsicik anik âya,
onihcikiskwapiwinihk, êkotê ê-~ ê-kî-ohci-pê-kîwêhtahicik aw
âya, nisis êkwa nisikos. ninîkihikwak ê-mêkwâ-wîcêwakik aya,
ê-mêkwâ-oskinîkiskwêwiyân, nik-êtwân, êkotê ê-kî-pê-kiyôtêcik,
êkotê ê-kî-pê-takohtêcik. êkwa kayâhtê êtokwê apisis
ê-kî-nisitawêyimicik âhkosîwikamikohk ê-kî-ayâyân, êkota ohc âw
âya, nisis ê-kî-pê-wâh-wîcêwât ninîkihikwa ê-pê-nitawâpamiyit.
ôta *Ponoka* ê-kî-asiwasoyân, cîki maskwacîsihk, êkwa ôta mân ê-~,
ita kâ-wîkicik ê-kî-pê-katikoniyit êsa mân êkota aya, ninîkihikwa
aya, kâ-pê-nitawâpamiyit aya, ê-kî-pê-wîcêwât mân âwa nisis aya,
Dan Minde, êkota ohc âna ê-kî-nisitawêyimit, ê-kî-â-~ ê-kî-ayâyân

think — that is my thinking, but perhaps it is given to me that I think like this: When a person tries to live righteously, she really respects her fellow-humans, she really talks to them with respect. She does not look upon them in such a way that they would be afraid of her, what she might think of them; the way God looks upon us, that is the way she looks upon them; He loves us all, and He looks upon us this way. He does not look upon our wrong-doings, only upon the things we do right; when we try to love him, our God looks upon that especially; Christians also think that way, they try to love their fellow-humans. That is my thinking which I am passing on to you.

An Arranged Marriage

[39]   And they, this was a digression (back to that which I had started out talking about, my father-in-law and my mother-in-law whom they —~ whom I was going to tell about; and now back to that, I will return to what I was telling about), these people, my husband's parents, I will say [*i.e.,* his father and *step*-mother], about the time when I came to live here at *maskwacîsihk* (I had not been staying with my parents for very long, perhaps two weeks), when my father-in-law and my mother-in-law came to fetch me at *onihcikiskwapiwinihk* and brought me here from over there. While I was still living with my parents as a young girl, I will say, they had travelled there to visit, they had come and arrived there. And they must have known me a little bit from before, as I had been in the hospital, because my [future] father-in-law had come along with my parents to come and see me. I had been in the hospital here at Ponoka, close to *maskwacîsihk*, and

âhkosîwikamikohk aya, tânitahto-pîsim êtokwê niwanikiskisin,
mâka nikî-~ nikî-sawêyimikowisin ka-pê-wayawîyân êkotê ohc âya
âhkosîwikamikohk; kâwi ê-kî-kîwêyân. êkwa mân âwa, nisis mân
âw âya (mwêstas ot[i] îyikohk ê-kî-~, êkos ê-itâhkômak), êwako
mâna ê-kî-pê-nitawâpamit ê-~, ninîkihikwak ôma
kâ-pê-nitawâpamicik. mâka namôy wîhkâc nôh-kaskihtân
ka-pîkiskwêyân, ê-kî-wanihtâyân nipîkiskwêwin êkospî. mâk
îyikohk êtokwê ê-kî-ayamihêstamâkawiyân, kâwi nikî-miyikowisin
ka-pîkiskwêyân. êkota ohci kâ-kî-ispayik ê-kî-nisitawêyimit
êtokwê, êkwa ê-kî-pê-kiyôtêcik aya, ê-kî-kîwêyân anim
ê-pê-kiyôtêcik aya, ê-nîpâ-ayamihâhk, êkotê ê-kiyokêcik,
kâ-kî-pê-nitawâpamâcik aya ninîkihikwa, ê-pê-mâmiskôtamawâcik
ôm âya, okosisa êyâpic ê-môsâpêwiyit, ê-kî-nitawêyimit okosisa
ka-wîcêwimak.[16]

[40]   kî-âyiman pimâtisiwin (êkw âwa niwîcêwâkan awa
     Mrs. Ahenakew, ê-nitawêyimit êwako k-âtotamân aya, tânis
ê-kî-pê-is-âyâyân ôta aya maskwacîsihk), aya mân ê-~ ê-itwêyân;
kayâs mân-~ aya, pêci-nâway ôtê kâ-kî-âtotamihk, kêhtê-ayak mân
ê-kî-mêkicik otawâsimisiwâwa, êkos ânim ê-~ ê-kî-is-âya-~, êkos âw
ê-kî-isi-nakiskawak nâpêw aya kâ-kî-nakasit awa, *Joe Minde*, môya
wîst ê-ohci-nisitawêyimit, êkwa môy nîst ê-ohci-nisitawêyimak.
mâk êkwa ôk âya, onîkihikomâwak ôki, wiyawâw êwako
ê-kî-wiyasiwâtahkik ôm âya, ê-kî-kakâyawisît awa, kwayask
ê-kî-tôtahk awa niwîkimâkan, ê-kî-atoskêt, ê-kî-nanahihtawât
ôhtâwiya. ê-kî-êtokwê-nisis-kakwê-miskamawât[17] iskwêwa aya,
tânih êkoni ka-kitimâkêyimikot, ê-kî-itêyihtahk êtokwê, wiy
ê-kî-nawasônamawât ôm âya okosisa, niya ka-wîcêwimak[18] —
tânêhk êtokwê kâ-kî-itôtahk, môy ôsâm ê-ohci-miyohtwâyân
[*ê-pâhpihk*]! êkwa, ê-kî-pê-kîwêhtahicik anim âya êkospî, itê aya,
nîsta kâ-kî-ohcîyân aya onihcikiskwapiwinihk, ê-kî-pê-kiyokêcik

my parents used to camp there at his [my father-in-law's] place when they came to see me, and my father-in-law, Dan Minde, used to come along with them, because of that he knew me, I had been at the hospital I forget for how many months, but I was blessed by divine grace so that I came out again from the hospital; and I did return back home. And my father-in-law (it was only later that I called him by that kinship term), he used to come to see me when my parents came to see me. But I was never able to speak, I had lost my voice at that time. But people must have said so many prayers for me that I was given my voice again. Because of what had happened, I guess, he knew me, and they travelled and came to visit, they travelled and came to visit after I had returned home, they were visiting for Midnight Mass on Christmas Eve, that was when they came to see my parents, discussing with them the fact that his son was still a bachelor and that he wanted me to marry his son.

[40]   Life used to be difficult (and my friend here, Mrs. Ahenakew, wants me to tell about that, how I came to be here in *maskwacîsihk*), that is what I usually say; it is told about times past that the old people in the old days used to arrange the marriages of their children, that is how I met this man who has now left me behind, Joe Minde, he did not know me and I did not know him. But it was for the parents, it was they who decided this, and he was a good worker, my husband did the right thing, he worked and he listened to his father. My father-in-law must have tried to find a wife for him, one who would love him, he must have thought, for he had made the choice for his son, for me to marry him — I wonder why he did that, for I was not very good-natured [*laughter*]! And then they brought me back here at that time, from over there where I for my part had been from, *onihcikiskwapiwinihk*, they had come there to

êkota. kî-âyiman mâk âya, ispî ê-kakwêcimit aya nôhtâwiy aya, "kiwî-wîcêwâw cî aw ôskinîkiw," ê-itikawiyân; kinwês môy nôh-pîkiskwân, osâm êkâ cêskw âhpô ohkwâkan ê-wâpahtamwak, kî-âyiman aya, ka-naskomoyân aya, ka-wîcêwak awa, 'Joe Minde' awa kâ-kî-isiyîhkâsot. piyisk ê-kîhkâmikawiyân ôm âya, êkâ ê-wî-naskomoyân. nik-êtwân anima, tânis ê-kî-itâspinêmikawiyân: "pâskac mâna, namôy kiwî-kakwê-âh-onâpêminâwâw,[19] êkwa mâna mwêstas ê-mâh-môhcowiyêk;" êkos ê-itâspinêmikawiyâhk. piyisk êkwa kâ-naskomoyân, "wiy ê-sîhkimiyan, 'êhâ!'[20] nik-êtwân êtokwê," k-êtwêyân. kî-âyiman niya nipimâtisiwin; nikî-miskamâkawin niya nâpêw ka-wîcêwak, mo-~ êkosi môy ê-ohci-nisitawêyimak, êkos ôtê êkwa kâ-kî-pêsîkawiyân maskwacîsihk.

[41]   ê-kî-mâtoyâhk anima nikâwiy aya, maywêsk ka-nakatamân anima nîkinân. ê-kî-âyimahk sôskwâc, ka-pê-ayâyân ôtê, ê-~ êkâ ê-ohci-nisitawêyimakik ayisiyiniwak. ê-tipiskâk ôm ôt[a] ê-kî-takohtêyâhk aya; âsay ê-kawisimocik ayisiyiniwak kâ-takohtêyâhk, ê-kî-pôsiyâhk pôsiwinihk, ê-âpihtâ-tipiskâk ê-takwâpôyoyâhk, êkwa ê-pipok. êkos ânim êkwa nikîwânân, ma kîkway êkospî aya wâsaskocêpayîs ohc-îhtakon, wâsaskotênikana mân ê-kî-saskahamihk aya, kâ-wî-wâsaskotênikêhk. ê-pîhtokwêyâhk ôma ê-wani-tipiskâk ôm âya, wîkiwâhk ê-takohtêyâhk, môy nikiskêyihtênân tânitê ê-nitawi-nîpawiyâhk, êk-~ êkos ôm âya (kotak piminawasowikamik ê-kî-ihtakok, êkwa kotak aya ê-âniskôstêk wâskahikan êkotê ê-ati-pîhtokwêyâhk, êkotê ês ôm âya, apîwikamik êkwa nipêwikamik aya, ê-ayâki ôhi); miton ês ôm âya, cîk ê-nitawi-nîpawiyân aw êkota ê-nipât aw âya, Joe Minde awa kâ-kî-wîcêwak. ispî êkwa ê-wâsaskotênikêhk aya, cîk ês ôma nipêwinihk ê-nîpawiyân; êkw âwa nicâhkos Justine aya, pêyakosâp êkospî ê-itahtopiponwêt, êkota wîst ê-nîpawit, "aw îta nistês kâ-pimisihk," ê-isit [ê-pâhpihk]. êkwa ês âwa, Joe Minde ês âwa, niwîkimâkan êkwa (nik-êtâhkômâw, âsay êkwa ê-kî-nakasit), ê-kî-akwanâhkwêyâmot êsa kâ-pîhtokwêyâhk [ê-pâhpihk]. êkos ânima niy ê-kî-isi-nakiskawak, ôyâ nâpêw kâ-kî-wîcêwak.

visit. But it was difficult then, when my father asked me, "Are you going to marry this young man?" was said to me; I did not speak for a long time, because I had not yet even seen his face, it was difficult for me to respond, to marry this Joe Minde as he was called. Finally I was scolded because I would not respond. I will say the scolding words which were said to me: "On top of it all, you girls make no effort to get married, and then later you go crazy and run around," those were the scolding words said to me. Finally I responded, "Since you urge me, I guess I will say yes," is what I said. For me, my life was difficult; a man had been found for me to marry and I did not know him, and so I was brought over here to *maskwacîsihk*.

[41]   We did cry, my mother and I, before I left home. It was difficult indeed for me to come and live over here, for I did not know the people. We arrived here at night; the people had already gone to bed when we arrived, we had travelled on the train, with the train arriving at midnight, and it was winter. And so we went home [from the station], there was no electricity then, you would light the lamps when you wanted light. It was dark as we went inside on arriving at their house, we did not know where to go and stand, and so (there was another kitchen, and another extension to the house, we went on in there, and there was a living room there and a bedroom); and so, very close to where I went to stand, there was Joe Minde sleeping, the one to whom I was married [but who is now dead]. Then, when they lit the lamp, here I was standing close to the bed; and my sister-in-law Justine was eleven years old at that time and she, too, stood there and said to me, "There he is, my older brother, lying there" [*laughter*]. This was Joe Minde, my husband (I will call him by that kinship term even though he has already left me behind), he had hidden his face under the covers when we came in

[42]   mâk âya, ê-ayamihâyân ohci, nik-êtwân, môy niya nikaskihtâwin,
wiya piko kimanitôminaw ka-wîci-~ ka-wîcihikoyahk kîkway
ka-kaskihtâyahk; piko ka-mawimoscikêyahk ka-nitotamawâyahk,
kîkway ê-miywâsik aya ka-miyikoyahk. nikî-kaskihtân awa
ka-sâkihak nâpêw aya, ispî ê-kî-kihci-wîkimak. nikî-manâcihâw,
êkwa nikiskêyihtên nîst ê-kî-sâkihit; nikî-sâki-~
nikî-êtokwê-aya-sâkihik wîsta, k-ôh-kî-têpêyimot ka-kihci-wîkimit;
êkosi mâna nititêyihtên. ê-kiht-~ ê-kihcêyihtâkwahk anima
kihci-wîkihtowin, êwakw ânim âyisiyiniwak, namôy
ka-kî-wanikiskisicik; pêci-nâway kotakak kâ-nakatikoyahkik
kêhtê-ayak, ê-kî-pê-anima-manâcihtâcik êwakw ânim âya,
'wîkihtowin' kî-isiyîhkâtamwak, kihci-wîkihtowin mâk âya,
kâ-nitawi-kihc-âsotamâ-~-n-~-tohk ayamihêwikamikohk
kâ-pîhtokwêhk, êwak ôhci 'kihci-wîkihtowin' k-ôh-isiyîhkâtêk. êwako
mîna mâna tâpitawi kiwîhtamâkawinânaw, ayamihêwiyiniwak
mihcêtiwak kiwîhtamâkaw-~, kihc-âyamihêwiyiniwak mîna
kiwîhtamâkonawak, kihci-wîkihtowin anima miton
ê-kîhkâtêyihtâkwahk. ahpô wiya cêsos²¹ ôhtâwîhkâwina,
'kihcihtwâwi-côsap' kâ-kî-isiyîhkâsot, êkwa okâwiya,
kihcihtwâwi-mariy,²² ê-kî-kihci-wîkihtoyit, cîsas²³ wîst âya, ê-kî-ayât
anim âya wîkiwin, ita ê-kî-kitimâkêyimikot, ôhtâwiya nik-êtwân êkwa
okâwiya; êkot[a] ê-kî-pamihikot êkwa ê-kî-kiskinohamâkot, tânisi
kit-êsi-sâkihât, tânisi mîna k-êsi-sâkihât ayisiyiniwa, tânisi mîna
k-êsi-atoskêt. êkw ânim âya, cêsos²⁴ ê-kî-kiskinohamâkoyahk
sâkihitowin; namôya katisk mâna p-~ pîkiskwêwinihk isi
ka-mâmiskôtamahk, kitêhinawa ohc âya kik-âpacihtâyahk,
ka-tôtamahk tâpwê, ka-kitimâkêyimâyahkik ayisiyiniwak;
ka-kakwê-wîcihâyahkik wîstawâw kwayask ka-kakwê-pimâtisicik,
taht ôk êkâ kâ-kiskêyihtahkik; âtiht ayisk ayisiyiniwak, namôy wîhkâc
kîkway aya wîhtamawâwak aya, onîkihikomâwak ôk âya,
kâ-wîhtamawâcik otawâsimisiwâwa; âtiht awâsisak, namôy wîhkâc
wîhtamawâwak êkoni ôhi. êwak ôhci, kêhtê-ayak ôh âya,

[*laughter*]. That is how I first met the man, the one no longer with us, to whom I was married.

[42] But because I was religious, I will say, the strength was not mine, for it is only our God who will help us to deal with things; we must pray and ask him to give us good things. I was able to love this man once I had become his wedded wife. I treated him with respect, and I know he loved me, too; he, too, must have loved me, since he had been willing to get married to me; that is what I usually think. Marriage is highly thought of, that is something people should not forget; in the past, the old people who have gone before us used to treat it with respect, they called it 'wedlock', proper marriage, when you go and make solemn promises to one another in church, that is why it is called 'holy matrimony'. We were told about that incessantly, there were numerous priests and bishops telling us about that, that holy matrimony is held in the highest esteem. Even in the case of Jesus, his step-father, Holy Joseph as he is called, and his mother, Holy Mary, had been properly married, and Jesus, too, had a home where they loved him, his father, I will say, and his mother; there they looked after him and taught him how to love them, and how to love people and also how to work. And Jesus taught us about love; not merely to talk about it in words, but to use it with our hearts and truly to do that, to care for people; to try to help them so that they, too, might try to live properly, all those that do not know; for some people are never told anything, when the parents tell their children; some children are never told about these things. That is why the old people should persevere, we are of course asked to counsel the young. Some people also want us to remind them about things. It is this, as I told you earlier today, that she, my mother-in-law, immediately began to counsel me, as soon as we had

ka-kî-âhkamêyimocik mân, âta wiya ê-nitotamâkawiyahk anima mân âya, ka-kakêskimâyahkik aya osk-âyak. mîn ôt[i] âyisiyiniwak âtiht mân ê-nitawêyimikoyahkik aya, kîkway ka-kiskisômâyahkik. êwak ôm âya, anohc kâ-wîhtamâtakok, ê-kî-kakêskimit ana sêmâk aya, mayaw ê-kîsi-kihci-wîkihtoyâhk aya, niwîkimâkan aya — môy niyanân aya, mihcêt ayisiyiniwak aya ohci-pê-itohtêwak kâ-kihci-wîkihtoyâhk, niyanân pikw âya nikî-pê-ispayinân aya, *Joe Minde* awa kâ-wî-kihci-wîkimak êkwa wîstâwa, '*Pete Wolfe*' ê-isiyîhkâsoyit; êkoni ê-kî-nawasônâcik ta-nîpawistamâkoyâhk, êkwa kisk-~ kiskinohamâtowikamikohk ohc âna nicâhkos, '*Mina Minde*' ê-kî-isiyîhkâsot (mâka kâ-kî-isi-nisitawêyimâyêk ôma, '*Mina Hudson*' êkwa kî-isiyîhkâsow, *Mrs. Hudson*, ê-kî-kihci-wîkimât *Fred Hudson* ê-isiyîhkâsoyit); êkonik aniki nîsw âyisiyiniwak ê-kî-nîpawistamâkoyâhkik kâ-kihci-wîkihtoyâhk. ayamihêwiyiniw piko, êkwa êkonik ôki nîsw âyisiyiniwak ê-kî-niyânaniyâhk piko aya — kotak ayamihêwikamik anim âya, kâ-kî-ohpimê-nitaw-âstâhk nîpisîhkopâhk kayâs-âyamihêwikamik, êkota ê-kî-kihci-wîkihtoyâhk aya niwîkimâkan. pêyakwan mistah âya nikî-miyawâtên, nikî-miywêyihtên —~

≈ / ≈

gotten married — for us, not many people had come to our wedding, only we had driven there when I was getting married to Joe Minde, and his brother-in-law called Pete Wolfe; they had chosen him to stand up for us, and from school my sister-in-law, she was called Mina Minde (but you knew her as Mina Hudson, her name was Mrs. Hudson since she had married Fred Hudson as he is called); these two stood up for us at our wedding. With the priest and these two people there were only five of us — it was another church, the one which was moved out to the place where the willows stand, it was the old church, that is where we were married, my husband and I. I had a very good time all the same, and I was happy —~

≈ / ≈

[EM:] êkosi cî ôm êkwa?

[FA:] êkos ânim âsay ê-sipwêpayik.

[EM:] ôh.

V

[43]   êkonik ôk âya, ê-nitawêyimit aw âya *Mrs. Ahenakew*
k-âcimakik aya, nisis êkwa aya nisikos, tânis
ê-kî-is-âya-~-is-~-ispayik, anima nistam kâ-wîkihtocik.
ê-kî-âcimostawit mân âya nisikos, nistam ôtê kâ-pê-ayâyân aya,
kiskinohamâtowikamikohk ohci wîst âya, êkota ohc ê-kî-wîcêwât
ôh âya nisisa, nistam kâ-kihci-wîkihtocik (kayâhtê awa nisis aya,
âsay nitâtotên êwako, kayâhtê kotaka ê-kî-wîcêwât), êkwa ôh âya,
oskinîkiskwêwa ês ây ê-kî-kiskinohamâkosiyit ôta, ôma
kayâsi-kiskinohamâtowikamik, êkota ês ôhci ê-kî-wîcêwât; ostêsa
êsa wiya nisikos ê-kî-mêkiyit wiya; wîsta namôy
ê-ohci-nakayâskawât ôhi nâpêwa, *'John Louis'* kî-isiyîhkâsoyiwa
ostêsa, êkon ês ê-kî-aya-sîhkimikot ka-wîcêwât ôhi nâpêwa,
ê-kî-êtokwê-aya-itêyihtamiyit, ka-miyo-pamihikot ôh êkoni ôhi
nâpêwa, osâm ê-kî-atoskêyit. êkwa mîn ê-kî-nakacihtâyit ôm âya,
âsay aya, awâsisa ê-kî-ayâwâyit, "ka-kitimâkêyimik êtokwê,"
ê-kî-itêyihtamiyit aya, êwak ôhci êkoni ôhi kâ-kî-wîcêwât wîsta
nâpêwa. mâk âwa aya nisikos kwayask kî-tôtam, êkos
ê-kî-isi-wâpamak, ê-kî-miyo-kiskinowâpahtihit aya,
ê-kî-kitimâkêyimât ôhi, nisis awa nimanâcimâkan aya,
kâ-mâmiskômak, *Dan Minde*; ê-kî-kitimâkêyimât êkwa kwayask

[EM:] Is it ready now?
[FA:] It is ready, it has started already.
[EM:] Oh.

V

The Marriage of Mary-Jane and Dan Minde

An Arranged Marriage

[43]   It is these Mrs. Ahenakew wants me to tell about, my father-in-law and my mother-in-law, how things used to be when they first got married. My mother-in-law had told me about it when I first moved over here, she, too, had come straight from boarding-school when she had married my father-in-law, when they first got married (my father-in-law had previously, I told about that already, he had previously been married to another), and this young woman [my mother-in-law] who had also [like me] been a student in the old boarding-school here, she also got married straight from there; her older brother had arranged the marriage for my mother-in-law; she also had not known the man, John Louis was her older brother's name, he had urged her to marry that man; he [her brother] must have thought that this man would be a good provider for her, because he worked. He was already used to having children, moreover, "I guess he will care for you," he [her brother] had thought, and because of that she, too, had married that man. But my mother-in-law acted properly, that is how I saw her, she showed me by her own good

ê-kî-pamihât. kâkikê ê-kî-~ ê-kî-kanâcinâkosit nisis,
ê-kî-wiyasiwêhkâniwit. nanâtohk isi mîn ê-kî-wâpahtamân
ê-wîcihikot aya owîkimâkana, ê-kî-kiskinohamâkosiyit, êkwa wiya
namôy ê-ohci-kiskêyihtahk nisis kik-êsi-masinahikêt, êkota anima
mistahi kî-wîcihik aya owîkimâkana, kîkway kâ-wî-masinaha-~
kâ-nitawêyihtahk ka-masinahikâtêyik kîkway, êwakw âwa mâna
nisikos aya ê-kî-masinahahk kahkiyaw kîkway, otisîhcikêwiniyiw
ohc ôma kâ-kî-aya-wiyasiwêhkâniwiyit nîkân; piyisk êkwa
kî-okimâhkâniwiw nisis. êkwa êtokwê aya, ê-kî-miywêyimikot
êtokwê ayisiyiniwa, ê-kî-~ ê-kî-kitimâkêyimât ayisiyiniwa; pêyak
kîkway mâna kâkikê ê-kî-pêhtawak awa nimanâcimâkan *Dan
Minde*, ê-kî-isi-sîhkimât aya ayisiyiniwa, môy pik ôsk-âya, sôskwâc
ayisiyiniwa ê-kî-pêhtawak mân ê-kî-itât, "kitimâkêyimihkok
kêhtê-ayak!" — êkosi mân ê-kî-itât, "kitimâkêyimihkok
kîwâc-âwâsisak!" tânitahtwâw nikî-pêhtawâw, êkos ê-itât
ayisiyiniwa ê-kakêskimât. mîna niyanân kâ-kakêskimikoyâhk
niwîkimâkan êkwa niya, êkosi mâna nikî-itikonân: "kihcêyimihkok
kêhtê-ayak, kitimâkêyimihkok kîwâc-âwâsisak!" — êkosi mân
ê-kî-itikoyâhk; êkoni miyo-pîkiskwêwina aya nikî-kiskisin. êkwa
nikî-manâcihâwak aya nîsta, ê-kî-wâpamak niwîkimâkan kwayask
ê-kitâpamât aya onîkihikwa, nîsta nikî-manâcihâwak nisikos êkwa
nisis; tânis ê-isi-sîhkimicik, tânisi ê-isi-nitawêyimicik, nikî-tôtên.
tâpwê âta, môy ê-ohci-nakayâskamân kîkway
kâ-kî-kiskinohamawicik, nikî-kakwâtakihtân mân âskaw mâk âya,
namôy wîhkâc nânitaw nôh-itwân, nikî-wî-kakwê-nanahihtên aya,
ka-kakwê-atamihakik ôk âya kâ-kî-wâhkômakik ayisiyiniwak; aniki
mîna kotakak aya, niwîkimâkan omisa nîso, êkonik mîna mân âya,
nikisk-~ nikiskisin mân ê-kî-kitimâkêyimicik, êkwa nîst
ê-kî-kitimâkêyimakik. ê-kî-pê-kâh-kiyokawicik mâna, êkwa
ê-kî-mâh-mihcêtôsêcik. âsônê an[a] ômisimâw, *Sophie Wolfe*,
ayiwâk êwako ê-kî-kitimâkêyimit, mîn âyiwâk êwako
ê-kî-mihcêtôsêt; nikî-pêhtên mâna, mîn ê-kî-wâpamak
ê-kî-miyohtwât êwakw ân[a] âya nicâhkos, ê-kî-kitimâkêyimât

example, she loved him, my father-in-law, my parent-in-law, the one I am talking about, Dan Minde; she loved him and she looked after him properly. My father-in-law always looked clean, he was a councillor. I also saw that his wife helped him in various ways, she had gone to school, and he, my father-in-law, did not know how to write, in that his wife helped him greatly, when he wanted to write something, when he wanted something written, it was my mother-in-law who would write everything, all his dealings as a councillor, first; and finally my father-in-law became chief. And the people must have liked him, because he loved the people; one thing I always used to hear my parent-in-law Dan Minde say was how he used to urge people, not only young ones, I heard him say to anybody, "Love the old people!" — he used to say that, "Love the orphans!" I used to hear him say that to the people many times as he counselled them. Also when he counselled us, my husband and me, he would say this to us: "Treat the old people with reverence! Love the orphans!" — he would say to us; these are good words, and I remember them. And I, too, treated them with respect, since I saw my husband properly looking upon his parents, I, too, treated my mother-in-law and my father-in-law with respect; what they urged me, what they wanted me to do, that I would do. Although, it is true that at times I had a difficult time, since I had not been used to the things they taught me, I never said anything, I was going to try and listen, I tried to please the people I now had as relatives; and also the other ones, my husband's older sisters, two of them, they too, I remember, loved me, and I in turn loved them. They used to come to visit me, and they both had many children. Especially the oldest sister, Sophie Wolfe, she especially used to love me, and she had more children [than her sister]; I used to hear

ayisiyiniwa, ê-kî-kitimâkêyimât kêhtê-aya; pêyak mâna
nôtokwêsiwa mîn ê-kî-kanawêyimât ê-kî-kitimâkêyimât.

[44]   êwako kayâs ôyâ ayahk, 'k-ôsihkosiwayâniw' kâ-kî-itiht ana
okimâhkân, êkoni ê-kî-wîcêwât ôhi nôtokwêsiwa, êkoni mâna
kâ-kî-kanawêyimât nicâhkos *Sophie*, ê-kî-nêhiyawiyîhkâsot êwakw
ân[a] âya nôcokwêsiw, 'oscikwânis' ê-kî-isiyîhkâsot; êwakw âna
mîna mâna nôtokwêsiw ê-kî-nihtâ-kakêskihkêmot, ê-kî-miyohtwât
mîn êwakw âna nôcokwêsiw. ê-kî-pêhtamân mân êkospî, miton
êtokwê kayâs êwakw âwa kâ-kî-pimâtisit aya (êwak ôma
k-ôh-wîhtamihk ôm âya, tipahaskân ita ôma k-âyâyâhk,
'*Ermineskin*' k-êsiyîhkâtêk; êwakw ân[a] âyahk, owîhowin ê-âpatahk
ôma aya tipahaskân kâ-kî-aya-wîhtamihk, '*Ermineskin*'
k-êsiyîhkâtêk aya, 'k-ôsihkosiwayâniw' ê-kî-isiyîhkâsot);
nikî-pêhtawâw mâna êwakw âwa nimanâcimâkan *Dan Minde*,
ê-kî-mâmiskômât, êkoni ôhi kisêyiniwa, ôh ôkimâhkâna; wîst ês
ê-kî-kakêskimikot êkoni anih ôkimâhkâna. ê-kî-kiskiwêhokot êsa,
êkâ cêskwa kîkway ê-~ ê-tâwinahk, ê-~ ê-kî-wîhtamâkot êsa niyâk
aya, ê-kî-wâpahtamiyit, ômis îs ê-kî-itikot: "ôtê nîkân
kiwî-okimâhkâniwin," ê-kî-itikot êsa, êkwa tânis âya,
ê-isi-miyopayik, kik-êsi-kanawâpamât aya, otiyinîma okimâhkân,
"ka-kitimâkêyimacik kitayisiyinîmak; ka-nâtamawacik
kitayisiyinîmak, ita ayahk, kâ-nayêhtâwipayicik." êwakw ânim ês
ê-kî-kwayâci-wîhtamâkot nisis aya, kayâs anih ôkimâhkâna aya,
'k-ôsihkosiwayâniw' kâ-kî-isiyîhkâsoyit. tâpwê ê-kî-wâpamak nisis
ê-kî-kitimâkêyimât ayisiyiniwa. kâ-wiyasiwâtimiht mân âya,
ê-kî-têpwâ-~ ê-kî-têpwâtikot mân ê-nitawi-pîkiskwêstamawât, êkây
êkwayikohk ka-mâyi-tôtâmiht aya, kâ-wiyasiwâtimiht ôm âya,
minihkwêwin ohc âhpô kotak kîkway ohci aya, kâ-mâyipayiyit

and I also used to see that this sister-in-law of mine was good-natured, she loved people, she loved old people; she also used to keep one old lady, lovingly.

Ermineskin's Counsel

[44]   Long ago he who is no longer with us was chief, *k-ôsihkosiwayâniw* as he was called, he had been married to this old lady, she was the one my sister-in-law Sophie used to keep, that old lady used to have a Cree name, her name was *oscikwânis*; that old lady also used to be good at counselling, and that old lady also used to be good-natured. I used to hear it at that time, it must have been long ago when he [Ermineskin] had still been alive (that is why they named this reserve where we live Ermineskin, as it is called; it is his name which was used when they named this reserve Ermineskin, as it is called, his name had been *k-ôsihkosiwayâniw* [*i.e.*, Has-an-Ermineskin]); I used to hear my parent-in-law Dan Minde talk about him, this old man, this chief; he, too, had been counselled by that chief. He had had prophesies uttered by him, about things which he [Dan Minde] had not yet encountered, he had been told by him about the future, he [Ermineskin] had seen it and he had said thus to him: "There in the future you are going to be chief," he had said to him, and how things might go well, how a chief should look after his people, "For you to care for your people; for you to take up for your people where they run into trouble." That is what my father-in-law was told in preparation by that chief of long ago, that *k-ôsihkosiwayâniw* as he was called. It is true, I saw that my father-in-law loved the people. When they went to court, they would call on him to go and speak for

k-ôtinimiht, êwako ê-kî-wâpamak nisis ê-kî-tôtahk; ê-kî-itohtêt
mâna, ê-nitawi-pîkiskwêstamawât otayisiyinîma. êkwa mîn âya,
k-êtwêyân, kâkikê ê-kî-kakêskimikoyâhk, kâkikê ê-kî-kakêskimât
okosisa, êkâ ka-pakitinamiyit atoskêwin, k-âhkamêyimoyit
k-âtoskêyit. wîsta kayâhtê êtokwê nisis, maywês k-âhkosit, mistah
ê-kî-atoskêt.

[45]   kî-nîsiwak ôki nisisak, pêyak ayahk, 'Sam Minde' kotak
kî-isiyîhkâsow. êwako mîna kî-wiyasiwêhkâniwiw pêyakwâw, êkwa
mîna kî-okimâhkâniwiw pêyakwâw. kahkiyaw êkonik ôki nîsw ây-~
ayisiyiniwak atoskêwin ê-kî-nôkohtâcik aya, ôta ôma maskwacîsihk;
ê-kî-okistikêwiyinîwicik, êkwa mostoswa mîn ê-kî-ayâwâcik mâna,
môya mihcêt oht-â-~ ohc-âyâwêw wiya nisis awa *Dan Minde*, mâka
wiy ô-~ osîma, mihcêt aya pisiskiwa, mostoswa êkwa misatimwa
ê-kî-ayâwâyit. êkwa ê-kî-wîcihiwêyit mîna mân îta aya kâ-têhtapihk
aya, ôki mâna kotiskâwêwatimwa k-âyâwâcik. pêyakwan nisis,
êwakw âya, ôta ê-pê-ay-ayâyân âsay kî-pônihtâw, kotiskâwêwatimwa
êsa mân ê-kî-ayâwât nisis, êkwa êsa mân ê-kî-papâmohtahât, êkos
êtokwê mân ê-kî-isi-sôniyâhkêt. êkwa mâna wiya ni-~ niwîkimâkan
aya ê-kî-ay-apit mâna, ê-kanawâpokêt êkwa mîna mân âya
ê-ay-atoskêt kistikâna —~ kistikânihk, kahkiyaw kîkway
ê-kî-nakacihtât, ôhtâwiya ê-kî-kiskinohamâkot, êwakw ânim ânohc
k-âtotamân aya, kotak anim âya âcimowin k-ôsîhtâyân, ayêhkwêwa
mân ê-kî-~ ê-kî-pîkopicikêhât kâ-mâci-okistikêwiyinîwit aya
niwîkimâkan, ê-~ ê-oskînî-~ ê-o-~ ê-oskinîkînîwîs-~
ê-oskinîkîwiyinîsiwit êkospî.
[46]   êkos êtokwê anim âya, ê-itêyihtamân mâna niya, kiyipa
ka-mâci-kiskinohamâhcik ôk âya, osk-âyak, ka-sâkihtâcik atoskêwin

them so that they would not be dealt with so harshly when they were in court for drinking or some other thing, when they were arrested on some charge, I used to see my father-in-law do that; he used to go there to go and speak for his people. And also, as I said, he would forever counsel us, he would forever counsel his son, not to let go of work and to persevere in work. My father-in-law himself must have worked hard previously, before he fell ill.

Teaching by Example

[45] My father-in-law was one of two brothers, he was one, and the other one was called Sam Minde. He [Sam Minde] also used to be a councillor once, and then he also was chief once. Both these people left evidence of all their work here at *maskwacîsihk*; they used to farm, and they also used to have cattle, my father-in-law Dan Minde, he did not have many, but his younger brother [Sam Minde] had many animals, cattle and horses. And he also used to be part of the riding circuit, he used to be one of those who have race-horses. The same with my father-in-law [Dan Minde], but that one had already quit by the time I came here; he used to have race-horses and had followed the circuit with them, that was how he must have made money. And my husband used to stay home keeping house and also working in the fields, he knew how to do everything, his father had taught him, that is what I told about earlier today, when I made the other recording, that my husband had used oxen to plough the land when he began farming, at a time when he was still a very young boy.

[46] I usually think you have to start early in training young people to love work, while they are still young, then they

aya, miyêkwâ-osk-âyiwitwâwi, miywêyihtamwak êkwa k-âtoskêcik.
êkos ê-kî-kisk-~-isi-kiskêyihtamân niwîkimâkan, ê-kî-miywêyihtahk
mân ê-atoskêt kistikânihk; êkwa mîna, pisiskiwa mâna mitoni
kwayask ê-kî-pamihât. êkoni ôhi nîso ayahk, k-âtotamân aya,
k-âcimakik ôki nîsw ât[a] âya ayisiyiniwak,
ê-kî-anima-miyo-kiskinowâpahtihiwêcik atoskêwin aya,
ê-kî-sâkihtâcik k-âtoskêcik; êkwa mîn ê-kî-kiskinohamawâcik
otawâsimisiwâwa k-ês-âtoskêyit.

[47]   kâh-kîhtwâm êwak ôma kiwîhtamâtinâwâw, môy âyisk kâkikê awa
misawâc sôniyâw ka-miyikawiyahk, awa mistahi sôniyâw
kâ-miyikawiyahk. pikw êkwa ayisiyiniwak ka-kîwêtotahkik
k-âtoskêcik ka-kakwê-pimâcihocik aya, awa sôniyâw, kisipipayiki.
âtiht môy tâpwêhtamwak mâk âya, môy kâkikê awa
ka-kî-miyikawinânaw awa sôniyâw kâ-miyikawiyahk; âsay
at-â-~-âstamipayiw awa sôniyâw kâ-miyikawiyahk êkota; piko kâwi
ka-kîwêtotamahk k-âtoskêyahk, ka-kakwê-pimâcihoyahk; kayâs
mâna kâ-kî-isi-pimâcihocik nâpêwak êkwa iskwêwak.

like to work. I know that is true of my husband, he liked working in the fields; and he also very much took proper care of the animals. These two [Dan and Sam Minde], the story I am telling, these two people whom I am telling about, they used to set a good example for people by their work, they loved to work; and they also showed their children how to work.

[47]   I have been telling you all over and over that we will not be getting this money [oil royalties] forever, in any case, the large sums of money we get. People will have to go back and work to try and make a living when this money, when the oil wells run out. Some do not believe this, but we will not be able forever to get this money that we are getting; already the sums of money we are getting are becoming less and less; so we will have to go back and work to try and make a living; the way men and women used to make a living long ago.

VI

[48]   kotak kîkway awa kâ-nitawêyihtamawit aw âya, iskwêw aw
âya, ôhi kâ-âh-otinahk²⁵ aya âcimowina, ê-n-~ ê-nôhtê-kiskêyihtahk
tânis îskwêwak kayâs ê-kî-tôtahkik aya, tânis ê-kî-isi-pimâcihocik
wîstawâw otawâsimisiwâwa aya, tânis ê-is-âya-pimâcihâcik. mihcêt
aniki ê-kî-kaskihtâcik aya ê-mîkisihkahcikêcik êkospî iskwêwak,
êkwa ayiwinisa mân ê-kî-osîhtâcik ê-kî-mîkisihkahtahkik mî-~ anih
âya, waskitasâkaya ê-kî-m-~, 'mîkisasâkaya' kî-isiyîhkâtêwa,
êkotowahk mân ê-kî-osîhtâcik, pahkêkinwêsâkaya. êkwa mîna
maskisina êkwa astisa, ê-kî-pê-wâpamakik êwakw ânim ê-tôtahkik,
mistahi ê-kî-mîkisihkahtahkik mâna kîkway k-ôsîhtâcik, maskisina
êkwa aya astisa. êkw ânihi mîna mân âya maskisina aya
ê-kî-misiwêminakinahkik, misiwê mân ê-kî-mîkisihkahtahkik anihi
maskisina aya, 'napakaskisina' mâna kî-isiyîhkâtêwa. êwakw ânima
n-~, êwakw âwa nisikos ê-kî-kiskinowâpamak êkoni ê-kî-tôtahk;
ê-kî-~ ê-kî-kiskinohamawit mîna tânisi k-êsi-mîkisihkahcikêyân.
êkwa mîn âya, êk-~ êkâya ê-ohci-nitawêyimit aya, ka-nâh-nayahtoyit
mîkisa, kwayask nikî-kiskinohamâk aya k-êsi-mîkisihkahcikêyân,
tânisi mitoni ka-tôtamân, ê-kî-~ ê-kî-kwayaski-kakêskimit, tânis êkâ
k-êsi-nayahtocik mîkisak [ê-pâhpit]. êkwa nikî-nanâskomâw nisikos,
sêmâk aya ê-kî-kiskinohamawit, mayaw kâ-pê-wîcêwakik, êkoni ôhi
ka-tôtamân, tânisi k-ês-âya-~-kanâcihtâyân wâskahikan mîn êwakw
âya, âta k-~ âs-~ ê-kî-kiskin-~, ât[a] âsay ê-kî-kiskinohamâkawiyân
kiskinohamâtowikamikohk, nikî-sîhkiskâk aya, ka-kanâcihtâyân
wâskahikan, ka-kisêpêkihtakinikêyân êkwa ka-kisêpêkinamân
wiyâkana. sôskwâc kahkiyaw kîkway ôm âya
kâ-kî-isi-kiskinohamâkawiyân, nikî-nitawêyimik êkoni
ka-pimitisahamân. êkwa nikî-manâcihâw, nikî-tôtên kahkiyaw êkoni.

VI

Self-Reliant Women

[48] Another thing this woman wants from me when she is recording these stories, she wants to know what women did long ago, how they themselves made a living and how they made a living for their children. Many of the women used to be able to do beadwork then, and they used to make clothes and beaded them, overcoats, beaded coats they were called, they used to make that kind, leather coats. And also moccasins and mittens, I used to see them then, they did that, they used to put a lot of beadwork on the things they made, moccasins and mittens. And these moccasins they covered with beadwork, they put beadwork all over the top of these moccasins, they used to be called flat moccasins. This —~, I learnt this by watching my mother-in-law making them; she also taught me how to bead. And she also did not want me to have beads climbing up on one another [if the thread is too tight], she showed me how to bead properly, exactly how to do it, she instructed me properly how not to have the beads climbing up on one another [*laughs*]. And I was thankful to my mother-in-law that she taught me right away, as soon as I came to live with them, how to do these things, how to clean house and that kind of thing, although I had already been taught at boarding-school, she urged me to clean house, to scrub floors and to wash dishes. She wanted me to follow strictly everything I had been taught. And I treated her with respect, I did all these things. Naturally, my mother had,

cikêmâ, âta wiya kayâhtê nikâwiy mîn êkos ê-kî-isi-kiskinohamawit,
ê-kî-sîhkimit êkoni kahkiyaw kîkway, ê-awâsisîwiyân ohc
ê-kî-sîhkiskawit ka-kâsîyâkanêyân ka-wêpahikêyân; êkoni
ka-tôtamân, êkwa mîn âya, ka-kakwê-kanâcihoyân, kahkiyaw kîkway
nikî-kiskinohamâk nikâwiy.

[49]   mistahi mâna nikî-sâkihâw nikâwiy, kêskêyihtamân[i] êyâpic ôma,
êyâpic ôm âya, kâ-mâmitonêyimak nikâwiy, ninanâskomâw, nisâkihâw
êyâpic, iyikohk kîkway ê-miywâsik ê-kî-pê-kiskinohamawit. mîn
ê-kî-kitahamawit, êkâ ka-mâyi-wîcêwakik aya
nîci-kiskinohamawâkanak, êwako mîna mâna kâkikê nikî-wîhtamâk,
êkâ ka-kâ-~ ka-nâh-nôtinakik, ka-kâ-~ êkâ ka-kâh-kîhkâmakik
nîci-kiskinohamawâkanak; êwako mîna kâkikê nikî-kitahamâk; môy
niya piko, nîtisâna mîna mâna kî-kitahamawêw. âta kâkikê
ê-kî-wî-kakwê-kiskinohamâkoyâhk aya, ka-miyo-wîcihiwêyâhk aya,
pikw âwiyak ôma kâ-wîc-âyâmâyâhk, tâpiskôc kiskinohamawâkanak,
êkwa ayamihêwiskwêwak êkwa ayamihêwiyiniwak ka-man-~
ka-manâcihâyâhkik; kahkiyaw êkoni ê-kî-wîhtamâkawiyâhk aya
ka-tôtamâhk, ninîkihikonânak êwako ê-kî-kaskihtâcik wiyawâw
ka-kis-~ ka-wîhtamâkoyâhkik. môy mîn ôhci-kostamwak wîhkâc aya,
ayamihêwikamikohk aya k-êtohtahikoyâhkik ka-nitawi-pêhtamâhk
anim âya, ayamihêwiyiniw aya kâ-kakêskihkêmot,
kisê-manitowi-pîkiskwêwin kâ-wîhtamâkoyâhk. êwak ôhc êtok ôm
ânohc aya, kahkiyaw wiyawâw aya, ê-wî-~ ê-wî-mamihcimakik
ê-kî-kiskinohamawicik ninîkihikwak aya, ayamihâwin ka-sâkihtâyân,
êwak ôhc ânohc êyâpic kâ-sâkihtâyân aya, kisiwâk êkwa ôta ê-wîkiyân
ôm îta ayamihêwikamik kâ-cimatêk, têpiyâhk katisk ê-pimohtêyân
êkwa ôta, ê-kitâpahtamân, tahto-kîsikâw ayamihêwikamik
ê-nitaw-âyamihâyân.

≈≈≈

[EM:]   kêkâc âs-~ âsay êkota anima, katisk mîn ê-miyopayik
ê-kîsîhtâyân anim âya, *the last word*, tâpiskôc anima kotak
mîn ânima kâ-kîsîhtâyahk.

of course, taught me the same things previously, she had urged me in all these things, from childhood on she had urged me along to wash dishes and to sweep; to do these things and also to try and keep myself clean, my mother had taught me everything.

[49]   I loved my mother very much, I still think of her whenever I feel lonesome, I thank her, I still love her, she had taught me so many good things. And she had warned me not to live on bad terms with my schoolmates; she forever used to tell me this, not to fight with them, not to scold my schoolmates; against that also she forever used to warn me; and not only me, she also used to warn my siblings against it. She forever used to try and teach us, of course, to get along well with people, with everyone we had to live with, such as the other schoolchildren, and to treat the nuns and the priests with respect; all these things she used to tell us to do, our parents, they used to be able to tell us that. They also were never afraid to take us to church so that we would go and listen to the priest preach and tell us the word of God. I guess that is why today I am going to speak proudly about my parents, all of them, that they taught me to love the church, that is why I still love it today, I live close to where the church stands now, I just have to walk a little ways and I just look at the church from here, I go to church every day.

≈≈≈

[EM:]   Almost —~ again it turned out well, just as I am finishing it, the last word, just like the other [tape] we finished.

[EM:]   âsay anima cî ê-yôhtênaman?

[FA:]   âha! âha.

[50]   êkwa ôk âya iskwêwak kâ-nitawêyimikawiyân aya kik-âcimakik
aya, ôta maskwacîsihk, tânis ê-kî-tôtahkik, maywês awa sôniyâw
ka-miyikawiyâhk mi-~, mîna kayâs ôta, aspin ohci
kâ-pê-wîcihiwêyân, tânisi kâ-pê-isi-wâpamakik iskwêwak aya,
mihcêt iskwêwak ê-kî-wâpamakik aya, mistah ê-kî-atoskêcik
ê-kî-kakâyawisîcik. êkwa nama wîhkâc ê-ohci-pêhtawakik
ka-kisiwiyocik. ê-kî-mâna-nâtahkik mihta sakâhk,
ê-kî-nâcimihtêcik, ê-pôsihtâcik ê-kinwâyiki, êkwa ê-pê-nîhtinahkik
ita kâ-wîkicik, êkwa wîkiwâhk mîn ê-~
ê-mosc-âya-nâh-nâtwâhahkik êkoni anihi aya mihta ka-pônahkik;
wiyawâw iskwêwak êwako ê-kî-wâpamakik ê-kî-tôtamâsocik, êkâ
—~, âta k-âya-~ k-ônâpêmicik, kotak kîkway k-ôtamiyoyit atoskêwin,
êkos ê-kî-isi-wîcihâcik onâpêmiwâwa, ê-kî-nikohtêstamâsocik mân
îskwêwak. âta wiya nîsta piyisk nikî-tôtên êwakw ânima,
nikî-yêyihikawin ê-nâh-nikohtêyân. nikî-yîwêyâskocinin mân
ê-mosci-nâcitâpêyân²⁶ nîpisîhtakwa, êkâ kîkway kâ-~ kâ-pônamân
aya nîkihk; ê-kiskisiyân iyikohk mân âskaw
ê-kî-yâh-yâyikâskociniyân kâ-nâtitâpêyân²⁷ nîpisîhtakwa. êkos ânim
âya ê-kî-is-âhkamêyimocik kayâs iskwêwak. nam-~ namôy âya
iskwêwak ohci-kitimâkinâsowak ât[a] âya, kâ-nakatikocik
onâpêmiwâwa aya, êkâ kîkway k-ômihtimicik, kî-astamâsowak mâna
mihta. êkwa piyê-takohtêtwâwi mâna nâpêwak kî-kîsowihkasowak,
onâpê-~ o-~ wîwiwâwa mân âya ê-kî-astamâsoyit aya mihta, ahpô
mitoni kâ-pwâtawihtâcik iskwêwak aya, mihta ka-kâhcitinahkik
ahpô nîpisîhtakwa, pîwihtakahikana mân ê-kî-pônahkik (mistahi
kî-ihtakonwa wiy ê-kî-mosci-nikohtêhk), êkotowahk mân
ê-kî-pônamâhk, pîwihtakahikana. mâk âni mâna nistam
kâ-mâci-kwâhkotênikêyâhk aya, ê-kî-kaskâpahtêk [ê-pâhpit].
nanâtohk kîkway ôm âya, âtiht osk-âyak itâwak môy
ê-tâpwêhtahkik, tânisi mân ê-kî-itâcihocik kayâs aya ôtê
ayisiyiniwak nâway. mîn ôh âyahk, kâ-mosci-pônamihk êkwa ôhi

[EM:]   Have you turned it on already?

[FA:]   Yes! Yes.

[50]   And it is these women I am expected to tell about, here
at *maskwacîsihk*, what they used to do before we were
getting this money [oil royalties], and also how I have seen
them here, from long ago, for all the time I have been
living here, how I used to see many women working a
great deal, they were hard workers. And I have never
heard them complain. They used to go for firewood in the
bush, they used to go for firewood, loading pole-length
wood and then unloading it back where they lived, and
also, at their homes, chopping the firewood into stove-
lengths to burn; I used to see the women themselves do
this for themselves, even though they had husbands, when
the men were busy doing something else, that is how
these women used to help their husbands, by cutting
firewood for themselves. I, too, finally used to do that, I
was tempted by their example to go cutting wood. I used
to get torn ragged from dragging willows home by hand,
when I had nothing to burn at my house. I remember how
ragged I used to get sometimes when I hauled willows
home; that is how women used to persevere in the old
days. The women did not feel sorry for themselves when
their husbands left them behind, and when they had no
wood, they used to lay in firewood for themselves. And
when the men would come home they used to warm
themselves by the fire because their wives had laid in
firewood for themselves; and when they were completely
unable to get firewood or willows, the women even used to
burn wood-chips (there used to be lots of them for wood
was chopped with an axe), that is what we used to burn,
wood-chips. But when we first started the fire, well, it
used to smoke. There are all kinds of things, it is said

kotawânâpiskwa, môy êkoni âtiht wâpahtamwak anohc ôk âya
kâ-pimâtisicik aya, mêkwâc ôk ôsk-âyak, nayêstaw ôm âya
wâsaskocêpayîs êkwa pimiy kâ-pônamihk, êkoni pikw
ê-wâpahtahkik; êkwa mân âya, ê-âcimostâkocik mâk-~ mân âtiht
onîkihikowâwa aya, mihta mân ê-kî-pônamihk aya, ka-piminawasohk
êkwa aya, ka-kîsowihkasocik ayisiyiniwak aya, wîkiwâw aya
ka-kisisahkik. êkosi mân ê-kî-is-âya-atoskêcik wiy âyisiyiniwak, êkwa
mîna mân ânihi wâsaskotênikana kâ-kî-âpacihtâcik aya,
ê-kî-mâna-kaskitêwâpahtêki, iskwêwak mîna mân êkoni
ê-kî-kanâcihtâcik maywês aya ka-wâsaskotênikêcik, 'askîwi-pimiy'
kî-isiyîhkâtêw mân ânima kâ-kî-aya-wâsaskotênikâkêhk.

[51]   êkwa aya, anima k-âtotamân aya, iskwêwak iyikohk
ê-kî-atoskêcik, kahkiyaw kîkway aya ê-kî-tôtamâsocik —
ê-kî-osîhtamâsocik, nik-êtwân; miskotâkaya ôhi kâ-kikiskahkik aya,
wiyawâw ê-kî-kaskikwâtamâsocik, papa-~ papakiwayânêkinwa mân
ê-kî-atâwêcik, êkwa mîna mân âya, otawâsimisiwâwa ôh âya,
ayiwinisisa kâ-kikiskamiyit aya, ê-kî-kaskikwâtamawâcik mân âya,
wiyawâw otawâsimisiwâwa, ê-kî-wiyisamâsocik êkwa
ê-kaskikwâtahkik êkw-~, môy, môy pikw âwiyak aya
kaskikwâswâkana anihi, môy pikw âwiyak ohc-âyâw,
ê-kî-moscikwâtahkik mân âya, iskwêwak ayiwinisa ôhi
k-ôsîhtamâsocik. êkwa tahto kâ-kî-kitimâkisiyâhk, âskaw ahpô môy
nôh-kaskihtânân papakiwayânêkinwa k-âtâwêstamâsoyâhk, êkwa
êkâ wîhkâc ê-ohci-papâmohtêyâhk aya, nayêstaw misatimwak êkwa
otâpânâskwak ê-kî-âpatisicik aya, nânitaw wâh-itohtêhki.
maskimotêkinwa mâna kâh-kanâtâpâwatâyâhki, êkoni mâna
nikî-âpacihtânân aya, itâmihk ôh âyiwinisa aya k-ôsîhtâyâhk,
iskwêwak mâna pîhtawêsâkâna ê-kî-osîhtamâsocik aya,
maskimotêkinwa anim îta mâna, pahkwêsikan kâ-kî-asiwasot.
papakiwayânêkinwa ayis kî-wâpiskâwa, mâk âya kî-masinahikâtêwa.
kâ-kisêpêkinahkik mân ânima kî-pawinamwak aya,
kâ-masinahikâtêyik anima; âtiht mîn ê-kî-ôsahkik,[28] êkosi mân
ê-kî-is-âya-pahkwatinahkik anih âya, kâ-masinahikâtêyiki.

about some young people that they do not believe how people used to live back there in the past. And some of those who live today, the young of today, have never seen a fire made or a wood-stove, they see only electric and kerosene heaters. Then some of them are told about it by their parents, that they used to burn firewood to cook and for people to keep warm, to keep their houses warm. For this is the work people used to do, and also the lamps they used to use, they used to give off black smoke, and the women also used to clean these before they lit them, it was called coal oil, that which was used for lighting.

[51]   And I have told about the fact that the women used to work so much, that they used to do everything for themselves — they made it for themselves, I will say; the dresses they wore, they used to sew for themselves; they would buy cloth, and also the clothes their children wore, they themselves used to sew for their children, they used to cut the patterns out for themselves and then sew them, not everyone had a sewing machine, the women used to sew by hand when they made clothes for themselves. And those of us who were poor, we sometimes were not even able to buy cloth for ourselves, and we never used to go anywhere [to shop], since only horses and wagons were used when you were going somewhere. Once we would have washed them clean, we used to use flour-bags to make underclothes, women used to make slips for themselves with these flour-bags in which the flour had come. For the cloth used to be white, but it carried writing. When they washed them, they took off the writing; some also used to boil them, that is how they would take the writing off.

[52]   ahpô êtokwê ka-kî-âtotamân, pêyak kîkway ayisiyiniwak
ê-kî-pâhpicik aya. môy êtokwê nânitaw k-âtotamân pêyak
ê-kî-pâhpihiht aya, oskinîkiskwêw ês âya, ê-kî-kihtimêyihtahk êsa
ka-pahkwatinahk anima kâ-~ kâ-masinahikâtêyik, sôskwâc ês êkos îs
ê-kî-osîhtât aya, pîhtawêsâkân aya, maskimotêkin ê-âpacihtât. mâk
êtokwê mitoni kî-pahpawiwêpinam, miton êtokwê kî-kâh-kâskaham
kwayask aya, aya, ka-k-~ êkâ êkwayikohk ka-sîtawâyik, êkos îsi
ê-kaskikwâtamâsot êtokwê pîhtawêsâkân. mâk êtokwê aya,
ê-sâkêkamoniyik êsa, *Mac's Best* ê-itastêyik êsa [*ê-pâhpihk*].

     [FA:]   êkos ê-isiyîhkâsot cî pahkwêsikan?

pahkwêsikan êkos ê-kî-isiyîhkâsot an[a] âya k-âskitit, êwakw ânim
êtokwê ê-sâkamoniyik êsa kâ-wâpahtamoht [*ê-pâhpihk*]! têpiyâhk
ka-pâhpihk ôm êwako k-â-~ k-âtotamân [*ê-pâhpihk*]. môy êtokw
âwa oskinîkiskwêw ê-~ ohci-kiskêyihtam êwakw ânim âya,
ê-kî-wâpahtamoht anim âya, êkâ ê-ohci-pahkwatinahk anima
masinahikêwin.

     ≈≈≈

[53]   ≠ êkw-~ êkw ânima mîn âya,
ê-kî-mân-âya-~-kahkiyaw-kîkway-tôtamâsocik iskwêwak. wiyâs
anim âya (ma kîkway anih âya âhkwatihcikana ohc-îhtakonwa),
wiyâs k-âyâcik mistahi aya, môso-wiyâs ahpô mostoso-wiyâs,
kâhkêwakwa mân ê-kî-osîhtâcik; ê-kî-osîhtâcik mân âya
wayawîtimihk anih âya, mwêhci mîkiwâhp ê-isîhtâcik. mistikwa
mân ê-kî-âpacihtâcik aya, êkota pîhc-âyihk ê-kaskâpasahkik anima
wiyâs aya, kâh-pânisahkwâwi, kâhkêwakwa mân ê-kî-osîhtâcik êkwa
ê-kî-kaskâpasahkik. ≠ pêyakwan kinosêwa, ê-kî-pâniswâcik mâna
kinosêwa êkwa ê-kî-kaskâpaswâcik. ≠ êkwa, kêkâc kahkiyaw
iskwêwak ê-kî-ayâcik kiscikânisa. pîwi-kiscikânisa mân âya
ê-kî-ayâcik, êkosi mân ânihi kî-isiyîhkâtêwa, ita aya k-ôhpikihtâcik
askipwâwa êkwa oskâtâskwa, 'pîwi-kiscikânisa' mâna

[52]   Perhaps I should tell about one incident people used to laugh about. I guess it's all right to tell it how one young woman was laughed at, she was too lazy to take the writing off, she simply made a slip like that, using a flour-bag. But she must have shaken it out and properly scraped it off [rather than washing or boiling it] so it would not be so stiff, and she must have sewn a slip for herself just like that. But, I guess, it was hanging out below her dress, and the writing said *Mac's Best* [*laughter*]!

[FA:]   Is that the name of the flour?

That was the name of that flour, uncooked [*i.e.*, not bannock], and that is what was showing, that was visible [*laughter*]. It is simply for a laugh that I am telling this [*laughter*]. This young woman did not know, I guess, that it was visible, that she had not taken off the writing.

≈≈≈

[53]   ≉ and it was also that, that the women used to do everything for themselves. The meat (there were no freezers), when people had lots of meat, moose meat or beef, they used to make dried meat; they used to build a structure outside, making it exactly like a tipi. They used to use poles, smoking the meat inside there, after cutting it into sheets, they used to make dried meat and smoke it. ≉ The same with fish, they used to cut them into sheets and smoke them. ≉ And nearly all the women used to have gardens. They used to have vegetable gardens, that is what they used to be called, where they grew potatoes and carrots, they used to call them vegetable gardens. Of the garden seeds, they never had very much of anything

kî-isiyîhkâtamwak. êkwa êkoni ôhi mân âya pîwi-kiscikânisa, êkamâ
ohc âya mist-~ ayiwâkipayicik²⁹ kîkway (ôta mân âya,
'asahkêwikamik' mâna kî-isiyîhkâtêw ôm îta k-ôh-~
k-ôh-paminahkik —~ k-ôh-paminiwêcik ôk ôkimâ-~, aya, okimânâhk
ohci, kâ-paminiwêcik ôki), êkotowahk mân ôhi ê-kî-miyikawiyâhk,
pîwi-kiscikânisa ka-kistikêyâhk. askipwâwa mâna piko
kâ-kî-atâwêyâhk, êkoni ê-kistikêyâhk. êkwa mîna mân
ê-kî-manisamâhk aya, maywêsk aya ka-pakitinamâhk aya asiskîhk,
ê-kî-~ ê-kî-pîkinisamâhk mâna, "êkos îsi kiyipikinwa,"
ê-kî-itikawiyâhk mâna.

[54]   êkoni kahkiyaw iskwêwak ê-kî-tôtahkik, mâka mân âya,
onâpêmiwâwa mîna kî-wî-~-wîcihikwak mân ê-pîkopitah-~,
ê-kî-pîkopitamâkocik mân âsiskiy, ita ka-kistikêcik; êkwa anim âya,
ka-w-~ ka-wêhcasiniyik aw îskwêw êkâ êkwayikohk k-âtoskêt; êkosi
mâna niya wiya niwîkimâkan ê-kî-isi-wîcihit aya, ê-kî-m-~
ê-kî-pimi-pîkopicikêt mân êkota ê-kî-pimi-pakitinamân ôh
âskipwâwa. mistahi mâna miton ê-kî-pakitinamân askipwâwa,
tâsipwâw môy kakêtihk mâna nikî-atoskânân aya, ôma mân âya,
macikwanâsa k-ôhpikihki,³⁰ mâka nikî-nakacihtânân piyisk aya,
wîpac kahkiyaw kâ-kawikahamâhk, môy wîhkâc mistah
ôhci-wîpâcikinwa anihi aya macikwanâsa. êkwa piyisk mîna
nikî-ayânân aya, ê-kî-atâwêyâhk môniyânâhk aya, ayahikâkana anihi,
pêyak misatim mân ê-kî-pim-âyahikêt, êkotowahk nikî-ayânân anim
âya âpacihcikanis, êkota ê-âpacihtâyâhk. êkwa aya, aya, pêyakwâw
ê-kiskisiyân iyikohk ê-kî-miyokihtâyâhk askipwâwa, êkosi mân
ê-kî-isi-tipahamâhk, mitâtahtomitanaw-maskimot ê-kî-ayâyâhk, êkwa
ê-kî-apisâsik wâtihkân anim îtê mân âya ê-kî-astâyâhk askipwâwa,
ê-kî-yahkâtihkâtamâhk, êkâ anima nânitaw ê-kî-astâyâhk anih
âskipwâwa; môy wayaw-~ wayawîtimihk wîhkâc nôh-ayahênân,
kahk-~ kahkiyaw mân ê-kî-pîhtokwatâyâhk. ≉
[55]   êkwa mîna mân âya, kayâhtê ohpimê nikî-âtotên, nikâwiy mâna
mistahi ê-kî-mawisot aya, mînisa, ê-kî-pâsahk, êkwa takwahiminâna
mîna ê-kî-pâsahk ê-kî-takwahahk mâna. êkwa âtiht mân
ê-kî-kaskâpiskahahk kotaka mînisa aya, 'iyinimina' mâna

(it was called the 'ration house' here, where they looked after it —~ where they looked after people on behalf of the government, the ones who looked after people [*i.e.,* the Indian agents]); there we were given that kind, garden seeds for us to plant. We only used to buy potatoes, and we planted them. And we also used to cut them up, before we put them down into the soil, we used to cut them small because "They grow faster that way," we had been told.

[54]   The women did all those things but their husbands also used to help them by ploughing the soil for them, where they would plant; so that it would be easy for the woman and she would not have to work so hard; that is how my husband helped me, too, he used to go along ploughing and I followed behind putting in the potatoes. I used to plant lots of potatoes, and we worked extremely hard, in fact, at the time when the weeds come up, but finally we knew what to do, when you cut them all down early, the weeds did not really take over. And finally we also had a hiller, we had bought it from a White place, one horse went along and did the hilling [of the potatoes], we used to have that kind of machine and used it. And I remember once, when we grew such a good crop of potatoes, that is how we measured them, we had one hundred bags, and the cellar where we stored potatoes was small, we dug it out to make it bigger, we had no place to put all of the potatoes; we never left them outside, covered with dirt, we used to haul them all inside. ⚘

[55]   And we also used to, I told about this before somewhere, my mother used to pick lots of berries, she used to dry them, and the chokecherries she used to both crush and dry. And some other berries she used to can,

kî-isiyîhkâtêwa êkwa aya, nikikomina; êkoni mân
ê-kî-kaskâpiskahahk aya, môtêyâpiskohk.

[56]   êkwa mîna mân ânim âya, mîn êwakw âsay nikî-âtotên,
ê-kî-pahkêkinohkêt mâna. wiy êwakw ânima niya môy nikaskihtân,
tahk âyiwâk ayisk âstamispî aya, osk-âyak kî-nêwo-~
kî-nêsowâtisiwak. mâk ôki kêhtê-ayak, mitoni kî-kaskihtâwak mân
âya, ê-osîhtamâsocik pahkêkinwa, âsônê anih âpisimôsoswayâna,
mitoni kî-wiya-~ kî-wêhcihêwak êkoni mitoni, ê-osîhtamâsocik.
nikî-wâp-~

⧣⧣⧣

—~ êkwa nicâhkos, ê-kî-osîhtamâsocik mân êkotowahk. êkoni ôhi
pahkêkinwa âtiht mâna nikâwiy kî-atoskêmow, ê-kî-âyimêyihtahk
êtokwê mân âya kik-ôsîhtât, osâm mâna mistahi mîn ê-kî-atoskêt
aya wâsakâm nîkin-~

≈≈≈

[57]   —~ âsay mîn êwako pakahkam nitâtotên, ê-kî-yîkinikêt kâkikê
nikâwiy, mostoswa ê-kî-ayâwât ê-miyosiyit, ⧸ ê-yîkinikêstamâsot
êkwa ascascwâs êkwa manahikan, tôhtôsâpoy, namôy wîhkâc
oht-ât-~ ohc-âya-atâwêw, mistahi mân êkotowahk aya,
ê-kî-aya-ohtâcihoyâhk. êkwa pahpahâhkwâna mîn ê-kî-ayâwât,
kôhkôsa mîn ê-kî-ayâwâcik, mostoswa mîn ôma k-êtwêyân, âskaw
kî-minahowak wiyâs, êkota ohc âya, ê-âpacihtâyâhk wiyâs, mâka
kayâs mîna tânis ê-kî-isi-wâpamakik ayisiyiniwak ê-tôtahkik, awiyak
mistahi wiyâs k-âyât, ê-kî-asamât mâna kotaka ayisiyiniwa;
ê-kî-nitomihcik mân âskaw ayisiyiniwak aya ka-pê-mîcisocik, êkwa
mân ê-miyihcik ka-kîwêhtatâcik wiyâs. ⧸ iyikohk
ka-misiwanâtaniyik anima wiyâs, êkos ânima mân ê-kî-tôtahkik,
ê-kî-nitomâcik mâna owîcêwâkaniwâwa, ka-pê-nâtamâsoyit wiyâs;
⧸ kêhtê-aya mîna mân ê-kî-asamâcik aya, wiyâs. ⧸ êwakw ânim

blueberries they used to be called, and wild black-
currants; these she used to can in jars.

[56]   And she also used to, and I have also told about this
already, she used to tan hides. I, by contrast, am not able
to do that, because as time went on young people became
weaker and weaker. But the old people were very much
able to tan hides for themselves, especially deer hides,
they used to have an easy time in tanning these for
themselves.

⚹⚹⚹

—~ and my sister-in-law, they used to make that kind for
themselves. With some of the hides, my mother had
someone else to do them for her, she must have found
them difficult to prepare, and she also worked too hard
around our house —~

≈≈≈

[57]   —~ I also told about that already, I think, that my
mother used to milk the cows all the time, she used to
have good milk cows, ⚹ she milked for herself, and she
never bought curds and cream, or milk, she never bought
very much of that kind, we used to live on that. She also
had chickens, they also had pigs, and sometimes, as I said,
they also used to butcher a cow for meat, and we used the
meat from that, but in the old days, as I saw people do it,
when someone had lots of meat he used to feed other
people; people were sometimes asked to come and eat,
and given some meat to take home with them. ⚹ Instead
of letting the meat spoil, that is what they used to do, they
invited their friends to come and get meat for themselves;
⚹ and they also used to feed meat to the old people. ⚹

âya, 'mâmawi-wîcihitowin' môniyâwak k-êsiyîhkâtahkik,
nik-âkayâsîmon êyâpic, 'share' k-êtwêcik, êkos ê-kî-tôtahkik kayâs
nêhiyawak. ê-kî-aya-~ kîkway k-âyiwâkipayicik, kayâcic[31] mân
ê-kî-miyitocik. êwak ôm êtokwê mîna môy nisitawêyihcikâtêw,
osâm êkwa mistahi ê-sôniyâwi-mâmitonêyihtamihk, kahkiyaw
kîkway nayêstaw ê-kakwê-sôniyâhkâtamihk. mîn ôk âyahk, namôy
mistahi wîhkâc êkwa aya ayisiyiniwak ê-~ ê-minahôstamâsocik,
nayêstaw ê-atâwâkêcik mostoswa aya; êkota k-ôhtinahkik kîkway
aya mîciwin k-âtawêstamâs-~

≋

[58]   —~ êkoni ôhi ê-kî-wâpahtamân aya, âsay âhkwatihcikana
ê-ihtakohki,[32] ê-apisâsik ê-kî-ayâyâhk âhkwatihcikan, ≉
kî-atoskêmow mân ê-nipahtamâht aya niwîkimâkan aya,
ayêhkwêsisa mân ê-kî-atotât aya, ôtênâhk aya, ka-minahôstamâkot,
êkwa anita ê-asiwatâyâhk akoc-~ âhkwatihcikanihk. ≉ môy êwako
kinwês nôh-tôtênân, êkos ânima wîpac kâ-kî-at-âhkosit
niwîkimâkan aya. ≉ kahkiyaw kîkway ati-pîkopayin ayisiyiniw
k-âhkosit, môy wiya miton ôhci-pîkopayiw êyâpic aya, mistahi
kistikâna kî-ayâwêw niwîkimâkan, êkwa mîn âya mostoswa
kî-ayâwêw. mâka masinahikan kî-osîhtâw, ê-kî-mâh-miyikoyâhk
êkoni, maywêsk ka-nakataskêt ≉. kahkiyaw nikî-atâwâkân aya
mostoswak, mâka kêswân môy mistah ê-ohc-îtakisocik. môy niya
nôh-kaskihtân ka-pamihakik ôki pisiskiwak, osâm aya ≉ âyiman
iskwêw wiya ka-pamihât pisiskiwa, êkosi môy âyiwâk
nôh-kanawêyimâwak ≉ mostoswak, kahkiyaw nikî-mêkin. êkw
ânihi mîn âya, askiya, kayâhtê wiya ê-kî-âh-atoskêmot, wiya
nistw-âskiy ê-kî-aya-âhkosit. kayâhtê ê-kî-awihiwêt aya, êkâ
ê-kaskihtât k-âtoskêt, kî-awihiwêw anih âya kistikâna; âtiht
nêhiyawa, âtiht môniyâwa kî-awihêw. mâk êkwa niy âya, namôy
kinwês êwako nôhc-âya-nôhtê-tôtên k-âya-~ k-âwihiwêyân.
nikî-miyâwak anih âya askiya nôsisimak; pêyak iskwêw, êkwa nîso
nâpêwak, nôsisimak nikî-miyâwak. môy kîkway

That is what the Whites call cooperation, I will say it in English again, sharing as they call it, that is what Crees used to do long ago. When they had a surplus of something, they used to give it to one another. This also is not well understood, I guess, as money is the general obsession now and you only try to make money from everything. The people also never really butcher for themselves now, they only sell cows; and with that they earn something to buy food for themselves —~

≈≈≈

[58]   —~ these things I used to see, there were freezers already, we used to have a small freezer, ≉ my husband used to have someone else butcher for him, he used to have steers butchered for him in town and we put the meat in there, in the freezer. ≉ We did not do that for a long time, it was shortly afterwards that my husband fell ill. ≉ Everything will fall apart when a person is ill, my husband did not really go broke, he still had a lot of grain and he also had cattle. But he made a will and gave these to each of us before he departed this world ≉. I sold all the cattle but, as it happened, they were not worth very much. I was not able to look after the animals myself because ≉ it is difficult for a woman to look after animals, so I did not keep cattle any longer, ≉ I gave them all away. And the land also, he himself had someone else work it for him, on an annual basis, beforehand, for he was ill for three years. He had rented it out to people beforehand, since he was unable to work, he had rented the fields out to people; some he rented out to Crees, some to White people. But as for me now, I did not want to do that for long, to rent it out to people. I gave the land to my grandchildren; one is a woman and two are men, I gave the land to my

nôhci-nôhtê-kanawêyihtên osâm aya, ê-ati-kêhtê-ayiwiyân mîn êkwa
ispî aya, ê-pamihikawiyân okimânâhk ohci, êkwa mîn ôta ôma
nêhiyânâhk ôm âya, ≠ ôki kâ-paminâcik kêhtê-aya, êkot[a]
ê-kî-ohci-pamihikawiyân. môy âyiwâk kîkway nôhci-nôhtê-ayân.

[59]   âstamispî êkwa, êkosi mwêhci kâ-kî-ispayik ôma kâ-kî-tôtamân,
nikî-taciwihâwak ôk âya, kêhtê-aya kâ-paminâcik, "môy
nitawêyimâwak ôki kâ-tipahamâhcik kêhtê-ayak, kîkway askiy
kik-âyâcik," nikî-itikawinân, ê-mâmawôpiyâhk. "âsay kahkiyaw
niya nikî-miyâwak nôsisimak," nititwân [ê-pâhpit], âsay niya
nikî-kîsi-miyâwak anik âya nôsisimak, pêyak *Theresa* okosisa, êkwa
nîsw âwa kâ-pê-pîhtokwêt *Kathleen* aya otânisa, êkwa êwako
kâ-kî-ohpikihak, omosôma sêmâk ê-kî-miyikot aya askiy, aya, êkota
anima k-ôsîhtâhk anim âya *will*, êkota kî-masinahikâtêyiw *Karen*
owîhowin, wiy ê-kî-ohpikihâyâhk, omosôma ê-kî-astâyit owîhowin.
êkwa aya, kotak nôsisim ana kâ-kî-pôni-pimâtisit, êwako
ê-kî-miyak aya, *Allen*, ≠ mâka êkây ê-pimâtisit, kotak an[a]
îyaskohc *Anthony* êkwa (êwakw âna sêmâk owâhkômâkana
kâ-kiskisototâkot, *Lester Frame*), ê-kî-miyât anih âya wîscâsa, "wiy
êwako kik-âyâw askiy," ê-kî-itikot, môy —~ âhkosîwikamikohk
ê-asiwasoyân, âsay ki-~ kî-kîsi-miyâw ana nôsisim, mâka mitoni
nimiywêyihtên nôsisim êwakw âw âya, nika-mamihcimâw nôsisim
ê-miyohtwât kwayask. kwayask ê-paminât aya owîkimâkana êkwa
otawâsimisa, êwako nâha [*pointing to a picture on the wall*] —~

≠≠≠

—~ k-ôcawâsimisicik; êwako sasîwiskwêwa kâ-wîcêwât, k-êtitân,
êwakw âw âwa *Anthony Young*, êkwa '*Wilma Starlight*' an[a]
ê-kî-isiyîhkâsot kâ-wîcêwât. êwako mîna —~

grandchildren. I did not want to keep anything because I was getting older, and also at that time I was getting a pension from the government and also from the reserve here, ⚮ these who look after the old people, I was getting a pension from there. I did not want anything else.

[59]   Later, it happened exactly as I had acted on it, I had gotten ahead of the ones who look after the old people, "I do not want the old people who are paid a pension to have any land," we were told, at a meeting. "As for me, I have already given all of it to my grandchildren," I said [*laughs*], I had already finished giving it to my grandchildren, one is Theresa's son, and two are the children of this one who just came in, Kathleen, and her daughter [Karen] is the one we had raised, her grandfather had given her land already, it was when the will was made, Karen's name was written in there for we had raised her, her grandfather had put her name in. And another grandchild of mine who has died, I had given it to that one, Allen, ⚮ but when he died, another was next in line now, Anthony (that one was remembered by his relative [Anthony] right away, Lester Frame), he [Anthony] gave it to him, his cross-cousin, "He shall have that land," the other had said to him [*references obscure*], not —~ I was in the hospital, the land had already been completely transferred to my grandchild, but I am very glad that my grandchild, I will speak with pride of my grandchild [Anthony], that he is truly good-natured. He looks after his wife and children properly, that one [*pointing to a picture on the wall*] —~

⚮⚮⚮

—~ who have children; the one who is married to a Sarcee woman, as I said to you, it is this one, Anthony Young, and Wilma Starlight is the name of the one who is married to him. And she also —~

—~ aw îskwêw. anim ânohc k-êtwêyahk, ê-wîcihitocik osk-âyak aya, kâ-kihci-wîkihtocik. pêyak iskwêw anohc êkos ê-isi-pîkiskwêyâhk aya, kotak iskwêw ê-wîtapimit ê-mîcisoyâhk, êkosi ê-itwêyâhk, ôsisima ê-~ ê-wîcihikoyit anih îskwêwa ê-~ ê-kihci-wîkimâyit, ê-miyohtwât an[a] îskwêw ê-wîcihât anih ôskinîkiwa, ta-pônihtâyit minihkwêwin; êkos ê-isi-miywêyihtahk an[a] âya iskwêw, ʻ*Louisa Wildcat*ʼ ê-isiyîhkâsot. êkw ân[a] êtokw-~

[EM:] —~ êkwa, môy âyiwâk êkwa kotak kîkway nikiskisin êkwa.
[FA:] mêkwâc?
[EM:] kâ-kiskisômiyan ôh âya, kahkiyaw êkoni nitâtotên, êha.

[FA:] âha.

≈≈≈

≉≉≉

—~ this woman. As we were saying here before, young people who are properly married help one another. A certain woman and I were just speaking like that, I was sitting with another woman as we were eating, and we said this, that her grandchild gets help from that woman whom he married, that that woman is good-natured and helps that young man to quit drinking; she was so happy, the woman [with whom I talked], Louisa Wildcat is her name. It must have been that one —~

≉≉≉

[EM:]   —~ and I cannot think of anything else now.
[FA:]   Right now?
[EM:]   I have told about everything of which you
          reminded me, yes.
[FA:]   Yes.

≈≈≈

VII

[60]   anohc êkwa ôma kâ-wî-aya-âtotamân aya, nisikos aya,
ê-wî-âcimak aw âya, môy kayâs ôta aya kâ-nakatikoyâhk,
ê-kî-nakataskêt aya, ayîki-pîsim ê-mêkwâ-akimiht, 'Mary Minde'
êwako kâ-kî-isiyîhkâsot; ôta kêhtê-ayak ita kâ-kanawêyimihcik,
êkot[a] ê-kî-kanawêyimiht. êwakw âwa mîn âya
ê-nitawêyihtamâkawiyân k-âcimak. êkosi mitoni nimiywêyihtên,
êwakw âwa k-âcimak aya, nisikos ê-kî-kitimâkêyimit. êwako mîna
mihcêt kîkway ê-miywâsik ê-kî-pê-kiskinohamawit, êkwa mihcêt
kîkway ê-kî-pê-kiskinowâpahtihit iyikohk kwayask, wîstawâw
kwayask ê-kî-pamihisocik aya, anihi kâ-kî-wîcêwât nâpêwa, 'Sam
Minde' kâ-kî-isiyîhkâsot êwako mîna kotak nisis. mistah âya
ê-kî-nihtâ-atoskêt mîn êwako ê-kî-okistikêwiyinîwit; êkwa mostoswa
mîna ê-kî-ohpikihât. êkotê ohc êtokwê mîna mâna niwîkimâkan
kî-kiskinohamâsow, tânis âya k-êsi-nihtâ-atoskêt;
ê-kî-mâh-masinahikêhikot êsa mân ôhcâwîsa
ê-kî-nitaw-âh-atoskêstamawât mâna kistikânihk, êkwa pisiskiwa
mîna mân êtokwê ê-kî-pamihtamawât. nistam ôta kâ-takohtêyân
aya, maskwacîsihk, nikî-wâpamâwak êkonik anik âyisiyiniwak miton
âya, ê-kî-miyo-pamihisocik, ê-kî-miyonâkohcikêcik wîkiwâhk êkwa
mîn âya, wâsakâm êkota. wâskahikana anih ê-kî-itaskitêyiki,
misatimokamikwa êkwa aya, kistikânikamikwa. êwakw âna nisis aya,
êkwayikohk ê-kî-miyomahcihot wiy âya, iyikohk
kâ-kî-miyonâkohcikêt êkwa mîn âya, ayisiyiniwa mâna
ê-kî-masinahikêhât aya, ka-wîcihikot aya, anima kistik-~
kâ-kî-okistikêwiyinîwit. kî-nan-~ nanâtohk mâna kî-~, atoskêwin,
nanâtohkôskân kî-aya-paminam, anima mîna mân âya, kayâs
kâ-kî-tahkopitamihk maskosiya, êkotowahk mîna mân ê-kî-paminahk
ê-masinahikêhât ayisiyiniwa, êwakw âw âya Sam Minde.

VII

Mary and Sam Minde at Work

[60]   What I am going to tell this time, I am going to
tell about my aunt; she left us behind here not long ago,
she departed this world in April, her name was Mary
Minde; here at the old folks' home, that is where she had
been kept. She is the one that I am expected to tell about.
So I am very happy to tell about that one, my aunt,
because she cared for me. She also taught me many good
things, and she taught me many things by her example, for
they, too, had made such a proper life for themselves, she
and the man she was married to, Sam Minde was the
name of my father-in-law's brother. He was very good at
working, and he also used to farm; and he also raised
cattle. My husband must have learnt from these, too, how
to be good at working; he used to be hired by his uncle,
and he used to go and work for him in the fields and, I
guess, also used to look after the animals for him. When I
first arrived here at *maskwacîsihk*, I saw that these people
used to make a good life for themselves, they used to
make things look prosperous, in their home and also
around it. There were buildings all around, horse-barns
and granaries. That uncle of mine stayed quite healthy, he
made his place look so prosperous and he also used to hire
people to help him with his farming. Various kinds of
work, he used to manage work of all kinds, as when they
used to bundle hay in the old days, he used to manage
that kind of work with hired people, this was Sam Minde.

[61]   êkwa owîkimâkana mistah âya kî-wîcihik, waskawîwinihk isi mîn
êwako mistahi ê-kî-wîcihikot aya, atoskêwinihk. êwakw âwa
nisikos, ê-kî-~ ê-kî-aya-âcimostawit mâna tânis ê-itahkamikisit
wîkiwâhk. tânitahto êtokwê mân âya (ôma mistah-âtoskêwin
k-âyâcik, tâpiskôc aya, kistikân kâ-manisoht êkwa kâ-kistikêhk),
tânitahto êsa mân âya oskayisiyiniwa oskinîkiwa ê-kî-atoskahâcik,
êkwa wîkiwâhk ê-kî-nipâyit. êwakw ânim âya nisikos
ê-kî-âcimostawit, *Mary Minde*: "miyêkwâ-nipâtwâwi mân ôk âya
atoskahâkanak, ê-kî-nitaw-âsamakik niya misatimwak," ê-itwêt,
"ê-kî-nitawi-pamihakik mân," ê-itwêt, êkwa kâh-kîsi-pamihâci
misatimwa aya, êkos ânim êtokwê mân ê-kî-~
ê-kî-kwayâci-kîspôhât, mân êkos ê-kî-wiyahpicikêcik ôki
kîsi-mîcisotwâwi, ê-mâc-âtoskêcik ôk ôskinîkiwak.
"ê-kî-pê-pîhtokwêyân êkwa mân ê-piminawatakik, êkwa
ê-koskonakik ka-mîcisocik;" êkos âya kâ-kî-itâcimostawit, êkos
ê-kî-isi-wîcihât owîkimâkana — pêyakwan êtokwê mân
ôwîkimâkana mîn ê-kî-na-nipâyit êtokwê mân âya,
k-ôh-kî-nitawi-pamihât wiy âya misatimwa.

[62]   êwakw ânima mîn âya, kotak ana mîna nisikos aya *Mary-Jane
Minde*, êkosi mâna nikî-isi-wâpamâw, kî-pâh-pamihêw mîna mân
êwakw âya misatimwa. mâskôc môy ôhci-pêyakowak, kayâs êtokwê
êkos îskwêwak ê-kî-isi-kakâyawisîcik aya, êkâ onâp-~ onâpêmiwâwa
kâh-pamihtamâkotwâwi misatimwa aya, ahpô nânitaw k-~
k-êtamahcihoyit, kâ-mâyamahcihoyit, iskwêwak mân
ê-kî-nitawi-pamihâcik misatimwa. êkwa o-~ mîna mostoswa
k-âyâwâcik, êkotowahk mîna mân ê-kî-nitaw-âsamâcik
ê-kî-pamihâcik. nîsta mîna mâna nikî-wâh-wîcihâw niwîkimâkan
aya, kâ-pamihât aya opisiskîma, kâ-nitaw-âsamât aya maskosiya,
êkwa âskaw kistikâna mîna mâna ka-~, kî-ihtakowak mân âya
ê-osîhihcik aya, 'asamastimwân' ê-kî-isiyîhkâsocik anik âya,
ê-askihtakosicik kistikânak êkos îsi ê-kî-manisohcik; êkotowahk
mîna mân âya ê-kî-asamihcik pisiskiwak. êkoni kahkiyaw
ê-kî-wâpahtamân tânis âya ê-kî-isi-paminahkik kîkway kâ-~,
kêhtê-ayak ôki kâ-kî-pê-ayâcik, kwayask kî-paminamwak.

[61]   And his wife helped him a great deal, she helped him a great deal with the work itself, with the labour. It was this aunt of mine who used to tell me about what she did around the house. I wonder how many (when they had lots of work, for example, when they were swathing grain and seeding), how many young people, young men they had working, and they all slept at their house. That is what my aunt, Mary Minde, told me: "While they were still sleeping, these hired hands, I used to go and feed the horses," she said, "I used to go and look after them," she said, and when she was done looking after them, I guess, she had the horses fully fed and ready, and so the young men harnessed them, after they had finished their own breakfast, and began to work. "I used to come inside then and cook for them, and wake them up to eat," that is what she used to tell me, that is how she used to help her husband — her husband must also still have been sleeping, like the others, I guess, that is why she used to go and look after the horses.

[62]   And the other one, too, my mother-in-law Mary-Jane Minde, I saw her do the same, she also used to look after the horses. Probably they were not alone, women long ago must have been hard workers in such things, when their husbands did not look after the horses for them; or when they [the men] were not feeling well, when they were feeling sick, the women used to go and look after the horses. And when they also had cattle, they used to go and feed that kind, too, and look after them. I, too, used to help my husband in looking after his animals, when he went to feed them hay and sometimes grain, there were also bundles made, green-feed as it was called, they were green sheaves of grain [usually oats] cut that way [green]; that kind also used to be fed to animals. I saw all these things, how they looked after things, what the old people had, they looked after properly.

[63]   êwa-~ êwakw êtokwê mân âya, kayâs mân âya ayisiyiniwak, miyâmitonêyimihtwâwi, êwak ôhci kwayask kâ-kî-pimâtisicik, osâm ê-kî-otamiyocik, mistahi mâna kîkway atoskêwin ê-kî-otamiyocik. mâka namôy ôhci-pakwâtamwak, kî-miywêyihtamwak anim âyisiyiniwak aya, k-âtoskêcik, ka-pamihisocik anim âya, otapwêsiwiniwâhk ohci kîkway ka-kaskihtamâsocik. êwakw ânim êkwa mistahi kâ-wanihtâyahk. môy kiyânaw piko, misiw îtê êtokwê aya êwakw ânim ê-wanihtâhk aya, nayêstaw ê-~ ê-wî-kakwê-wêhtisihk êkwa aya, ka-sôniyâhkêhk êkwa êkota ohci ka-pimâcihohk. mâka mân âskaw miyâmitonêyihtamahki, "matwân cî kêtahtawê aya, êkâ kîkway ohpikici kistikân, matwân cî ka-kaskihtânânaw sôniyâw ka-mowâyahk?" — êkosi mân ê-itwêyân, osâm mistah âtiht ayiwâkêyimêwak sôniyâwa.

[FA:]   êha!

"matwân cî kêtahtawê êkâ kîkway ohpikihki,[33] matwân cî sôniyâw ka-mowânaw?" — êkosi mân ê-itwêyân, ê-pâhpiyân mân âskaw, niwîcêwâkanak mân êkos ê-itakik. tâpwê ayisk êtokwê kâh-kî-ihkin kêtahtawê, êkâ kîkway k-ôhpikik aya; kotaka ôh âskiya, akâmaskîhk ôtê, iyikohk mihcêt ayisiyiniwak ê-nipahâhkatosocik, ma kîkway ê-ohpikiniyik aya; kîkway kâ-kistikêcik, môy ê-ohtinikêcik. môy —~ môy ôsâm aya anima —~, môy ânim ôsâm êkâ kîkway ê-ohpikiniyik aya (ê-ayamihtâyân mân âya, âskaw ê-pê-itisahamâkawiyân âcimowina aya), akâmaskîhk âta kîkway k-ôhpikik aya, manicôsak êsa mân ê-kitâcik kistikâna, ê-misikiticik. kîkw-âyak[34] êtokwê êkonik aniki manicôsak aya, *locusts*, êkos ê-isiyîhkâtâcik aya, ê-kitâyit êsa mân ôkistikâniwâwa. êwak ôhc ânim âya, k-ôh-nipahâhkatosocik mihcêt ayisiyiniwak êkotê, ≠ êkwa nôtinitowin mîn ôhci, êwak ôhci k-ôh-nipahâhkatosocik.

≈≈≈

[63]   When you think of the people of long ago, I guess, that must be the reason why they lived properly, because they kept busy, they kept busy with lots of work. But they did not dislike work, the people liked to work in order to look after themselves and to earn things for themselves by their sweat. That is what we have largely lost now. Not we alone, it must be like that all over, that this was lost and that people are only going to try the easy way to make money on which to live. But when we think about it sometimes, "I wonder if one day, when there is no grain growing, I wonder if we will be able to eat money?" — that is what I usually say, some people put too much emphasis on money.

[FA:]   Yes.

"I wonder if one day, when nothing grows, I wonder if we will eat money?" — that is what I usually say, and sometimes I laugh and say that to my friends. For it could indeed happen someday, I guess, that nothing would grow; there are other countries, over there across the ocean, where so many people are starving to death and nothing is growing; whatever they plant, they do not get any harvest from it. It is not, however, that nothing grows (I read about it, sometimes I get these stories sent to me), even when something grows in these places overseas, insects eat the entire crops, and big ones. I wonder what kinds of insects these are, locusts, that is what they call them, they devour their entire crops. And that is why many people are starving to death over there, ≉ and also because of war, that is why they are starving to death.

≈≈≈

VIII

[64]   aya, êkwa awa, kêhcinâ êwako kâ-nôhtê-âcimak, êwako
ka-kî-âcimak, nisikos *Mary Minde*, pêyakwâw ê-kî-pêhtawak
ômatowihk ê-~- ê-kî-aya-âcimot aya, itowihk ôma k-âcimoyân,
nitânis *Theresa* ê-kî-âcimôhât ôhkoma. êkospî ê-kî-nitohtawak awa
nisikos ê-âtotahk, "nistam awa kâ-kihci-wîkimak nâpêw aya,
ê-kî-aya-~, mistahi ê-kî-kitimâkisiyâhk," itwêw. mâk âwa
k-âcimôhit, ê-nitawêyimit anim âya, tânis êwakw âwa mîn
ê-kî-is-âya-wîcê-~ ê-kî-~ ê-kî-is-ôh-âya-onâpêmit[35] ôh âya *Sam
Minde*. êwako mîna kiskinohamâtowikamikohk ohc âya,
ê-kî-ohc-âya-wayawît, êkoni ôh âya kâ-kihci-wîkimât *Sam Minde*.
êwakw ês âwa mân âya, ê-kî-atoskawât êsa mân âyamihêwiskwêwa,
êkwa iyikohk ê-kî-nihtâ-atoskêt aya, kwayask ê-kî-tôtahk,
ayamihêwiskwêwak êsa mistah âya, ê-kî-takahkêyimâcik ôh âya
oskinîkiwa, iyikohk ê-kakâyawisîyit. êkwa êtokwê mîn âwa *Mary
Minde* aya, kwayask ê-kî-tôtahk, ayamihêwiskwêwa mîn êwako
ê-kî-aya-atamihât, kâ-wîhtamâkot ês âya, "môy âya
kinitawêyimitinân aya —~"

    ≈ / ≈

    [FA:]   —~ kâ-pôyoyan.

[65]   aya anima —~ k-âcimostawit anim âya, kâ-miywêyimâcik anih âya
oskinîkiwa ê-miyohtwâyit, êkwa anihi mîn ôskinîkiskwêwa

VIII

The Marriage of Mary and Sam Minde

An Arranged Marriage

[64]   Now she certainly was the one I wanted to tell about, the one I should tell about, my aunt Mary Minde. Once I had heard her telling a story on this kind [the tape-recorder], the kind I am telling on, my daughter Theresa had her great-aunt tell a story. At that time I listened to my aunt telling about it, "When I first got married to this man, we were very poor," she said. But this one [Freda Ahenakew] who is having me tell about this, she wants me to tell about how she had taken this man, Sam Minde, as her husband. She also had come straight out of boarding-school when she got married to Sam Minde. He had used to work for the nuns, and he had been so good at his work, he did things properly, the nuns very much liked this young man because he was such a good worker. And Mary Minde also must have done things properly, and the nuns were happy with her, too; so they told her, "We do not want you —~"

≈ / ≈

[FA:]   —~ when you stopped.

[65]   She told me about it, that they liked that good-natured young man and also the good-natured young woman, and

ê-miyohtwâyit aya, iskwêyâc anim ômosôma aya, êkâ
ê-nitawêyimiht ka-kîwêtotawât osâm aya, êkospî wiy
âyamihêwiskwêwak mân âya ê-kî-pakwâtahkik anim ê-pêhtahkik
aya, osâm êtokwê mân âwa kisêyiniw aya, anima pawâmiwin
ê-kî-aya-nôcihtât. "môy, môy ka-kîwêtotawâw aw âya, kimosôm,
osâm aya kik-âsôskamâk anima êkâ kwayask ê-itâtisit," ê-kî-itikot
êsa; "ka-miskamâtinân awiyak ka-wîcêwat," ê-kî-itikot êsa, êkwa
êkoni ôh êsa kâ-kî-miskamâkocik, ê-nisitawêyimâyit aya, *Sam
Minde*, ê-kî-~ ê-kî-itikot êkoni ka-kihci-wîkimât, êkos êkoni
kâ-kî-kihci-wîkimât êkwa aya. tâpwê mitoni kwayask ê-kî-tôtahkik,
âta wiya mâna wîst âya, kî-minihkwêyiwa aya, owîkimâkana ⚭,
k-êtwêyân aya. êwakw âna mâna nisis, *Sam Minde*, kî-atoskêw
pêyakwan âta kâ-minihkwêt; kî-pakitinam mâna minihkwêwin, môy
ôhci-nawaswâtam, iyikohk kâ-tawâyik aya, êkâ kîkway k-ôtamiyot
ahpô k-ôtâkosik, êkota mâna piko kâ-kî-minihkwêcik ôk
âyisiyiniwak, ê-kî-kaskihtâcik kâh-kipîhci mân ê-pônihtâcik. ahpô
kâh-kinwês âsaw, môy ê-ohci-minihkwêcik, môy tahto-kîsikâw
ê-ohc-îsîhkahkik minihkwêwin. êwako ê-kî-kaskihtâcik ôki, osâm
ê-kî-~ ê-kî-sâkihtâcik êtokwê aya otatoskêwiniwâw. ê-kî-aya-~,
itâwak mân ôki niwâhkômâkanak, *Mindes* k-êtihcik,
ê-kî-kihc-~-kihcêyihtahkik anima opimâtisiwiniwâw
k-êsi-pimâtisicik. ê-wî-~ ê-kî-wî-kakwê-miy-ôsîhtâcik aya
owîhowiniwâw, ayisiyinînâhk, ayisk ê-kî-pê-kitimâk-ôhpikihikocik
okâwîwâwa; kwayask êtokwê ê-kî-ohpikihikocik okâwîwâwa.

[66]   êkonik mân ôk âya iskwêwak, kâ-pêyak-ôhpikihtamâsocik
otawâsimisiwâwa — pêyak kî-omisiwak. môy âhpô nikiskisin aya,
kwayask anim ôwîhowin aya, kêhcinâ owîhowin nik-êtwân,
onêhiyawi-wîhowin piko ê-kî-kiskêyihtamân ê-kî-omisicik,
ê-kî-isiyîhkâsoyit. 'wâpanohtêw' ê-kî-isiyîhkâsot êwakw ân[a] âya

at the end of school they did not want her to go back to her grandfather because the nuns did not use to like what they heard at that time, that the old man must have dealt with spirit power. "No, you will not go home to your grandfather because he will infect you with his wicked ways," they had said to her. "We will find you a husband," they said to her, and they found Sam Minde for her, she knew him, and they told her to get married to him, and so she married him. They very much did things properly, although her husband, he used to drink ≉, as I said. My father-in-law's brother, Sam Minde, still used to work the same, even when he drank; he would leave drink alone, he did not chase after drinking, only when there was time, when he was not busy or in the evening, only then did these people drink, and they were able to quit at any time. Sometimes they did not drink even for long periods, they did not bother with drink every day. They were able to do that because they must have loved their work. It used to be said about my relatives, the Mindes as they are called, that they thought highly of the way in which they lived their lives. They tried to make their name respectable among the people, for they had been raised under difficult circumstances by their mother; they must have been raised properly by their mother.

The Minde Family

[66]   And it was these women who raised their children by themselves — they [Dan and Sam Minde] had one older sister. I do not even remember her right name, her real name, I will say, I only know the Cree name of their older sister, what she was called. *wâpanohtêw* was the

nôtokwêsiw, kayâs êkâ kâ-pimâtisit. êkoni anihi ê-kî-omisicik, êkwa wiyawâw aya, ê-kî-nisticik nâpêwak. ê-~ ostêsiwâwa anih âya, 'kayâsiyâkan' êwakw ân[a] ê-kì-isiyîhkâsot, 'Old-Pan' k-êtwêyân anohc, êkota ohc ânik êkonik aniki. iyaskohc êkwa êkota aya, nisis awa, *Dan Minde*, 'kâ-mahihkani-pimohtêw' êwako kî-isiyîhkâsow. êkwa aw âya, ê-kî-~ ê-kî-osîmimâwit awa *Sam Minde* awa, 'okikocêsîs' êwako kî-isiyîhkâsow; kahkiyaw ê-kî-nêhiyawiyîhkâsocik. êkwa aya, êwakw âwa nisis aya, nikî-kihc-~ nikî-kihcêyihtamawâw mân ânim âya, ê-kî-itâcihot aya, kwayask ê-kî-paminahk wîkiwâw êkwa mîna kwayask aya, anih âya, otihtâwin anim îta; ê-kî-ayât mâna misatimokamikwa, kistikânikamikwa, êkwa okistikâna kwayask ê-kî-paminahk, môy wîhkâc ohc-ôhpikihtâw aya macikwanâsa; anima mâna kâ-kwayâtastâhk, ≠ êkosi mân ê-kî-isi-kwayâtastât. pêyakwan êkosi mân âw ê-kî-tôtahk niwîkimâkan, êkot[a] êtokwê mîn êwako ê-kî-ohtinahk ê-kiskinowâpamât, âta wiy ôhtâwiya mîna mistahi kîkway kâ-kî-kiskinohamâkot atoskêwin. ≠ êkwa, êwakw âwa *Mrs. Minde* aya, iyikohk kâ-kî-kaskihoyit onâpêma, osâm mistah âya ê-kî-kakâyawisît, ê-kî-wîcihât. wâwâc mân ê-kî-âcimostawit, ê-kî-miciminamawât misatimwa aya kâ-nakayâhâyit, ê-kî-miciminamôhikot, mistah êsa mâna ê-kî-kostât.

[67]   kêtahtawê k-âcimostawit mîna, pêyakwâw ês ê-ispayit, âhcanisa ê-kikiskawât, ok-~ okihc-~ okihci-wîkihtow[i]-âhcanisa; êkoni ôhi kâ-miciminât misatimwa ê-sâ-simacîyit, ê-tâpisikopayiyit ês ôcâhcanisihk aya, anih âya, tâpitonêhpicikanihk êtokwê nânitaw ê-s-~ ê-sêkopayiniyik pîwâpisk, kêkâc ês ê-kî-kîskicihcêpitikot, ê-simacîyit. tânis êtokwê ê-kî-isi-pask-~ ≠ êtokwê ê-kî-wîcihikowisit, ta-kêcikopitahk ocihciy, êkos ê-kî-itâcimostawit, iyikohk mân âya, ê-kî-âyimaniyik ot-~ otatoskêwin. êkwa aya, piko kîkway môy ê-ohci-kostahk êwakw âw ê-kî-wâpamak awa *Mrs. Minde*.

[68]   mistahi mîna ê-kî-nihtâ-mîkisihkahcikêt. ê-kî-miywâsiniyiki an[a] ôtayiwinisa aya, nisis ana, *Sam Minde* aya, êkoni anihi pahkêkinwêsâkaya ê-mîkisiwiyiki ê-kî-osîhtamâkot mâna. êkwa

name of that old lady, she died long ago. She was their older sister, and there were three brothers. Their older brother was called *kayâsiyâkan*, Old-Pan as I said here, that is where these [the Old-Pans whom Freda Ahenakew had met] are descended from. The next one in line was my father-in-law, Dan Minde, *kâ-mahihkani-pimohtêw* was his name. And Sam Minde was the youngest, *okikocêsîs* was his name; they all had Cree names. And this one, my father-in-law's brother [Sam Minde], I thought highly of the way he lived, he looked after their home properly, and also after his farm there; he used to have horse-barns and granaries, and he worked his fields well, he never grew weeds; when you prepare the land [in the fall], ≉ he prepared his fields in that way. My husband did the same, he must have taken it from there, by following his example, although he had also been taught a great deal about work by his father. ≉ And that Mrs. Minde [Mary Minde], her husband [Sam Minde] did so well for himself, because she was such a good worker, and she helped him. She even held the horses for him, she told me, when he broke them, he would have her holding them and she was very much afraid of them.

[67]   At one time, she also told me about what happened to her once, as she was wearing a ring, her wedding ring; she was holding that horse as it reared up, and it caught on her ring, the metal on the bridle must have gotten caught under the ring somehow, and the horse almost tore her finger off when it reared up. She must have escaped —∼ ≉ she must have had divine help to pull her hand out, she told me that, her work was so difficult. And she was not afraid of anything, I used to see that Mrs. Minde.

[68]   She also was very good at beadwork. My father-in-law's brother, Sam Minde, used to have beautiful clothes, she used to make beaded buckskin coats for him. And the

anihi mîna mân âya, kâ-nîmihitocik kâ-kikiskahkik mîkisayiwinisa,
êkotowahk ê-kî-ayât; ana mîna kotak aya nisis aya, *Dan Minde*,
owîkimâkana mîna êwako mân ê-kî-osîhtamâkot mîkisayiwinisa. ≠
êkosi kahkiyaw ê-kî-is-âya-~-isi-nihtâwiminakinikêcik ôki nisikosak
nîs ôki kâ-mâmiskômakik. êkwa anihi mîna mâna 'têhtapîwitâsa'
kî-isiyîhkâtêwak, êkotowahk mîna mân ê-mîkisiwiyiki
ê-kî-osîhtamâkot aw âya *Sam Minde*, owîkimâkana, ≠ ê-kî-kikiskahk
mân êkotowahk ê-mîkisiwiyiki. ≠ mistah âniki mâna
ê-kî-mîkisihkahcikêcik kayâs aya iskwêwak, êkwa mitoni kwayask
ê-kî-aya-osîhtâcik, âtiht mân âya kêyâpic[36] ê-kanawêyihtamân
ê-kî-wâh-wiyisamawit nisikos, wâpikwaniya[37] ê-masinahahkik êkwa
ê-~ ê-manisahkik, êkoni ê-masinihtatâyâhk
kâ-wî-aya-kîkway-osîhtâyâhk, maskisina ahpô aya, astisak. ≠
mistahi mâna ê-kî-miyosîhtâcik, ê-masinahamâsocik aya, kîkway
kâ-mîkisihkahtahkik, êkwa anihi mîn âya nêhiyaw-masinîwina,[38]
mîn êkoni ê-kî-kaskihtâcik. sôskwâc kî-miywâsiniyiwa aya
otôsîhcikêwiniwâwa.

[69]   êkwa mâna, tânis ê-kî-tôtâkocik onâpêmiwâwa, nik-~
ê-isi-nîsicik êkwa nik-âcimâwak. ê-kî-mâna-mitoni-pômêcik,
kîkway kâ-kî-osîh-~ kâh-osîhtamawâtwâwi ê-kî-mêkiyit mâna
[*ê-pâhpihk*]. êkwa mâna kotak kîkway mân êkwa
ê-kî-nitotamâkocik k-ôsîhtamawâcik.

[FA:]   ma cî ê-kî-kitimâkisicik mîna mistahi?

êwakw ânim âya, kêhcinâ aya, kâ-nôhtê-âtotamân, iyikohk ê-~
ê-kî-kitimâkisicik êkonik ôk âya, *Sam Minde* êkwa *Mary Minde*.
anim âya, ayamihêwiskwêwak kâ-mêkicik aya *Mary Minde*,
ka-wîcêwâyit *Sam Minde*, kî-kihci-wîkihtowak ês êkwa

beaded clothes they wear when dancing, he had that kind; and the other, my father-in-law, Dan Minde, his wife also used to make him beaded clothes. ⚹ In this way they were all good at beadwork, both my mother-in-law and the wife of my father-in-law's brother, the two women about whom I am talking. And also those which they used to call riding-pants, that kind, too, and beaded, Sam Minde's wife used to make for him, ⚹ he used to wear beaded ones. ⚹ The women used to do a lot of beadwork long ago, and very well, I still keep some of the cut-outs my mother-in-law had made for me, they would draw flowers and cut them out, and we would use these as patterns when we were going to make something, mocassins or mittens. ⚹ They used to make them very beautiful, drawing designs for themselves, when they did some beadwork, and they were also able to do Cree motifs. Anything they made used to be beautiful.

Sisters-in-Law

[69]   And how they used to be treated by their husbands, both of them, I will tell about them now. They used to be very disappointed when they had made something for them and their husbands would give it away [*laughter*]. And then they would be asked to make something else for them.

[FA:]   Weren't they very poor, too?

It was that which I definitely wanted to tell about, that they used to be so poor, Sam Minde and Mary Minde. When the nuns arranged for Mary Minde to marry Sam Minde, they had a church wedding and then went to live

kî-nitaw-âya-wîcêwêwak ostêsa aya, *Sam Minde* aw ôstêsa anihi
Dan Minde ê-kî-nitawi-wîcêwâcik, ê-kî-nitawi-wîtokwêmâcik êkotê,
êtokwê môy —~, môy êtokwê kîkway êk ôhc-âyâwak aya wîkiwin,
êkwa ê-kî-nitawi-wîtokwêmâcik ês âya, ostêsa awa *Sam*, êkwa ôk
îskwêwak mîn êsa mâna kîkway ê-kî-kiskinohamâtocik. mâk âwa,
Mary Minde aw âyiwâk ê-kî-ispîhtisît iyikohk *Jane Minde*. ≉ êkwa
mân âya, wiya nîkân aya, pakahkam (môy kwayask nititâcimon);
wiya nîkân ana *Mary Minde* ê-kî-onâpêmit, êkwa wiyawâw wîkiwin
ê-kî-ayâcik, mâk ôkâwîya awa *Sam Minde* ê-kî-pimâtisiyit, êkoni
ê-kî-wîtokwêmâcik nistam kâ-wî-~ kâ-wîcêwât aw ônâpêma. êkwa
aw îspî awa kâ-mâyipayit aw âya, owîkimâkana awa, *Dan Minde*,
awa nisis, mwêstas êkwa an[a] âya, *Mary-Jane Minde*
kâ-kihci-wîkimât, êkota êkwa ôk âya, kî-owîkiwak[39] êkwa, *Sam
Minde* êkwa *Mary Minde*, êkota êtokwê kanak (kanak, môy kinwês)
êtokwê ê-kî-nitawi-wîtokwêmâcik. ≉ êkwa aya, piyisk ês âya,
kotaka wîkiwina kî-âh-ayâwak pâh-pêyak, wâh-wâhyawês, êkota
piyisk anima nîstanân kâ-kî-wîkiyâhk aya, êkota ôki nisis êkwa
nisikos ê-kî-mêkwâ-wîkicik anima wâskahikan, ≉ oski-wâskahikan
êsa *Sam Minde* ê-kî-aya-osîhtamâsot êkotê, êkwa nêtê ô-~
wâhyawîs[40] miton âya kotakak aniki nisis an[a] ôstêsimâw *Dan*
ê-kî-wîkicik, êkwa awasitê ês âw ôski-wâskahikan
ê-kî-nitaw-ôsîhtât — kêyâpic[41] êwakw ânima ê-cimatêk wâskahikan,
ê-kî-okistikânikamikot niwîkimâkan. êkwa aya, êwak ôm âya, ôk
îskwêwak êsa mân îyikohk ê-kî-wîcihitocik aya, mîkisihkahcikêwin
≉ êkwa mîn ânih âya, miskotâkaya êkwa aya maskisina k-ôsîhtâcik,
ây-âhci[42] ê-kî-kiskinohamâtocik, êkosi mân ê-kî-isit awa nisikos,
Mary-Jane Minde.

[70]   mâk ânim âya, êkwa kâ-wî-âtotamân aya, nistam êkotê
kâ-nitawi-wîkicik *Mary Minde* êkwa *Sam Minde*, iyikohk ês
ê-kî-kitimâkisicik. nama kîkway misatimwa ês ê-ohc-âyâwâcik,
êkwa êtokwê ât[a] ê-nôhtê-pamihisocik, mâka namôy êyâpic (êkota
nik-êtwân), namôy ês ôhci-kitimâkinâsow nisis êkwa mîna nisikos
aya, osâm ê-kwîtâpacihtâcik.[43] êkota kisiwâk ê-kî-wîkit an[a] âya
nâpêw, namôya wâhyaw êkota sôskwâc êtokwê mân ê-kî-itohtêt aya

with his older brother, Sam Minde's older brother, Dan Minde, they went to live with them, they went to stay with them over there, they did not have any home then, I guess, and they went to stay with him, Sam's older brother, and the women also taught each other. But Mary Minde was older than Jane [*i.e.*, Mary-Jane] Minde. ≉ And she was first, I think (I have not told it right); Mary Minde took a husband first, and they did have a home, but Sam Minde's mother was still alive and they stayed with her when she was first married to her husband. And at the time when my father-in-law, Dan Minde, lost his [first] wife, later when Mary-Jane Minde got married to him, at that time Sam Minde and Mary Minde lived there, at that time they must have gone to stay with them temporarily (not for long). ≉ And then finally they had other homes, each of them, quite a little ways apart, it was there, finally, that we, too, lived, when my father-in-law and my mother-in-law were living in that house, ≉ Sam Minde had built himself a new house over there, and the others, my father-in-law Dan Minde, the oldest brother [excluding Old-Pan], and his family lived quite a little ways away yonder, and he [Dan Minde] had gone beyond that and built a new house — that house still stands today, my husband used it as a granary. And these women used to help each other so much in their beadwork ≉ and when they made coats and mocassins, they used to teach each other at one house or another, that is what my mother-in-law Mary-Jane Minde used to say to me.

[70]   But what I was going to tell about, when Mary Minde and Sam Minde first went to live over there, they were so poor. They did not have any horses, they must have wanted to make a living for themselves, but (I will say that about that time) my father-in-law's brother still did not feel sorry for himself, and neither did my aunt, just because they lacked tools. Close by there lived that man, he did not

Sam, êkotê ê-nitaw-âtoskawât êkoni ôh ôtatâwêwa, ê-kî-otatâwêwit
an[a] êwako mîn âya, ê-kî-nêhiyawiyîhkâsot nâpêw, ê-kî-pêhtamân
mâna, mâka kahkiyaw wiy êwako nikiskêyihtên owîhowina. *'Alec
Whitebear'* ê-kî-isiyîhkâsot, êkwa anima onêhiyawi-wîhowin, aya,
'câpihcicikan' ê-kî-isiyîhkâsot, onêhiyawi-wîhowin; êwakw âw êsa
kâ-kî-otatâwêwit. mâk ôki kêswân ôk âyisiyiniwak miton
ê-kî-miywêyihtahkik k-âtoskêcik, êwakw âwa ê-kî-kakâyawisît ês
âw âya, *Alec Whitebear* awa, ê-kî-kakâyawisît. nisis mîn êwako
ê-kî-pêhtawak, "kî-pimi-mâna-~ kîkisêpâ mitoni
kî-pimi-wâsaskotêw mâna ê-nitawi-pamihât pisiskiwa,
ê-papâmi-wâsaskotêk mân ê-kî-~ ê-kî-wâpahtamân, êyâpic
ê-tipiskâk ê-kî-mâcatoskêt[44] mân," ê-itât êkon ôhi ayisiyiniwa, ⚹
iyikohk êtokwê kwayask ê-kî-pamihisot mîn êwako. ⚹ êkwa,
êwakw âwa nâpêw ês âya kâ-kî-otatâwêwit, êkotê êsa mân êkwa
awa kâ-kî-nitaw-âtoskêt aya, *Sam Minde*, ê-nitawi-kîspinatât anihi
misatimwa. ê-nôhtê-kiscikêsit wîsta, kâh-kîspinatâci ês êkwa mâna
kâ-kî-pê-pîkopitahk êsa mân îta, ê-kistikêt apisis, êkoni anih ê-kî-~
kîspin-~ [45]

⚹⚹⚹

—~ kiscikânis.

[71] êkwa awa nisikos aya, êtokwê mân ôma kâ-nit-~
kâ-nitaw-âtoskêyit aya, iyikohk ê-kî-kitimâkisicik; nama kîkway êsa
mân ê-ohci-mîcit, k-êtitân, anima ê-kî-mâh-manipitahk êsa mân âya
ocêpihka, otêhiminâni-cêpihka[46] êsa mân ê-kanâcihtât, ê-kî-mîcit
êkoni [ê-pâhpit]. "êkwayikohk ê-kî-kitimâkisiyân, êkotowahk mân
ê-kî-mîciyân, iyikohk ê-nôhtêhkatêyân," ê-kî-itwêt. ⚹ êkwa piyisk
mân âskaw ê-kî-môskomot aya, k-âcimostâkoyâhk anima êkotê
nîhc-âyihk ê-~ nitânis wîkihk, *Theresa* ê-kî-nitaw-âcimôhât aya,
ôhkoma, piyisk ê-kî-mâh-môskomot aya nisikos aya, iyikohk ês
ê-kî-kitimâkisicik onâpêma, aya, ⚹ —~ [nama] kîkway êsa mân

have far to go, I guess, Sam went to work over there for that trader, he used to keep the store, the man also had a Cree name, I used to hear it, but I know all his names. Alec Whitebear he was called, and his Cree name was this, he was called *câpihcicikan* by his Cree name; he was the one who used to keep the store. But it so happened that these people really liked to work, and this one used to be a hard worker, this Alec Whitebear, he used to be a hard worker. I used to hear my father-in-law's brother say, "Early in the morning a lantern used to go by as he went to look after the animals, I used to see a lantern move about, it was still dark when he used to begin to work," he said about this man, ⚹ so well did that one also use to look after himself. ⚹ Now it was this storekeeper, it was over there that Sam Minde used to go to work, going to earn enough for a horse. He, too, wanted to farm, on a small scale, when he would have earned enough for a horse and had come to plough and planted a little, when he would have earned that [horse] —~

⚹⚹⚹

—~ a little field.

[71] And my aunt, when he went to work there, I guess, they were so poor, she used to have nothing to eat, as I told you before [off-tape], she would pull up roots, cleaning strawberry-roots, and these she used to eat [*laughs*]. "I was that poor, I was so hungry that I would eat that kind," she used to say. ⚹ And sometimes she used to end up crying when telling us about this, down the hill there at my daughter's house, Theresa used to go and have her great-aunt tell stories, and my aunt used to end up crying, so poor had she and her husband been —~

ê-ohci-mîcicik,[47] êkwa iyikohk kaskihtâcik[48] êsa mân âya, kîkway
ê-~ ê-kî-wî-kakwê-miskahkik ≠ ka-mîcicik aya, mâcik ânihi, môy
nânitaw ohpimê k-êtohtêt, sôskwâc ê-mâh-manipitahk anihi
ocêpihkisa, ê-mâh-mîcit êkoni (ê-kî-yôskâyiki êtokw âhpô mitoni),
ê-kî-kanâcihtât êkoni.

≠≠≠

nimihtâtênân anim ânima ê-kî-wanihtâhk anim îyikohk aya —

[FA:]   ê-kî-wanihtâhk?

êha, ê-kî-takahkihtâkwahk anima, êwakw ânima âcimowin, mitoni
ê-kî-nitawêyihtamâhk ê-~ *Theresa* awa nicânis, ka-pêhtahkik
ayisiyiniwak, tânisi kayâs ayisiyiniwak iyikohk ê-~
ê-kî-sâ-sîpihkêyihtahkik êkwa ê-kî-aya-miton-âya-wîhkôcik, kwayask
ê-wî-itôtahkik, kwayask ê-wî-kakwê-itâcihocik. êkâ —~ êkây êtokwê
ê-ohci-nôhtê-kimoticik êwak ôma kâ-kî-tôtahkik aya, wâwâc awa
nâpêw kâ-kî-kîspinatât misatimwa, aya, ≠ kâ-mâci-kist-~
ka-mâcihtât aya, aya, kistikân, k-ôkistikêwiyinîwit. tahk âyiwâk
êtokwê kîkway kî-ati-kâhcitinam ahpô êtokwê piyisk mîna
misatimwa aya, kî-kîspinatêw, êkota ohc âya, ka-sipwê-pamihisot
êkwa aya, k-ôkistikêwiyinîwit. êkonik ôki mistahi ê-kî-kistikêcik
mâna, mâk âyiwâk *Sam Minde* mista-~

≈≈≈

[72]   —~ ôtê ês êkwa ê-kî-âhc-âyâcik aya, sâkâstê-~ sâkâstênohk
êkwa êkotê aya, ôsisimiwâwa mêkwâc kâ-wîkiyit, ê-kî-mâh-misâki

≉ they had nothing to eat and, as much as they could, they tried to find things ≉ to eat, for instance those little roots, she did not have to go anywhere far off, she simply pulled up those little roots (they must have been quite soft) and cleaned and ate them.

≉≉≉

We were sorry that this [recording of Mary Minde] was lost, it was so —

  [FA:]   It was lost?

Yes, that story was good to listen to, my daughter Theresa and I very much wanted people to hear how much the people of old used to endure and how they pulled through, trying to do their best and trying to live right. They did not want to steal, I guess, when they did this [persevere despite privations], this man even earned enough for a horse ≉ to start a farm, to farm. Gradually he must have acquired things, and finally he must even have earned enough for a horse, to start to make a living for himself with that, and to farm. They used to farm a lot, but Sam Minde more so —~

≈≈≈

Daily Life

[72]   —~ then they moved over here, over there towards the east, where their grandchildren still live now, those

êkoni kistikâna, êkotê ê-kî-âhc-âyât aya, osâm êtokwê
ê-kî-tatâyawâk anim îtê aya, ostêsa kâ-kî-wîkicik. êkotê ês ôm âya,
napakikamikos êsa, asiskîwikamikos kî-nitaw-ôsîhtamâsow ôtê,
ê-nitawi-mâc-âya-pîkopicikêt, kistikâna anihi ê-nitaw-ôsîhtât, êkwa
ôma wâskahikan aya, oski-wâskahikan kâ-kî-ayât, ê-kî-nakatamawât
ês ôstêsa.

༝༝༝

—~ ê-kî-wîkicik ôki nisis, *Sam Minde*, êkota, k-êtitân kâ-~, êyâpic
ê-kî-wîkicik kâ-pê-ayâyân. *nineteen-twenty-seven* kâ-pê-ayâyân ôta
aya, maskwacîsihk, êkota êyâpic —~

༝༝༝

—~ kwayask miton êtokwê ê-kî-osîhcikâtêk êwakw ânim âya, ༝
mistikokamik, kâ-kî-mâna-sisopêk-~ kâ-kî-~ mâna ༝ itowahk anim
âya, mâna kayâs, nayêstaw êkotowahk ôta kâ-kî-aya-cimatêki
mistikokamikwa; êkwa mân âya, kî-sisoskiwakinamwak mân êkwa
kî-wâpiskahamwak mâna, wâpatoniska ahpô aya, 'asiniy kâ-kîsisot'
kî-isiyîhkâtamwak mân âya, anim âya, ê-kî-wâpisk-~ [49]

༝༝༝

—~ kî-masinahikêhêwak mân âskaw aya,

[FA:]   iskwêwa

nâpêwa êkwa iskwêwa ka-tôtamâkocik mâka mân âya,
ê-kî-wâpamak mâna wiya nisikos, *Mary Minde*, ê-kî-tôtamâsot mân
ê-kî-sisoskiwakinikêt. mîn êwakw ânima namôy
ê-ohc-âtawêyihtahkik iskwêwak, môy êtokw âw âya nisikos —
kotakak mân îskwêwak mîn ê-kî-âcimihcik ê-kî-sisoskiwakinikêcik.
êwako niya môy nôh-kaskihtân.

fields were big, he moved over there, it must have become too crowded there where he and his older brother had lived. Over there he went and built a little flat shack, a little mud-shack for himself, he went and began to break the sod and get the fields ready, and the house, the new house he used to have, he left for his older brother.

彡彡彡

—~ my father-in-law's brother, Sam Minde, and his family used to live there, as I told you, they still lived there when I came to live here. It was 1927 when I came to live here in *maskwacîsihk*, at that time they still —~

彡彡彡

—~ it must have been made very well, ≁ a log house, they used to mud them ≁ that kind, long ago there were only log houses standing here; and they used to mud them and then whitewash them, with white clay or with lime, they used to call it, they used to white-~

彡彡彡

—~ sometimes they hired

[FA:]   women

men and women to do this for them, but I used to see my aunt, Mary Minde, do it for herself, she used to do the mudding. And women also did not think anything of this work, not my aunt, I guess, and it was also told about other women that they did the mudding. That I was not able to do.

kî-kosikwan ayisk mân âya, kwayask anima ka-kikamohtâcik aya,
maskosiya mân ê-kî-kikinahkik, môy nikah-sâkôhtân[50] anim âya,
kâ-kî-wêpinahkik mân âya, ita anim âya, mistikwa —

[FA:]   ita kâ-nîswapicik

— êha, ita kâ-tawâyik anima, êkota mân ê-kî-aya-sôhkêhtatâcik mân
âya, nikî-kitâpamâwak mâna, niwîkimâkan êkwa nâpêwa mân
ê-kî-nitomât ê-kî-sisoskiwakinikêcik mâna — mâk âtiht môy
kwayask ohci-tôtamwak; osâm anih âya, asiskiya môy âya
ohci-misisîhtâwak êkwa aya, kî-sâpoyowêwa mâna âskaw, osâm êkâ
kwayask ê-sisoskiwakinikêcik. ≠ êwako mîna kî-âyiman aya, pikw
âwiyak ka-maskawisît ka-sisoskiwakinikêt. mâka wiya niwîkimâkan
mistah âya, kî-miyôw anim ê-sisoskiwakinikêt, misatimokamikwa
mîna mân ê-kî-sisoskiwakinahk; misatimokamik êkotowahk
ê-kî-ayât, êkwa ê-kî-sisoskiwakinamâsot mân êkotowahk.
[73]   êkwa mistahi ê-kî-kisiki wâskahikana; ispî ôma kâ-~ kâ-~
kâ-pîwaniyôtik, kiyâm pikoyikohk kâ-pônamâhk awaswâkan,
kotawânâpisk ê-kî-ayâyâhk, môy ê-ohci-kaskihtâyâhk
ka-kîsowihkasoyâhk, ê-kî-wêwêkapiyâhk mâna wâsakâm aya, êkota
awasowi-kotawânâpiskohk, ê-akwanahoyâhk akohpa; êkwayikohk
mîn ê-kî-âyimahk ê-kawacihk [ê-pâhpit].

[FA:]   ahpô piko pîhtikwê-âwacimihtêwin ahpô.

êwako mîn ê-kî-âyimahk ka-pîhtokwê-âwacimihtêhk, wâwâc mân
âwâsisak aya, ê-kî-tôtamôhihcik, môy mihcêt ê-tahkonahkik, mâka
m-~ mihcêtwâw pêmohtêtwâwi, piyisk mâna kî-sâkaskinahtâwak
anima mâna mistikowat mân îta aya, mihta ê-kî-asiwatâhk.
ê-kî-mamihcisit mân ân[a] âya, kâ-kî-nakatikoyâhk ana nitânis
ê-apisîsisit, niyâcimihtêyici mân ômisa ê-kî-pimitisahikêt ('Clara'

[FA:]   It was heavy.

For it used to be heavy for them to put it on right, they mixed it with straw, I would not be able to lift it, when they threw it on —

[FA:]   where the logs come together

— yes, into the chinks in between the logs, there they would throw it hard, I used to watch them, my husband and the men he had asked, as they used to do the mudding — but some did not do it right; they did not make the clumps of mud big enough, and sometimes the wind would blow through because they did not do the mudding right. ✳ That was also difficult, one had to be strong to do the mudding. But my husband used to be very good at mudding, he also mudded the barn; he had that kind of barn, and he used to mud that kind for himself.

[73]   And the houses were very cold, at times when there was a blizzard it did not matter how much wood you put in the heater, we used to have a stove, and we did not manage to get warm, we would sit around the stove wrapped in blankets, there by the heating-stove, covered in blankets; it used to be that hard when you were cold [*laughs*].

[FA:]   Even just hauling the firewood inside.

That also used to be hard, to haul the firewood inside, even the children were made to do it, they did not carry much, but when they went back and forth many times, they would finally fill up the wooden box in which the wood was kept. My daughter, the one who has left us behind, used to be proud when she was small, every time

ana kâ-kî-isiyîhkâsot nitânis, kâ-kî-nakatikoyâhk, têpakohposâp
ê-itahtopiponwêt êkâ ê-ohci-pimâtisit), pêyak mân
ê-kî-pê-tahkonahk aya, wîsta mihti ê-pê-pakitinahk. "tâpwê mistah
âwa kakâyawisîw," ê-kî-itak mân, âspin mân ê-kî-wayawîpahtât, âsay
mîna kotak ê-nâtahk [*ê-pâhpihk*]. îh, êkos ânima mâna
ê-kî-is-âya-~-mâci-aya-~-miyo-kîsihihcik awâsisak kîkway
ka-wîcihtâsocik, ê-kî-pîhtokwatamâkêcik mân âya mihta. nipiy
mîna mâna ê-kî-nâtahkik, apisis askihkosihk ê-~ ê-pimohtatâcik, ≠
kâ-kwâpikêhk, wîstawâw mâna ê-apisîsiyit askihkosa
ê-kî-tahkonâcik.

≠≠≠

—~ êkwa aya, êwakw âwa nisikos aya, namôy ê-kî-kiskisiyân aya,
kîkwây anim ê-âtotahk, kâ-kî-mâtot —~

≠≠≠

—~ k-êtwêyân âta wiya, êwako mîna kî-tôtam.
ê-kî-mosci-nâtitâpêt[51] êsa mâna mihta, ê-~ ê-pâstêyiki
kâ-wî-pônahk. êkwa aya ê-nikohtêt, êkwa ê-pîhtokwatât. maywês
awâsisak k-âyâwâyâhkik, êkosi nîstanân mâna nikî-tahk-~

≠≠≠

—~ [môy] nôh-~ nôh-nakacihtân[52] aya, k-êsi-nikohtêyân.
ê-kî-âsôhtatâyân mân êkota ê-nikohtâtamân aya, ê-kîskatahamân
aya mihta. êkwa, ôk êkâ kâ-nakacihtâcik aya, ayisiyiniwak aya
nikohtêwin, ê-kî-câh-cîkahosocik mîna mân ôsitiwâhk [*ê-pâhpit*] —

[FA:]   kêhcinâ!

— kî-âyiman kahkiyaw kîkway êkospî.

her older sisters hauled firewood, she would follow along (the name of my daughter was Clara, the one who has left us behind, she was seventeen when she died), she used to carry one stick at a time, and she, too, would come and put it down. "This one is truly a hard worker," I used to say to her, and immediately she would run out and fetch another one again [*laughs*]. Look! that was the way children were given good habits to help with things, they brought wood in for you. They also went for water, carrying a little in a small pail, ≉ when you got water, they, too, would carry little pails.

≉≉≉

—∼ and this aunt of mine, I cannot remember what it was she told about, when she used to cry —∼

≉≉≉

—∼ as I said, she also used to do that. She used to get wood and drag it home, dry firewood, when she was going to make a fire. And she chopped wood and brought it inside, we, too, used to do that before we had children —∼

≉≉≉

—∼ I was not good at cutting wood. I used to lean the wood against something and chopped on it as I cut the wood. And the people who were not used to chopping wood, they also used to chop their feet [*laughs*] —

[FA:]   for sure!

— everything was difficult in those days.

[74]   mâka, ayiwâk ayisiyiniwak ê-itêyihtamân êkospî
ê-kî-miyawâtahkik. iyikohk mân ê-kî-pâhpicik kayâs ayisiyiniwak,
ê-âcimostâtocik, kahkiyaw kîkway ê-âcimostâtocik, tâpiskôc ôm â-~
k-ês-âcimostâtân. mihcêtwâw kîkway ê-miywâsik
ê-kî-mâmiskôtahkik ayisiyiniwak aya, mîn ê-kâh-kiskisomitocik[53] aya,
tânis âtoskêwin aya, wiyawâw ê-isi-wâh-wîkicik, tânis ê-itôtahkik
atoskêwin. ≠ tâpiskôc k-êtwêyân aya, kahkiyaw kîkway
ê-kî-osîhtamâsocik; akohpa mîna mân ê-kî-nanâtohkokwâsocik, êkwa
mân ê-kî-moscikwâtahkik. ê-kî-kispakikwâtahkik mâna kîkway aya,
ê-kî-osîhtâcik ≠ ê-kîsowâyiki. êk ôm êkwa nikiskisopayin,
wâposwayânakohpa mîn ê-kî-osîhtâcik ê-kî-kîsowâyiki.

[FA:]   sîsîp-~

≠≠≠

êkwa mîn âtiht aya, anih âya, sîsîpipîwaya mîna mân âya,
kâ-kî-pâh-piskihcikwâtahkik, êkoni mîna ê-kî-yâhkasiki ê-kî-~
ê-kî-kîsowâki aya, aya, akohpa ê-kî-osîhtâcik âstamispî êkoni; nîkân
anih âya, wâposwayâna mâna, wâposwayânakohpa kâ-kî-osîhtâcik.
pita mân âya, pakahkam aya, ê-kî-aya-~ ê-kî-o-~
ê-kî-mâh-manisahkik aya, ê-âh-apiscisasicik anih âya, pahkêkinwa,
wâposo-~ wâposwayâna anihi, wâposwayâna. ê-kî-maniswâcik
êkwa aya, ê-âh-âniskôkwâtahkik anih âya, kâ-manisahkik, êkwa ê-~,
nânitaw is ê-kî-apihkâtahkik. itâmihk êkoni êkwa
ê-pîhtawêkwâtahkik, waskic êkwa ê-pîhtawêkwâtahkik. mâk âya,
mistahi kî-sakâpâtamwak mîna, êkâ aya ka-yîkatêpayiyiki. êkoni
mîna kî-yâhkasinwa mâna, wâpos-~

≠≠≠

—~ êha. môy kayâs ohc âya atâwêwikamikohk ohc-îspahtâwak
ayisiyiniwak,

[74]   But people used to have more fun, I think, in those days. People used to laugh so much long ago, telling one another stories, telling one another stories about everything, just as I am telling you. People would often talk about good things and also remind one another, what work they were doing at their homes, what kind of work they did. ≉ As I said, they used to make everything for themselves; they used to sew patchwork blankets, and they used to sew them by hand. They used to sew them thick, they used to make them ≉ warm. And it just comes back to me that they also used to make rabbitskin blankets, and they used to be warm.

[FA:]   duck-~

≉≉≉

And some also were made of duck-feathers, which they used to sew in squares, and they used to be light-weight and warm, they used to make these blankets later on; the first ones were rabbitskin, when they used to make rabbitskin blankets. As a first step, I believe, they used to cut them up into small pieces of hide, the rabbitskins. They used to cut the rabbitskins, sewing them together one adjoining to another when they had cut them, and then they used to braid these strips. They sewed these between covers, they sewed them in between something outside. But they also sewed them firmly, so that they [the braided strips] would not move sideways [but stay in place]. And they also used to be light-weight, these rabbit-~

≉≉≉

—~, yes. People did not use to run to the store long ago,

sôskwâc mâna kîkway kî-tôtamâsowak, êkos îs ôma mâna
ê-kî-nanâtohkokwâsocik. ahpô aw âya, maywês ka-nakataskêt,
maywês aya, êkâ —~, maywês ka-wanihtât owâpiwin aya, awa
nisikos, êyâpic mân ê-kî-aya-nanâtohkokwâsot ≠ ê-moscikwâsot.

[FA:]   tânimayikohk ê-kî-itahtopiponêt, êkwa?

kâ-pôni-pimâtisit anim âya, kêkâ-mitâtahtomitanaw ayiwâk niyânan
ê-itahtopiponwêt, kêkâc ôm êkwa ka-kî-otihtahk aya (tânis êtokwê
ê-isi-nêhiyawi-wîhiht an[a] âya, *August*, ohpahowi-pîsim),

[FA:]   êha

êkota an[a] ê-~, mân ê-otihtahk, ê-kî-otihtahk
otihtahtopiponwêwin, êkot[a] êkwa kêkâ-mitâtahtomitanaw ayiwâk
nikotwâsik ka-kî-otihtahk; *ninety-six* ka-kî-itahtopiponwêt.
[75]   êkwa ôm âya, âsay êtokwê êkospî nânitaw aya, nânitaw
ka-kî-itahtopiponwêw *eighty-nine*, êyâpic
kâ-kî-aya-nanâtohkokwâsot. ê-kî-mâh-miyât mân âya, otânisa êkwa
ôsisima êkoni akohpa kâ-kî-~

[FA:]   ê-moscikwâtahk

≠≠≠

—~ kwayask ê-kî-~, ê-moscikwâtahk êkwa ê-kî-pîhtawêkwâtahk —
êkâ wanikiskisiyâni, ka-wâpahtihitin pêyak ê-kî-miyit. nêtê êwakw
ânim âya, nêm âya, wîhkwêhtakâhk anim âya, nipêwin k-âstêk,
êkota astêw, êwakw ânim âkohp ê-kî-miyit, "osâm mân âya,
piyôsihiyan[i] âya, nikâh-kawacin, ôma k-âspapiyan," ê-kî-isit.
ê-kî-kâh-kawatimak aya, êkos îsi mân âya, êkâ kîkway ê-ohc-âstâyân

[FA:]   for everything

they simply used to do things for themselves, they used to sew patchwork blankets just like that. Even my aunt [Mary Minde], before she departed this world, before she lost her eye-sight, she still used to sew patchwork blankets ≉ and she was sewing by hand.

[FA:]   How old was she now?

When she died she was ninety-five years old, she would soon have reached (what is the Cree name for August, flying-up month),

[FA:]   yes

then she would have reached her birthday, then she would have reached the age of ninety-six; she would have been ninety-six years old.

[75]   And at that time she must have already been about, she would have been eighty-nine when she was still sewing patchwork blankets. She used to give the blankets to her daughters and grandchildren —~

[FA:]   sewing them by hand

≉≉≉

—~ properly sewing them by hand, and then she used to sew them between covers — if I don't forget, I will show you one she gave me. It is that one over there, in the corner where the bed is, there is that blanket she gave me, "Because every time you give me a ride I get cold, this is for you to sit on," she had said to me. I used to get her

akohp êkwa ê-kî-pâh-pôsihak, êkwa êsa mâna ê-kî-kâh-kawacit;
kâ-miyit êkwa akohp k-âspapiyâhk êkota, mâk êkwa êkotê aya, ôki
mâna kâ-pê-aya-ôta-nipâcik aya niwâhkômâkanak, ê-âpacihtâcik
mân êwakw ânim âkohp, ⚹ êkotê ê-kî-astâyân êwako. ⚹ —~
êkwayikohk aya ê-kî-miywêyihtahk aw ê-atoskêt awa *Mary Minde*,
âhci piko mân ê-kî-aya-nanâtohkokwâsot; êyâpic ahpô êtokwê
ôsisima âtiht ayâyiwa anihi, anih âya kâ-kî-osîhtât nanâtohk-~ ⚹ —~
iyikohk ê-kî-kisêwâtisit mân âya, âhci piko mân
ê-kî-âhkami-kaskikwâsot, êkwa ê-mâh-miyât kîkway otânisa êkwa
ôsisima.

⚹⚹⚹

—~ âta wiy êyâpic êtokwê ihtakowak âtiht aya, kêhtê-ayak êkosi
ê-isi-kitimâkêyimâcik —~

⚹⚹⚹

—~ kîkway kâ-kaskihtâcik kîkway ê-osîhtamawâcik.

⚹⚹⚹

—~ kaskihtâw mîna mân âya, pakahkam, ê-ay-~

≈≈≈

[76]   —~ kahkiyaw ayisk mân ôhi —

    [FA:]   ê-itapihkêt[54]

— êha, kahkiyaw ayisk kiskinohamawâkanak ôk âya kâ-kihci-wîkicik
aya, ayamihêwiskwêwa kâ-kî-paminikocik, kahkiyaw
nikî-kiskinohamâkawinân asikanak tânisi k-ês-ôsîhtamâsoyâhk,
ê-kî-apihkâtâyâhkik,

cold, it was that way, I did not put down any blanket when I used to give her rides, and she used to be cold; then she gave me a blanket for us to sit on, but it is over there, when my relatives come to sleep here, they use that blanket, ⚹ I have put it over there. ⚹ —~ so much did Mary Minde use to love working that she still would sew patchwork blankets; her grandchildren probably still have them, those she made —~ ⚹ —~ she was so kind, she still persevered in sewing, and then giving things to her daughters and grandchildren.

⚹⚹⚹

—~ although there must be still some old people that care for them —~

⚹⚹⚹

—~ anything they were able to do, they made for them.

⚹⚹⚹

—~ she was also able to, I believe, —~

≈≈≈

[76]   —~ for all of these —

   [FA:]   she was knitting

— yes, for all the students who were in residence, where the nuns looked after them, we all learned to make stockings for ourselves, we used to knit them,

—~ ê-kî-kaskitêsicik mâna ê-kî-kinosicik. mâka mâna nistam
kâ-nitaw-âyâyâhk, nikî-nayêhtâwêyimânânak, iyikohk ê-kî-kâsisicik
[*ê-pâhpit*]. ayisk ana, *pure wool* ana, ê-kâsisit, êkotowahk mân
ê-kî-aya-~, anihi mâna kâ-kî-osîhtamâsocik aya, mâyatihkopîwaya
ohci kâ-kî-osîhtamâsocik — kî-ayâwak ayisk mîn ânim âya (sêstakwa,
êkon ê-osîhâcik, ayamihêwiskwêwak ê-kî-osîhâcik) *spinning-wheel*
ê-kî-ayâwâcik. êkwa mân êtokwê anima ê-kî-kaskitêwatiswâcik,
êwak ôhc ânima mâna kâ-kî-kaskitêsicik aya nitasikaninânak, êkwa
ôk âya, k-âpisîsisicik ôk îskwêsisak aya, ê-kî-aya-~, êkâ
ê-ohci-kaskihtâcik sêmâk k-ês-âpihkêcik; sîskêpisona mân
ê-kî-apihkâtahkik. mâka pîminahkwânisa wiya êkoni aya —~ môy
pîminahkwânisa, ê-kî-titipihtik mîn êwakw ânim âya, pîminahkwânis
aya, *green*, ê-kî-askihtakwâk, ê-kî-oskaskosîwinâkwahk. êkoni mân
âya, ômis îsi mê-~ kwêh-kwêkwask, ômis îs ê-kî-itapihkâtamâhk,
tâpiskôc ôma, sîskwê-~ sîskêpisona mân ê-kî-osîhtamâsoyâhk.
êwakw ânim êkw-~, k-êsi-nihtâ-apihkêyâhk
ê-kî-kiskinohamâkawiyâhk. mitoni mân ômayikohk êtokwê ê-kî-~
ê-kî-ispîhcâki, osâm wiy ôma apis-~ apisâsin.

—~ mân âya, mihcêt mân ê-kî-osîhtâyâhk, kotakak ôki
kiskinohamawâkanak mîn ê-kî-osîhtamawâyâhkik, êkwa aniki mîna
mân âsikanak aya, môy piko pêyakw-âyak nôsîhânânak, taht ôki
kâ-kaskihtâcik k-âpihkâtâcik, ✻ mihcêt mâna kî-osîhêwak.
kêtahtawê êkwa ayamihêwiskwêwak aya — ê-kî-âyimîcik êtokwê
mân ôtê misitihk k-âpihkâtâcik ôki iskwêsisak, kêtahtawê êkwa mîn
âya (namôy ôtê, êtokwê êwakw ânim âya ê-wanêyihtamân,
miskâtihk osâm kinwês ê-kî-nôcihtâyâhk, anik ê-kî-kinosicik),
kêtahtawê aya, k-âtâwêcik aya, âpacihcikan, anima *machine*, namôy
nikiskêyihtên tânisi k-êtamân anim âya, apihkêpicikan, êkosi
nik-êtwân, ê-kî-wâwiyêyâk; ayamihêwiskwêw mâna

※※※

—~ they were black and they were long. But when we first went to stay there, we felt awful about them because they were so rough [*laughs*]. For pure wool is rough, when they made that kind for themselves, when they made it for themselves from sheep's wool — they also used to have that (they made yarn, the nuns used to make it), they used to have a spinning-wheel. And they must have dyed it black, that is why our stockings used to be black, and the little girls, they were not able to knit right away; they used to knit garters. But those were made of string, not string, it was twisted and it was green string; it was the green, it was the colour of fresh grass. These we used to knit like this [*gesture*], back and forth like this [*gesture*], and we used to make things like garters for ourselves. With that we learnt to be good at knitting. They were this [*gesture*] big, this [*gesture*] is too small.

※※※

—~ we used to make many, we also used to make them for other students, and also these stockings, we did not only make one pair, as many as they were able to knit, ※ they used to make lots of them. At one time the nuns — I guess these girls had a hard time knitting the feet over here [*gesture*], at one time (it was not that over here [*gesture*], I guess I am mixed up, we took too long on the legs, they were long stockings), at one time they bought a machine, a machine, I don't know what to call it, a knitting-machine, I will say, it was round; when the nun had threaded the yarn on, she would just crank it, the

kâh-kikamôhâc[i] ânihi sêstakwa, sôskwâc mân ê-kî-wâskânahk
anim âya, apihkêpicikan anima, êkwa iyikohk ê-iskosiyit mân âya
asikana, ê-kî-osîhât, êkwa êkota ê-paskinât. êkwa nîso mâna
kâ-kîsihâcik pêyak iskwêsis aya, ê-miyiht, misita aya, mahkwan
êkwa êkwa misit-~ misita aya, ê-kîsapihkâtahk êwako, êkos
ê-kî-isi-mihcêt-osîhâyâhkik. êwak ôm âya, wîstawâw êtok ôma
mâna êkosi kî-~ kî-tôtamwak ôki *Mary Minde*.

≠≠≠

êwako kanihk[55] mîn âya —~

[FA:]   tâni ?[56]
[EM:]   êha.

[77]   kotak kîkway êkwa kâ-kiskisiyân k-âtotamân aya, iyikohk
ê-kî-aya-~, okâwîmâwak ôk îskwêwak ê-kî-aya-~, kahkiyaw kîkway
ê-kî-kakwâtakîcik aya, kâ-tôtamâsocik, ê-kî-mosci-kisêpêkinikêcik
mân ânih âya, n-~ 'sinikohtakinikana' kî-isiyîhkâtêwa
ê-kî-âpacihtâcik, êkwa mahkahkwa ê-kî-capahcâsiki, êkota mân âya,
nipiy ê-kî-âwatamâsocik mân âya; âskaw aya, îhkatawâhk ohci nipiy
ê-kî-âwatâcik êkwa ê-kisâkamisahkik, ê-kisêpêkinikêcik aya, êkos
ânima ê-kî-tôtahkik kâ-kisêpêkinikêcik. êkosi kahkiyaw kîkway
ê-kî-kisêpêkinahkik, mitâsa, ôk ôwîkimâkaniwâwa kâ-kikiskawâyit,
êkwa wiyawâw otayiwinisiwâwa, miskotâkaya, êkwa itâmihk ôh
âyiwinisa kâ-kikiskamihk, 'pîhtawêwayiwinisa' mâna
kâ-kî-isiyîhkâtêki; wâwâc akohpa êkota ê-kî-kisêpêkinahkik êkwa
ê-kî-mosci-sînahkik. nama kîkway ohc-âyâwak aya, ka-wîcihikocik
aya, êkâ êkwayikohk k-âyimisicik kîkway tiyôtahkwâwi. mâka
êtokwê ôm âya, iyikohk kâ-kî-atoskêcik iskwêwak aya,
kî-maskawâtisiwak; ê-kî-osîhtamâsocik anima maskawisîwin, kîkway
ka-tôtamâsocik.

[78]   âskaw mân âhpô aya, k-âsiwatahki mahkahkohk aya, wîpayiwinisa,
êkwa sinikohtakinikan êkota mîn âya ê-âswastâhk, âh-âyîtaw mân

knitting-machine, and then she would make the stocking until it was long enough, and then she would break off the yarn. And when they had finished two of the legs, they were given to one girl who would then finish knitting the feet, the heel and the feet, and that is how we made many. They, too, must have done that, Mary Minde and her friends.

❊❊❊

And also this, I forgot —~

[FA:] which?
[EM:] yes.

[77]   Another thing I remember to tell about, to what extent these mothers, these women, had a hard time with everything when they did things for themselves, when washing their clothes simply by hand, using what were called wash-boards, and low tubs, in these they used to haul water for themselves; sometimes they used to haul water from the slough, and heated it and washed clothes, that is what they used to do when they washed clothes. In that way they washed everything, their husband's pants and their own clothes, dresses, and the underclothes one wore, 'in-between-clothes' [between skin and clothes] as they used to be called. They even used to wash blankets and then they used to wring them out by hand. They had nothing to help them, to make it easier for them, when they did this. But because the women worked so hard, I guess, they used to be strong; they made themselves strong so that they could do things for themselves.

[78]   Sometimes, perhaps, when the dirty clothes were put in the tub and the washboard was placed to lean against the

ê-kî-itinamihk, îhkatawâhk mân âya ê-kî-itohtatâhk êkoni
wîpayiwinisa, êkwa êkotê ê-pônamihk, aya, wayawîtimihk mohcihk.
êkwa ê-nât-~ ê-sâsâkihtihk ê-nâtamihk nipiy, ê-pahkopêhk
ê-nitawi-kwâpahamihk êkwa ê-kisâkamisikêhk aya, ita
kâ-misi-pôh-pônamihki nîpisîhtakwa, kisâkamitêwâpoy aya
k-âpacihtâhk kisêpêkinikêhki. êkwa âskaw mîna mân ê-kî-osamiht
kîkway, êkâ kâ-kaskihtâhk aya ka-pahkwatinamihk aya,
wîpâtayiwinisa âskaw aya, ayiwâk nêtawêyihtamihki ka-kanâtahki,
ê-kî-mân-âya-pakâhtâhk mân âya, kisêpêkinikan ê-âpat-~ ê-âpatahk
ahpô aya, pih-~ 'pihkwâpoy' mâna kî-isiyîhkâtêw, *lye* êkospîhk piko
ê-kî-ihtakok. êwakw âpisis ê-kî-sîkinamihk, ka-pahkwatinamihk
kîkway aya, k-âkô-wiyîpâk, *stains* k-êtamihk, ka-pahkwatinamihk.
êkosi mân ê-kî-isi-pahkwatinahkik iskwêwak, ê-kî-pakâhtâcik
ayiwinisa aya, pahk-~ wâh-pahkwatinahkwâw[i] âsiskiy, kâ-~
k-âkô-wiyîpâki ôhi ayiwinisa. êkoni ôh âya, âtiht êtok ôk ôsk-âyak
ka-miywêyihtamwak ka-pêhtahkik, tânimayikohk
ê-kî-pê-kakâyawisîyit ôtê nâway aya kêhtê-aya — êwako mîna mân
âskaw ka-kî-wîhtahkik ayisiyinînâhk, iyikohk ê-kî-kakâyawâtisicik
kêhtê-ayak, iyikohk ê-kî-aya-~ ê-kî-nihtâ-waskawîstamâsocik aya,
tânisi k-ês-âya-miyo-pimâtisicik, êkwa mîna tânisi k-êsi-kanâcihocik,
êkwa mîna tânisi k-ês-âya-asamisocik, k-êsi-pimâcihocik. êkoni mân
âskaw ka-kî-wîhtahkik ayisiyiniwak, taht ôk âya,
kâ-pê-otisâpahtahkik aya. niya pêyak kâ-kî-pê-otisâpahtamân êkwa
ôk âyisiyiniwak aya kâ-wîc-îspîhcisîmakik, wîstawâw êkoni
ê-pê-wâpahtahkik, ê-kî-mosci-kisêpêkinikêyâhk mân âya,
wâh-kanâcihtâyâhki nitayiwinisinâna; êkwa mân âya, îhkatawâhk
kâ-nitawi-kisêpêkinikêyâhk, nîpisîhk mân ê-kî-akociwêpinamâhk
ayiwinisa, êkota mân âya ê-kî-pâstêki. wîpac mâna kî-pâstêwa
kâ-kîsopwêk, k-âkociwêpinamihk nîpisîhk ayiwinisa. mâka mâna
niya wiya, mîn êtokwê kotakak ayisiyiniwak, mistahi
nikî-miywêyihtênân mân âya, îhkatawâhk
ka-nitawi-kisêpêkinikêyâhk ê-pahkopêyâhk; kiyîsopwêki, iyikohk
ê-miywâsik aya, ka-sâpopatâhk miskâta tahkikamâpôhk aya,
ka-pahkopêhk aya, tâpiskôc ayiwâk ayisiyiniw aya ê-kakâyawâtisit,

edge, they would hold it on either side and take the dirty clothes to the slough, making a fire there, outside, on the ground. And you went barefoot to get water, you waded into the water and went to dip it up and heated it where you kept making a big fire with willows, in order to use hot water to do the wash. And sometimes you also brought them to a boil when you could not take the dirt out, when you sometimes wanted your dirty clothes cleaner, you used to boil them with soap or lye, it was called, lye was the only thing that existed in those days. You poured in a little of that in order to remove stubborn soiling, stains as they are called, in order to remove them. That is how the women got it out, by boiling the clothes, when they were getting the dirt out, when the clothes were badly soiled. Some of the young people, I guess, will like to hear about these things, how the old people used to be such hard workers back then — and they should also tell about that sometimes among the people, that the old people were such hard workers, that they were so good at fending for themselves, how to live well and how to keep clean and also how to feed themselves, how to make a living. People sometimes should tell about these things, as many as have lived to see them. I am one who has lived to see these things, and the people who are my age-mates, they, too, have seen them, we used to do the laundry by hand, when we were going to clean our clothes; and when we went to do the laundry at the slough, we would throw our clothes on the willow bushes and dry them there. They used to dry quickly on a warm day, when you threw the clothes on the willow bushes. But I, and perhaps other people as well, I very much liked going to do the laundry at the slough, walking into the water when it was warm, it was so good to immerse your legs, to walk into the cold water, it seemed a person was more active, and when you walked

êkwa êkâ êkwayikohk ê-kisisot kâ-pahkopêt. mwêhci mâna niya wiy
âya, "âskaw ê-nitawi-mêtawêyân," nikî-itêyihtên, îhkatawâhk
kâ-nitawi-kisêpêkinikêyân, "*picnic* ê-kî-ayâyân," nikî-itêyihtên mâna
[*ê-pâhpit*].

[FA:]   ê-kî-nîmâyêk?

âskaw mâna, kinwês k-âyâyâhk, nikî-nîmânân mâna,
nikî-tahkonênân kîkway ka-mîciyâhk.

≈≈≈

[FA:]   -~-monahâwasoyêk kayâs ôma —~

⚹⚹⚹

[79]   —~ pîhc-âyihk mân âya, êkamâ kahkiyaw kîkway ohc-âyâhk aya,
sôskwâc mâna kâsîhkwêwiyâkanihk aya, kî-pakâsimonahâwak
awâsisak.

⚹⚹⚹

ahpô aya, sôskwâc mân ê-kî-anâskêhk akohpisahk,[57] êkwa aya,
ê-kî-âpacihtâhk aya, kâsîhkwêwiyâkan êkwa aya, pâhkohkwêhon
anima, pâhkohkwêhonis aya, ê-ohci-mosci-kisêpêkinihcik.
'*sponge-bath*' mân êwako isiyîhkâtamwak, êkosi mâna
kî-isi-pakâsimonahâwasowak, osâm pikw êkosi kî-tôcikâtêw, osâm —
môya kahkiyaw kîkway ohc-âyâniwiw êkospîhk ita k-âkohcimihcik,
osîhcikâtêwa êkwa mân îta, awâsisak ê-akohcimihcik; sôskwâc mân
ê-kî-mosci-kisêpêkinâcik, kâsîhkwêwiyâkan mân ê-kî-âpacihtâcik.
[80]   êkwa aya, âstamispî ôma niy âya, kâ-nitawi-nihtâwikit an[a] âya,
tastawayask nitânis, *Kathleen*, mistahi kîkway nikî-kiskinohamâkwak
aya maskihkîwiskwêwak, tânisi k-êsi-kanâcihak aya, aw âya,

into the water you were not as hot. To me it sometimes seemed just as if I was going to play, when I went to do the laundry at the slough, I used to think, "I am having a picnic" [*laughs*].

[FA:]   Did you use to take food along?

Sometimes, when we were there for a long time, we used to take food along, we used to carry something to eat.

≈≈≈

[FA:]   —~ and bathing babies in the old days —~

≉≉≉

[79]   —~ indoors, of course, we did not have everything, the children simply used to be washed in a basin.

≉≉≉

Or you simply used to lay out some little blankets and use a basin and a towel, a face-cloth, and they were washed simply with those. They called this a sponge bath, that way they used to wash their children, it was mostly done that way, they did not have anything in those days for them to be put into the water, nowadays there are tubs made where you can put the children into the water; they simply used to wash them using a basin.

[80]   And later, when my middle daughter Kathleen was going to be born, the nurses taught me a lot, how to clean the newborn which had been given to me by divine grace.

oskawâsis awa kâ-~ kâ-kî-miyikowisiyân. êkos ânim ê-kî-isicik,
"anâskê mân âkohpisa aya! mîcisowinâhtikohk êkwa, otina
kâsîhkwêwiyâkan êkwa aya, kisêpêkinikan otina, anima mâna
kâ-kâsîhkwâkêhk!" êkwa kotak mîna mâna kîkway
ê-kî-kiskinohamawicik aya, 'boric' ê-kî-isiyîhkâtêk, 'boric acid'
ê-kî-isiyîhkâtêk, ohpimê nânitaw wiyâkanisihk aya, kisâkamicêwâpôs
aya ka-sîkinamân, êkwa anihi mâna kâ-yôskâki aya, 'absorbent cotton'
isiyîhkâtêwa ê-âkayâsîmohk, ê-yôskâki mân ê-âpacihtâhk, ☀
êkotowahk mân âya ê-akohtitâhk, êkwa anim âya, êkota ê-~
ê-pîwêwêpinamihk anim ê-pîwêyâwahkwâk aya boric acid, êkwa
ê-kisêpêkinamoht aya ocônisiwâwa, aya, itâmihk ê-kisêpêkinamoht
aya ocônisiwâwa, êkâ aya ka-môskipayicik, ê-kî-itwêt ana
maskihkîwiskwêw. êkwa, "wâh-nôhaci mîna mâna, êwak ôma
k-ôh-kisêpêkinacik aya, k-ôh-~ wâh-nônitwâwi k-ôh-~
k-ôh-kisêpêkinisoyan, êkâ ka-pîkokonêwêpayicik;" êkos âya mân
ê-kî-isicik aya maskihkîwiskwêwak. êkosi mân âstamispî niyanân
ê-kî-isi-paminâyâhkik oskawâsisak.

☀☀☀

—~ nitânisak mîn âya, ê-kî-aya-kâh-kihci-wîkihtocik êkwa
ê-ayâwâcik oskawâsisa, nikî-kiskinohamawâwak êkonik kahkiyaw
ôhi, êkosi kit-êsi-paminâcik otawâsimisiwâwa.

☀☀☀

—~ anima mîna mân âya, kâw êkwa nika-pê-kîwêtotên anima
kisêpêkinikêwin, kâ-kî-mosci-kisêpêkinikêcik. kâ-pipok ôm âya,
kâ-kisêpêkinikêyâhk pîhc-âyihk, môy nôh-kaskihtânân mâna
k-âkotâyâhk mihcêt kâ-kisêpêkinamâhk ôh âyiwinisa,
wayawîtimihk mân ê-kî-nitaw-âkotâyâhk ê-âhkwatiki. êkwa aya,
âskaw êkâ kâ-pâstêki, ay-âskawi mâna nikî-pîhtokwatânân,
pîhc-âyihk ê-pâsamâhk; ☀ êkosi mân ê-kî-tôtamâhk ôm âya.
mihcêt ayisk mân ôh âya, awâsisak k-âyâhcik, wayawîtimihk mâna

That is what they said to me, "Lay out some little blankets on the table and take a basin and take some soap, the one used to wash your face!" And they also taught me another thing, boric it was called, boric acid it was called, to pour a little warm water into a separate little bowl and, using that soft stuff that is called absorbent cotton in English, it is soft, ≉ you put that kind into the water and sprinkle that powdery boric acid on it, and then you wash their little mouths, you wash the inside of their little mouths so that they won't get a rash, that nurse said. And, "Each time you are going to nurse the baby, you use this to wash them, each time they are going to suckle, you wash yourself with it so that their mouths will not break out in blisters;" that is what the nurses said to me. And that is how we treated babies later on.

≉≉≉

—~ my daughters, too, when they got married and had babies, I used to teach them all of these things, how to look after their children.

≉≉≉

—~ and that, too, I will come back to the topic of doing the laundry, when they used to do the laundry by hand. In the winter, when we did the laundry indoors, we were unable to hang up many of the clothes we had washed, and we would go outside and hang them up to freeze. And then, sometimes when they were not dry, we would bring in a few at a time, drying them indoors; ≉ that is what we used to do. For there was lots of laundry when you had children, we

nikî-akotânân sôskwâc. mâk ôk âtiht kâ-nakacihtâcik iskwêwak,
pêyak nikî-âcimostâk, miton ês ê-kî-kwayask-tôtahk, êwakw ân[a]
ê-manâ-kawatimisot aya (âsiyânak mân ê-kî-mosci-kisêpêkinihcik,
êkwa âtiht mân ê-kî-nitaw-âkociwêpinâhcik wayawîtimihk aya
k-âhkwaciyit, mâk êkonik êtokwê mân âya kî-kawaciwak); aw
îskwêw, mistiyâkanihk êsa mân âya ê-kî-ahât kâ-kîsi-kisêpêkinât,
sôskwâc aya ê-isi-wayawît, ê-kî-wayawîpakitinât êkota
ê-âhkwaciyit; êkwa mâna mwêstas ê-pîht-~ ê-pîhtokwahât,
ay-âskaw ê-pâswât, êkw êsa mitoni kî-nakacihtâw êkâ
ka-kawatimisot kâ-kî-tôtahk. êwakw ânima ê-kî-miywêyihtamân
awa ê-pêhtaw-~ ê-pêhtawak, osâm mân âya kâ-kisêpêkinikêhk aya,
ê-apwêsihk anima kâ-mosci-kisêpêkinikêhk, êkwa nikî-pêhonân
mân âtiht aya, êkâ ê-wayawîyâhk iskw âya kâ-pâhkopayiyâhk ôma
k-âpwêsiyâhk, mwêstas ≠ ê-itohtatâyâhk wayawîtimihk [ê-pâhpit].

[FA:]   kî-nayêhtâwan êtikwê mîna wayawîwin, ≠ awâsisak wâwîs
kâ-pipohk.

[81]   êwako mîn âya, pîhc-âyihk mân âya, askihkwak
ê-kî-kanawêyimihcik aya, wiy ê-kî-kakâyawâtisicik iskwêwak,
kî-ihtakonwa mâna wayawîtimihk ôh âya wâskahikanisa ita aya,
ayisiyiniwak mân âya ê-nitawi-wayawîstamâsocik, nik-êtwân. êkwa
ôki pîhc-âyihk kâ-kî-kanawêyimâyâhkik askihkwak, nipiy mâna
nikî-sîkinênân aya, pîhc-âyihk k-âpacihâyâhkik, êkwa
k-ât[i]-âkwâtaskinêcik, êkotowihk mâna aya, 'mîsîwikamikwa'
kî-isiyîhkâtêwa [ê-pâhpit], êkotê mân ê-kî-nitawi-sîkiwêpinamâhk
ôma. êkos ânima mân ê-kî-~ ê-kî-isi-paminisohk kayâs, askihkwak
mân âya, mîna kî-ihtakowak piyisk ê-atâwâkêhk aya,
ê-akwanâpowêhikâsocik, êkonik mâna pîhc-âyihk
ê-kî-kanawêyimâyâhkik.

≠≠≠

would simply hang the clothes outside. But some of the women who know these things, one of them told me that she really did it right, she avoided getting herself cold (diapers used to be washed by hand, and then some would go outside and throw them high up to freeze, but those [women] probably got cold); this woman would put them in a large bowl when she was finished washing them, and then she simply put them down outside, just by the door, and let them freeze; bringing them inside later and drying a few at a time, that one certainly knew how not to get herself cold when she did this. I really liked what I heard that woman say because when you do the laundry by hand, you sweat, when you do the laundry by hand, and some of us would wait so as not to go outside until we were dry from the sweat, ⚹ taking the laundry outside later [*laughs*].

    [FA:]   It must also have been difficult with relieving oneself, ⚹ especially for children in winter.

[81]   That, too, pails were kept indoors, for the women used to be very energetic [in doing all these chores], there used to be little houses outdoors where people would go to relieve themselves, I will say. And these pails which we kept indoors, we used to pour water in there when we made use of them indoors, and then, when they would be over half-full, we would go and pour them out over there, in the outhouses, they used to be called [*laughs*]. That is how people used to look after themselves long ago, and finally there also used to be pails sold with covers, these used to be kept indoors.

⚹⚹⚹

—~ niwîkimâkan aya, nistam an[a] âya, awâsis kâ-kî-ayâwâyâhk,
iskwêsis, ispî ê-wî-kiskinohamawâyâhk aya k-êsi-nahapit,
ê-kî-osîhtât apiwinis aya, niwîkimâkan aya, napakihtakwa
ê-kî-âpacihtât, êkwa anita ita k-âpiwiht ê-kî-payipisahk, êkwa êkotê
askihkos sîpâ ê-kî-ahâyâhk. êkosi ê-kî-is-âya-mâci-kiskinohamawâyâhk
Theresa k-êsi-nahapit. wîpac kî-kiskêyihtam aya êwakw ânima,
mwêstas aniki kotakak kâ-kiskinohamawâyâhkik ≠ mîn êkoni.

[82]   nanâtohk mâna kî-isi-wîcihisowak sôskwâc ayisiyiniwak, tânis âya
k-êsi-kanâci-paminisocik, êkâ konita kîkway ôm âya ka-wêpinahkik
mîn âya, ê-kî-kanâcihtâcik mâna wâskahikana; nawac tâpiskôc
kayâs kêhtê-ayak mistahi ê-kî-kanâcihocik, ê-itêyihtamân.
ê-kî-ocihkwanapicik —

[FA:]   ê-kî-kanâtapicik

— êha, ê-kî-ocihkwanapicik mân ânim âya, 'sinikohtakinikan' mâna
kî-isiyîhkâtêw mîn êwakw âya, 'sinikohtakahikan' kî-isiyîhkâtêw aya,
'*brush*' k-êsiyîhkâtamâhk êwako. wâwâc ê-kî-wâpamakik âtiht, pihko
ê-siswêwêpinahkik êkwa êwako ê-ohci-wâpiskahahkik aya, anih âya
napakihtakwa kâ-kî-kisêpêkinahkik. ≠ mitoni mân ê-kî-wâpiskâyiki
napakihtakwa. êkwa mîna mân ê-kî-manâ-pahkikawinahkik pimiy
aya, aya, kâ-mîcisocik ôm âya, ê-~ ê-kî-mâna-kîhkânâkwahk kîkway
kâ-tômâk; napakihtakwa ôhi kâ-~ ê-wâpiskihtakâki; mitoni mân
ê-kî-kîhkânâkwahki kâ-tômâki —~

≠≠≠

—~ nikâwiy ê-kâh-kisiwâhak kâ-sâ-sîkipicikêyân, kâ-kanâci-~

≈≈≈

[83]   —~ ê-sêsâwipayit [*ê-pâhpit*].

—~ my husband, when we had our first child, a little girl, at the time when we were going to train her to use the toilet, my husband made a little seat, he used lumber and cut it out there where you sit, and then we put a potty underneath. And that is how we began to train Theresa to use the toilet. Soon she was trained in that, and later we trained ⚹ the others in that also.

[82]   People simply used to help themselves in all kinds of ways, how to keep themselves clean, how not to throw garbage around, and they used to clean their houses; the old people of long ago used to keep much cleaner, it seems to me. They used to be on their knees —

[FA:]   they used to live in clean houses

— yes, they were on their knees with a scrubber, it used to be called, scrub-brush it used to be called, what we call a brush. Some I even saw sprinkle ashes about and use that to wash the floor white when they washed the floor-boards. ⚹ The floor-boards used to be really white. And then they also used to be careful not to drop any grease when they were eating, anything greasy used to show on these white floor-boards; grease-spots really used to show, —~

⚹⚹⚹

—~ my mother would be angry with me when I spilt things —~

≈≈≈

[83]   —~ becoming stretched [*laughs*].

[FA:] ê-kî-ma-mostohtêhk ôma; aya mîna, nikiskisin, êkây —~
êkây wîhkâc kîkway mîciwin ê-ohci-wêpinamohk, ahpô mân
ôh ôtitâmiyawa iyikohk kwayask —~

êha, êkoni mîn âya, wînâstakay êkwa omâw, êkwa anihi mîna
mitakisiya mostosw-âya, ê-kî-kanâcihtâhk, mîn êkoni mân âya,
iskwêwak ê-kî-pâsahkik mân êkâ ka-misiwanâtaniyiki, mwêstas
êkoni ê-~ ê-mîcicik, anih ôti kêhcinâ aya, otakisiya anihi, mêtoni
mân ê-kî-kanâcihtâcik êkwa mân ê-kî-kaskâpasahkik. êkosi mân
ê-kî-isîhtât nikâwiy, êwak ôhci k-ôh-kiskêyihtamân aya, tânis
ê-itôtamihk. mitoni mâna kwayask ê-kî-kisêpêkinahk êkwa
ê-kî-wiyinowiki,[58] êkwa ê-kî-âpotahahk, itâmihk mân ânim âya,
wiyin ê-kî-ihtatahk,[59] êkwa waskic miton ê-kanâcihtât êkwa
ê-kî-pâsahk mân îta anim âya, kâ-kî-aya-osikwânâsahk kîkway, êkos
âyisk mâna kî-itwêwak, 'ê-osikwânâsamihk' kî-itamwak kîkway
kâ-kaskâpasahkik; êwakw ânima ê-osikwânâsahk.

[84]   pêyakwan, pahkêkin mîn âya, kâ-kaskâpasahkik, ⚹
ê-osikwânâsahkik mîna êwako; ⚹ ê-osikwânâstêk ⚹ —
ê-kî-wîhtamihk mâna kîkway, pahkêkin âtiht ayisk mîna môy âya
osikwânâsamwak, êwako mâna kâ-wâpiskâk pahkêkin.

[FA:]   âha, miywâsin.

⚹⚹⚹

êkos ânima mân âya, ê-kî-is-âya-~, wâwâc môy ê-ohci-wêpinahkik
oskana. ê-kî-mân-âya-~, anihi kâ-cîhcîkosahkik mâna miskana aya,
kâ-pânisâwêcik; ê-kî-nîswahpitahkik mân ôhi oskana, mîn êkoni
ê-akotâcik aya, ê-kaskâpasahkik. êkwa mân âya, mîcimâpoy mâna
ê-kî-~[60]

≈ / ≈

[FA:]   You just used to walk; and I also remember that
        no food was ever thrown away, even the innards
        were so properly —~

Yes; you also used to clean those, the tripe and the bible
[*i.e.*, paunch and manyplies], and the guts, in cattle, and
the women also dried these so that they would not spoil, as
they ate them later, they certainly used to clean those guts
out thoroughly and smoke them. My mother used to
prepare them like that, that is how I know what you do
with them. She used to clean them very thoroughly, they
were fat and she turned them inside out, the fat was on the
inside, and she really cleaned the surface, and then she
dried them where she used to smoke-dry things, for that is
what they used to say, you smoke-dry it, they used to call it
when they smoked things; she smoke-dried them.

[84]   The same with leather, when they smoked it, ⚹ they
also smoke-dried that; ⚹ it was smoke-dried ⚹ — they
used to name things, for there is also some leather which
they did not smoke-dry, that is the leather which is white.

[FA:]   Yes, it is beautiful.

⚹⚹⚹

It used to be like that, they did not even throw away the
bones. When they had cut all the meat off the bones,
when they had cut the meat into sheets, they used to tie
the bones together in pairs and hang them up and smoke
them. And then they used to make soup —~

≈ / ≈

[FA:] wîni.

[EM:] wîni.

[FA:] êkosi; âha.

[85] —~ miskanihk[61] mân ânim âya, 'wîni' mân êwako kî-isiyîhkâtêw, aya, 'oskani-pimiy' mîna mâna kî-isiyîhkâtêw, pakahkam. êwakw ânim âya, kâ-kas-~ kâ-kaskâpasahkik anih âya oskana, ê-kî-pakâhtâcik mân âya, mîcimâpoy ê-osîhtâcik; êkwa anih ôskana mân âya ê-kî-pâst-~ ê-kî-~ ê-kî-pâstatahahkik mâna, anima wîni ê-otinahkik, êwakw ânim ê-kî-~, mistah ê-kî-wîhkasik êwako. êwakw ânima niya ê-kî-wîhkistamân wîni, môy wîhkâc ê-ohc-âya-paswêskôyoyân êkotowahk kâ-mîciyân, mâka wiyin wiya mâna nikî-paswêskôyon, môy nôh-kaskihtân wiyin ka-mîciyân. mâk ânihi otakisiya, nikâwiy mîna kâ-kî-osîhtât, mistahi mîn êkoni ê-kî-wîhkasiki, môy wîhkâc â-~ ohci-paswêyâwa, ê-kî-pakâhtât mân âya, ≉ êkwa miton âya, ê-kî-kaskâciwasahk. maskawâwa ayis anih âya otakisiya; tâpiskôc mîn ânihi, piko mitoni ka-kaskâciwasamihk aya, wînâstakay êkwa omâw, mitoni piko mîn êkoni ka-kaskâciwahtêki.

[86] êkwa kotaka anihi kikî-mâmiskôtên mîna wiyâs aya, waskatay anima, êwako mîn ê-~, mitoni mîn êwako ê-maskawâk, piko mîn êwako mitoni ka-kaskâciwahtêk. iyikohk mân âtiht ê-nîh-~ ê-nihtâwitêpocik, nikâwiy ê-kî-âcimostawit aya, pêyak nisîmis ê-wî-wîkihtot nâpêw, "mistahi pêyak ê-nihtâ-piminawasot iskwêw ê-kî-nitomiht," ê-itwêt, "êwak ôma waskatay ê-tâsawisâwâtahk, êkwa ê-titipinahk," ê-itwêt. "êkwa ê-tahkopitahk pîminahkwânisa ohc," îtwêw, "êkwa êkoni êkwa ê-pakâhtât ê-kaskâciwasahk," ê-itwêt.

≉≉≉

" —~ [êkosi] k-êsîhtât,[62] mistah ês ê-wîhkasiki anim âya, ê-titipinahk êkwa ê-tahkopitahk; mistah ê-wîhkasiki ê-isîhtât," ê-itwêt, "ê-mâh-manisahk mwêstas ê-kîsitêyiki," ê-itwêt.

[FA:]	Bone-marrow.
[EM:]	Bone-marrow.
[FA:]	In that way; yes.

[85]   —~ this was in the bone, bone-marrow it used to be
called, it also used to be called bone-grease, I believe.
After they had smoked the bones, they used to boil that
and make soup; and they used to break the bones with a
tool and take the bone-marrow out, it tasted very good. I
really used to like that bone-marrow, I never got sick from
eating too richly when I ate that kind, but with fat, on the
other hand, I would get sick, I could not eat fat. But the
guts, my mother also used to prepare them, they also
tasted very good, they were not too rich, she used to boil
them ⋇ and cook them until they were really tender. For
the guts are tough; just like these others, the tripe and the
bible, you have to cook them until they are tender, they
also have to be cooked until they are really tender.

[86]   And that other meat you have mentioned, the belly
[*i.e.*, the abdominal wall, layered with fat], that also is
tough, that also has to be cooked until it is tender. Some
are such good cooks, my mother used to tell me about the
time when one of my younger brothers was going to get
married, "A certain woman who was a very good cook was
asked to come," she said, "she cut into the middle of the
belly and then rolled it up," she said, "and then she tied it
up with string," she said, "and then she boiled it until
tender," she said.

⋇⋇⋇

"—~ the way she made it, it tasted very good, she rolled
and tied it; it tasted very good the way she prepared it,"
she said, "and later, when it was cooked done, she sliced
it," she said.

❀❀❀

—~ *bologna* êtokwê ê-kî-osîhtât [*ê-pâhpihk*]!

[FA:] âha. nêki mîna nôhkom êkwa nimosôm mâna
    kâ-minahoyâhk ê-kî-pê-kiskinahamawicik aya, ❀ *blood*
    sausage ka-osîhtâyân.

êha, êkotowahk mâka mîn ê-kî-osîhtamâsocik, ê-kî-aswahahkik
mâna mihko, êkwa mân âya kîkway ê-kî-kikinahkik aya, wiy-~ wiyin
êtokwê mâna kî-kikinamwak, êkwa nikâwiy wiya ê-wâpamak
êkotow[a] ê-osîhtât, ê-sikosahk mîna wîhcêkaskosiya, êkota ê-astât,
ê-sîpahahk anim âya, aya, aya sôskwâc aya — kani sôskwâc pit[a]
ê-âh-asiwatât aya, môy mâk êtokw ê-sâkaskinahtât, êkot[a] êkwa
ê-sîkinahk anim âya, mihko anima. mîna kotak êkwa ê-takwastât,
êkos îs ânima ê-kî-pakâhtât ê-kî-kâh-kipwahpitahk. êkoni anih
ôtakisiya mîn ê-âpacihtâcik aya, ❀ *blood sausage* anim âya,
otakisîhkân êtokwê.

[FA:] âha, kakwâyaki-wîhkasin êtikwê.

êha, mihtko[63] ohci, otakisîhkân, mistahi kî-wîhkasin.
kî-takahkisîhtâwak mâna kahkiyaw kîkway; mâk âyis, ma kîkway
ohci-kiht-~-kihtimêyihtamwak wiy êkospî ayisiyiniwak. mitoni
kahkiyaw kîkway —~

❀❀❀

—~ êkoni ôhi kahkiyaw kîkway, ma kîkway ê-ohci-wêpinahkik.

[FA:] namwâc.

môy ka-tâpwêhtamihk mîna mân âtiht aya, anima mân âya,
'otamiskay' kâ-kî-isiyîhkâtêk aya, pahkêkinohk ê-kî-kikamok. êwako

—~ she must have made bologna [*laughter*]!

   [FA:]   Yes, my grandfather and my grandmother, they
           used to come and teach me when we butchered,
           ෫ how to make blood-sausage.

Yes; they also used to make that kind for themselves, they
used to collect the blood and mix something with it, I
guess they put fat into it, and I saw my mother prepare
that kind, she also chopped onions and put them in,
simply stretching the — I forget, she first put it inside but,
I guess, she did not fill them all the way up, and then she
poured the blood into them. And she also added other
things [pepper and salt], and she used to boil them like
that, having tied each one shut. They also used the guts ෫
for this blood-sausage, this sausage, I guess.

   [FA:]   Yes; it tasted exceedingly good, I guess.

Yes; sausage made from blood, it tasted very good! They
used to prepare everything extremely well; for people were
not too lazy to do anything in those days. Absolutely
everything —~

෫෫෫

—~ [they made use of] everything, they did not throw
anything away.

   [FA:]   Nothing at all.

You wouldn't believe, some also used to use the meat that
is stuck to the hide, what used to be called hide-scrapings.

mân ânim âya ê-kî-aya-pahkwatahahkik; êwakw ânima mân êkwa
êtokwê kâ-kî-itwêcik aya, 'ê-kî-mihkitahkik' mân âya, ê-kâ-~
ê-pahkwaciwêpahahkik anim ôtamiskay. êwakw ânima mîna mân
ê-kî-mîcicik, otamiskay. ≠ ê-kî-mân-âya-sêkwâpiskinahkik,
ê-kâspisahkik. êwakw ânima mîna ê-kî-mîcicik, anima otamiskay.

[87]   mitoni nama kîkway ê-ohci-wêpinahkik. wiyakâc êkwa mâna
mênahotwâwi, wâwâc pahkêkinwa ê-wêpinahkik; osâm êkâ aya
ê-kiskêyihtahkik k-ês-ôsîhtâcik. mistah ôm êkwa aya
ê-misiwanâcihtâyahk kîstanaw kîkway kâ-nêhiyâwiyahk, —~

≠≠≠

—~ êkwa ê-itwêyahk, "môy nikaskihtân," ê-itwêyahk, mâka mâna
ka-kî-mêkicik anihi kâ-kaskihtâyit kîkway, ka-kî-miyâcik pahkêkinwa
mâna. kâ-pipok ka-kî-âhkwatihtâcik êkwa k-âsawinamawâcik[64]
ayisiyiniwa aya, ≠ anihi tahto kâ-nihtâ-pahkêkinohkêyit, ≠
ka-kî-aya-miyâcik ≠ mâna, âta wiy âtiht êkos êkwa tôtamwak.
nikî-wîhtamâkwak âtiht ôki nêhiyawak, awasi-nîpinohk
ê-kî-atâmakik pêyak pahkêkinos,

≠≠≠

~-[apisimôsos]wayâna,[65] êkwa nitânis wiy âya, môso-~
môso-pahkêkin kî-atâmêw. pêyak ês ôtê aya (tânis ôma
k-êsiyîhkâtêk êwako *Rocky Mountain House*), êkotê mâna pêyak ês
îskwêw ê-osîhtât pahkêkinwa, êkoni ê-nitawi-miyâcik. ≠ âpihtaw
êsa mân ê-miyâcik, êkwa âpihtaw ê-miyikocik kâ-kîsîhtâyit; êkos
ê-isi-tipahamawâcik.

[EM:]   êkosi mâk êkwa aya ka-kîsîhtânânaw, osâm aya, nêtê piko
        mîna k-âcimostâkawiyan kotak ≠ nikiskêyihtên ôm âya,
        ê-nîsôhkamâtoyâhk ôma k-âtotamâhk.
[FA]   â, *thank you*, kinanâskomitin mistahi.

They used to knock that off; I guess that is what they meant by the term 'scraping meat off the hide', when they knocked off the hide-scrapings. And they also used to eat that, the hide-scrapings. ⚹ They used to roast them in the oven, cooking them crisp. And they also used to eat them, those hide-scrapings.

[87]   They really did not throw anything away. It is too bad today when they butcher and even throw the hide away; because they do not know how to prepare it. We, too, we Crees really are throwing a great deal away now.

⚹⚹⚹

—~ and we say, "I cannot do it," we say, but they should give it away to someone who does know how to do it, they should give the hides to that one. In the winter they should freeze them and then pass them on to people, ⚹ they should give them to those ⚹ who are good at tanning hides, although some do that now. The winter before last some Crees told me that, I bought one little hide from them,

⚹⚹⚹

—~ a deer-hide, and my daughter bought a moose-hide. One woman over there (what is it called, Rocky Mountain House), she prepares hides, and they go and give them to her. ⚹ They give her half, when she is finished she gives them back half [of the hides]; that is how they pay her.

[EM:]   And with that we will finish now; because you must also be told stories over there ⚹ I know that there are two of us at work telling stories.

[FA:]   Well, thank you, I thank you very much.

Notes to the Text

1   nowâhc [*?sic*]
2   niwî-kakwê-kiskisomâwak [*sic:* -o-; *cf.* kiskisôm– EM *passim*]
3   ka-wîcêwimak [*sic:* -êwi-]
4   kaskihtâyân [*sic: simple conjunct*]
5   ê-kî-pê-is-ôhp-~ [*sc.* ê-kî-pê-is-ôhpikiyân]
6   kikiskêyihtê-~ [*sc.* kikiskêyihtênânaw]
7   kwîtawêyihcikâtêwa [*sic:* -î-]
8   êkwa ânohc [*sic:* â-]
9   ê-kî-mâcatoskêt [*sic:* -ca-; *cf.* kâ-kî-mâc-âtoskêt EM27, EM61; *cf.* mâtatoskê–]
10   nikah-miywêyihtên [*sic:* nikah]
11   tahto-aya [*sic:* -o, a-; *cf.* tahtw-âskiy EM3]
12   niwî-nêhiyawâh [*sc.* niwî-âkayâsîmoh]
13   ka-nêhiyawêyân [*sc.* ka-âkayâsîmoyân]
14   kêyâpic [*sic; cf.* êyâpic EM *passim*]
15   nowâhc [*?sic*]
16   ka-wîcêwimak [*sic:* -êwi-]
17   ê-kî-êtokwê-nisis-kakwê-miskamawât [*sic*]
18   ka-wîcêwimak [*sic:* -êwi-]
19   kiwî-kakwê-âh-onâpêminâwâw [*sic:* âh]
20   êhâ [*sic:* -â]
21   cêsos [*sic; cf.* cîsas EM *infra*]
22   kihcihtwâwi-mariy [*sic:* -a-]
23   cîsas [*sic; cf.* cêsos EM *supra, infra*]
24   cêsos [*sic; cf.* cîsas EM *supra*]
25   kâ-âh-otinahk [*sic:* âh]

26 ê-mosci-nâcitâpêyân [*sic:* nâci-]

27 kâ-nâtitâpêyân [*sic:* nâti-]

28 ê-kî-ôsahkik [*sic:* -ô-]

29 ayiwâkipayicik [*sic: simple conjunct*]

30 k-ôhpikihki [*sic:* -hki; *cf.* -ki EM63]

31 kayâcic [?*sic*]

32 ê-ihtakohki [*sic:* -hki; *cf.* -ki EM *passim*]

33 ohpikihki [*sic:* -hki; *cf.* -k EM63; *simple conjunct*]

34 kîkw-âyak [*sic*]

35 ê-kî-is-ôh-âya-onâpêmit [*sic*]

36 kêyâpic [*sic; cf.* êyâpic EM *passim*]

37 wâpikwaniya [*sic:* -wa-]

38 nêhiyaw-masinîwina [*sic; cf.* nêhiyawi- EM *passim*]

39 kî-owîkiwak [*sic; cf.* wîki- EM *passim*]

40 wâhyawîs [*sic; cf.* wâhyawês EM77]

41 kêyâpic [*sic; cf.* êyâpic EM *passim*]

42 ây-âhci [*sic:* â- ; *cf.* ay, âh]

43 ê-kwîtâpacihtâcik [*sic:* -î-]

44 ê-kî-mâcatoskêt [*sic:* -ca-; *cf.* kâ-kî-mâc-âtoskêt EM27, EM61; *cf.* mâtatoskê–]

45 kîspin-~ [*sc.* kîspinatâci]

46 otêhiminâni-cêpihka [*sic:* c-; *cf.* ocêpihka EM71]

47 —~ [*sc.* nama] kîkway êsa mân ê-ohci-mîcicik

48 kaskihtâcik [*sic: simple conjunct*]

49 ê-kî-wâpisk-~ [*sc.* ê-kî-wâpiskahikêcik]

50 nikah-sâkôhtân [*sic:* nikah]

51 ê-kî-mosci-nâtitâpêt [*sic:* nâti-]

52 —~ [*sc.* môy] nôh-~ nôh-nakacihtân

53 ê-kâh-kiskisomitocik [*sic:* -o-; *cf.* kiskisômito– EM30]

54 ê-itapihkêt [?*sic*]

55 kanihk [*sic; cf.* kani]

56 tâni [?*sic*]

57 akohpisahk [*sic; sc.* akohpisa(h)]

58 ê-kî-wiyinowiki [*sic:* -owiki; *cf.* -oyiki]

59 ê-kî-ihtatahk [*sic; both stem and gloss tentative*]

60 ê-kî-~ [*sc.* ê-kî-osîhtâcik]

61 miskanihk [?*sic*]

62 —~ [*sc.* êkosi] k-êsîhtât

63 mihtko [?*sic; cf.* mihko EM86]

64 k-âsawinamawâcik [*sic:* -awi-]

65 ~-[*sc.* apisimôsos]wayâna

Cree–English Glossary

STEM-CLASS CODES

NA	animate noun
NI	inanimate noun
NDA	animate noun, dependent
NDI	inanimate noun, dependent
VAI	verb of type AI (animate actor, usually intransitive)
VII	verb of type II (inanimate actor, intransitive)
VTA	verb of type TA (animate goal, transitive)
VTI	verb of type TI (inanimate goal, usually transitive)
PR	pronoun
IPC	indeclinable particle
IPV	indeclinable preverb particle
INM	indeclinable nominal

All noun and verb entries in this glossary end in a hyphen, indicating that the form given in the glossary is a stem.

Only some stems are identical to words; most Cree words consist of stems combined with inflectional endings. In the case of noun stems in post-consonantal -w-, the stem-final -w- does not appear in the singular form of the word.

Dependent noun stems (listed as a set at the start of the glossary) have a hyphen both at the end and at the beginning: such stems also require a personal prefix.

FOR TRANSITIVE VERB stems belonging to the VTA and VTI types, the primary goal (or object) for which the verb is inflected is indicated by the notations *s.o.* and *s.t.*, to be read 'someone' and 'something', respectively:

kitâpam– *VTA* look at s.o.
kitâpaht– *VTI* look at s.t.

The secondary goal (or object), which is not specified by inflection, is conventionally indicated by the notation *(it/him)*:

pamihtamaw– *VTA* tend to (it/him) for s.o., look after (it/him) for s.o.
(*cf.* **pamih–** *VTA* tend to s.o., look after s.o.)

For transitive verb stems belonging to the VAI type, the corresponding notation is *(it)*:

âpacihtâ– *VAI* use (it), make use of (it)

(For a fuller survey of verb types and their syntactic relations *cf.* Wolfart 1996: 402–4.)

Lexical entries used exclusively in Freda Ahenakew's comments are marked by an asterisk.

–**ahkwan**– *NDI* heel [*e.g.*, mahkwan]
–**askatay**– *NDI* abdominal wall, belly (of animal) [*e.g.*, waskatay]
–**awâsimis**– *NDA* child [*e.g.*, kitawâsimisinawak]
–**ayisiyinîm**– *NDA* people, followers [*usually plural;*
      e.g., kitayisiyinîmak]
–**câhkos**– *NDA* female cross-cousin; sister-in-law (woman speaking)
      [*e.g.*, nicâhkos]
–**cânis**– *NDA* daughter [*diminutive; e.g.*, nicânis]
–**cihciy**– *NDI* hand [*e.g.*, ocihciy]
–**ciwâm**– *NDA* male parallel cousin (man speaking); [*Christian:*] brethren
      [*e.g.*, kiciwâminawak]
–**cônis**– *NDI* mouth [*diminutive; e.g.*, ocônisiwâwa]
–**hkwâkan**– *NDI* face [*e.g.*, ohkwâkan]
–**iyinîm**– *NDA* people, followers [*usually plural; e.g.*, otiyinîma]
–**îcayisiyiniw**– *NDA* fellow person, fellow human
      [*sic:* -a-; *e.g.*, kîcayisiyinînaw]
–**îci-kiskinohamawâkan**– *NDA* fellow student, school-mate
      [*e.g.*, nîci-kiskinohamawâkanak]
–**îk**– *NDI* house, dwelling, home [*e.g.*, nîkihk]
–**îscâs**– *NDA* male cross-cousin; brother-in-law (man speaking) [*diminutive;*
      e.g., wîscâsa]
–**îstâw**– *NDA* male cross-cousin; brother-in-law (man speaking) [*e.g.*, wîstâwa]
–**îtisân**– *NDA* sibling [*e.g.*, nîtisânak]
–**îw**– *NDA* wife [*e.g.*, wîwiwâwa]
–**kâwiy**– *NDA* mother, mother's sister [*e.g.*, kikâwînawak]
–**kâwîs**– *NDA* mother's sister; step-mother [*e.g.*, nikâwîs]
–**kosis**– *NDA* son [*e.g.*, okosisa]
–**manâcimâkan**– *NDA* father-in-law (woman speaking)
      [*e.g.*, nimanâcimâkan]
–**mis**– *NDA* older sister [*e.g.*, omisa]
–**mosôm**– *NDA* grandfather, grandfather's brother [*e.g.*, kimosôm]
–**nâpêm**– *NDA* husband [*e.g.*, onâpêmiwâwa]
–**nîkihikw**– *NDA* parent [*e.g.*, ninîkihikonânak]
–**ôhcâwîs**– *NDA* father's brother; step-father [*e.g.*, ôhcâwîsa]
–**ôhkom**– *NDA* grandmother, grandmother's sister, "great-aunt"
      [*e.g.*, nôhkom]
–**ôhtâwiy**– *NDA* father, father's brother; [*Christian:*] Heavenly Father
      [*e.g.*, kôhtâwînaw]
–**ôhtâwîhkâwin**– *NDA* godfather; "step-father" [*e.g.*, ôhtâwîhkâwina]
–**ôsisim**– *NDA* grandchild [*e.g.*, kôsisiminawak]
–**sikos**– *NDA* father's sister, mother's brother's wife; mother-in-law,
      father-in-law's brother's wife, "aunt" [*e.g.*, nisikosak]

–sis– NDA mother's brother, father's sister's husband; father-in-law, father-in-law's brother [*e.g.*, nisisak]

–sit– NDI foot [*e.g.*, misita]

–sîmis– NDA younger sibling [*e.g.*, nisîmis]

–skan– NDI bone [*e.g.*, miskana]

–skât– NDI leg [*e.g.*, miskâta]

–stês– NDA older brother [*e.g.*, nistês]

–takisiy– NDI intestines, guts, entrails [*e.g.*, mitakisiya]

–tawêmâw– NDA male parallel cousin; female cross-cousin's husband (woman speaking) [*e.g.*, nitawêmâw]

–tânis– NDA daughter [*e.g.*, nitânisak]

–tâs– NDA leggings, trousers, pants [*e.g.*, mitâsa]

–têh– NDI heart [*e.g.*, kitêhinawa]

–wâhkômâkan– NDA relative [*e.g.*, niwâhkômâkanak]

–wîcêwâkan– NDA companion, partner [*e.g.*, kiwîcêwâkaniwâwak]

–wîkimâkan– NDA spouse, housemate [*e.g.*, niwîkimâkan]

ah– VTA place s.o.

ahpô IPC even, or

akâmaskîhk IPC across the water, overseas

akâwât– VTI wish for s.t., desire s.t.

akihtê– VII be counted

akim– VTA count s.o.

akociwêpin– VTA throw s.o. over top (*e.g.*, onto willow bushes)

akociwêpin– VTI throw s.t. over top (*e.g.*, onto willow bushes)

akohcim– VTA immerse s.o. in water (*e.g.*, baby)

akohp– NI blanket

akohpis– NI small blanket [*diminutive*]

akohtitâ– VAI put (it) in water, add (it) to water (*e.g.*, boric acid)

akotâ– VAI hang (it) up

akwanaho– VAI cover oneself, be covered (*e.g.*, by a blanket)

akwanâhkwêyâmo– VAI cover one's face in flight, flee with one's face covered; hide by rapidly covering one's face

akwanâpowêhikâso– VAI be covered as vessel capable of containing liquid, have a lid (*e.g.*, pot)

amiskw– NA beaver

ana PR that [*demonstrative*; *e.g.*, ana, aniki, anihi; anima, anihi]

anâskê– VAI spread a blanket

ani IPC [*emphatic enclitic*]

anima IPC it is that; the fact that [*predicative*]

anita IPC at that place, there

anohc IPC now, today

apahkwât– VTI make a roof over s.t.

apahkwâtê– VII have a roof, be roofed

api– *VAI* sit, be situated; stay
apihkât– *VTA* braid s.o.; knit s.o. (*e.g.,* stocking)
apihkât– *VTI* braid s.t.; knit s.t.
apihkê– *VAI* knit, do knitting
apihkêpicikan– *NI* knitting machine
apisâsin– *VII* be small
apiscis– *VTI* cut s.t. into small pieces
apiscisasi– *VAI* cut (it) into very small pieces [*diminutive; cf.* apiscis–]
apisimôsos– *NA* deer
apisimôsoswayân– *NA* deer-hide
apisis *IPC* a little
apisîsisi– *VAI* be small
apiwinis– *NI* seat, chair
apîwikamikw– *NI* sitting room, living room
apwêsi– *VAI* sweat, perspire
apwêsiwin– *NI* sweating, labouring
asahkêwikamikw– *NI* ration house
asam– *VTA* feed s.o., give s.o. to eat
asamastimwân– *NA* green-feed, oats [*sic:* NA *with reference to oats*]
asamiso– *VAI* feed oneself
asawâpam– *VTA* watch out for s.o., lie in watch for s.o.
ascascwâs– *NI* curds, cottage cheese
ascikêwikamikw– *NI* storage room, storage building
asên– *VTA* reject s.o.
asên– *VTI* reject s.t., turn s.t. back; shirk s.t., run away from s.t.
asikan– *NA* sock, stocking
asiniy– *NA* rock, stone [*e.g.,* asiniy kâ-kîsisot 'quick-lime']
asiskiy– *NI* earth, soil, dirt; clay
asiskîwihkwê– *VAI* have soil on one's face, have dirt on one's face
asiskîwikamikos– *NI* mud shack [*diminutive*]
asiwaso– *VAI* be inside
asiwatan– *VII* be inside
asiwatâ– *VAI* put (it) inside
askihkos– *NA* little pail, little pot [*diminutive*]
askihkw– *NA* pail, pot
askihtakosi– *VAI* be green
askihtakwâ– *VII* be green
askipwâw– *NI* potato
askiti– *VAI* be raw, be uncooked (*e.g.,* flour)
askiy– *NI* earth, land, country; [*pl.:*] fields under cultivation, pieces
        of farmland
askîwi-pimiy– *NI* coal oil, petroleum
aspapi– *VAI* sit against something, sit on something (*e.g.,* blanket)

aspastâkan– *NI* apron
aspin *IPC* off, away; the last I knew
astamâso– *VAI* place (it/him) for oneself
astâ– *VAI* place (it)
astê– *VII* be placed
astinwân– *NI* sinew
astis– *NA* mitten, glove
aswah– *VTI* catch s.t. as it drips
atamih– *VTA* make s.o. grateful, make s.o. indebted, please s.o.
atâm– *VTA* buy (it/him) from s.o.
atâwâkê– *VAI* sell things
atâwê– *VAI* buy (it)
atâwêstamâso– *VAI* buy (it/him) for oneself
atâwêwikamikw– *NI* store
ati *IPV* progressively
atis– *VTI* dye s.t.
atoskah– *VTA* make s.o. work, employ s.o., hire s.o.
atoskahâkan– *NA* employee, hired man
atoskaw– *VTA* work for s.o., be employed by s.o.
atoskât– *VTI* work at s.t.
atoskê– *VAI* work
atoskêmo– *VAI* get people to do things, employ people, hire people
atoskêstamaw– *VTA* work for s.o., do s.o.'s work for her/him
atoskêwin– *NI* work
atot– *VTA* ask s.o. to do something
awa *PR* this [*demonstrative; e.g.,* awa, ôki, ôhi; ôma, ôhi]
awasi-nîpinohk *IPC* the summer before last
awasitê *IPC* further over there
awasowi-kotawanâpiskw– *NI* warming-stove, heater [*sic:* NI]
awaswâkan– *NI* heater [*sic:* NI]
awâsis– *NA* child
awâsisîwi– *VAI* be a child
awâsisîwiwin– *NI* being a child, childhood
awih– *VTA* lend (it/him) to s.o.; rent (it/him) out to s.o.
awihiwê– *VAI* lend (it/him) to people; rent (it/him) out to people
awiyak *PR* someone, somebody; [*in negative clause:*] anyone, anybody; [*indefinite; e.g.,* awiyak, awiya]
awîna *PR* who [*interrogative; e.g.,* awîna]
ay-api– *VAI* sit, be seated [*reduplicated*]
ay-âhci *IPC* from one to another
ay-âskawi *IPC* from time to time, a few at a time [*reduplicated*]
aya *IPC* ah, well [*hesitatory; cf.* ayahk, ayi]
ayah– *VTI* cover s.t. with earth; hill s.t. (*e.g.,* potatoes)

ayahikâkan– *NI* hiller, tool for covering potatoes with earth

ayahikê– *VAI* cover things with earth, hill things (*e.g.,* potatoes)

ayahk *IPC* ah, well [*hesitatory; cf.* aya, ayi]

ayamihâ– *VAI* pray, say prayers; participate in a religious observance

ayamihâhtah– *VTA* make s.o. go to church, take s.o. to mass

ayamihâwin– *NI* prayer, saying prayers; religious observance; religion; the Roman Catholic church

ayamihcikêwin– *NI* reading; [*Christian:*] bible verse

ayamihêstamaw– *VTA* say prayers for s.o.

ayamihêwâtisi– *VAI* be of religious disposition

ayamihêwi-kîsikâw– *NI* Sunday

ayamihêwi-saskamon– *NA* the host; Holy Communion

ayamihêwikamikw– *NI* church, church building

ayamihêwiskwêw– *NA* nun

ayamihêwiyiniw– *NA* priest

ayamihtâ– *VAI* read (it)

ayâ– *VAI* be there, live there

ayâ– *VAI* have (it)

ayâ– *VII* be there, exist

ayâw– *VTA* have s.o.

ayâwahkahw– *VTA* bury s.o. in the ground

ayêhkwêsis– *NA* young castrated bull; steer [*diminutive*]

ayêhkwêw– *NA* castrated bull; ox

ayi *IPC* ah, well [*hesitatory; cf.* aya, ayahk]

ayinânêwimitanaw *IPC* eighty

ayis *IPC* for, because [*cf.* ayisk]

ayisiyiniw– *NA* person, human being

ayisiyinîwi– *VAI* be a person, be a human being

ayisk *IPC* for, because [*cf.* ayis]

ayiwâk *IPC* more; [*in numeral phrases:*] plus

ayiwâkêyim– *VTA* think more of s.o., regard s.o. more highly

ayiwâkipayi– *VAI* have more than enough, have a surplus, have plenty

ayiwêpi– *VAI* rest, take a rest

ayiwinis– *NI* clothes

ayiwinisis– *NI* clothes [*diminutive*]

ayîki-pîsimw– *NA* the month of April

â *IPC* ah, oh [**; exclamatory; cf.* âw]

âcim– *VTA* tell s.o., tell something to s.o.

âcimo– *VAI* tell things, tell a story

âcimostaw– *VTA* tell s.o. about (it), tell s.o. a story

âcimostâto– *VAI* tell one another about (it), tell stories to one another

âcimowin– *NI* story, what is being told

âcimôh– *VTA* make s.o. tell about (it), make s.o. tell a story

âh-âyîtaw *ipc* on both sides [*reduplicated*]

âha *ipc* yes [*; *cf.* êha]

âhc-âyâ– *vai* move one's abode, move from one place to another

âhcanis– *na* ring

âhci piko *ipc* still, nevertheless [*adversative*]

âhkamêyimo– *vai* persist in one's will

âhkami *ipv* persistently, unceasingly, unwaveringly

âhkosi– *vai* be sick

âhkosîwikamikw– *ni* hospital

âhkwaci– *vai* freeze, be frozen

âhkwatihcikan– *ni* refrigerator; freezer

âhkwatihtâ– *vai* let (it) freeze, freeze (it)

âhkwatin– *vii* be frozen

âhkwâtisi– *vai* be stern, be sharp, be of severe disposition

âkayâsîmo– *vai* speak English

âkô *ipv* covered, shielded

âkô-wiyipâ– *vii* be covered in dirt

âkwâtaskinê– *vai* be quite full (*e.g.,* pail), be more than half full

âniskôkwât– *vti* sew s.t. on as an extension

âniskôstê– *vii* extend, be extended

âpacih– *vta* use s.o., make use of s.o.

âpacihcikan– *ni* tool, appliance, machine

âpacihcikanis– *ni* small tool, small appliance [*diminutive*]

âpacihtâ– *vai* use (it), make use of (it)

âpatan– *vii* be used, be useful

âpatisi– *vai* be used, be useful

âpihtaw *ipc* half

âpihtâ-tipiskâ– *vii* be midnight

âpotah– *vti* turn s.t. upside down, turn s.t. inside out

âsawi *ipv* in passing something on

âsawinamaw– *vta* pass (it/him) on to s.o. [*sic:* -awi-; *cf.* âsônamaw–]

âsay *ipc* already

âsiyân– *na* loin-cloth, diaper

âskaw *ipc* once in a while

âsôhtatâ– *vai* lean (it) across something

âsônê *ipc* especially, in particular

âsôskamaw– *vta* infect s.o.

âstamipayi– *vai* become less, run low (*e.g.,* money)

âstamispî *ipc* more recently

âswastâ– *vai* place (it) to lean against something

âta *ipc* although

âtawêyiht– *vti* reject s.t.

âtiht *IPC* some

âtot– *VTI* tell about s.t.

âw *IPC* ah, oh [*exclamatory*]

âwacimihtê– *VAI* haul firewood

âwatamâso– *VAI* haul (it/him) for oneself

âwatâ– *VAI* haul (it)

âyiman– *VII* be difficult

âyimanohk *IPC* in a difficult place

âyimêyiht– *VTI* consider s.t. difficult

âyimisi– *VAI* have a difficult time; be of difficult disposition

âyimî– *VAI* have a difficult time, have a difficult task

âyimôm– *VTA* gossip about s.o.

capahcâsin– *VII* be low [*diminutive*]

câpihcicikan– *NA* [*man's name:*] Handle

cêskwa *IPC* wait; [*in negative clauses:*] not yet

cêsos– *NA* Jésus [*sic, as in French; cf.* cîsas–]

cikêmâ *IPC* of course, naturally

cimatê– *VII* stand erect

cî *IPC* [*question marker*]

cîhcîkos– *VTI* cut meat off s.t. (*e.g.,* bone)

cîkahoso– *VAI* chop oneself

cîki *IPC* close by

cîsas– *NA* Jesus [*sic, as in English; cf.* cêsos–]

côsap– *NA* Joseph

êha *IPC* yes

êkamâ *IPC* it is not the case [*predicative*]

êkâ *IPC* not [*cf.* êkây, êkâya]

êkây *IPC* not [*cf.* êkâ, êkâya]

êkâya *IPC* not [*cf.* êkâ, êkây]

êkos îsi *IPC* thus, in that way; that is how it is

êkosi *IPC* thus, in this way

êkospî *IPC* then, at that time

êkota *IPC* there, at that place

êkotê *IPC* over there

êkotowahk *IPC* of that kind

êkotowihk *IPC* in that place

êkwa *IPC* then; and

êkwayâc *IPC* only now, for the first time [*]

êkwayikohk *IPC* up to that point

êsa *IPC* reportedly

êskwa *IPC* wait [*; cf.* cêskwa]

êtikwê *IPC* presumably, I guess [*; sic: -i-; cf.* êtokwê]

êtokwê *IPC* presumably, I guess

êwako *PR* that one [*resumptive demonstrative*; *e.g.,* êwako, êkonik, êkoni; êwako, êkoni]

êyâpic *IPC* still [*also* kêyâpic]

hêy *IPC* hey [*exclamatory*]

ihkin– *VII* occur, take place

ihtahtopiponwêwin– *NI* having so many years, the number of one's years, one's age [*sic:* iht-; *cf.* itahtopiponwê–]

ihtako– *VAI* exist

ihtakon– *VII* exist

ihtasi– *VAI* be so many, be as many

ihtatan– *VII* exist there [*?sic; both stem and gloss tentative*]

ihtâwin– *NI* abode, place of residence

isi *IPC* thus

isi *IPV* thus

isiyîhkâso– *VAI* be called thus, have such a name

isiyîhkât– *VTA* call s.o. thus, give s.o. such a name

isiyîhkât– *VTI* call s.t. thus, give s.t. such a name

isiyîhkâtê– *VII* be called thus, have such a name

isîh– *VTA* make s.o. thus

isîhcikêwin– *NI* what is thus done, such activities

isîhk– *VTI* bother with s.t. thus

isîhkaw– *VTA* bother s.o. thus

isîhtâ– *VAI* make (it) thus

isko *IPC* so far

isko *IPV* so far

iskonikowisi– *VAI* be left over (*e.g.,* to survive) by the powers

iskosi– *VAI* be so tall, be of such height

iskwêsis– *NA* girl, little girl

iskwêw– *NA* woman, female adult

iskwêyâc *IPC* at last, at the end

ispahtâ– *VAI* run there or thus

ispastâ– *VAI* place (it) so high, pile (it) so high

ispayi– *VAI* move thus, drive there

ispayin– *VII* occur thus, happen thus

ispî *IPC* at such a time, then

ispîhcâ– *VII* extend thus, be of such size (*e.g.,* country)

ispîhtisî– *VAI* extend thus, be of such age

it– *VTA* say thus to s.o., say thus of s.o.

it– *VTI* say thus of s.t., say thus about s.t.

ita *IPC* there

itahkamikisi– *VAI* do things thus

itahtopiponê– *VAI* be so many years old [*; sic:* -nê-; *cf.* itahtopiponwê–]

itahtopiponwê– *VAI* be so many years old

itakiso– *VAI* be counted thus, cost so much; be held in such esteem

itamahciho– *VAI* feel thus, be in such health [*e.g.,* nânitaw itamahciho– 'feel unwell']

itapihkât– *VTI* braid s.t. thus; knit s.t. thus

itapihkê– *VAI* braid thus; knit thus [**; ?sic: record*]

itaskitê– *VII* stand thus (*e.g.,* lodges)

itastâ– *VAI* place (it) thus

itastê– *VII* be placed thus; be written thus

itâciho– *VAI* travel thus, lead one's life thus

itâcihowin– *NI* travelling thus, leading one's life thus

itâcimo– *VAI* tell thus, tell a story thus

itâcimostaw– *VTA* tell s.o. thus about (it), tell s.o. such a story

itâhkôm– *VTA* be thus related to s.o., have s.o. as such a relative, use such a kin-term for s.o.

itâmihk *IPC* inside (*e.g.,* mouth); underneath (*e.g.,* one's clothes)

itâpatan– *VII* be thus used, be of such use

itâspinêm– *VTA* call s.o. thus in anger, angrily call s.o. such a name, thus scold s.o. in anger

itâtisi– *VAI* act thus, be of such a disposition

itê *IPC* there, over there

itêyiht– *VTI* think thus of s.t.

itêyihtâkwan– *VII* be thought of

itêyim– *VTA* think thus of s.o.

itin– *VTI* hold s.t. thus

itisahamaw– *VTA* send (it/him) to s.o. thus

itito– *VAI* say thus to one another, say thus about one another

itohtah– *VTA* take s.o. there or thus

itohtatâ– *VAI* take (it) there or thus

itohtê– *VAI* go there or thus

itowahk *IPC* this kind

itowihk *IPC* in this place

itôt– *VTI* do thus, act thus [*cf.* tôt–]

itôtamôh– *VTA* make s.o. act thus

itwê– *VAI* say thus

iyaskohc *IPC* next in sequence

iyâyaw *IPC* preferably, rather

iyikohk *IPC* so much, to such an extent

iyinimin– *NI* blueberries

iyinîsi– *VAI* be clever

iyisâho– *VAI* resist, resist temptation, exercise restraint

iyisâhowin– *NI* resistance, resisting temptation, restraint

îh *IPC* lo! look! [*exclamatory*]

îhkatawâw– *NI* slough, marsh

k-ôsihkosiwayâniw *INM* [*man's name:*] Ermineskin
[*literally* Has-an-Ermineskin]

kahkiyaw *IPC* every, all

kakâyawâtisi– *VAI* be hard-working, be of industrious disposition

kakâyawisî– *VAI* be hard-working, be industrious

kakêskihkêmo– *VAI* counsel people, preach at people

kakêskim– *VTA* counsel s.o., preach at s.o.

kakêskimiso– *VAI* counsel oneself

kakwâtakêyiht– *VTI* be tormented, be tormented about s.t.

kakwâtakihtâ– *VAI* suffer because of (it), have difficulties because of (it)

kakwâtakî– *VAI* suffer, have difficulties

kakwâyaki *IPV* greatly, extremely [*]

kakwê *IPV* try, attempt to

kakwêcim– *VTA* ask s.o. a question

kanak *IPC* for a short while

kanawâpam– *VTA* look at s.o.; look after s.o.

kanawâpokê– *VAI* look after a household, keep house

kanawêyiht– *VTI* look after s.t., take care of s.t.

kanawêyihtamôh– *VTA* ask s.o. to look after (it/him), leave (it/him) to be looked after by s.o.

kanawêyim– *VTA* look after s.o., take care of s.o.

kanâci *IPV* clean

kanâcih– *VTA* clean s.o.

kanâciho– *VAI* clean oneself

kanâcihtâ– *VAI* clean (it), clean (it) out (*e.g.*, intestine)

kanâcinâkosi– *VAI* look clean, give a clean appearance

kanâtan– *VII* be clean

kanâtapi– *VAI* live in a clean house [*]

kanâtâpâwatâ– *VAI* wash (it) clean with water

kani *IPC* oh yes, I just remembered, I had forgotten [*cf.* kanihk]

kanihk *IPC* oh yes, I just remembered, I had forgotten [*cf.* kani]

kaskâciwahtê– *VII* be boiled until tender

kaskâciwas– *VTI* boil s.t. until tender

kaskâpahtê– *VII* be smoked

kaskâpas– *VTI* smoke s.t.

kaskâpasw– *VTA* smoke s.o.

kaskâpiskah– *VTI* can s.t., preserve s.t.

kaskiho– *VAI* be able, be competent

kaskihtamâso– *VAI* earn (it) for oneself

kaskihtâ– *VAI* be able to do (it)

kaskihtâwin– *NI* ability to do (it), competence

kaskikwâso– *VAI* sew, do one's sewing

kaskikwâsopayihcikanis– *NI* sewing machine [*diminutive*]

kaskikwâsopayihcikâkê– *VAI* do machine-sewing with (it), use (it) to machine-sew

kaskikwâswâkan– *NI* sewing machine

kaskikwât– *VTI* sew s.t.

kaskikwâtamaw– *VTA* sew (it/him) for s.o.

kaskikwâtamâso– *VAI* sew (it/him) for oneself

kaskikwâtiso– *VAI* sew for oneself

kaskitêsi– *VAI* be black

kaskitêwatisw– *VTA* dye s.o. (*e.g.*, stocking) black

kaskitêwâpahtê– *VII* give off black smoke

katâc *IPC* insistently; [*in negative clause:*] necessarily

katikoni– *VAI* sleep over, spend the night

katisk *IPC* just now, exactly; [*in negative clause:*] not merely

kawaci– *VAI* be cold, experience cold

kawatim– *VTA* get s.o. cold, expose s.o. to cold

kawatimiso– *VAI* get oneself cold

kawikah– *VTI* chop s.t. down, cut s.t. down

kawisimo– *VAI* lie down, go to bed

kayâcic *IPC* the spare, the surplus [*?sic; both record and gloss highly tentative*]

kayâhtê *IPC* before, previously

kayâs *IPC* long ago

kayâsi *IPN* long-ago, old-time

kayâsiyâkan– *NA* [*man's name:*] Old-Pan

kâ-mahihkani-pimohtêw *INM* [*man's name:*] Walks-like-a-Wolf

kâh-kipîhci *IPC* stopping now and then [*reduplicated*]

kâh-kîhtwâm *IPC* again and again [*reduplicated*]

kâhcitin– *VTI* catch s.t.

kâhkêwakw– *NI* dried meat

kâkikê *IPC* always, forever

kâsisi– *VAI* be sharp, be scratchy (*e.g.*, wool)

kâsîhkwâkê– *VAI* wash one's face with (it), use (it) to wash one's face

kâsîhkwêwiyâkan– *NI* wash-basin

kâsînamaw– *VTA* wipe (it) off for s.o.; [*Christian:*] forgive s.o.

kâsînamâso– *VAI* wipe (it) off for oneself; [*Christian:*] have one's sins forgiven, obtain forgivenness

kâsînamâto– *VAI* wipe (it) off for one another; [*Christian:*] forgive one another

kâsîyâkanê– *VAI* wash dishes, do the dishes

kâskah– *VTI* scrape s.t. off

kâso– *VAI* hide, hide oneself

kâspis– *VTI* heat s.t. until crisp

kâwi *IPC* again

kêcikopit– *VTI* pull s.t. free, pull s.t. out

kêhcinâ *IPC* surely, for certain

kêhtê-ay– *NA* old person, elder [*e.g.,* kêhtê-ayak]

kêhtê-ayiwi– *VAI* be an old person, be an elder

kêhtêskwêw– *NA* old woman, old lady

kêkâ-mitâtahtomitanaw *IPC* ninety

kêkâc *IPC* almost

kêswân *IPC* by coincidence

kêtahtawê *IPC* suddenly; at one time

kêyâpic *IPC* still [*sic; cf.* êyâpic]

kihc-âyamihêwiyiniw– *NA* bishop

kihc-ôkimâw– *NA* king; government [*e.g.,* kihc-ôkimânâhk 'the government']

kihcêyiht– *VTI* think highly of s.t.

kihcêyihtamaw– *VTA* think highly of (it/him) for s.o.

kihcêyihtâkwan– *VII* be highly thought of

kihcêyim– *VTA* think highly of s.o.

kihci-kîsikw– *NI* heaven

kihci-wîki– *VAI* live formally; [*Christian:*] live in residence

kihci-wîkihto– *VAI* be formally married in church

kihci-wîkihtowin-âhcanis– *NA* wedding ring

kihci-wîkihtowin– *NI* formal marriage, Holy Matrimony

kihci-wîkim– *VTA* marry s.o. formally in church

kihcihtwâwi *IPN* of exalted character; venerable, holy [*e.g.,* kihcihtwâwi-côsap 'Holy Joseph']

kihtimêyiht– *VTI* be tired of s.t.

kikamohtâ– *VAI* attach (it), put (it) on something

kikamon– *VII* be attached, be on something

kikamôh– *VTA* attach s.o., put s.o. (*e.g.,* yarn) on something

kikin– *VTI* put s.t. on something, add s.t. in (*e.g.,* baking-powder)

kikisk– *VTI* wear s.t.

kikiskaw– *VTA* wear s.o. (*e.g.,* stocking, ring)

kimiwan– *VII* rain, be rainy

kimoti– *VAI* steal (it); be a thief

kinosêw– *NA* fish

kinosi– *VAI* be long, be tall

kinwâ– *VII* be long, be tall

kinwês *IPC* for a long time

kipwahpit– *VTI* pull s.t. close, tie s.t. close

kisâkamicêwâpôs– *NI* warm water [*diminutive*]

kisâkamis– *VTI* heat s.t. up as liquid

kisâkamisikê– *VAI* heat a liquid; make tea

kisâkamitêwâpoy– *NI* hot water

kisât– *VTI* stay with s.t., hold fast to s.t.

kiscikânis– *NA* grain, seed [*diminutive*]

kiscikânis– *NI* garden [*diminutive*]

kiscikêsi– *VAI* plant seeds; have a small garden [*diminutive*]

kisê-manitow– *NA* God the kind, the compassionate God; [*Christian:*] Merciful God

kisê-manitowi-pîkiskwêwin– *NI* God's word

kisêpêkihtakinikê– *VAI* wash a wooden floor, wash floor-boards

kisêpêkin– *VTA* wash s.o.

kisêpêkin– *VTI* wash s.t.

kisêpêkinikan– *NI* soap

kisêpêkinikê– *VAI* wash things, do the laundry

kisêpêkinikêwin– *NI* laundry, doing the laundry

kisêpêkiniso– *VAI* wash oneself

kisêwâtisi– *VAI* be kind, be of compassionate disposition

kisêwâtisiwin– *NI* kindness, compassion

kisêyiniw– *NA* old man, elder

kisin– *VII* be very cold weather

kisipipayin– *VII* come to an end, run out

kisis– *VTI* warm s.t. up, heat s.t. up

kisiso– *VAI* be warm, be hot

kisiwâh– *VTA* anger s.o., make s.o. angry

kisiwâk *IPC* nearby

kisiwiyo– *VAI* complain about work, be angry about one's work

kisîkitot– *VTA* speak to s.o. in anger [*sic:* -î-]

kisîm– *VTA* anger s.o. by speech

kisîstaw– *VTA* be angry with s.o., stay angry with s.o.

kiskêyiht– *VTI* know s.t.

kiskêyihtamâ– *VAI* have spiritual knowledge

kiskinahamaw– *VTA* teach s.o., teach (it) to s.o. [*; *sic:* -a-; *cf.* kiskinohamaw–]

kiskinohamaw– *VTA* teach s.o., teach (it) to s.o.

kiskinohamawâkan– *NA* student

kiskinohamâkê– *VAI* teach things

kiskinohamâkosi– *VAI* be a student, be in school

kiskinohamâkosiwin– *NI* being a student, going to school; schoolwork, homework

kiskinohamâso– *VAI* teach oneself

kiskinohamâto– *VAI* teach one another

kiskinohamâtowikamikw– *NI* school, school-house

kiskinohamâtowin– *NI* teaching, education

kiskinowâpahtih– *VTA* teach s.o. by example

kiskinowâpahtihiwê– *VAI* teach people by example

kiskinowâpam– *VTA* watch s.o.'s example

kiskisi– *VAI* remember

kiskisom– *VTA* remind s.o. [*sic; cf.* kiskisôm–]

kiskisomito– *VAI* remind one another [*sic; cf.* kiskisômito–]

kiskisopayi– *VAI* think of something, suddenly remember

kiskisototaw– *VTA* remember s.o.

kiskisôm– *VTA* remind s.o. [*also* -o-]

kiskisômito– *VAI* remind one another [*also* -o-]

kiskiwêh– *VTI* utter s.t. as a prophesy, utter prophesies

kiskiwêhw– *VTA* utter prophesies to s.o., utter prophesies about s.o.

kispakikwât– *VTI* sew s.t. thickly

kistikân– *NA* grain, seed; sheaf of grain

kistikân– *NI* field, arable land

kistikânikamikw– *NI* granary

kistikê– *VAI* seed things, plant things

kitahamaw– *VTA* advise s.o. against (it/him)

kitâ– *VAI* eat (it) up, eat (it) completely

kitâpaht– *VTI* look at s.t.

kitâpam– *VTA* look at s.o.

kitimah– *VTA* be mean to s.o., treat s.o. badly

kitimâk-ôhpikih– *VTA* raise s.o. in poverty; raise s.o. as an orphan

kitimâkêyihto– *VAI* feel pity towards one another, love one another

kitimâkêyihtowin– *NI* feeling pity towards one another, loving one another

kitimâkêyim– *VTA* feel pity towards s.o., be kind to s.o., love s.o.

kitimâkinaw– *VTA* take pity upon s.o., lovingly tend s.o.

kitimâkinâso– *VAI* pity oneself, feel sorry for oneself

kitimâkisi– *VAI* be pitiable, be poor

kitot– *VTA* speak to s.o., address s.o.

kiya *PR* you (sg.) [*]

kiyawâw *PR* you (pl.)

kiyâm *IPC* let it be, let there be no further delay; please

kiyânaw *PR* we-and-you (incl.)

kiyipa *IPC* soon

kiyipikin– *VII* grow quickly

kiyokaw– *VTA* visit s.o.

kiyokâto– *VAI* visit one another

kiyokê– *VAI* visit people, pay a visit

kiyôtê– *VAI* visit afar, travel to visit

kîhkâm– *VTA* scold s.o.

kîhkânâkwan– *VII* be clearly visible

kîhkâtêyihtâkwan– *VII* be held in high esteem, be prominent

kîhkâtêyim– *VTA* hold s.o. in high esteem

kîhtwâm *IPC* again

kîkisêpâ *IPC* early in the morning

kîkw-ây– *NA* which one; what kind [*e.g.,* kîkw-âyak]

kîkway *PR* something, thing; [*in negative clause:*] anything, any; [*indefinite*]

kîkwây *PR* what [*interrogative*]

kîmôc *IPC* secretly, stealthily

kîsapihkât– *VTI* braid s.t. to completion; knit s.t. to completion

kîsi *IPV* completely, to completion

kîsih– *VTA* complete s.o. (*e.g.,* stocking), finish preparing s.o.
       [*sic:* -ih-]

kîsikâ– *VII* be day, be daylight

kîsikâw– *NA* day, daylight

kîsis– *VTI* cook s.t. to completion

kîsiso– *VAI* be cooked to completion

kîsitê– *VII* be cooked to completion

kîsîhtâ– *VAI* finish (it), complete (it)

kîskatah– *VTI* chop s.t. through

kîskicihcêpit– *VTA* tear s.o.'s hand off, tear s.o.'s finger off

kîskipotâ– *VAI* saw (it) through

kîsopwê– *VII* be hot weather

kîsowâ– *VII* be warm, provide warmth

kîsowihkaso– *VAI* warm oneself by fire, keep oneself warm by fire

kîspin *IPC* if

kîspinat– *VTA* earn enough to buy s.o. (*e.g.,* horse)

kîspinat– *VTI* earn enough to buy s.t.

kîspôh– *VTA* feed s.o. until full, get s.o. (horse) fully fed

kîstanaw *PR* we-and-you (incl.), too; we-and-you (incl.) by contrast

kîwâc-âwâsis– *NA* orphan

kîwâtisi– *VAI* be orphaned, be an orphan

kîwê– *VAI* return home

kîwêhtah– *VTA* take s.o. home

kîwêhtatâ– *VAI* take (it) home

kîwêtinohk *IPC* in the north

kîwêtot– *VTI* return home to s.t.

kîwêtotaw– *VTA* return home to s.o.

konita *IPC* in vain

kosikwan– *VII* be heavy

koskoh– *VTA* startle s.o., surprise s.o.

koskon– *VTA* wake s.o. up

kost– *VTA* fear s.o.

kost– *VTI* fear s.t.

kotak PR other, another [*e.g.*, kotakak, kotaka]

kotawânâpiskw– NI stove [*sic:* NI]

kotiskâwêwatimw– NA race-horse [*sic:* -a-]

kôhkôs– NA pig

kwayask IPC properly, right

kwayaski IPV properly

kwayâc IPC ready, prepared

kwayâci IPV in readiness, in preparation

kwayâtastamaw– VTA put (it/him) aside in readiness for s.o.

kwayâtastamâso– VAI put (it/him) aside in readiness for oneself

kwayâtastâ– VAI place (it) in readiness, put (it) aside in readiness

kwâhkotênikê– VAI start a fire, set things aflame

kwâpah– VTI dip s.t. out

kwâpikê– VAI go for water, haul water

kwêh-kwêkwask IPC back and forth [*reduplicated*]

kwêskî– VAI turn around

kwîtawêyihcikâtê– VII be missed, be in short supply

kwîtâpacihtâ– VAI be short of (it) to use, lack tools

ma cî IPC is it not the case [*; *predicative*]

ma kîkway PR nothing

mac-âyiwi– VAI be bad, be evil

maci IPV bad, evil

macikwanâs– NI weed

mahkahkw– NI barrel, tub

mahti IPC let's see, please

mamihcim– VTA boast about s.o.

mamihcimo– VAI be boastful

mamihcisi– VAI be proud

mamisî– VAI place reliance

mamisîtotaw– VTA rely on s.o.

manahikan– NI cream

manâ IPC avoiding to do something, careful not to

manâcih– VTA treat s.o. with respect

manâcihtâ– VAI treat (it) with respect

manâcim– VTA speak to s.o. with respect, speak of s.o. with respect

manêsi– VAI have run out of (it), lack (it)

manicôs– NA insect, bug

manipit– VTI pull s.t. free, pull s.t. out

manis– VTI cut s.t.

manisw– VTA cut s.o.

manitow– NA God

manitowi-masinahikan– NI God's book, the Bible

mariy– NA Marie, the Virgin Mary [*sic, as in French* Marie]

masinah– *VTI* mark s.t., draw s.t.; write s.t.

masinahamâso– *VAI* draw (it) for oneself; write (it) for oneself, write oneself

masinahikan– *NI* book; written document, will

masinahikâtê– *VII* have marks, have writing; be written

masinahikê– *VAI* write things; write, be literate

masinahikêh– *VTA* hire s.o.

masinahikêwin– *NI* writing; letter, character

masinihtatâ– *VAI* trace (it), use (it) as pattern

masinipayiwin– *NI* picture, photograph

maskawâ– *VII* be hard, be strong

maskawâtisi– *VAI* be strong, be of strong disposition

maskawisî– *VAI* be strong

maskawisîwin– *NI* strength

maskihkîwiskwêw– *NA* nurse

maskimotêkinw– *NI* sacking, cloth from flour-sacks

maskisin– *NI* moccasin, shoe

maskosiy– *NI* grass, hay

maskwacîsihk *INM* [*place-name:*] Hobbema, Alberta [*locative; literally* at Bear's Hill]

matwân cî *IPC* I believe, I wonder

mawimoscikê– *VAI* pray, wail

mawiso– *VAI* pick berries

mayaw *IPC* as soon as

maywês *IPC* before [*cf.* maywêsk]

maywêsk *IPC* before [*cf.* maywês]

mâcatoskê– *VAI* start to work [*sic:* -c-, -a-]

mâci *IPV* begin

mâcihtâ– *VAI* begin doing (it)

mâcika *IPC* for instance

mâcipayin– *VII* begin to run (*e.g.*, tape–recorder) [*]

mâcî– *VAI* hunt, go hunting

mâka *IPC* but

mâmaw-ôhtâwîmâw– *NA* All-Father, Father-of-All

mâmawi *IPN* all together, all as a group [*e.g.*, mâmawi-ayisiyiniw–]

mâmawi-wîcihitowin– *NI* all helping together, general cooperation

mâmawôhkamâto– *VAI* work together at (it/him) as a group

mâmawôpi– *VAI* sit together, hold a meeting

mâmiskôm– *VTA* talk about s.o., discuss s.o.

mâmiskôt– *VTI* talk about s.t., discuss s.t.

mâmiskôtamaw– *VTA* discuss (it/him) for s.o.

mâmitonêyihcikan– *NI* mind; thought, worry

mâmitonêyiht– *VTI* think about s.t., worry about s.t.

mâmitonêyihtêstamâso– *VAI* think about (it/him) for oneself, plan
    for oneself

mâmitonêyim– *VTA* think about s.o., worry about s.o.

mâna *IPC* usually, habitually

mâskôc *IPC* perhaps, I suppose [*cf.* mâskôt]

mâskôt *IPC* perhaps, I suppose [*cf.* mâskôc]

mâto– *VAI* cry, wail

mâyamahciho– *VAI* fare ill, be sick

mâyatihkopîway– *NI* sheep's fleece; wool

mâyâtan– *VII* be ugly, be bad

mâyi *IPV* bad, evil

mâyi-tôt– *VTI* do s.t. evil

mâyi-tôtaw– *VTA* do evil to s.o., harm s.o.

mâyinikêwin– *NI* wrong-doing, evil deed

mâyipayi– *VAI* fare badly; suffer a death, be bereaved

mêki– *VAI* give (it/him) away, release (it/him); give (her) in marriage

mêkwâ *IPV* while, during

mêkwâc *IPC* while, during

mêstinikê– *VAI* use things up, exhaust things, spend it all

mêtawê– *VAI* play; gamble

mêtoni *IPC* really [*cf.* mitoni]

micimin– *VTA* hold on to s.o.

miciminamaw– *VTA* hold on to (it/him) for s.o.

miciminamôh– *VTA* make s.o. hold on to (it/him)

mihcêt *IPC* many, much

mihcêti– *VAI* be numerous, be plentiful

mihcêtôsê– *VAI* have many children, have numerous offspring

mihcêtwâw *IPC* many times

mihkit– *VTI* scrape s.t. (meat) off the hide

mihkw– *NI* blood [*e.g.,* mihko]

miht– *NI* firewood, piece of firewood [*e.g.,* mihti, mihta]

mihtât– *VTI* regret s.t.

minaho– *VAI* kill an animal, make a kill

minahôstamaw– *VTA* kill an animal for s.o., make a kill for s.o.

minahôstamâso– *VAI* kill an animal for oneself, succeed in a kill

minihkwê– *VAI* drink (it), have a drink; drink, abuse alcohol

minihkwêski– *VAI* habitually abuse alcohol, be an alcoholic

minihkwêwin– *NI* drinking, alcohol abuse

misakâmê *IPC* all the way

misatimokamikw– *NI* horse-barn

misatimw– *NA* horse

misatimwâyow– *NI* horse-tail; tail-hair of a horse

misawâc *ipc* in any case
misâ– *vii* be big
misâskwatômin– *ni* saskatoon berry
misi *ipv* big, greatly
misikiti– *vai* be big (in height or girth)
misipocikê– *vai* run things (*e.g.,* hide) over a sharp edge
misipotâ– *vai* run (it) (*e.g.,* hide) over a sharp edge
misisîhtâ– *vai* make (it) big
misiw îtê *ipc* all over, everywhere
misiwanâcihiso– *vai* ruin oneself, destroy oneself; commit suicide
misiwanâcihtâ– *vai* ruin (it), destroy (it)
misiwanâtan– *vii* be ruined, be destroyed
misiwê *ipc* all over
misiwêminakin– *vti* put beads all over s.t.; cover s.t. with beads
misk– *vti* find s.t.
miskamaw– *vta* find (it/him) for s.o.
miskaw– *vta* find s.o.
miskotâkay– *ni* coat, dress
mistahi *ipc* very many, lots
mistikokamikw– *ni* log-house
mistikowat– *ni* wooden box, trunk
mistikw– *ni* pole, log, rail
mistiyâkan– *ni* big dish, platter, large bowl
mitâtahtomitanaw *ipc* one hundred
mitâtahtomitanaw-maskimot *ipc* a hundred bags, one hundred bags
mitoni *ipc* really [*cf.* mêtoni]
miy– *vta* give (it/him) to s.o.
miyawât– *vti* enjoy s.t.; have fun, be joyful
miyawâtamowin– *ni* enjoyment; fun, joyfulness
miyikowisi– *vai* be given (it/him) by the powers
miyito– *vai* give (it/him) to one another
miyo *ipv* good
miyo-kakêskihkêmowin– *ni* good counselling, good preaching
miyo-kîsih– *vta* finish s.o. well; educate s.o. well
miyo-pîkiskwêwin– *ni* good speech; [*Christian:*] the good news
miyo-tôt– *vti* do s.t. good
miyo-tôtamowin– *ni* good deed, good works
miyo-tôtaw– *vta* do s.o. a good turn
miyoht– *vti* like the sound of s.t.
miyohtah– *vta* guide s.o. well
miyohtwâ– *vai* be good-natured, be of pleasant character
miyokihtâ– *vai* be good at growing (it)

miyomahciho– *VAI* fare well, feel well, be in good health or spirit

miyonâkohcikê– *VAI* have one's property look nice, have things look prosperous

miyonâkwan– *VII* look good, have a nice appearance, look prosperous

miyopayin– *VII* work well, run well

miyosi– *VAI* be good, be beautiful

miyosîhtâ– *VAI* make (it) good, make (it) beautiful

miyoskamin– *VII* be early spring

miyô– *VAI* be good at something

miywâpisin– *VAI* like the look of something

miywâsin– *VII* be good

miywêyiht– *VTI* consider s.t. good, like s.t.

miywêyim– *VTA* consider s.o. good, like s.o.

mîci– *VAI* eat (it)

mîcimâpoy– *NI* broth, soup

mîciso– *VAI* eat, have a meal

mîcisowinâhtikw– *NI* dining table, table

mîciwin– *NI* food

mîkis– *NA* bead

mîkisasâkay– *NI* beaded coat, beaded jacket

mîkisayiwinis– *NI* beaded clothing

mîkisihkahcikê– *VAI* bead things, do beadwork

mîkisihkahcikêwin– *NI* beading, beadwork

mîkisihkaht– *VTI* bead s.t., put beads on s.t.

mîkisiwi– *VII* be beaded

mîkiwâhp– *NI* lodge, tipi

mîna *IPC* also, again

mînis– *NI* berry

mînom– *VTA* straighten s.o. out, correct s.o. verbally

mîsîwikamikw– *NI* outhouse, toilet

mohcihk *IPC* on the bare ground

mosci *IPV* merely, without instrument

moscikwâso– *VAI* sew by hand

moscikwât– *VTI* sew s.t. by hand

mostohtê– *VAI* walk (without conveyance)

mostoso-wiyâs– *NI* beef

mostosw– *NA* cattle, cow

mostosw-âya *IPC* of a cow, in matters bovine

mostoswayân– *NA* cow-hide

mow– *VTA* eat s.o. (*e.g.,* bread)

môhcowi– *VAI* be crazy, be silly

môniyâw– *NA* non-Indian, Whiteman

môsâpêwi– *VAI* be a bachelor, be unmarried, be single

môsihtâ– VAI sense (it), feel (it)

môskipayi– VAI break out in a rash, in sores (*e.g.,* with thrush)

môskomo– VAI talk oneself into crying, cry while talking

môso-pahkêkin– NI finished moose-hide

môso-wiyâs– NI moose-meat

môsw– NA moose [*e.g.,* môswa]

môtêyâpiskw– NI bottle

môy kakêtihk IPC a great many

môya IPC not [*cf.* namôya]

mwêhci IPC exactly

mwêstas IPC later, subsequently

nahapi– VAI sit down in one's place, be properly seated

nahastâ– VAI put (it) in its place, put (it) away

nahin– VTA bury s.o., hold a funeral for s.o.

nakacihtâ– VAI be familiar with doing (it), be practised at (it)

nakat– VTA leave s.o. behind; die and leave s.o. behind

nakat– VTI leave s.t. behind

nakatamaw– VTA leave (it/him) behind for s.o.

nakataskê– VAI leave the earth behind, depart the world, die

nakayâh– VTA get s.o. accustomed to something, break s.o.
(*e.g.,* horse)

nakayâsk– VTI be accustomed to s.t., be comfortable with s.t.

nakayâskaw– VTA be accustomed to s.o., be comfortable with s.o.,
be familiar with s.o.

nakiskaw– VTA encounter s.o., meet s.o.

nakî– VAI stop, come to a stop

nama kîkway IPC nothing

nama wîhkâc IPC never

namatê– VAI be nonexistent, have disappeared

namôya IPC not [*cf.* môya]

namwâc IPC no, not [*]

nanahiht– VTI listen well to s.t., obey s.t.

nanahihtaw– VTA listen well to s.o., obey s.o.

nanâskom– VTA thank s.o., speak words of thanks to s.o.

nanâtohk IPC variously, various kinds

nanâtohkokwâso– VAI sew patchwork blankets

nanâtohkôskân IPC all kinds of things

naniwêyatwê– VAI joke, tell a joke

napakaskisin– NI flat moccasin

napakâ– VII be flat

napakihtakw– NI flat lumber, board

napakikamikos– NI flat-roofed log-house [*diminutive*]

naskomo– VAI respond, make a verbal response

nawac *ipc* more, better, rather

nawac piko *ipc* sort of, kind of, approximately; more or less

nawasôn– *vta* choose s.o.

nawasôn– *vti* choose s.t.

nawasônamaw– *vta* choose (it/him) for s.o.; make a choice for s.o.

nawaswât– *vta* pursue s.o., chase after s.o.

nawaswât– *vti* pursue s.t., chase after s.t.

nayaht– *vti* carry s.t. on one's back

nayahto– *vai* carry one another on one's back; ride up on one another (*e.g.,* beads)

nayêhtâwan– *vii* be difficult, be troublesome [*]

nayêhtâwêyim– *vta* find s.o. difficult, find s.o. troublesome

nayêhtâwipayi– *vai* run into difficulties, experience trouble

nayêstaw *ipc* only

nâcimihtê– *vai* fetch firewood, go for firewood

nâcitâpê– *vai* go and drag (it) back, fetch (it) by cart [*sic; cf.* nâtitâpê–]

nâha *pr* that one yonder [*demonstrative, e.g.,* nâha, nêki; nêma]

nânitaw *ipc* simply; something, anything; something bad, anything bad

nâpêsis– *na* boy, little boy

nâpêw– *na* man, male adult

nâpêwasikan– *na* men's socks

nât– *vta* fetch s.o.

nât– *vti* fetch s.t.

nâtamaw– *vta* fetch (it/him) for s.o.

nâtamâso– *vai* fetch (it/him) for oneself

nâtâmototaw– *vta* flee to s.o., seek refuge with s.o.

nâtitâpê– *vai* go and drag (it) back, fetch (it) by cart [*also* nâcitâpê–]

nâtwâh– *vti* chop s.t. off something

nâway *ipc* behind; in the past

nêhiyaw– *na* Cree Indian, Indian

nêhiyaw-masinîwin– *ni* Cree design, Cree motif, Indian design, Indian motif [*sic:* -w-]

nêhiyawê– *vai* speak Cree

nêhiyawêwin– *ni* speaking Cree, the Cree language

nêhiyawi *ipv* Cree, Indian

nêhiyawi-wîhowin– *ni* Cree name, Indian name

nêhiyawiyîhkâso– *vai* have a Cree name, have an Indian name

nêhiyâwi– *vai* be a Cree Indian, be an Indian

nêpêwih– *vta* shame s.o., put s.o. to shame

nêpêwisi– *vai* be ashamed, be shy

nêsowâtisi– *vai* be weak, have a weak constitution

nêsowisi– *vai* be weak, be near death

nêtê *IPC* over there

nihtâ *IPV* good at, competent, practised

nihtâwiki– *VAI* be born

nihtâwiminakinikê– *VAI* be good at sewing on beads

nihtâwisîhcikê– *VAI* be good at making things

nihtâwitêpo– *VAI* be good at cooking

nikikomin– *NI* a certain berry [*literally* otter-berry]

nikohtât– *VTI* chop s.t. for firewood

nikohtê– *VAI* collect firewood, chop firewood

nikohtêstamâso– *VAI* make firewood for oneself, make one's own firewood

nikohtêwin– *NI* making firewood

nikotwâsik *IPC* six

nikotwâsomitanaw-askiy *IPC* sixty years

nipahâhkatoso– *VAI* starve to death, die from starvation

nipahiso– *VAI* kill oneself, commit suicide

nipahtamaw– *VTA* kill (it/him) for s.o., make a kill for s.o.

nipâ– *VAI* sleep, be asleep

nipêwikamikw– *NI* bedroom

nipêwin– *NI* bed

nipiy– *NI* water

nipîmakan– *VII* be dead

nisitawêyihcikâtê– *VII* be recognised

nisitawêyim– *VTA* recognise s.o.

nisitoht– *VTI* understand s.t.

nisitohtaw– *VTA* understand s.o.

nistam *IPC* first, at first, for the first time

nisti– *VAI* be three in number

nisto *IPC* three

nistopiponwê– *VAI* be three years old

nistosâp *IPC* thirteen

nistw-âskiy *IPC* three years

nitawâpam– *VTA* go to see s.o., go to visit s.o.

nitawâwê– *VAI* go looking for eggs, go to collect eggs

nitawêyiht– *VTI* want s.t.

nitawêyihtamaw– *VTA* want (it/him) for s.o., want (it/him) from s.o.

nitawêyim– *VTA* want s.o., want (it/him) of s.o.

nitawi *IPV* go and

nitâhtâm– *VTA* borrow (it/him) from s.o.

nitohtaw– *VTA* listen to s.o.

nitohtâkowisi– *VAI* be heard by the powers

nitom– *VTA* invite s.o.

niton– *VTI* look for s.t.

nitotamaw– *VTA* ask s.o. for (it/him)

niya *PR* I

niyanân *PR* we (excl.)

niyâk *IPC* in the future

niyânan *IPC* five

niyânani– *VAI* be five in number

nîhc-âyihk *IPC* down, below

nîhcipit– *VTA* pull s.o. down, drag s.o. down

nîhtin– *VTI* take s.t. down, unload s.t.

nîkân *IPC* in front, in the lead

nîmâ– *VAI* take provisions

nîmihito– *VAI* dance with one another, dance

nîmihitowin– *NI* dance

nîpawi– *VAI* stand, stand up, stand erect, stand fast

nîpawistamaw– *VTA* stand up for s.o., be a witness (*e.g.,* at wedding) for s.o.

nîpâ-ayamihâ– *VAI* celebrate midnight mass (at Christmas)

nîpêpi– *VAI* sit up with someone dead or dying; hold a wake

nîpin– *VII* be summer

nîpisiy– *NI* willow, willow bush

nîpisîhkopâw– *NI* stand of willows, willow-patch

nîpisîhtakw– *NI* willow piece, willow trunk

nîpisîs– *NI* willow branch, willow switch; little willow [*diminutive*]

nîsi– *VAI* be two in number

nîso *IPC* two

nîsôhkamâto– *VAI* work together at (it/him) as two

nîsta *PR* I, too; I by contrast

nîstanân *PR* we (excl.), too; we (excl.) by contrast

nîsw-âskiy *IPC* two years

nîsw-âyamihêwi-kîsikâw *IPC* two weeks

nîswahpiso– *VAI* be harnessed as two, be a team of two

nîswahpit– *VTI* tie s.t. together as two (*e.g.,* bones)

nîswapi– *VAI* sit as two, be situated as two, come together as two [*]

nîswâw *IPC* twice [*]

nowâhc *IPC* ?better, ?more properly [*?sic; ?*nowâc; *both record and gloss highly tentative*]

nôcih– *VTA* pursue s.o., hunt s.o.

nôcihcikê– *VAI* trap things

nôcihcikêwaskiy– *NI* trapping territory, trapline

nôcihtâ– *VAI* pursue (it), work at (it)

nôcikinosêwê– *VAI* be engaged in fishing

nôcisipê– *VAI* be engaged in duck-hunting

nôcokwêsiw– *NA* old woman, old lady [*diminutive; also* nôtokwêsiw–]

nôh– *VTA* suckle s.o., nurse s.o.

nôhtê *IPV* want to, desire to

nôhtêhkatê– *VAI* be hungry, want food
nôhtêpayi– *VAI* run short, be in want
nôhtêsin– *VAI* be played out
nôkohtâ– *VAI* let (it) appear, show (it)
nôkosi– *VAI* be visible; be born
nôni– *VAI* suck at the breast, be nursed
nôtin– *VTA* fight s.o., fight with s.o.
nôtin– *VTI* fight s.t., fight with s.t.
nôtinikê– *VAI* fight people, put up a fight; take part in war
      (*e.g.,* World War II)
nôtinitowin– *NI* fighting
nôtokwêsiw– *NA* old woman, old lady [*sic; cf.* nôcokwêsiw–]
ocawâsimisi– *VAI* have a child, have (her/him) as child [*diminutive*]
ocêpihk– *NI* root
ocêpihkis– *NI* little root [*diminutive*]
ocihkwanapi– *VAI* kneel
ocîhkwêhikan– *NI* pleated moccasin
ohci *IPC* thence, from there
ohci *IPV* thence, from there; [*in negative clause:*] past
ohcipayin– *VII* come from there, result from that
ohcitaw *IPC* purposely; it has to be [*predicative*]
ohcî– *VAI* come from there, be from there
ohpahowi-pîsimw– *NA* the month of August
ohpiki– *VAI* grow up
ohpikih– *VTA* raise s.o.
ohpikihtamâso– *VAI* make (it) grow for oneself
ohpikihtâ– *VAI* make (it) grow
ohpikin– *VII* grow
ohpimê *IPC* off to the side, elsewhere
ohtâciho– *VAI* make one's living from there
ohtin– *VTI* take s.t. from there, obtain s.t. from there
ohtinikê– *VAI* take things from there, obtain things from there
ohtohtê– *VAI* come walking from there
okâwîmâw– *NA* mother
okikocêsîs– *NA* [*man's name:*] Hooked-Nose [*?sic; gloss highly tentative*]
okimâhkân– *NA* chief, elected chief
okimâhkâniwi– *VAI* be chief, serve as elected chief
okimâhkâniwin– *NI* chieftaincy
okimâw– *NA* chief, leader, boss; Band Council [*e.g.,* okimânâhk
      'Band Council, band authorities']
okiskinohamâkêw– *NA* teacher
okistikânikamiko– *VAI* have a granary
okistikêwiyinîwi– *VAI* be a farmer, be engaged in agriculture

okistikêwiyinîwiwin– *NI* farming, farm-work

omâw– *NA* "bible", manyplies, omasum (*i.e.*, third stomach of ruminant)

omihtimi– *VAI* have one's firewood, have (it) as one's firewood

omisi– *VAI* have an older sister, have (her) as older sister

omisimâw– *NA* oldest sister

onâcowêsis– *NA* [*personal name*] [*?cf.* the name sometimes rendered
    Natuasis]

onâpêmi– *VAI* have a husband, be married (woman)

onihcikiskwapiwinihk *INM* [*place-name:*] Saddle Lake, Alberta [*locative;
    ?literally* at the place of the indistinct dark figure]

onîkihikomâw– *NA* parent

os– *VTI* boil s.t.

osâm *IPC* too much; because

oscikwânis– *NA* [*woman's name:*] Little-Head

osikwânâs– *VTI* smoke-dry s.t.

osikwânâstê– *VII* be smoke-dried

osîh– *VTA* make s.o., prepare s.o. (*e.g.*, bread)

osîhcikâtê– *VII* be made, be prepared

osîhcikêwin– *NI* what is made, handiwork, product

osîhtamaw– *VTA* make (it/him) for s.o.

osîhtamâso– *VAI* make (it/him) for oneself

osîhtâ– *VAI* make (it), prepare (it)

osîmimâw– *NA* youngest sibling

osîmimâwi– *VAI* be the youngest sibling

osîmisi– *VAI* have a younger sibling, have (him/her) as younger sibling

osk-ây– *NA* young person [*e.g.*, osk-âyak]

osk-âyiwi– *VAI* be young

oskani-pimiy– *NI* bone-marrow

oskaskosîwinâkwan– *VII* look green, have a green appearance

oskawâsis– *NA* young child, infant

oskayisiyiniw– *NA* young person [*sic:* -a-]

oskâtâskw– *NI* carrot

oski *IPN* young, fresh, new

oskinîki– *VAI* be a young man

oskinîkiskwêw– *NA* young woman

oskinîkiskwêwi– *VAI* be a young woman

oskinîkiw– *NA* young man

oskinîkîwiyinîsiwi– *VAI* be a young man

ostêsimâw– *NA* oldest brother

otakisîhkân– *NI* sausage

otamiskay– *NI* hide-scrapings (meat scraped from hide)

otamiyo– *VAI* busy oneself, keep busy, be preoccupied

otatâwêw– *NA* store-keeper, store-manager

otatâwêwi– *vai* be the store-keeper, be the store-manager

otayamihâw– *na* Christian, adherent of Christianity

otâhkosiw– *na* sick person

otâkosin– *vii* be evening

otânisi– *vai* have a daughter, have (her) as daughter

otâpânâskw– *na* wagon, automobile

otêhiminâni-cêpihk– *ni* strawberry root [*sic; cf.* ocêpihk–]

oti *ipc* [*emphatic enclitic*]

otiht– *vti* reach s.t.

otin– *vta* take s.o., steal s.o.

otin– *vti* take s.t., steal s.t.

otinikowisi– *vai* be taken by the powers

otinito– *vai* take one another; marry each other

otisâpaht– *vti* have lived long enough to see s.t.

otitâmiyaw– *ni* innards [*]

otôtêmi– *vai* have a kinsman or friend, have (her/him) as kinsman
　　　　or friend

owâwi– *vai* lay eggs

owîcêwâkani– *vai* have a companion or partner, have (her/him) as
　　　　companion or partner

owîhowini– *vai* have a name, have (it) as one's name

owîki– *vai* live there, have one's home there [*sic; cf.* wîki–]

owîtisâni– *vai* have a sibling, have (her/him) as sibling [*sic:* o-]

ôh *ipv* from there; [*in negative clause:*] past

ôma *ipc* it is this; the fact that [*predicative*]

ômatowihk *ipc* in this place

ômayikohk *ipc* this much, to this degree, to this extent

ômisi *ipc* thus

ôta *ipc* here

ôtê *ipc* over there

ôtênaw– *ni* town, settlement

ôyâ *pr* that one no longer here [*absentative, e.g.,* ôyâ]

paci *ipv* wrongly, in error

paci-tôtaw– *vta* wrong s.o.

paciyawêh– *vta* wrong s.o. by one's utterance, provoke s.o.'s anger

pahkêkinohkê– *vai* make dressed hides, make leather

pahkêkinos– *ni* small dressed hide, small piece of leather [*diminutive*]

pahkêkinw– *ni* dressed hide, finished hide, leather

pahkêkinwêsâkay– *ni* leather coat, leather jacket

pahkikawin– *vti* let s.t. drip

pahkisin– *vai* fall

pahkopê– *vai* walk into water

pahkwaciwêpah– *vti* knock s.t. off, pry s.t. off (*e.g.*, hide-scrapings)

pahkwatah– *VTI* knock s.t. off (*e.g.*, hide-scrapings)

pahkwatin– *VTI* take s.t. off by hand (*e.g.,* caked dirt from laundry)

pahkwêsikan– *NA* bannock, bread; flour

pahkwêsikaniwat– *NI* flour-bag

pahpahâhkwân– *NA* domestic chicken

pahpakwaciho– *VAI* amuse oneself

pahpawiwêpin– *VTI* shake s.t. out

pakahkam *IPC* I believe

pakamahw– *VTA* strike s.o., hit s.o.

pakâhtâ– *VAI* boil (it) in water

pakâsimonah– *VTA* immerse s.o., bathe s.o.

pakâsimonahâwaso– *VAI* immerse one's children, bathe one's children

pakitin– *VTA* let s.o. go, release s.o.; permit (it) to s.o.

pakitin– *VTI* let s.t. go, release s.t., give s.t. up; put s.t. in
        (*e.g.,* seed potatoes)

pakitinikowisi– *VAI* be permitted by the powers

pakwât– *VTA* hate s.o., disapprove of s.o.

pakwât– *VTI* hate s.t., disapprove of s.t.

pamih– *VTA* tend to s.o., look after s.o.

pamihiso– *VAI* tend oneself, look after oneself

pamihtamaw– *VTA* tend to (it/him) for s.o., look after (it/him) for s.o.

pamihtamâso– *VAI* tend to (it/him) for or by oneself, look after (it/him) for
        or by oneself

pamin– *VTA* tend to s.o., look after s.o.

pamin– *VTI* tend to s.t., look after s.t.

paminiso– *VAI* tend to oneself, look after oneself

paminiwê– *VAI* tend to people, look after people

papakiwayân– *NI* shirt

papakiwayânêkinw– *NI* thin cloth, cotton; canvas

papâmi *IPV* about, around, here and there

papâmipici– *VAI* move about, camp here and there

papâmohtah– *VTA* take s.o. about, take s.o. here and there

papâmohtatâ– *VAI* take (it) about, take (it) here and there

papâmohtê– *VAI* walk about, go here and there

pasastêhw– *VTA* whip s.o.

paskêwihito– *VAI* leave one another; separate, divorce

paskin– *VTA* break s.o. off (*e.g.,* thread)

paspaskiw– *NA* partridge

paswêskôyo– *VAI* get sick from eating excessively fatty food

paswêyâ– *VII* be excessively fatty

patinikê– *VAI* make a mistake, take a wrong step, transgress; [*Christian:*] sin

pawâmiwin– *NI* spirit power; [*Christian:*] witchcraft

pawin– *VTI* shake s.t. out

payipis– *VTI* cut s.t. out, cut a hole in s.t.

pâh-pahki *IPC* part of this, part of that; here and there [*reduplicated*]

pâh-pêyak *IPC* one each [*reduplicated*]

pâh-pîtos *IPC* each differently [*reduplicated*]

pâhkohkwêhon– *NI* towel

pâhkohkwêhonis– *NI* small towel [*diminutive*]

pâhkopayi– *VAI* get dry, dry out

pâhpi– *VAI* laugh

pâhpih– *VTA* laugh at s.o.

pânis– *VTI* cut s.t. (*e.g.*, meat) into sheets

pânisâwê– *VAI* cut meat into sheets

pânisw– *VTA* cut s.o. (*e.g.*, animal) into sheets

pâs– *VTI* dry s.t.

pâskac *IPC* to top it all

pâstatah– *VTI* break s.t. (*e.g.*, bones) by tool

pâstâho– *VAI* breach the natural order, transgress; [*Christian:*] sin,
  be a sinner

pâstê– *VII* be dry

pâsw– *VTA* dry s.o.

pê *IPV* hither

pêci-nâway *IPC* from back then; down from the distant past

pêho– *VAI* wait

pêht– *VTI* hear s.t.

pêhtamowin– *NI* what is heard

pêhtaw– *VTA* hear s.o.

pêhtâkwan– *VII* be heard

pêsiw– *VTA* bring s.o. hither

pêtâ– *VAI* bring (it) hither

pêyak *IPC* one; alone, single

pêyako– *VAI* be alone, be the only one

pêyakosâp *IPC* eleven

pêyakw-ây– *NA* a single one (*e.g.*, stocking); one pair [*e.g.*, pêyakw-âyak]

pêyakwan *IPC* the same

pêyakwâw *IPC* once

pihêw– *NA* prairie-chicken

pihkoho– *VAI* free oneself, escape; [*Christian:*] be saved

pihkw– *NI* ash [*e.g.*, pihko]

pihkwâpoy– *NI* lye

piko *IPC* only [*enclitic*]

piko *IPC* must, have to [*clause-initial predicative*]

pikoyikohk *IPC* no matter how much, to any extent

pikw âwiyak *IPC* anyone, everyone

pikw îta *IPC* in any place, everywhere

pimâcih– *VTA* make s.o. live, give life to s.o.; make a living for s.o., sustain s.o.

pimâcihiso– *VAI* make oneself live; make a living for oneself

pimâciho– *VAI* make a life for oneself, live

pimâcihowin– *NI* way of life; livelihood

pimâtisi– *VAI* live, be alive

pimâtisiwin– *NI* life

pimâtisîtot– *VTI* live one's life; live one's life by s.t.

pimi *IPV* along, in a linear fashion

piminawaso– *VAI* cook, do the cooking

piminawasowikamikw– *NI* cookhouse, kitchen

piminawat– *VTA* cook for s.o.

pimipayin– *VII* work, function; go on

pimisin– *VAI* lie extended

pimitisah– *VTI* follow s.t.

pimitisahikê– *VAI* follow people, tag along, be a follower

pimiy– *NI* fat, oil; crude petroleum

pimohtatâ– *VAI* carry (it) along, travel with (it)

pimohtê– *VAI* go along, walk along

pinkow– *NI* bingo

pipon– *VII* be winter

piscipo– *VAI* be poisoned

piscipohtâ– *VAI* poison (it)

piscipôskaw– *VTA* poison s.o.

pisiskiw– *NA* animal; domestic animal

piskihcikwât– *VTI* sew an extension on s.t.

pita *IPC* first, for a while

piyisk *IPC* finally, at last

pîhc-âyihk *IPC* inside

pîhtawêkwât– *VTI* sew s.t. as lining into a garment; sew s.t. in between covers, sew covers on s.t.

pîhtawêsâkân– *NI* slip, undergarment

pîhtawêwayiwinis– *NI* underclothes, underwear

pîhtikwê-âwacimihtêwin– *NI* hauling firewood inside [*; *sic:* -i-; *cf.* pîhtokwê–]

pîhtokwah– *VTA* take s.o. inside

pîhtokwatamâkê– *VAI* bring (it/him) inside for people

pîhtokwatâ– *VAI* bring (it) inside

pîhtokwê– *VAI* enter, go inside

pîhtokwêyâmo– *VAI* flee inside

pîhtwâwin– *NI* smoking; [*Christian:*] cannabis abuse

pîkinis– *VTI* cut s.t. into small pieces

pîkiskwât– *VTA* speak to s.o.

pîkiskwê– *VAI* speak

pîkiskwêh– *VTA* make s.o. speak, get s.o. to speak

pîkiskwêstamaw– *VTA* speak for s.o., speak on s.o.'s behalf

pîkiskwêwin– *NI* what is being said, speech; word; voice

pîkokonêwêpayi– *VAI* have cracks in one's mouth, have one's mouth break out in blisters (*e.g.,* from thrush)

pîkopayi– *VAI* break down, be broken; go broke, go bankrupt

pîkopayin– *VII* break down, be broken

pîkopicikâtê– *VII* be ploughed soil, be cultivated

pîkopicikê– *VAI* plough, do the ploughing

pîkopicikêh– *VTA* make s.o. plough, use s.o. (*e.g.,* oxen) in ploughing

pîkopit– *VTI* break s.t. (*e.g.,* soil), plough s.t. (*e.g.,* field)

pîkopitamaw– *VTA* break (it) for s.o., plough (it) for s.o.

pîminahkwânis– *NI* string [*diminutive*]

pîtos *IPC* strange, different

pîwaniyôtin– *VII* be a blizzard

pîwâpiskw– *NI* metal, metal object; steel blade

pîwêwêpin– *VTI* scatter s.t., sprinkle in a pinch of s.t.

pîwêyâwahkwâ– *VII* be powdery

pîwêyimo– *VAI* think little of oneself, have low self-esteem; [*Christian:*] be humble

pîwi-kiscikânis– *NA* garden seeds [*diminutive*]

pîwi-kiscikânis– *NI* vegetable garden [*diminutive*]

pîwihtakahikan– *NI* wood-chips

postayiwinisah– *VTA* clothe s.o., make clothes for s.o.

postayiwinisahiso– *VAI* clothe oneself, make clothes for oneself

postayiwinisê– *VAI* put clothes on, get dressed

pômê– *VAI* be discouraged; give up

pômêh– *VTA* make s.o. discouraged, disappoint s.o.

pôn– *VTI* build a fire; make a fire with s.t.

pônêyihtamaw– *VTA* forgive s.o.

pônêyihtamâto– *VAI* forgive one another

pôni *IPV* cease, stop

pôni-pimâtisi– *VAI* cease to be alive, be dead

pônihtâ– *VAI* cease of (it)

pôsi– *VAI* board a conveyance

pôsih– *VTA* make s.o. board a conveyance, give s.o. a ride

pôsihtâ– *VAI* put (it) on a conveyance, load (it) on

pôsiwin– *NA* train

pôyo– *VAI* cease, quit [*]

pwâtawihtâ– *VAI* be thwarted at (it), fail of (it)

sakâpât– *VTI* attach s.t. by sewing, sew s.t. on

sakâw– *NI* bush, woodland

sakâwi-pihêw– NA wood-cock, wood-partridge, wood-chicken

sasîhciwih– VTA make s.o. ashamed, embarrass s.o.

sasîwiskwêw– NA Sarci woman

saskah– VTI light s.t. (*e.g.,* lamp)

sawêyim– VTA be generous towards s.o., bless s.o.

sawêyimikowisi– VAI be blessed by the powers

sâkamon– VII stick out, project

sâkaskinahtâ– VAI make (it) full, fill (it)

sâkâstênohk IPC in the east

sâkêkamon– VII stick out as cloth, project as cloth

sâkih– VTA love s.o., be attached to s.o.

sâkihito– VAI love one another

sâkihitowin– NI mutual love, charity

sâkihtâ– VAI love (it), be attached to (it)

sâkôcih– VTA overcome s.o., beat s.o.

sâkôhtâ– VAI overcome (it), accomplish (it); be able to lift (it) up

sâpopatâ– VAI get (it) thoroughly wet

sâpoyowê– VII have the wind blowing through

sâsâkihti– VAI be barefoot

sêkopayin– VII run beneath, go underneath, get caught underneath

sêkwâpiskin– VTI put s.t. under the coals, into the oven

sêmâk IPC right away, immediately

sêsâwipayi– VAI stretch, become stretched

sêstakw– NA yarn, thread

sikos– VTI chop s.t. small

sikwahcisikê– VAI cultivate, harrow

simacî– VAI stand upright; rear up (*e.g.,* horse)

simâkanisihkâniwi– VAI be a soldier; take part in war
(*e.g.,* World War II)

sinikohtakahikan– NI scrub-brush, floor brush, brush for wood

sinikohtakinikan– NI scrubber, brush; wash-board

sipwê IPV departing, leaving, starting off

sipwêhtê– VAI leave, depart

sipwêpayin– VII start off to run (*e.g.,* tape-recorder) [*]

sipwêpici– VAI leave with one's camp

sisikotêyiht– VTI be surprised, be shocked

sisoskiwakin– VTI mud s.t. (*e.g.,* log-house), plaster s.t.

sisoskiwakinamâso– VAI do the mudding for oneself

sisoskiwakinikâtê– VII be mudded

sisoskiwakinikê– VAI do the mudding

siswêwêpin– VTI sprinkle s.t. about (*e.g.,* ashes in cleaning)

sîhkim– VTA urge s.o. by speech

sîhkiskaw– VTA urge s.o. bodily

sîkin– *VTI* pour s.t.

sîkipicikê– *VAI* spill things

sîkiwêpin– *VTI* pour s.t. out

sîn– *VTI* wring s.t. out

sînâskwah– *VTI* wring s.t. out with a wooden tool

sîpah– *VTI* stretch s.t.

sîpâ *IPV* beneath, underneath

sîpihkêyiht– *VTI* endure s.t. by strength of mind; persevere

sîsîp– *NA* duck

sîsîpipîway– *NI* duck feathers, duck-down

sîskêpison– *NI* garters

sîtawâ– *VII* be stiff

sôhkêhtatâ– *VAI* throw (it) hard, throw (it) forcefully

sôniyâhkât– *VTI* make money at s.t.

sôniyâhkê– *VAI* make money; earn wages

sôniyâw– *NA* money; wages

sôniyâwi *IPC* with respect to money, in financial matters

sôskwâc *IPC* simply, immediately, without further ado

taciwih– *VTA* get ahead of s.o.

tahk âyiwâk *IPC* increasingly, more and more

tahkâ– *VII* be cold

tahkikamâpoy– *NI* cold water

tahkon– *VTA* carry s.o.

tahkon– *VTI* carry s.t.

tahkopit– *VTI* tie s.t. fast

tahto *IPC* so many, as many

tahto-aya *IPC* so many [*sic*: -o-]

tahto-kîsikâw *IPC* every day, daily

tahtw-âskiy *IPC* so many years, as many years

tahtw-âyamihêwi-kîsikâw *IPC* every Sunday

tahtwâw *IPC* so many times

takahkêyim– *VTA* consider s.o. nice, like s.o.

takahkihtâkwan– *VII* sound nice

takahkisîhtâ– *VAI* make (it) nice

takohtê– *VAI* arrive walking

takwah– *VTI* crush s.t.

takwahiminân– *NI* chokecherries

takwastâ– *VAI* add (it) in

takwâkin– *VII* be fall, be autumn

takwâpôyo– *VAI* arrive by rail, arrive by train

tasôh– *VTA* trap s.o. under something, catch s.o. in a trap

tastawayas *IPC* in between, in the middle

tatâyawâ– *VII* be crowded

tawâ– *VII* be open, have room

tânêhki *IPC* why

tâni *PR* which one [*interrogative; e.g.,* tânihi; tânima]

tânimayikohk *IPC* to which extent

tânisi *IPC* how

tânitahto *IPC* how many; so many

tânitahto-pîsim *IPC* how many months; what month is it [*predicative*]; so many months

tânitahtwâw *IPC* how many times; so many times

tânitê *IPC* where over there

tâpapîstamaw– *VTA* sit in s.o.'s place, succeed s.o. in office

tâpisikopayi– *VAI* get caught in something

tâpiskôc *IPC* as if, seemingly, apparently

tâpitawi *IPC* all the time

tâpitonêhpicikan– *NI* bridle

tâpwê *IPC* truly, indeed

tâpwêht– *VTI* agree with s.t., believe s.t.

tâpwêhtaw– *VTA* agree with s.o., believe s.o.

tâpwêwakêyiht– *VTI* hold s.t. to be true, believe in s.t.

tâsawisâwât– *VTI* cut into the middle of s.t., slice s.t. open (*e.g.,* veal belly cordon-bleu)

tâsipwâw *IPC* as a matter of fact

tâwin– *VTI* encounter s.t., bump into s.t.

têhtapi– *VAI* be mounted, be on horseback

têhtapîwitâs– *NA* riding breeches

têpakiht– *VTI* count s.t. up

têpakohp-askiy *IPC* seven years

têpakohposâp *IPC* seventeen

têpêyimo– *VAI* be content, be willing

têpiyâhk *IPC* merely; barely; so long as

têpwât– *VTA* call out to s.o., yell at s.o.

têtipêwêyâmo– *VAI* flee around in a circle

tipah– *VTI* measure s.t.

tipahamaw– *VTA* pay s.o. for (it/him), repay a debt to s.o.; pay s.o. a pension

tipahaskân– *NI* reserve

tipêyiht– *VTI* own s.t., control s.t.

tipêyim– *VTA* own s.o., control s.o.

tipiskâ– *VII* be night

tipiyaw *IPC* personally, really

titipihtin– *VII* be rolled up, be twisted

titipikwanah– *VTI* sew s.t. in overcast stitch (*e.g.,* the spiral loops around the vamp of a moccasin)

titipin– *VTI* roll s.t. up

tôcikâtê– *VII* be done

tôhtôsâpoy– *NI* milk

tômâ– *VII* be greased, be greasy

tôt– *VTI* do s.t. [*cf.* itôt–]

tôtamaw– *VTA* do (it) for s.o.

tôtamâso– *VAI* do (it) for oneself

tôtamôh– *VTA* make s.o. do (it)

tôtaw– *VTA* do (it) to s.o., treat s.o. so

tôtâso– *VAI* do (it) to oneself

wacaskw– *NA* muskrat

wanêyiht– *VTI* have one's mind blurred, be confused

wani *IPV* indistinctly, blurred

wani-tipiskâ– *VII* be dark night

wanih– *VTA* lose s.o.

wanihikê– *VAI* set traps

wanihtâ– *VAI* lose (it)

wanikiskisi– *VAI* forget (it), be forgetful

wanwêhkaw– *VTA* confuse s.o.

waskawîstamâso– *VAI* work for oneself, be enterprising

waskawîwin– *NI* being active, enterprise

waskic *IPC* on top, on the surface

waskitasâkay– *NI* overcoat

waskitaskamik *IPC* on the face of the earth

wawânêyiht– *VTI* worry about s.t., be worried

wawêyîst– *VTI* prepare s.t., be prepared

wayawî– *VAI* go outside; go to relieve oneself; leave school, leave hospital

wayawîpahtâ– *VAI* run outside

wayawîpakitin– *VTA* put s.o. (*e.g.*, diapers) down outside

wayawîstamâso– *VAI* go outside for oneself, go to relieve oneself

wayawîtimihk *IPC* outside

wayawîwin– *NI* going outside, going to the toilet [*]

wâhkêyêyiht– *VTI* be easily swayed; [*Christian:*] be too weak

wâhkôm– *VTA* be related to s.o.

wâhyaw *IPC* far

wâhyawês *IPC* quite far [*cf.* wâhyawîs]

wâhyawîs *IPC* quite far [*cf.* wâhyawês]

wânaskêwin– *NI* being at peace with oneself

wâpaht– *VTI* see s.t.

wâpahtih– *VTA* make s.o. see (it), show (it) to s.o.

wâpam– *VTA* see s.o.

wâpanohtêw *INM* [*woman's name:*] Walks-til-Dawn [*?sic; gloss tentative, cf.* Walks-at-Dawn, Comes-Back-at-Dawn]

wâpatonisk– *NA* white clay [*?sic* NA]

wâpikwaniy– *NI* flower

wâpiskah– *VTI* whitewash s.t.

wâpiskahikê– *VAI* do the whitewashing

wâpiskâ– *VII* be white

wâpiskihtakâ– *VII* be white boards, be white floor

wâpiwin– *NI* eye-sight

wâposw– *NA* rabbit

wâposwayân– *NA* rabbitskin

wâposwayânakohp– *NI* rabbitskin blanket

wâsakâm *IPC* around, in a circuit

wâsaskocêpayîs– *NI* lamp, electric light [*diminutive*]

wâsaskotê– *VII* be light, be lit; be a lantern

wâsaskotênikan– *NI* light, lamp, lantern

wâsaskotênikâkê– *VAI* light things with (it), use (it) to have light

wâsaskotênikê– *VAI* light things, have light

wâskahikan– *NI* house

wâskahikanis– *NI* little house [*diminutive*]

wâskamisî– *VAI* settle down; be of quiet disposition

wâskân– *VTI* make s.t. go around, turn s.t. (*e.g.*, treadle), crank s.t.

wâtihkân– *NI* hole, cellar

wâwâc *IPC* especially, even

wâwiyêyâ– *VAI* be round

wâwîs cî *IPC* especially

wâwîs *IPC* especially [*]

wêhcasin– *VII* be easy

wêhcih– *VTA* have an easy time with s.o. (*e.g.*, hide)

wêhtisi– *VAI* have it easy

wêpahikê– *VAI* sweep things, do the sweeping

wêpin– *VTA* throw s.o. away; abandon s.o. (*e.g.*, child)

wêpin– *VTI* throw s.t. away

wêtinahk *IPC* quietly

wêwêkapi– *VAI* sit wrapped up, sit bundled up

wiya *IPC* for, because [*clause-initial causal conjunction*]

wiya *IPC* by contrast [*enclitic*]

wiya *PR* he, she

wiyahpicikê– *VAI* do the harnessing

wiyakâc *IPC* it is regrettable [*predicative*]

wiyasiwât– *VTA* decide about s.o.; sit in judgment on s.o., hold court over s.o.

wiyasiwât– *VTI* decide s.t.

wiyasiwêhkâniwi– *VAI* be a band councillor

wiyawâw *PR* they

wiyâkan– *NI* dish, vessel

wiyâkanis– *NI* small dish, small bowl [*diminutive*]

wiyâs– NI meat

wiyino– VII be fat

wiyinw– NI fat, animal fat

wiyis– VTI cut s.t. out, cut s.t. to a pattern

wiyisamaw– VTA cut a pattern for s.o.

wiyisamâso– VAI cut a pattern for oneself, cut one's own pattern

wiyipâ– VII be soiled, be dirty

wî IPV intend to

wîc-âyamihâm– VTA pray with s.o.

wîc-âyâm– VTA live with s.o.

wîc-îspîhcisîm– VTA be of the same age as s.o., have s.o. as one's age-mate

wîc-ôhpikîm– VTA grow up with s.o., be raised together with s.o.

wîcêht– VTI go along with s.t., cooperate with s.t.

wîcêhto– VAI live with one another

wîcêw– VTA accompany s.o., live with s.o.

wîci-kiskinohamâkosîm– VTA be in school with s.o., have s.o. as a fellow-student

wîcih– VTA help s.o.

wîcihikowisi– VAI be helped by the powers

wîcihiso– VAI help oneself

wîcihito– VAI help one another, cooperate with one another

wîcihiwê– VAI join in, participate, be part of something

wîcihtâso– VAI help with things

wîh– VTA name s.o., mention s.o. by name

wîhcêkaskosiy– NI onion

wîhcêkaskosîwi-sâkahikanihk INM [*place-name:*] Onion Lake, Saskatchewan [*locative; literally* at Onion Lake]

wîhkasin– VII taste good

wîhkâc IPC ever

wîhkist– VTI like the taste of s.t.

wîhkô– VAI strain oneself, use all one's force

wîhkwêhtakâw– NI corner made by wooden walls

wîhowin– NI name

wîht– VTI name s.t., mention s.t. by name

wîhtamaw– VTA tell s.o. about (it/him)

wîhtamâto– VAI tell one another about (it/him)

wîki– VAI live there, have one's home there [*also* owîki–]

wîkihto– VAI live with each other, be married

wîkihtowin– NI living together, matrimony

wîkim– VTA live with s.o., be married to s.o.

wîkiwin– NI household; [*Christian:*] home

wîn– NI bone-marrow [*e.g.*, wîni]

wînâstakay– NI "tripe", paunch (*i.e.*, largest stomach of ruminant)

wîpac *IPC* soon, early

wîpayiwinis– *NI* dirty clothes

wîpâcikin– *VII* grow out of place, grow wild, grow as weeds

wîpâtayiwinis– *NI* dirty clothes

wîsakitêhê– *VAI* have a heavy heart

wîsakîmin– *NI* cranberry

wîsâm– *VTA* ask s.o. along, take s.o. along

wîsta *PR* he, too; she, too; he by contrast, she by contrast

wîstawâw *PR* they, too; they by contrast

wîtapim– *VTA* sit with s.o.

wîtokwêm– *VTA* share a dwelling with s.o., live with s.o.

yahkâtihkât– *VTI* dig out more of a hole or cellar, push out the size of an existing hole or cellar

yâhkasin– *VII* be light in weight

yâyikâskocin– *VAI* tear one's clothes on wood (*e.g.*, in bush)

yêyih– *VTA* get s.o. excited by one's action, tempt s.o. by one's action

yîkatêhtê– *VAI* walk off to the side; [*Christian:*] walk away

yîkatêpayin– *VII* move off to the side, move sideways (*e.g.*, braided strips of rabbitskin)

yîkatêstaw– *VTA* go off to the side from s.o., go away from s.o.

yîkinikan– *NA* milk-cow

yîkinikê– *VAI* do the milking

yîkinikêstamâso– *VAI* do the milking for oneself

yîwêyâskocin– *VAI* tear one's clothes ragged on wood (*e.g.*, in bush)

yôhtên– *VTI* open s.t.

yôskâ– *VII* be soft

yôskipotâ– *VAI* soften (it) by scraping (*e.g.*, hide)

English Index to the Glossary

This is a *selective* index of the English glosses that correspond to each Cree stem. As a rough guide to the entries in the glossary, it should not be confused with the English-Cree part of a bilingual dictionary.

It often takes several English words or phrases to capture the meaning of a single Cree stem, *e.g.,*

> **itakiso–** VAI be counted thus, cost so much; be held in such esteem.

In its literal sense, this stem appears under COUNT and COST (while no effort has been made to include stems of this type under headwords like THUS, SO, SUCH); in its transferred sense, it is indexed under ESTEEM. A single Cree stem may give rise to several entries in the English index.

Conversely, the entries listed under a single headword are arranged simply in alphabetical order; no attempt has been made to group them semantically (*e.g.,* 'hide oneself' versus 'dressed hide' under HIDE) or syntactically (*e.g.,* 'anger s.o.' versus 'scold s.o. in anger' under ANGER).

Although the headwords themselves may be ambiguous, the individual entries which are listed under them are fully identified by stem, stem-class code and an explicit gloss. The distinction between headword and cited entry emphasises the fact that this is not a dictionary but merely an index.

ABANDON
wêpin– *VTA* throw s.o. away; abandon s.o. (*e.g.,* child)

ABDOMINAL
–askatay– *NDI* abdominal wall, belly (of animal) [*e.g.,* waskatay]

ABILITY
kaskihtâwin– *NI* ability to do (it), competence

ABLE
kaskiho– *VAI* be able, be competent
kaskihtâ– *VAI* be able to do (it)

ABODE
âhc-âyâ– *VAI* move one's abode, move from one place to another
ihtâwin– *NI* abode, place of residence

ABOUT
papâmi *IPV* about, around, here and there
papâmipici– *VAI* move about, camp here and there
papâmohtah– *VTA* take s.o. about, take s.o. here and there
papâmohtatâ– *VAI* take (it) about, take (it) here and there
papâmohtê– *VAI* walk about, go here and there

ACCOMPANY
wîcêw– *VTA* accompany s.o., live with s.o.

ACCOMPLISH
sâkôhtâ– *VAI* overcome (it), accomplish (it); be able to lift (it) up

ACCUSTOMED
nakayâh– *VTA* get s.o. accustomed to something, break s.o. (*e.g.,* horse)
nakayâsk– *VTI* be accustomed to s.t., be comfortable with s.t.
nakayâskaw– *VTA* be accustomed to s.o., be comfortable with s.o., be familiar with s.o.

ACROSS
akâmaskîhk *IPC* across the water, overseas

ACT
itâtisi– *VAI* act thus, be of such a disposition
itôt– *VTI* do thus, act thus [*cf.* tôt–]
itôtamôh– *VTA* make s.o. act thus

ACTIVE
waskawîwin– *NI* being active, enterprise

ACTIVITIES
isîhcikêwin– *NI* what is thus done, such activities

ADD
akohtitâ– *VAI* put (it) in water, add (it) to water (*e.g.,* boric acid)
kikin– *VTI* put s.t. on something, add s.t. in (*e.g.,* baking-powder)
takwastâ– *VAI* add (it) in

ADDRESS
kitot– *VTA* speak to s.o., address s.o.

ADVISE AGAINST
kitahamaw– *VTA* advise s.o. against (it/him)

AFLAME
kwâhkotênikê– *VAI* start a fire, set things aflame

AGAIN
kâh-kîhtwâm *IPC* again and again [*reduplicated*]
kâwi *IPC* again
kîhtwâm *IPC* again
mîna *IPC* also, again

AGE
ihtahtopiponwêwin– *NI* having so many years, the number of one's years, one's age [*sic:* iht-; *cf.* itahtopiponwê–]
ispîhtisî– *VAI* extend thus, be of such age
wîc-îspîhcisîm– *VTA* be of the same age as s.o., have s.o. as one's age-mate

AGREE
tâpwêht– *VTI* agree with s.t., believe s.t.
tâpwêhtaw– *VTA* agree with s.o., believe s.o.

AH
aya *IPC* ah, well [*hesitatory; cf.* ayahk, ayi]

AHEAD
taciwih– *VTA* get ahead of s.o.

ALCOHOL
minihkwê– *VAI* drink (it), have a drink; drink, abuse alcohol
minihkwêski– *VAI* habitually abuse alcohol, be an alcoholic
minihkwêwin– *NI* drinking, alcohol abuse

ALIVE
pimâtisi– *VAI* live, be alive

ALL
kahkiyaw *IPC* every, all
misakâmê *IPC* all the way
misiwê *IPC* all over
nanâtohkôskân *IPC* all kinds of things
tâpitawi *IPC* all the time

ALMOST
kêkâc *IPC* almost

ALONE
pêyak *IPC* one; alone, single
pêyako– *VAI* be alone, be the only one

ALONG

pimi *IPV* along, in a linear fashion

pimohtatâ– *VAI* carry (it) along, travel with (it)

pimohtê– *VAI* go along, walk along

wîcêht– *VTI* go along with s.t., cooperate with s.t.

wîsâm– *VTA* ask s.o. along, take s.o. along

ALREADY

âsay *IPC* already

ALSO

mîna *IPC* also, again

ALTHOUGH

âta *IPC* although

ALWAYS

kâkikê *IPC* always, forever

AMUSE

pahpakwaciho– *VAI* amuse oneself

AND

êkwa *IPC* then; and

ANGER, ANGRY

itâspinêm– *VTA* call s.o. thus in anger, angrily call s.o. such a name, thus scold s.o. in anger

kisiwâh– *VTA* anger s.o., make s.o. angry

kisiwiyo– *VAI* complain about work, be angry about one's work

kisîkitot– *VTA* speak to s.o. in anger [*sic:* -î-]

kisîm– *VTA* anger s.o. by speech

kisîstaw– *VTA* be angry with s.o., stay angry with s.o.

paciyawêh– *VTA* wrong s.o. by one's utterance, provoke s.o.'s anger

ANIMAL

pisiskiw– *NA* animal; domestic animal

ANOTHER

kotak *PR* other, another [*e.g.,* kotakak, kotaka]

ANY

kîkway *PR* something, thing; [*in negative clause:*] anything, any; [*indefinite*]

misawâc *IPC* in any case

pikw îta *IPC* in any place, everywhere

ANYONE

awiyak *PR* someone, somebody; [*in negative clause:*] anyone, anybody; [*indefinite; e.g.,* awiyak, awiya]

pikw âwiyak *IPC* anyone, everyone

ANYTHING

kîkway *PR* something, thing; [*in negative clause:*] anything, any; [*indefinite*]

nânitaw *IPC·* simply; something, anything; something bad, anything bad

APPARENTLY
tâpiskôc *IPC* as if, seemingly, apparently

APPLIANCE
âpacihcikan– *NI* tool, appliance, machine
âpacihcikanis– *NI* small tool, small appliance [*diminutive*]

APRIL
ayîki-pîsimw– *NA* the month of April

APRON
aspastâkan– *NI* apron

AROUND
kwêskî– *VAI* turn around
têtipêwêyâmo– *VAI* flee around in a circle
wâsakâm *IPC* around, in a circuit
wâskân– *VTI* make s.t. go around, turn s.t. (*e.g.,* treadle), crank s.t.

ARRIVE
takohtê– *VAI* arrive walking
takwâpôyo– *VAI* arrive by rail, arrive by train

ASH
pihkw– *NI* ash [*e.g.,* pihko]

ASHAMED
nêpêwisi– *VAI* be ashamed, be shy
sasîhciwih– *VTA* make s.o. ashamed, embarrass s.o.

ASK
atot– *VTA* ask s.o. to do something
kakwêcim– *VTA* ask s.o. a question
kanawêyihtamôh– *VTA* ask s.o. to look after (it/him), leave (it/him) to be
  looked after by s.o.
nitotamaw– *VTA* ask s.o. for (it/him)
wîsâm– *VTA* ask s.o. along, take s.o. along

ASLEEP
nipâ– *VAI* sleep, be asleep

ATTACH
kikamohtâ– *VAI* attach (it), put (it) on something
kikamon– *VII* be attached, be on something
kikamôh– *VTA* attach s.o., put s.o. (*e.g.,* yarn) on something
sakâpât– *VTI* attach s.t. by sewing, sew s.t. on

ATTACHED
sâkih– *VTA* love s.o., be attached to s.o.
sâkihtâ– *VAI* love (it), be attached to (it)

ATTEMPT
kakwê *IPV* try, attempt to

AUGUST
ohpahowi-pîsimw– *NA* the month of August

AUTOMOBILE
otâpânâskw– *NA* wagon, automobile

AUTUMN
takwâkin– *VII* be fall, be autumn

AVOIDING
manâ *IPC* avoiding to do something, careful not to

AWAY
aspin *IPC* off, away; the last I knew

BACHELOR
môsâpêwi– *VAI* be a bachelor, be unmarried, be single

BACK
kwêh-kwêkwask *IPC* back and forth [*reduplicated*]

pêci-nâway *IPC* from back then; down from the distant past

BAD
mac-âyiwi– *VAI* be bad, be evil

maci *IPV* bad, evil

mâyâtan– *VII* be ugly, be bad

mâyi *IPV* bad, evil

mâyipayi– *VAI* fare badly; suffer a death, be bereaved

nânitaw *IPC* simply; something, anything; something bad, anything bad

BAG
mitâtahtomitanaw-maskimot *IPC* a hundred bags, one hundred bags

BAND
okimâw– *NA* chief, leader, boss; Band Council [*e.g.,* okimânâhk 'Band Council, band authorities']

wiyasiwêhkâniwi– *VAI* be a band councillor

BANNOCK
pahkwêsikan– *NA* bannock, bread; flour

BARE
mohcihk *IPC* on the bare ground

BAREFOOT
sâsâkihti– *VAI* be barefoot

BARELY
têpiyâhk *IPC* merely; barely; so long as

BARREL
mahkahkw– *NI* barrel, tub

BATHE
pakâsimonah– *VTA* immerse s.o., bathe s.o.

pakâsimonahâwaso– *VAI* immerse one's children, bathe one's children

BEADS, BEADING
misiwêminakin– *VTI* put beads all over s.t.; cover s.t. with beads

mîkis– *NA* bead

mîkisasâkay– *NI* beaded coat, beaded jacket

mîkisayiwinis– *NI* beaded clothing
mîkisihkahcikê– *VAI* bead things, do beadwork
mîkisihkahcikêwin– *NI* beading, beadwork
mîkisihkaht– *VTI* bead s.t., put beads on s.t.
mîkisiwi– *VII* be beaded
nihtâwiminakinikê– *VAI* be good at sewing on beads

BEAUTIFUL
miyosi– *VAI* be good, be beautiful
miyosîhtâ– *VAI* make (it) good, make (it) beautiful

BEAVER
amiskw– *NA* beaver

BECAUSE
ayisk *IPC* for, because [*cf.* ayis]
osâm *IPC* too much; because
wiya *IPC* for, because [*clause-initial causal conjunction*]

BED
nipêwin– *NI* bed

BEDROOM
nipêwikamikw– *NI* bedroom

BEEF
mostoso-wiyâs– *NI* beef

BEFORE
kayâhtê *IPC* before, previously
maywêsk *IPC* before [*cf.* maywês]

BEGIN
mâci *IPV* begin
mâcihtâ– *VAI* begin doing (it)
mâcipayin– *VII* begin to run (*e.g.,* tape-recorder) [*]

BEHIND
nâway *IPC* behind; in the past

BELIEVE
pakahkam *IPC* I believe
tâpwêht– *VTI* agree with s.t., believe s.t.
tâpwêhtaw– *VTA* agree with s.o., believe s.o.
tâpwêwakêyiht– *VTI* hold s.t. to be true, believe in s.t.

BELLY
–askatay– *NDI* abdominal wall, belly (of animal) [*e.g.,* waskatay]

BELOW
nîhc-âyihk *IPC* down, below

BENEATH
sêkopayin– *VII* run beneath, go underneath, get caught underneath
sîpâ *IPV* beneath, underneath

BEREAVED
mâyipayi– *VAI* fare badly; suffer a death, be bereaved
BERRY
mawiso– *VAI* pick berries
misâskwatômin– *NI* saskatoon berry
mînis– *NI* berry
nikikomin– *NI* a certain berry [*literally* otter-berry]
BETWEEN
tastawayas *IPC* in between, in the middle
BIBLE
omâw– *NA* "bible", manyplies, omasum (*i.e.,* third stomach of ruminant)
BIG
misâ– *VII* be big
misi *IPV* big, greatly
misikiti– *VAI* be big (in height or girth)
misisîhtâ– *VAI* make (it) big
BINGO
pinkow– *NI* bingo
BISHOP
kihc-âyamihêwiyiniw– *NA* bishop
BLACK
kaskitêsi– *VAI* be black
kaskitêwatisw– *VTA* dye s.o. (*e.g.,* stocking) black
kaskitêwâpahtê– *VII* give off black smoke
BLANKET
akohp– *NI* blanket
akohpis– *NI* small blanket [*diminutive*]
anâskê– *VAI* spread a blanket
wâposwayânakohp– *NI* rabbitskin blanket
BLESS
sawêyim– *VTA* be generous towards s.o., bless s.o.
sawêyimikowisi– *VAI* be blessed by the powers
BLISTERS
pîkokonêwêpayi– *VAI* have cracks in one's mouth, have one's mouth break
out in blisters (*e.g.,* from thrush)
BLIZZARD
pîwaniyôtin– *VII* be a blizzard
BLOOD
mihkw– *NI* blood [*e.g.,* mihko]
BLOW THROUGH
sâpoyowê– *VII* have the wind blowing through
BLUEBERRIES
iyinimin– *NI* blueberries

BLURRED

wanêyiht– *VTI* have one's mind blurred, be confused

wani *IPV* indistinctly, blurred

BOARD

pôsi– *VAI* board a conveyance

pôsih– *VTA* make s.o. board a conveyance, give s.o. a ride

BOARDS

napakihtakw– *NI* flat lumber, board

wâpiskihtakâ– *VII* be white boards, be white floor

BOAST

mamihcim– *VTA* boast about s.o.

mamihcimo– *VAI* be boastful

BOIL

kaskâciwahtê– *VII* be boiled until tender

kaskâciwas– *VTI* boil s.t. until tender

os– *VTI* boil s.t.

pakâhtâ– *VAI* boil (it) in water

BONE

–skan– *NDI* bone [*e.g.,* miskana]

BONE-MARROW

oskani-pimiy– *NI* bone-marrow

wîn– *NI* bone-marrow [*e.g.,* wîni]

BOOK

masinahikan– *NI* book; written document, will

BORN

nihtâwiki– *VAI* be born

nôkosi– *VAI* be visible; be born

BORROW

nitâhtâm– *VTA* borrow (it/him) from s.o.

BOSS

okimâw– *NA* chief, leader, boss; Band Council [*e.g.,* okimânâhk 'Band Council, band authorities']

BOTHER

isîhk– *VTI* bother with s.t. thus

isîhkaw– *VTA* bother s.o. thus

BOTTLE

môtêyâpiskw– *NI* bottle

BOWL

mistiyâkan– *NI* big dish, platter, large bowl

wiyâkanis– *NI* small dish, small bowl [*diminutive*]

BOX

mistikowat– *NI* wooden box, trunk

BOY
    nâpêsis– NA boy, little boy

BRAID
    apihkât– VTA braid s.o.; knit s.o. (*e.g.,* stocking)
    apihkât– VTI braid s.t.; knit s.t.
    itapihkât– VTI braid s.t. thus; knit s.t. thus
    itapihkê– VAI braid thus; knit thus [*; *?sic: record*]
    kîsapihkât– VTI braid s.t. to completion; knit s.t. to completion

BRANCH
    nîpisîs– NI willow branch, willow switch; little willow [*diminutive*]

BREACH
    pâstâho– VAI breach the natural order, transgress; [*Christian:*] sin, be a
    sinner

BREAD
    pahkwêsikan– NA bannock, bread; flour

BREAK
    môskipayi– VAI break out in a rash, in sores (*e.g.,* with thrush)
    paskin– VTA break s.o. off (*e.g.,* thread)
    pâstatah– VTI break s.t. (*e.g.,* bones) by tool
    pîkokonêwêpayi– VAI have cracks in one's mouth, have one's mouth break
    out in blisters (*e.g.,* from thrush)
    pîkopayi– VAI break down, be broken; go broke, go bankrupt
    pîkopayin– VII break down, be broken
    pîkopit– VTI break s.t. (*e.g.,* soil), plough s.t. (*e.g.,* field)
    pîkopitamaw– VTA break (it) for s.o., plough (it) for s.o.

BREECHES
    têhtapîwitâs– NA riding breeches

BRIDLE
    tâpitonêhpicikan– NI bridle

BRING
    pêsiw– VTA bring s.o. hither
    pêtâ– VAI bring (it) hither
    pîhtokwatamâkê– VAI bring (it/him) inside for people
    pîhtokwatâ– VAI bring (it) inside

BROTH
    mîcimâpoy– NI broth, soup

BROTHER
    –mosôm– NDA grandfather, grandfather's brother [*e.g.,* kimosôm]
    –ôhcâwîs– NDA father's brother; step-father [*e.g.,* ôhcâwîsa]
    –ôhtâwiy– NDA father, father's brother; [*Christian:*] Heavenly Father
    [*e.g.,* kôhtâwînaw]
    –sis– NDA mother's brother, father's sister's husband; father-in-law,
    father-in-law's brother [*e.g.,* nisisak]

–**stês**– *NDA* older brother [*e.g.,* nistês]

ostêsimâw– *NA* oldest brother

BROTHER-IN-LAW

–**îscâs**– *NDA* male cross-cousin; brother-in-law (man speaking) [*diminutive;*
   e.g., wîscâsa]

–**îstâw**– *NDA* male cross-cousin; brother-in-law (man speaking)
   [*e.g.,* wîstâwa]

BRUSH

sinikohtakahikan– *NI* scrub-brush, floor brush, brush for wood

sinikohtakinikan– *NI* scrubber, brush; wash-board

BUG

manicôs– *NA* insect, bug

BUNDLED UP

wêwêkapi– *VAI* sit wrapped up, sit bundled up

BURY

ayâwahkahw– *VTA* bury s.o. in the ground

nahin– *VTA* bury s.o., hold a funeral for s.o.

BUSH

nîpisiy– *NI* willow, willow bush

sakâw– *NI* bush, woodland

BUSY

otamiyo– *VAI* busy oneself, keep busy, be preoccupied

BUT

mâka *IPC* but

BUY

atâm– *VTA* buy (it/him) from s.o.

atâwê– *VAI* buy (it)

atâwêstamâso– *VAI* buy (it/him) for oneself

kîspinat– *VTA* earn enough to buy s.o. (*e.g.,* horse)

kîspinat– *VTI* earn enough to buy s.t.

CALL

itâspinêm– *VTA* call s.o. thus in anger, angrily call s.o. such a name, thus
   scold s.o. in anger

têpwât– *VTA* call out to s.o., yell at s.o.

CAMP

papâmipici– *VAI* move about, camp here and there

sipwêpici– *VAI* leave with one's camp

CAN

kaskâpiskah– *VTI* can s.t., preserve s.t.

CANVAS

papakiwayânêkinw– *NI* thin cloth, cotton; canvas

CAREFUL

manâ *IPC* avoiding to do something, careful not to

CARROT
  oskâtâskw– *NI* carrot
CARRY
  nayaht– *VTI* carry s.t. on one's back
  nayahto– *VAI* carry one another on one's back; ride up on one another
    (*e.g.,* beads)
  pimohtatâ– *VAI* carry (it) along, travel with (it)
  tahkon– *VTA* carry s.o.
  tahkon– *VTI* carry s.t.
CASTRATED
  ayêhkwêsis– *NA* young castrated bull; steer [*diminutive*]
  ayêhkwêw– *NA* castrated bull; ox
CATCH
  aswah– *VTI* catch s.t. as it drips
  kâhcitin– *VTI* catch s.t.
  tasôh– *VTA* trap s.o. under something, catch s.o. in a trap
  tâpisikopayi– *VAI* get caught in something
CATTLE
  mostosw– *NA* cattle, cow
CEASE
  pôni *IPV* cease, stop
  pôni-pimâtisi– *VAI* cease to be alive, be dead
  pônihtâ– *VAI* cease of (it)
  pôyo– *VAI* cease, quit [*]
CELLAR
  wâtihkân– *NI* hole, cellar
  yahkâtihkât– *VTI* dig out more of a hole or cellar, push out the size of an
    existing hole or cellar
CERTAINLY
  kêhcinâ *IPC* surely, for certain
CHAIR
  apiwinis– *NI* seat, chair
CHASE
  nawaswât– *VTA* pursue s.o., chase after s.o.
  nawaswât– *VTI* pursue s.t., chase after s.t.
CHICKEN
  pahpahâhkwân– *NA* domestic chicken
CHIEF
  okimâhkân– *NA* chief, elected chief
  okimâhkâniwi– *VAI* be chief, serve as elected chief
  okimâhkâniwin– *NI* chieftaincy
  okimâw– *NA* chief, leader, boss; Band Council [*e.g.,* okimânâhk 'Band
    Council, band authorities']

CHILD
–awâsimis– *NDA* child [*e.g.,* kitawâsimisinawak]
awâsis– *NA* child
awâsisîwi– *VAI* be a child
awâsisîwiwin– *NI* being a child, childhood
mihcêtôsê– *VAI* have many children, have numerous offspring
ocawâsimisi– *VAI* have a child, have (her/him) as child [*diminutive*]
oskawâsis– *NA* young child, infant

CHOKECHERRIES
takwahiminân– *NI* chokecherries

CHOOSE
nawasôn– *VTA* choose s.o.
nawasôn– *VTI* choose s.t.
nawasônamaw– *VTA* choose (it/him) for s.o.; make a choice
    for s.o.

CHOP
cîkahoso– *VAI* chop oneself
kawikah– *VTI* chop s.t. down, cut s.t. down
kîskatah– *VTI* chop s.t. through
nâtwâh– *VTI* chop s.t. off something
nikohtât– *VTI* chop s.t. for firewood
nikohtê– *VAI* collect firewood, chop firewood
sikos– *VTI* chop s.t. small

CHRISTIAN
otayamihâw– *NA* Christian, adherent of Christianity

CHURCH
ayamihâhtah– *VTA* make s.o. go to church, take s.o. to mass
ayamihêwikamikw– *NI* church, church building

CIRCLE
têtipêwêyâmo– *VAI* flee around in a circle

CLAY
asiskiy– *NI* earth, soil, dirt; clay
wâpatonisk– *NA* white clay [*?sic* NA]

CLEAN
kanâci *IPV* clean
kanâcih– *VTA* clean s.o.
kanâciho– *VAI* clean oneself
kanâcihtâ– *VAI* clean (it), clean (it) out (*e.g.,* intestine)
kanâcinâkosi– *VAI* look clean, give a clean appearance
kanâtan– *VII* be clean
kanâtapi– *VAI* live in a clean house [*]
kanâtâpâwatâ– *VAI* wash (it) clean with water

CLEVER
iyinîsi– *VAI* be clever

CLOSE
kipwahpit– *VTI* pull s.t. close, tie s.t. close

CLOSE BY
cîki *IPC* close by

CLOTH
papakiwayânêkinw– *NI* thin cloth, cotton; canvas
sâkêkamon– *VII* stick out as cloth, project as cloth

CLOTHES
ayiwinis– *NI* clothes
ayiwinisis– *NI* clothes [*diminutive*]
mîkisayiwinis– *NI* beaded clothing
postayiwinisah– *VTA* clothe s.o., make clothes for s.o.
postayiwinisahiso– *VAI* clothe oneself, make clothes for oneself
postayiwinisê– *VAI* put clothes on, get dressed
wîpayiwinis– *NI* dirty clothes
wîpâtayiwinis– *NI* dirty clothes
yâyikâskocin– *VAI* tear one's clothes on wood (*e.g.*, in bush)
yîwêyâskocin– *VAI* tear one's clothes ragged on wood (*e.g.*, in bush)

COAL OIL
askîwi-pimiy– *NI* coal oil, petroleum

COALS
sêkwâpiskin– *VTI* put s.t. under the coals, into the oven

COAT
miskotâkay– *NI* coat, dress
mîkisasâkay– *NI* beaded coat, beaded jacket
pahkêkinwêsâkay– *NI* leather coat, leather jacket

COINCIDENCE
kêswân *IPC* by coincidence

COLD
kawaci– *VAI* be cold, experience cold
kawatim– *VTA* get s.o. cold, expose s.o. to cold
kawatimiso– *VAI* get oneself cold
kisin– *VII* be very cold weather
tahkâ– *VII* be cold
tahkikamâpoy– *NI* cold water

COLLECT
nikohtê– *VAI* collect firewood, chop firewood
nitawâwê– *VAI* go looking for eggs, go to collect eggs

COME
ohcipayin– *VII* come from there, result from that
ohcî– *VAI* come from there, be from there

COMPANION

–wîcêwâkan– *NDA* companion, partner [*e.g.*, kiwîcêwâkaniwâwak]

owîcêwâkani– *VAI* have a companion or partner, have (her/him) as companion or partner

COMPASSION

kisêwâtisi– *VAI* be kind, be of compassionate disposition

kisêwâtisiwin– *NI* kindness, compassion

COMPASSIONATE

kisê-manitow– *NA* God the kind, the compassionate God; [*Christian:*] Merciful God

COMPETENT

kaskiho– *VAI* be able, be competent

kaskihtâwin– *NI* ability to do (it), competence

nihtâ *IPV* good at, competent, practised

COMPLAIN

kisiwiyo– *VAI* complain about work, be angry about one's work

COMPLETE

kitâ– *VAI* eat (it) up, eat (it) completely

kîsapihkât– *VTI* braid s.t. to completion; knit s.t. to completion

kîsi *IPV* completely, to completion

kîsih– *VTA* complete s.o. (*e.g.*, stocking), finish preparing s.o. [*sic:* -ih-]

kîsis– *VTI* cook s.t. to completion

kîsiso– *VAI* be cooked to completion

kîsitê– *VII* be cooked to completion

kîsîhtâ– *VAI* finish (it), complete (it)

CONFUSE

wanêyiht– *VTI* have one's mind blurred, be confused

wanwêhkaw– *VTA* confuse s.o.

CONTENT

têpêyimo– *VAI* be content, be willing

CONTROL

tipêyiht– *VTI* own s.t., control s.t.

tipêyim– *VTA* own s.o., control s.o.

COOK

kîsis– *VTI* cook s.t. to completion

kîsiso– *VAI* be cooked to completion

kîsitê– *VII* be cooked to completion

nihtâwitêpo– *VAI* be good at cooking

piminawaso– *VAI* cook, do the cooking

piminawasowikamikw– *NI* cookhouse, kitchen

piminawat– *VTA* cook for s.o.

COOPERATE
mâmawi-wîcihitowin– *NI* all helping together, general cooperation
wîcêht– *VTI* go along with s.t., cooperate with s.t.
wîcihito– *VAI* help one another, cooperate with one another

CORNER
wîhkwêhtakâw– *NI* corner made by wooden walls

CORRECT
mînom– *VTA* straighten s.o. out, correct s.o. verbally

COST
itakiso– *VAI* be counted thus, cost so much; be held in such esteem

COTTAGE CHEESE
ascascwâs– *NI* curds, cottage cheese

COTTON
papakiwayânêkinw– *NI* thin cloth, cotton; canvas

COUNCILLOR
wiyasiwêhkâniwi– *VAI* be a band councillor

COUNSEL
kakêskihkêmo– *VAI* counsel people, preach at people
kakêskim– *VTA* counsel s.o., preach at s.o.
kakêskimiso– *VAI* counsel oneself
miyo-kakêskihkêmowin– *NI* good counselling, good preaching

COUNT
akihtê– *VII* be counted
akim– *VTA* count s.o.
itakiso– *VAI* be counted thus, cost so much; be held in such esteem
têpakiht– *VTI* count s.t. up

COUNTRY
askiy– *NI* earth, land, country; [*pl.:*] fields under cultivation, pieces of farmland

COURT
wiyasiwât– *VTA* decide about s.o.; sit in judgment on s.o., hold court over s.o.

COUSIN
–ciwâm– *NDA* male parallel cousin (man speaking); [*Christian:*] brethren [*e.g.,* kiciwâminawak]
–tawêmâw– *NDA* male parallel cousin; female cross-cousin's husband (woman speaking) [*e.g.,* nitawêmâw]

COVER
akwanaho– *VAI* cover oneself, be covered (*e.g.,* by a blanket)
akwanâhkwêyâmo– *VAI* cover one's face in flight, flee with one's face covered; hide by rapidly covering one's face
akwanâpowêhikâso– *VAI* be covered as vessel capable of containing liquid, have a lid (*e.g.,* pot)

ayahikê– *VAI* cover things with earth, hill things (*e.g.,* potatoes)

âkô *IPV* covered, shielded

âkô-wiyipâ– *VII* be covered in dirt

misiwêminakin– *VTI* put beads all over s.t.; cover s.t. with beads

COW

mostosw– *NA* cattle, cow

mostosw-âya *IPC* of a cow, in matters bovine

mostoswayân– *NA* cow-hide

CRACKS

pîkokonêwêpayi– *VAI* have cracks in one's mouth, have one's mouth break
  out in blisters (*e.g.,* from thrush)

CRANBERRY

wîsakîmin– *NI* cranberry

CRANK

wâskân– *VTI* make s.t. go around, turn s.t. (*e.g.,* treadle), crank s.t.

CRAZY

môhcowi– *VAI* be crazy, be silly

CREAM

manahikan– *NI* cream

CREE

nêhiyaw– *NA* Cree Indian, Indian

nêhiyaw-masinîwin– *NI* Cree design, Cree motif, Indian design, Indian
  motif [*sic:* -w-]

nêhiyawê– *VAI* speak Cree

nêhiyawêwin– *NI* speaking Cree, the Cree language

nêhiyawi *IPV* Cree, Indian

nêhiyawi-wîhowin– *NI* Cree name, Indian name

nêhiyawiyîhkâso– *VAI* have a Cree name, have an Indian name

nêhiyâwi– *VAI* be a Cree Indian, be an Indian

CRISP

kâspis– *VTI* heat s.t. until crisp

CROSS-COUSIN

–câhkos– *NDA* female cross-cousin; sister-in-law (woman speaking)
  [*e.g.,* nicâhkos]

–îscâs– *NDA* male cross-cousin; brother-in-law (man speaking)
  [*diminutive; e.g.,* wîscâsa]

–îstâw– *NDA* male cross-cousin; brother-in-law (man speaking)
  [*e.g.,* wîstâwa]

CROWDED

tatâyawâ– *VII* be crowded

CRUSH

takwah– *VTI* crush s.t.

CRY
mâto– *VAI* cry, wail
môskomo– *VAI* talk oneself into crying, cry while talking
CULTIVATE
sikwahcisikê– *VAI* cultivate, harrow
CURDS
ascascwâs– *NI* curds, cottage cheese
CUT
apiscis– *VTI* cut s.t. into small pieces
apiscisasi– *VAI* cut (it) into very small pieces [*diminutive; cf.* apiscis–]
cîhcîkos– *VTI* cut meat off s.t. (*e.g.,* bone)
manis– *VTI* cut s.t.
manisw– *VTA* cut s.o.
payipis– *VTI* cut s.t. out, cut a hole in s.t.
pânis– *VTI* cut s.t. (*e.g.,* meat) into sheets
pânisâwê– *VAI* cut meat into sheets
pânisw– *VTA* cut s.o. (*e.g.,* animal) into sheets
pîkinis– *VTI* cut s.t. into small pieces
tâsawisâwât– *VTI* cut into the middle of s.t., slice s.t. open (*e.g.,* veal belly cordon-bleu)
wiyis– *VTI* cut s.t. out, cut s.t. to a pattern
wiyisamaw– *VTA* cut a pattern for s.o.
wiyisamâso– *VAI* cut a pattern for oneself, cut one's own pattern
DANCE
nîmihito– *VAI* dance with one another, dance
nîmihitowin– *NI* dance
DARK
wani-tipiskâ– *VII* be dark night
DAUGHTER
–cânis– *NDA* daughter [*diminutive; e.g.,* nicânis]
–tânis– *NDA* daughter [*e.g.,* nitânisak]
otânisi– *VAI* have a daughter, have (her) as daughter
DAY
kîsikâ– *VII* be day, be daylight
kîsikâw– *NA* day, daylight
tahto-kîsikâw *IPC* every day, daily
DEAD
mâyipayi– *VAI* fare badly; suffer a death, be bereaved
nêsowisi– *VAI* be weak, be near death
nipîmakan– *VII* be dead
nîpêpi– *VAI* sit up with someone dead or dying; hold a wake
pôni-pimâtisi– *VAI* cease to be alive, be dead

DEBT

tipahamaw– *VTA* pay s.o. for (it/him), repay a debt to s.o.;
pay s.o. a pension

DECIDE

wiyasiwât– *VTA* decide about s.o.; sit in judgment on s.o., hold court
over s.o.

wiyasiwât– *VTI* decide s.t.

DEED

mâyinikêwin– *NI* wrong-doing, evil deed

miyo-tôtamowin– *NI* good deed, good works

DEER

apisimôsos– *NA* deer

apisimôsoswayân– *NA* deer-hide

DEPART

sipwêhtê– *VAI* leave, depart

DESIGN

nêhiyaw-masinîwin– *NI* Cree design, Cree motif, Indian design, Indian
motif [*sic*: -w-]

DESIRE

akâwât– *VTI* wish for s.t., desire s.t.

nôhtê *IPV* want to, desire to

DESTROY

misiwanâcihiso– *VAI* ruin oneself, destroy oneself; commit suicide

misiwanâcihtâ– *VAI* ruin (it), destroy (it)

misiwanâtan– *VII* be ruined, be destroyed

DIAPER

âsiyân– *NA* loin-cloth, diaper

DIE

nakat– *VTA* leave s.o. behind; die and leave s.o. behind

nakataskê– *VAI* leave the earth behind, depart the world, die

nipahâhkatoso– *VAI* starve to death, die from starvation

DIFFERENT

pîtos *IPC* strange, different

DIFFICULT

âyiman– *VII* be difficult

âyimanohk *IPC* in a difficult place

âyimêyiht– *VTI* consider s.t. difficult

âyimisi– *VAI* have a difficult time; be of difficult disposition

âyimî– *VAI* have a difficult time, have a difficult task

nayêhtâwan– *VII* be difficult, be troublesome [*]

nayêhtâwêyim– *VTA* find s.o. difficult, find s.o. troublesome

nayêhtâwipayi– *VAI* run into difficulties, experience trouble

DIG

yahkâtihkât– *VTI* dig out more of a hole or cellar, push out the size of an existing hole or cellar

DIP OUT

kwâpah– *VTI* dip s.t. out

DIRT

asiskiy– *NI* earth, soil, dirt; clay

asiskîwihkwê– *VAI* have soil on one's face, have dirt on one's face

âkô-wiyipâ– *VII* be covered in dirt

wiyipâ– *VII* be soiled, be dirty

wîpayiwinis– *NI* dirty clothes

wîpâtayiwinis– *NI* dirty clothes

DISAPPEAR

namatê– *VAI* be nonexistent, have disappeared

DISAPPOINT

pômêh– *VTA* make s.o. discouraged, disappoint s.o.

DISAPPROVE

pakwât– *VTA* hate s.o., disapprove of s.o.

pakwât– *VTI* hate s.t., disapprove of s.t.

DISCOURAGED

pômê– *VAI* be discouraged; give up

pômêh– *VTA* make s.o. discouraged, disappoint s.o.

DISCUSS

mâmiskôm– *VTA* talk about s.o., discuss s.o.

mâmiskôt– *VTI* talk about s.t., discuss s.t.

mâmiskôtamaw– *VTA* discuss (it/him) for s.o.

DISH, DISHES

kâsîyâkanê– *VAI* wash dishes, do the dishes

mistiyâkan– *NI* big dish, platter, large bowl

wiyâkan– *NI* dish, vessel

wiyâkanis– *NI* small dish, small bowl [*diminutive*]

DIVORCE

paskêwihito– *VAI* leave one another; separate, divorce

DO

itahkamikisi– *VAI* do things thus

itôt– *VTI* do thus, act thus [*cf.* tôt–]

miyo-tôt– *VTI* do s.t. good

tôcikâtê– *VII* be done

tôt– *VTI* do s.t. [*cf.* itôt–]

tôtamaw– *VTA* do (it) for s.o.

tôtamâso– *VAI* do (it) for oneself

tôtamôh– *VTA* make s.o. do (it)

tôtaw– *VTA* do (it) to s.o., treat s.o. so

tôtâso– *VAI* do (it) to oneself

DOWN

kawikah– *VTI* chop s.t. down, cut s.t. down

kawisimo– *VAI* lie down, go to bed

nahapi– *VAI* sit down in one's place, be properly seated

nîhc-âyihk *IPC* down, below

nîhcipit– *VTA* pull s.o. down, drag s.o. down

nîhtin– *VTI* take s.t. down, unload s.t.

DRAG

nâcitâpê– *VAI* go and drag (it) back, fetch (it) by cart [*sic; cf.* nâtitâpê–]

nâtitâpê– *VAI* go and drag (it) back, fetch (it) by cart [*also* nâcitâpê–]

nîhcipit– *VTA* pull s.o. down, drag s.o. down

DRAW

masinah– *VTI* mark s.t., draw s.t.; write s.t.

masinahamâso– *VAI* draw (it) for oneself; write (it) for oneself, write oneself

DRESS

miskotâkay– *NI* coat, dress

postayiwinisê– *VAI* put clothes on, get dressed

DRINK

minihkwê– *VAI* drink (it), have a drink; drink, abuse alcohol

minihkwêwin– *NI* drinking, alcohol abuse

DRIP

aswah– *VTI* catch s.t. as it drips

pahkikawin– *VTI* let s.t. drip

DRY

pâhkopayi– *VAI* get dry, dry out

pâs– *VTI* dry s.t.

pâstê– *VII* be dry

pâsw– *VTA* dry s.o.

DUCK

nôcisipê– *VAI* be engaged in duck-hunting

sîsîp– *NA* duck

sîsîpipîway– *NI* duck feathers, duck-down

DURING

mêkwâ *IPV* while, during

mêkwâc *IPC* while, during

DYE

atis– *VTI* dye s.t.

kaskitêwatisw– *VTA* dye s.o. (*e.g.*, stocking) black

EACH
pâh-pêyak *IPC* one each [*reduplicated*]
pâh-pîtos *IPC* each differently [*reduplicated*]

EARLY
kîkisêpâ *IPC* early in the morning
wîpac *IPC* soon, early

EARN
kaskihtamâso– *VAI* earn (it) for oneself
kîspinat– *VTA* earn enough to buy s.o. (*e.g.*, horse)
kîspinat– *VTI* earn enough to buy s.t.

EARTH
asiskiy– *NI* earth, soil, dirt; clay
askiy– *NI* earth, land, country; [*pl.*:] fields under cultivation, pieces of
    farmland
ayahikê– *VAI* cover things with earth, hill things (*e.g.*, potatoes)
waskitaskamik *IPC* on the face of the earth

EAST
sâkâstênohk *IPC* in the east

EASY
wêhcasin– *VII* be easy
wêhcih– *VTA* have an easy time with s.o. (*e.g.*, hide)
wêhtisi– *VAI* have it easy

EAT
asam– *VTA* feed s.o., give s.o. to eat
kitâ– *VAI* eat (it) up, eat (it) completely
mîci– *VAI* eat (it)
mîciso– *VAI* eat, have a meal
mow– *VTA* eat s.o. (*e.g.*, bread)

EDUCATION
kiskinohamâtowin– *NI* teaching, education
miyo-kîsih– *VTA* finish s.o. well; educate s.o. well

EGGS
nitawâwê– *VAI* go looking for eggs, go to collect eggs
owâwi– *VAI* lay eggs

EIGHTY
ayinânêwimitanaw *IPC* eighty

ELDER
kêhtê-ay– *NA* old person, elder [*e.g.*, kêhtê-ayak]
kêhtê-ayiwi– *VAI* be an old person, be an elder
kisêyiniw– *NA* old man, elder

ELECTRIC LIGHT
wâsaskocêpayîs– *NI* lamp, electric light [*diminutive*]

ELEVEN
pêyakosâp *IPC* eleven

ELSEWHERE
ohpimê *IPC* off to the side, elsewhere

EMBARRASS
sasîhciwih– *VTA* make s.o. ashamed, embarrass s.o.

EMPLOY
atoskah– *VTA* make s.o. work, employ s.o., hire s.o.
atoskahâkan– *NA* employee, hired man
atoskaw– *VTA* work for s.o., be employed by s.o.
atoskêmo– *VAI* get people to do things, employ people, hire people

ENCOUNTER
nakiskaw– *VTA* encounter s.o., meet s.o.
tâwin– *VTI* encounter s.t., bump into s.t.

END
iskwêyâc *IPC* at last, at the end
kisipipayin– *VII* come to an end, run out

ENDURE
sîpihkêyiht– *VTI* endure s.t. by strength of mind; persevere

ENGLISH
âkayâsîmo– *VAI* speak English

ENJOY
miyawât– *VTI* enjoy s.t.; have fun, be joyful
miyawâtamowin– *NI* enjoyment; fun, joyfulness

ENTER
pîhtokwê– *VAI* enter, go inside

ENTERPRISE
waskawîstamâso– *VAI* work for oneself, be enterprising
waskawîwin– *NI* being active, enterprise

ENTRAILS
–takisiy– *NDI* intestines, guts, entrails [*e.g.,* mitakisiya]

ERECT
cimatê– *VII* stand erect
nîpawi– *VAI* stand, stand up, stand erect, stand fast

ERMINESKIN
k-ôsihkosiwayâniw *INM* [*man's name:*] Ermineskin
[*literally* Has-an-Ermineskin]

ERROR
paci *IPV* wrongly, in error

ESCAPE
pihkoho– *VAI* free oneself, escape; [*Christian:*] be saved

ESPECIALLY
âsônê *IPC* especially, in particular

wâwâc *IPC* especially, even

wâwîs cî *IPC* especially

wâwîs *IPC* especially [*]

ESTEEM

itakiso– *VAI* be counted thus, cost so much; be held in such esteem

kîhkâtêyihtâkwan– *VII* be held in high esteem, be prominent

kîhkâtêyim– *VTA* hold s.o. in high esteem

pîwêyimo– *VAI* think little of oneself, have low self-esteem; [*Christian:*] be humble

EVEN

ahpô *IPC* even, or

wâwâc *IPC* especially, even

EVENING

otâkosin– *VII* be evening

EVER

wîhkâc *IPC* ever

EVERY

kahkiyaw *IPC* every, all

tahtw-âyamihêwi-kîsikâw *IPC* every Sunday

EVERYONE

pikw âwiyak *IPC* anyone, everyone

EVERYWHERE

misiw îtê *IPC* all over, everywhere

pikw îta *IPC* in any place, everywhere

EVIL

mac-âyiwi– *VAI* be bad, be evil

maci *IPV* bad, evil

mâyi *IPV* bad, evil

mâyi-tôt– *VTI* do s.t. evil

mâyi-tôtaw– *VTA* do evil to s.o., harm s.o.

mâyinikêwin– *NI* wrong-doing, evil deed

EXACTLY

katisk *IPC* just now, exactly; [*in negative clause:*] not merely

mwêhci *IPC* exactly

EXAMPLE

kiskinowâpahtih– *VTA* teach s.o. by example

kiskinowâpahtihiwê– *VAI* teach people by example

kiskinowâpam– *VTA* watch s.o.'s example

EXCITE

yêyih– *VTA* get s.o. excited by one's action, tempt s.o. by one's action

EXHAUST

mêstinikê– *VAI* use things up, exhaust things, spend it all

EXIST
  ayâ– *VII* be there, exist
  ihtako– *VAI* exist
  ihtakon– *VII* exist
  ihtatan– *VII* exist there [*?sic; both stem and gloss tentative*]
EXTEND
  âniskôstê– *VII* extend, be extended
  ispîhcâ– *VII* extend thus, be of such size (*e.g.*, country)
  ispîhtisî– *VAI* extend thus, be of such age
  pimisin– *VAI* lie extended
  piskihcikwât– *VTI* sew an extension on s.t.
EXTENT
  iyikohk *IPC* so much, to such an extent
  ômayikohk *IPC* this much, to this degree, to this extent
  pikoyikohk *IPC* no matter how much, to any extent
  tânimayikohk *IPC* to which extent
EXTREMELY
  kakwâyaki *IPV* greatly, extremely [*]
EYE-SIGHT
  wâpiwin– *NI* eye-sight
FACE
  –hkwâkan– *NDI* face [*e.g.*, ohkwâkan]
  asiskîwihkwê– *VAI* have soil on one's face, have dirt on one's face
  kâsîhkwâkê– *VAI* wash one's face with (it), use (it) to wash one's face
FACT
  anima *IPC* it is that; the fact that [*predicative*]
  ôma *IPC* it is this; the fact that [*predicative*]
  tâsipwâw *IPC* as a matter of fact
FAIL
  pwâtawihtâ– *VAI* be thwarted at (it), fail of (it)
FALL
  pahkisin– *VAI* fall
  takwâkin– *VII* be fall, be autumn
FAMILIAR
  nakacihtâ– *VAI* be familiar with doing (it), be practised at (it)
  nakayâskaw– *VTA* be accustomed to s.o., be comfortable with s.o., be
    familiar with s.o.
FAR
  isko *IPC* so far
  isko *IPV* so far
  wâhyaw *IPC* far
  wâhyawês *IPC* quite far [*cf.* wâhyawîs]
  wâhyawîs *IPC* quite far [*cf.* wâhyawês]

FARE
  mâyamahciho– *VAI* fare ill, be sick
  mâyipayi– *VAI* fare badly; suffer a death, be bereaved
  miyomahciho– *VAI* fare well, feel well, be in good health or spirit

FARM
  askiy– *NI* earth, land, country; [*pl.:*] fields under cultivation, pieces of farmland
  okistikêwiyinîwi– *VAI* be a farmer, be engaged in agriculture
  okistikêwiyinîwiwin– *NI* farming, farm-work

FAST
  tahkopit– *VTI* tie s.t. fast

FAT
  paswêskôyo– *VAI* get sick from eating excessively fatty food
  paswêyâ– *VII* be excessively fatty
  pimiy– *NI* fat, oil; crude petroleum
  wiyino– *VII* be fat
  wiyinw– *NI* fat, animal fat

FATHER
  mâmaw-ôhtâwîmâw– *NA* All-Father, Father-of-All
  –ôhtâwiy– *NDA* father, father's brother; [*Christian:*] Heavenly Father [*e.g.,* kôhtâwînaw]

FATHER-IN-LAW
  –manâcimâkan– *NDA* father-in-law (woman speaking) [*e.g.,* nimanâcimâkan]
  –sis– *NDA* mother's brother, father's sister's husband; father-in-law, father-in-law's brother [*e.g.,* nisisak]

FEAR
  kost– *VTA* fear s.o.
  kost– *VTI* fear s.t.

FEATHERS
  sîsîpipîway– *NI* duck feathers, duck-down

FEED
  asam– *VTA* feed s.o., give s.o. to eat
  asamiso– *VAI* feed oneself
  kîspôh– *VTA* feed s.o. until full, get s.o. (horse) fully fed

FEEL
  itamahciho– *VAI* feel thus, be in such health [*e.g.,* nânitaw itamahciho– 'feel unwell']
  miyomahciho– *VAI* fare well, feel well, be in good health or spirit
  môsihtâ– *VAI* sense (it), feel (it)

FELLOW
  –îcayisiyiniw– *NDA* fellow person, fellow human [*sic:* -a-; *e.g.,* kîcayisiyinînaw]

–**îci-kiskinohamawâkan**– *NDA* fellow student, school-mate
[*e.g.*, nîci-kiskinohamawâkanak]

wîci-kiskinohamâkosîm– *VTA* be in school with s.o., have s.o. as a
fellow-student

FETCH

nâcimihtê– *VAI* fetch firewood, go for firewood

nâcitâpê– *VAI* go and drag (it) back, fetch (it) by cart [*sic; cf.* nâtitâpê–]

nât– *VTA* fetch s.o.

nât– *VTI* fetch s.t.

nâtamaw– *VTA* fetch (it/him) for s.o.

nâtamâso– *VAI* fetch (it/him) for oneself

nâtitâpê– *VAI* go and drag (it) back, fetch (it) by cart [*also* nâcitâpê–]

FIELD

askiy– *NI* earth, land, country; [*pl.:*] fields under cultivation, pieces of
farmland

kistikân– *NI* field, arable land

FIGHT

nôtin– *VTA* fight s.o., fight with s.o.

nôtin– *VTI* fight s.t., fight with s.t.

nôtinikê– *VAI* fight people, put up a fight; take part in war
(*e.g.,* World War II)

nôtinitowin– *NI* fighting

FINALLY

piyisk *IPC* finally, at last

FIND

misk– *V̆TI* find s.t.

miskamaw– *VTA* find (it/him) for s.o.

miskaw– *VTA* find s.o.

FINISH

kîsîhtâ– *VAI* finish (it), complete (it)

miyo-kîsih– *VTA* finish s.o. well; educate s.o. well

FIRE

kîsowihkaso– *VAI* warm oneself by fire, keep oneself warm by fire

kwâhkotênikê– *VAI* start a fire, set things aflame

pôn– *VTI* build a fire; make a fire with s.t.

FIREWOOD

âwacimihtê– *VAI* haul firewood

miht– *NI* firewood, piece of firewood [*e.g.,* mihti, mihta]

nâcimihtê– *VAI* fetch firewood, go for firewood

nikohtât– *VTI* chop s.t. for firewood

nikohtê– *VAI* collect firewood, chop firewood

nikohtêstamâso– *VAI* make firewood for oneself, make one's own firewood

nikohtêwin– *NI* making firewood

omihtimi– *VAI* have one's firewood, have (it) as one's firewood

pîhtikwê-âwacimihtêwin– *NI* hauling firewood inside
[*; *sic:* -i-; *cf.* pîhtokwê–]

FIRST

nistam *IPC* first, at first, for the first time

pita *IPC* first, for a while

FISH

kinosêw– *NA* fish

nôcikinosêwê– *VAI* be engaged in fishing

FIVE

niyânan *IPC* five

niyânani– *VAI* be five in number

FLAT

napakaskisin– *NI* flat moccasin

napakâ– *VII* be flat

napakihtakw– *NI* flat lumber, board

napakikamikos– *NI* flat-roofed log-house [*diminutive*]

FLEE

akwanâhkwêyâmo– *VAI* cover one's face in flight, flee with one's face covered; hide by rapidly covering one's face

nâtâmototaw– *VTA* flee to s.o., seek refuge with s.o.

pîhtokwêyâmo– *VAI* flee inside

têtipêwêyâmo– *VAI* flee around in a circle

FLEECE

mâyatihkopîway– *NI* sheep's fleece; wool

FLOOR

kisêpêkihtakinikê– *VAI* wash a wooden floor, wash floor-boards

sinikohtakahikan– *NI* scrub-brush, floor brush, brush for wood

wâpiskihtakâ– *VII* be white boards, be white floor

FLOUR

maskimotêkinw– *NI* sacking, cloth from flour-sacks

pahkwêsikan– *NA* bannock, bread; flour

pahkwêsikaniwat– *NI* flour-bag

FLOWER

wâpikwaniy– *NI* flower

FOLLOW

pimitisah– *VTI* follow s.t.

pimitisahikê– *VAI* follow people, tag along, be a follower

FOOD

mîciwin– *NI* food

FOOT

–sit– *NDI* foot [*e.g.,* misita]

FOR
ayisk *ipc* for, because [*cf.* ayis]
wiya *ipc* for, because [*clause-initial causal conjunction*]

FORCE
wîhkô– *vai* strain oneself, use all one's force

FOREVER
kâkikê *ipc* always, forever

FORGET
wanikiskisi– *vai* forget (it), be forgetful

FORGIVE
kâsînamaw– *vta* wipe (it) off for s.o.; [*Christian:*] forgive s.o.
kâsînamâso– *vai* wipe (it) off for oneself; [*Christian:*] have one's sins forgiven, obtain forgivenness
kâsînamâto– *vai* wipe (it) off for one another; [*Christian:*] forgive one another
pônêyihtamaw– *vta* forgive s.o.
pônêyihtamâto– *vai* forgive one another

FREE
kêcikopit– *vti* pull s.t. free, pull s.t. out
manipit– *vti* pull s.t. free, pull s.t. out
pihkoho– *vai* free oneself, escape; [*Christian:*] be saved

FREEZE
âhkwaci– *vai* freeze, be frozen
âhkwatihcikan– *ni* refrigerator; freezer
âhkwatihtâ– *vai* let (it) freeze, freeze (it)
âhkwatin– *vii* be frozen

FRESH
oski *ipn* young, fresh, new

FRIEND
otôtêmi– *vai* have a kinsman or friend, have (her/him) as kinsman or friend

FROM
ohtâciho– *vai* make one's living from there
ohtin– *vti* take s.t. from there, obtain s.t. from there
ohtinikê– *vai* take things from there, obtain things from there
ohtohtê– *vai* come walking from there
ôh *ipv* from there; [*in negative clause:*] past

FRONT
nîkân *ipc* in front, in the lead

FULL
âkwâtaskinê– *vai* be quite full (*e.g.*, pail), be more than half full
sâkaskinahtâ– *vai* make (it) full, fill (it)

FUN
> **miyawât–** *VTI* enjoy s.t.; have fun, be joyful
> **miyawâtamowin–** *NI* enjoyment; fun, joyfulness

FUNCTION
> **pimipayin–** *VII* work, function; go on

FUNERAL
> **nahin–** *VTA* bury s.o., hold a funeral for s.o.

FURTHER
> **awasitê** *IPC* further over there

FUTURE
> **niyâk** *IPC* in the future

GAMBLE
> **mêtawê–** *VAI* play; gamble

GARDEN
> **kiscikânis–** *NI* garden [*diminutive*]
> **kiscikêsi–** *VAI* plant seeds; have a small garden [*diminutive*]
> **pîwi-kiscikânis–** *NA* garden seeds [*diminutive*]
> **pîwi-kiscikânis–** *NI* vegetable garden [*diminutive*]

GARTERS
> **sîskêpison–** *NI* garters

GENEROUS
> **sawêyim–** *VTA* be generous towards s.o., bless s.o.

GIRL
> **iskwêsis–** *NA* girl, little girl

GIVE
> **mêki–** *VAI* give (it/him) away, release (it/him); give (her) in marriage
> **miy–** *VTA* give (it/him) to s.o.
> **miyikowisi–** *VAI* be given (it/him) by the powers
> **miyito–** *VAI* give (it/him) to one another

GIVE UP
> **pômê–** *VAI* be discouraged; give up

GLOVE
> **astis–** *NA* mitten, glove

GO
> **itohtê–** *VAI* go there or thus
> **nitawi** *IPV* go and
> **pimohtê–** *VAI* go along, walk along
> **wayawîstamâso–** *VAI* go outside for oneself, go to relieve oneself
> **wîcêht–** *VTI* go along with s.t., cooperate with s.t.
> **yîkatêstaw–** *VTA* go off to the side from s.o., go away from s.o.

GOD
> **kisê-manitow–** *NA* God the kind, the compassionate God; [*Christian:*] Merciful God

kisê-manitowi-pîkiskwêwin– *NI* God's word

manitow– *NA* God

manitowi-masinahikan– *NI* God's book, the Bible

GODFATHER

–ôhtâwîhkâwin– *NDA* godfather; step-father [*e.g.,* ôhtâwîhkâwina]

GOOD

miyo *IPV* good

miyo-pîkiskwêwin– *NI* good speech; [*Christian:*] the good news

miyo-tôt– *VTI* do s.t. good

miyo-tôtamowin– *NI* good deed, good works

miyo-tôtaw– *VTA* do s.o. a good turn

miyohtwâ– *VAI* be good-natured, be of pleasant character

miyokihtâ– *VAI* be good at growing (it)

miyonâkwan– *VII* look good, have a nice appearance, look prosperous

miyosi– *VAI* be good, be beautiful

miyosîhtâ– *VAI* make (it) good, make (it) beautiful

miyô– *VAI* be good at something

miywâsin– *VII* be good

miywêyiht– *VTI* consider s.t. good, like s.t.

miywêyim– *VTA* consider s.o. good, like s.o.

nihtâ *IPV* good at, competent, practised

nihtâwiminakinikê– *VAI* be good at sewing on beads

nihtâwisîhcikê– *VAI* be good at making things

nihtâwitêpo– *VAI* be good at cooking

wîhkasin– *VII* taste good

GOSSIP

âyimôm– *VTA* gossip about s.o.

GOVERNMENT

kihc-ôkimâw– *NA* king; government [*e.g.,* kihc-ôkimânâhk 'the government']

GRAIN

kiscikânis– *NA* grain, seed [*diminutive*]

kistikân– *NA* grain, seed; sheaf of grain

GRANARY

kistikânikamikw– *NI* granary

okistikânikamiko– *VAI* have a granary

GRANDCHILD

–ôsisim– *NDA* grandchild [*e.g.,* kôsisiminawak]

GRANDFATHER

–mosôm– *NDA* grandfather, grandfather's brother [*e.g.,* kimosôm]

GRANDMOTHER

–ôhkom– *NDA* grandmother, grandmother's sister, great-aunt [*e.g.,* nôhkom]

GRASS
 maskosiy– *NI* grass, hay
GRATEFUL
 atamih– *VTA* make s.o. grateful, make s.o. indebted, please s.o.
GREASY
 tômâ– *VII* be greased, be greasy
GREATLY
 kakwâyaki *IPV* greatly, extremely [*]
 misi *IPV* big, greatly
GREEN
 askihtakosi– *VAI* be green
 askihtakwâ– *VII* be green
 oskaskosîwinâkwan– *VII* look green, have a green appearance
GREEN-FEED
 asamastimwân– *NA* green-feed, oats [*sic:* NA with reference to oats]
GROUND
 mohcihk *IPC* on the bare ground
GROW
 kiyipikin– *VII* grow quickly
 miyokihtâ– *VAI* be good at growing (it)
 ohpiki– *VAI* grow up
 ohpikihtamâso– *VAI* make (it) grow for oneself
 ohpikihtâ– *VAI* make (it) grow
 ohpikin– *VII* grow
 wîc-ôhpikîm– *VTA* grow up with s.o., be raised together with s.o.
 wîpâcikin– *VII* grow out of place, grow wild, grow as weeds
GUIDE
 miyohtah– *VTA* guide s.o. well
GUTS
 –takisiy– *NDI* intestines, guts, entrails [*e.g.,* mitakisiya]
HABITUALLY
 mâna *IPC* usually, habitually
HALF
 âpihtaw *IPC* half
HAND
 –cihciy– *NDI* hand [*e.g.,* ocihciy]
 kîskicihcêpit– *VTA* tear s.o.'s hand off, tear s.o.'s finger off
HANDLE
 câpihcicikan– *NA* [*man's name:*] Handle
HANG UP
 akotâ– *VAI* hang (it) up
HARD
 maskawâ– *VII* be hard, be strong

HARD-WORKING
kakâyawâtisi– _VAI_ be hard-working, be of industrious disposition
kakâyawisî– _VAI_ be hard-working, be industrious

HARM
mâyi-tôtaw– _VTA_ do evil to s.o., harm s.o.

HARNESS
nîswahpiso– _VAI_ be harnessed as two, be a team of two
wiyahpicikê– _VAI_ do the harnessing

HARROW
sikwahcisikê– _VAI_ cultivate, harrow

HATE
pakwât– _VTA_ hate s.o., disapprove of s.o.
pakwât– _VTI_ hate s.t., disapprove of s.t.

HAUL
âwacimihtê– _VAI_ haul firewood
âwatamâso– _VAI_ haul (it/him) for oneself
âwatâ– _VAI_ haul (it)
kwâpikê– _VAI_ go for water, haul water
pîhtikwê-âwacimihtêwin– _NI_ hauling firewood inside [*; _sic:_ -i-; _cf._ pîhtokwê–]

HAVE
ayâ– _VAI_ have (it)
ayâw– _VTA_ have s.o.

HAY
maskosiy– _NI_ grass, hay

HE
wiya _PR_ he, she

HEALTH
itamahciho– _VAI_ feel thus, be in such health [_e.g.,_ nânitaw itamahciho– 'feel unwell']
miyomahciho– _VAI_ fare well, feel well, be in good health or spirit

HEAR
nitohtâkowisi– _VAI_ be heard by the powers
pêht– _VTI_ hear s.t.
pêhtaw– _VTA_ hear s.o.
pêhtamowin– _NI_ what is heard
pêhtâkwan– _VII_ be heard

HEART
–têh– _NDI_ heart [_e.g.,_ kitêhinawa]
wîsakitêhê– _VAI_ have a heavy heart

HEAT
kâspis– _VTI_ heat s.t. until crisp
kisâkamis– _VTI_ heat s.t. up as liquid

kisâkamisikê– *VAI* heat a liquid; make tea
kisis– *VTI* warm s.t. up, heat s.t. up

HEATER
awasowi-kotawanâpiskw– *NI* warming-stove, heater [*sic:* NI]
awaswâkan– *NI* heater [*sic:* NI]

HEAVEN
kihci-kîsikw– *NI* heaven

HEAVY
kosikwan– *VII* be heavy
wîsakitêhê– *VAI* have a heavy heart

HEEL
–ahkwan– *NDI* heel [*e.g.,* mahkwan]

HEIGHT
iskosi– *VAI* be so tall, be of such height

HELP
mâmawi-wîcihitowin– *NI* all helping together, general cooperation
wîcih– *VTA* help s.o.
wîcihikowisi– *VAI* be helped by the powers
wîcihiso– *VAI* help oneself
wîcihito– *VAI* help one another, cooperate with one another
wîcihtâso– *VAI* help with things

HERE
ôta *IPC* here

HEY
hêy *IPC* hey [*exclamatory*]

HIDE
kâso– *VAI* hide, hide oneself
mihkit– *VTI* scrape s.t. (meat) off the hide
otamiskay– *NI* hide-scrapings (meat scraped from hide)
pahkêkinohkê– *VAI* make dressed hides, make leather
pahkêkinos– *NI* small dressed hide, small piece of leather [*diminutive*]
pahkêkinw– *NI* dressed hide, finished hide, leather

HIGHLY
ayiwâkêyim– *VTA* think more of s.o., regard s.o. more highly
kihcêyiht– *VTI* think highly of s.t.
kihcêyihtamaw– *VTA* think highly of (it/him) for s.o.
kihcêyihtâkwan– *VII* be highly thought of
kihcêyim– *VTA* think highly of s.o.
kîhkâtêyihtâkwan– *VII* be held in high esteem, be prominent
kîhkâtêyim– *VTA* hold s.o. in high esteem

HILL
ayahikâkan– *NI* hiller, tool for covering potatoes with earth
ayahikê– *VAI* cover things with earth, hill things (*e.g.,* potatoes)

HIRE
  atoskah– *VTA* make s.o. work, employ s.o., hire s.o.
  atoskahâkan– *NA* employee, hired man
  atoskêmo– *VAI* get people to do things, employ people, hire people
  masinahikêh– *VTA* hire s.o.

HIT
  pakamahw– *VTA* strike s.o., hit s.o.

HITHER
  pê *IPV* hither

HOBBEMA
  maskwacîsihk *INM* [*place-name:*] Hobbema, Alberta [*locative; literally* at Bear's Hill]

HOLD
  itin– *VTI* hold s.t. thus
  micimin– *VTA* hold on to s.o.
  miciminamaw– *VTA* hold on to (it/him) for s.o.
  miciminamôh– *VTA* make s.o. hold on to (it/him)

HOLE
  payipis– *VTI* cut s.t. out, cut a hole in s.t.
  wâtihkân– *NI* hole, cellar
  yahkâtihkât– *VTI* dig out more of a hole or cellar, push out the size of an existing hole or cellar

HOLY
  ayamihêwi-saskamon– *NA* the host; Holy Communion
  kihcihtwâwi *IPN* of exalted character; venerable, holy [*e.g.,* kihcihtwâwi-côsap 'Holy Joseph']

HOME
  –îk– *NDI* house, dwelling, home [*e.g.,* nîkihk]
  kîwê– *VAI* return home
  kîwêhtah– *VTA* take s.o. home
  kîwêhtatâ– *VAI* take (it) home
  kîwêtot– *VTI* return home to s.t.
  kîwêtotaw– *VTA* return home to s.o.
  owîki– *VAI* live there, have one's home there [*sic; cf.* wîki–]
  wîki– *VAI* live there, have one's home there [*also* owîki–]

HOMEWORK
  kiskinohamâkosiwin– *NI* being a student, going to school; schoolwork, homework

HOOKED-NOSE
  okikocêsîs– *NA* [*man's name:*] Hooked-Nose [*?sic; gloss highly tentative*]

HORSE
  misatimokamikw– *NI* horse-barn
  misatimw– *NA* horse

HORSEBACK
têhtapi– *VAI* be mounted, be on horseback

HOSPITAL
âhkosîwikamikw– *NI* hospital

HOST
ayamihêwi-saskamon– *NA* the host; Holy Communion

HOT
kisâkamitêwâpoy– *NI* hot water
kisiso– *VAI* be warm, be hot
kîsopwê– *VII* be hot weather

HOUSE
–îk– *NDI* house, dwelling, home [*e.g.,* nîkihk]
asahkêwikamikw– *NI* ration house
wâskahikan– *NI* house
wâskahikanis– *NI* little house [*diminutive*]

HOUSEHOLD
wîkiwin– *NI* household; [*Christian:*] home

HOUSEMATE
–wîkimâkan– *NDA* spouse, housemate [*e.g.,* niwîkimâkan]

HOW
pikoyikohk *IPC* no matter how much, to any extent
tânisi *IPC* how
tânitahto *IPC* how many; so many
tânitahto-pîsim *IPC* how many months; what month is it [*predicative*];
so many months
tânitahtwâw *IPC* how many times; so many times

HUNDRED
mitâtahtomitanaw *IPC* one hundred
mitâtahtomitanaw-maskimot *IPC* a hundred bags, one hundred bags

HUNGRY
nôhtêhkatê– *VAI* be hungry, want food

HUNT
mâcî– *VAI* hunt, go hunting
nôcih– *VTA* pursue s.o., hunt s.o.

HUSBAND
–nâpêm– *NDA* husband [*e.g.,* onâpêmiwâwa]
onâpêmi– *VAI* have a husband, be married (woman)

I
niya *PR* I
nîsta *PR* I, too; I by contrast

IF
kîspin *IPC* if

ILL

mâyamahciho– *VAI* fare ill, be sick

IMMEDIATELY

sêmâk *IPC* right away, immediately

sôskwâc *IPC* simply, immediately, without further ado

IMMERSE

akohcim– *VTA* immerse s.o. in water (*e.g.,* baby)

pakâsimonah– *VTA* immerse s.o., bathe s.o.

pakâsimonahâwaso– *VAI* immerse one's children, bathe one's children

INCREASINGLY

tahk âyiwâk *IPC* increasingly, more and more

INDEED

tâpwê *IPC* truly, indeed

INDIAN

nêhiyaw– *NA* Cree Indian, Indian

nêhiyaw-masinîwin– *NI* Cree design, Cree motif, Indian design, Indian motif [*sic:* -w-]

nêhiyawi *IPV* Cree, Indian

nêhiyawi-wîhowin– *NI* Cree name, Indian name

nêhiyawiyîhkâso– *VAI* have a Cree name, have an Indian name

nêhiyâwi– *VAI* be a Cree Indian, be an Indian

INDISTINCTLY

wani *IPV* indistinctly, blurred

INDUSTRIOUS

kakâyawâtisi– *VAI* be hard-working, be of industrious disposition

INFANT

oskawâsis– *NA* young child, infant

INFECT

âsôskamaw– *VTA* infect s.o.

INNARDS

otitâmiyaw– *NI* innards [*]

INSECT

manicôs– *NA* insect, bug

INSIDE

asiwaso– *VAI* be inside

asiwatan– *VII* be inside

asiwatâ- *VAI* put (it) inside

itâmihk *IPC* inside (*e.g.,* mouth); underneath (*e.g.,* one's clothes)

pîhc-âyihk *IPC* inside

pîhtikwê-âwacimihtêwin– *NI* hauling firewood inside [*; *sic:* -i-; *cf.* pîhtokwê–]

pîhtokwah– *VTA* take s.o. inside

pîhtokwatamâkê– *VAI* bring (it/him) inside for people

pîhtokwatâ– *VAI* bring (it) inside

pîhtokwê– *VAI* enter, go inside

pîhtokwêyâmo– *VAI* flee inside

INSISTENTLY

katâc *IPC* insistently; [*in negative clause:*] necessarily

INSTANCE

mâcika *IPC* for instance

INTEND

wî *IPV* intend to

INTESTINES

–takisiy– *NDI* intestines, guts, entrails [*e.g.,* mitakisiya]

INVITE

nitom– *VTA* invite s.o.

JACKET

mîkisasâkay– *NI* beaded coat, beaded jacket

pahkêkinwêsâkay– *NI* leather coat, leather jacket

JESUS

cêsos– *NA* Jésus [*sic, as in French; cf.* cîsas–]

cîsas– *NA* Jesus [*sic, as in English; cf.* cêsos–]

JOIN

wîcihiwê– *VAI* join in, participate, be part of something

JOKE

naniwêyatwê– *VAI* joke, tell a joke

JOSEPH

côsap– *NA* Joseph

JOYFUL

miyawât– *VTI* enjoy s.t.; have fun, be joyful

miyawâtamowin– *NI* enjoyment; fun, joyfulness

JUDGMENT

wiyasiwât– *VTA* decide about s.o.; sit in judgment on s.o., hold court over s.o.

KILL

minaho– *VAI* kill an animal, make a kill

minahôstamaw– *VTA* kill an animal for s.o., make a kill for s.o.

minahôstamâso– *VAI* kill an animal for oneself, succeed in a kill

nipahiso– *VAI* kill oneself, commit suicide

nipahtamaw– *VTA* kill (it/him) for s.o., make a kill for s.o.

KIND

êkotowahk *IPC* of that kind

itowahk *IPC* this kind

kisêwâtisi– *VAI* be kind, be of compassionate disposition

kisêwâtisiwin– *NI* kindness, compassion

kitimâkêyim– *VTA* feel pity towards s.o., be kind to s.o., love s.o.

kîkw-ây– *NA* which one; what kind [*e.g.,* kîkw-âyak]

nanâtohkôskân *IPC* all kinds of things

nawac piko *IPC* sort of, kind of, approximately; more or less

KING

kihc-ôkimâw– *NA* king; government [*e.g.,* kihc-ôkimânâhk 'the government']

KINSMAN

otôtêmi– *VAI* have a kinsman or friend, have (her/him) as kinsman or friend

KITCHEN

piminawasowikamikw– *NI* cookhouse, kitchen

KNEEL

ocihkwanapi– *VAI* kneel

KNIT

apihkât– *VTA* braid s.o.; knit s.o. (*e.g.,* stocking)

apihkât– *VTI* braid s.t.; knit s.t.

apihkê– *VAI* knit, do knitting

apihkêpicikan– *NI* knitting machine

itapihkât– *VTI* braid s.t. thus; knit s.t. thus

itapihkê– *VAI* braid thus; knit thus [*; ?sic: record*]

kîsapihkât– *VTI* braid s.t. to completion; knit s.t. to completion

KNOCK OFF

pahkwaciwêpah– *VTI* knock s.t. off, pry s.t. off (*e.g.,* hide-scrapings)

pahkwatah– *VTI* knock s.t. off (*e.g.,* hide-scrapings)

KNOW

kiskêyiht– *VTI* know s.t.

KNOWLEDGE

kiskêyihtamâ– *VAI* have spiritual knowledge

LACK

kwîtâpacihtâ– *VAI* be short of (it) to use, lack tools

LAMP

wâsaskocêpayîs– *NI* lamp, electric light [*diminutive*]

wâsaskotênikan– *NI* light, lamp, lantern

LAND

askiy– *NI* earth, land, country; [*pl.:*] fields under cultivation, pieces of farmland

kistikân– *NI* field, arable land

LANGUAGE

nêhiyawêwin– *NI* speaking Cree, the Cree language

LANTERN

wâsaskotê– *VII* be light, be lit; be a lantern

wâsaskotênikan– *NI* light, lamp, lantern

LAST
awasi-nîpinohk *IPC* the summer before last
iskwêyâc *IPC* at last, at the end

LATER
mwêstas *IPC* later, subsequently

LAUGH
pâhpi– *VAI* laugh
pâhpih– *VTA* laugh at s.o.

LAUNDRY
kisêpêkinikê– *VAI* wash things, do the laundry
kisêpêkinikêwin– *NI* laundry, doing the laundry

LEADER
okimâw– *NA* chief, leader, boss; Band Council [*e.g.,* okimânâhk 'Band Council, band authorities']

LEAN
âsôhtatâ– *VAI* lean (it) across something
âswastâ– *VAI* place (it) to lean against something

LEATHER
pahkêkinohkê– *VAI* make dressed hides, make leather
pahkêkinos– *NI* small dressed hide, small piece of leather [*diminutive*]
pahkêkinw– *NI* dressed hide, finished hide, leather
pahkêkinwêsâkay– *NI* leather coat, leather jacket

LEAVE
iskonikowisi– *VAI* be left over (*e.g.,* to survive) by the powers
nakat– *VTA* leave s.o. behind; die and leave s.o. behind
nakat– *VTI* leave s.t. behind
nakatamaw– *VTA* leave (it/him) behind for s.o.
nakataskê– *VAI* leave the earth behind, depart the world, die
paskêwihito– *VAI* leave one another; separate, divorce
sipwêhtê– *VAI* leave, depart
sipwêpici– *VAI* leave with one's camp
wayawî– *VAI* go outside; go to relieve oneself; leave school, leave hospital

LEG
–skât– *NDI* leg [*e.g.,* miskâta]

LEGGINGS
–tâs– *NDA* leggings, trousers, pants [*e.g.,* mitâsa]

LEND
awih– *VTA* lend (it/him) to s.o.; rent (it/him) out to s.o.
awihiwê– *VAI* lend (it/him) to people; rent (it/him) out to people

LESS
âstamipayi– *VAI* become less, run low (*e.g.,* money)

LETTER
masinahikêwin– *NI* writing; letter, character

LID

akwanâpowêhikâso– *VAI* be covered as vessel capable of containing liquid, have a lid (*e.g.,* pot)

LIE

kawisimo– *VAI* lie down, go to bed

pimisin– *VAI* lie extended

LIFE

pimâciho– *VAI* make a life for oneself, live

pimâcihowin– *NI* way of life; livelihood

pimâtisiwin– *NI* life

LIGHT

saskah– *VTI* light s.t. (*e.g.,* lamp)

wâsaskocêpayîs– *NI* lamp, electric light [*diminutive*]

wâsaskotê– *VII* be light, be lit; be a lantern

wâsaskotênikan– *NI* light, lamp, lantern

wâsaskotênikâkê– *VAI* light things with (it), use (it) to have light

wâsaskotênikê– *VAI* light things, have light

yâhkasin– *VII* be light in weight

LIKE

miyoht– *VTI* like the sound of s.t.

miywâpisin– *VAI* like the look of something

miywêyiht– *VTI* consider s.t. good, like s.t.

miywêyim– *VTA* consider s.o. good, like s.o.

takahkêyim– *VTA* consider s.o. nice, like s.o.

LINING

pîhtawêkwât– *VTI* sew s.t. as lining into a garment; sew s.t. in between covers, sew covers on s.t.

LIQUID

kisâkamis– *VTI* heat s.t. up as liquid

kisâkamisikê– *VAI* heat a liquid; make tea

LISTEN

nanahiht– *VTI* listen well to s.t., obey s.t.

nanahihtaw– *VTA* listen well to s.o., obey s.o.

nitohtaw– *VTA* listen to s.o.

LITERATE

masinahikê– *VAI* write things; write, be literate

LITTLE

apisis *IPC* a little

pîwêyimo– *VAI* think little of oneself, have low self-esteem; [*Christian:*] be humble

LITTLE-HEAD

oscikwânis– *NA* [*woman's name:*] Little-Head

LIVE

ayâ– *VAI* be there, live there
kanâtapi– *VAI* live in a clean house [*]
kihci-wîki– *VAI* live formally; [*Christian:*] live in residence
ohtâciho– *VAI* make one's living from there
otisâpaht– *VTI* have lived long enough to see s.t.
owîki– *VAI* live there, have one's home there [*sic; cf.* wîki–]
pimâcih– *VTA* make s.o. live, give life to s.o.; make a living for s.o., sustain s.o.
pimâcihiso– *VAI* make oneself live; make a living for oneself
pimâciho– *VAI* make a life for oneself, live
pimâtisi– *VAI* live, be alive
pimâtisîtot– *VTI* live one's life; live one's life by s.t.
wîc-âyâm– *VTA* live with s.o.
wîcêhto– *VAI* live with one another
wîcêw– *VTA* accompany s.o., live with s.o.
wîki– *VAI* live there, have one's home there [*also* owîki–]
wîkihto– *VAI* live with each other, be married
wîkihtowin– *NI* living together, matrimony
wîkim– *VTA* live with s.o., be married to s.o.
wîtokwêm– *VTA* share a dwelling with s.o., live with s.o.

LIVELIHOOD

pimâcihowin– *NI* way of life; livelihood

LIVING ROOM

apîwikamikw– *NI* sitting room, living room

LOAD

pôsihtâ– *VAI* put (it) on a conveyance, load (it) on

LODGE

mîkiwâhp– *NI* lodge, tipi

LOG

mistikokamikw– *NI* log-house
mistikw– *NI* pole, log, rail
napakikamikos– *NI* flat-roofed log-house [*diminutive*]

LOIN-CLOTH

âsiyân– *NA* loin-cloth, diaper

LONG

kinosi– *VAI* be long, be tall
kinwâ– *VII* be long, be tall
kinwês *IPC* for a long time

LONG AGO

kayâs *IPC* long ago
kayâsi *IPN* long-ago, old-time

LOOK

îh *IPC* lo! look! [*exclamatory*]

kanawâpam– *VTA* look at s.o.; look after s.o.

kanâcinâkosi– *VAI* look clean, give a clean appearance

kitâpaht– *VTI* look at s.t.

kitâpam– *VTA* look at s.o.

miyonâkwan– *VII* look good, have a nice appearance, look prosperous

miywâpisin– *VAI* like the look of something

niton– *VTI* look for s.t.

LOOK AFTER

kanawâpam– *VTA* look at s.o.; look after s.o.

kanawâpokê– *VAI* look after a household, keep house

kanawêyiht– *VTI* look after s.t., take care of s.t.

kanawêyihtamôh– *VTA* ask s.o. to look after (it/him), leave (it/him) to be looked after by s.o.

kanawêyim– *VTA* look after s.o., take care of s.o.

pamih– *VTA* tend to s.o., look after s.o.

pamihiso– *VAI* tend oneself, look after oneself

pamihtamaw– *VTA* tend to (it/him) for s.o., look after (it/him) for s.o.

pamihtamâso– *VAI* tend to (it/him) for or by oneself, look after (it/him) for or by oneself

pamin– *VTA* tend to s.o., look after s.o.

pamin– *VTI* tend to s.t., look after s.t.

paminiso– *VAI* tend to oneself, look after oneself

paminiwê– *VAI* tend to people, look after people

LOSE

wanih– *VTA* lose s.o.

wanihtâ– *VAI* lose (it)

LOVE

kitimâkêyihto– *VAI* feel pity towards one another, love one another

kitimâkêyihtowin– *NI* feeling pity towards one another, loving one another

kitimâkêyim– *VTA* feel pity towards s.o., be kind to s.o., love s.o.

sâkih– *VTA* love s.o., be attached to s.o.

sâkihito– *VAI* love one another

sâkihitowin– *NI* mutual love, charity

sâkihtâ– *VAI* love (it), be attached to (it)

LOW

capahcâsin– *VII* be low [*diminutive*]

LUMBER

napakihtakw– *NI* flat lumber, board

LYE

pihkwâpoy– *NI* lye

MACHINE

âpacihcikan– *NI* tool, appliance, machine

kaskikwâsopayihcikanis– *NI* sewing machine [*diminutive*]

kaskikwâsopayihcikâkê– *VAI* do machine-sewing with (it), use (it) to
machine-sew

kaskikwâswâkan– *NI* sewing machine

MAKE

isîh– *VTA* make s.o. thus

isîhtâ– *VAI* make (it) thus

misisîhtâ– *VAI* make (it) big

nihtâwisîhcikê– *VAI* be good at making things

osîh– *VTA* make s.o., prepare s.o. (*e.g.,* bread)

osîhcikâtê– *VII* be made, be prepared

osîhcikêwin– *NI* what is made, handiwork, product

osîhtamaw– *VTA* make (it/him) for s.o.

osîhtamâso– *VAI* make (it/him) for oneself

osîhtâ– *VAI* make (it), prepare (it)

takahkisîhtâ– *VAI* make (it) nice

MALE

nâpêw– *NA* man, male adult

MAN

kisêyiniw– *NA* old man, elder

nâpêw– *NA* man, male adult

oskinîki– *VAI* be a young man

oskinîkiw– *NA* young man

oskinîkîwiyinîsiwi– *VAI* be a young man

MANY

ihtasi– *VAI* be so many, be as many

mihcêt *IPC* many, much

mihcêtôsê– *VAI* have many children, have numerous offspring

mihcêtwâw *IPC* many times

mistahi *IPC* very many, lots

môy kakêtihk *IPC* a great many

tahto *IPC* so many, as many

tahto-aya *IPC* so many [*sic:* -o-]

tahtw-âskiy *IPC* so many years, as many years

tahtwâw *IPC* so many times

tânitahto *IPC* how many; so many

tânitahto-pîsim *IPC* how many months; what month is it [*predicative*];
so many months

tânitahtwâw *IPC* how many times; so many times

MANYPLIES

omâw– *NA* "bible", manyplies, omasum (*i.e.,* third stomach of ruminant)

MARK

masinah– *VTI* mark s.t., draw s.t.; write s.t.

masinahikâtê– *VII* have marks, have writing; be written

MARRY

kihci-wîkihto– *VAI* be formally married in church

kihci-wîkihtowin– *NI* formal marriage, Holy Matrimony

kihci-wîkim– *VTA* marry s.o. formally in church

mêki– *VAI* give (it/him) away, release (it/him); give (her) in marriage

onâpêmi– *VAI* have a husband, be married (woman)

otinito– *VAI* take one another; marry each other

wîkihto– *VAI* live with each other, be married

wîkim– *VTA* live with s.o., be married to s.o.

MARSH

îhkatawâw– *NI* slough, marsh

MARY

mariy– *NA* Marie, the Virgin Mary [*sic, as in French* Marie]

MASS

ayamihâhtah– *VTA* make s.o. go to church, take s.o. to mass

nîpâ-ayamihâ– *VAI* celebrate midnight mass (at Christmas)

MATRIMONY

wîkihtowin– *NI* living together, matrimony

MEAN

kitimah– *VTA* be mean to s.o., treat s.o. badly

MEASURE

tipah– *VTI* measure s.t.

MEAT

kâhkêwakw– *NI* dried meat

pânis– *VTI* cut s.t. (*e.g.,* meat) into sheets

pânisâwê– *VAI* cut meat into sheets

wiyâs– *NI* meat

MEET

nakiskaw– *VTA* encounter s.o., meet s.o.

MEETING

mâmawôpi– *VAI* sit together, hold a meeting

MERELY

mosci *IPV* merely, without instrument

têpiyâhk *IPC* merely; barely; so long as

METAL

pîwâpiskw– *NI* metal, metal object; steel blade

MIDDLE

tastawayas *IPC* in between, in the middle

tâsawisâwât– *VTI* cut into the middle of s.t., slice s.t. open (*e.g.,* veal belly cordon-bleu)

MIDNIGHT
âpihtâ-tipiskâ– *VII* be midnight
nîpâ-ayamihâ– *VAI* celebrate midnight mass (at Christmas)

MILK
tôhtôsâpoy– *NI* milk
yîkinikan– *NA* milk-cow
yîkinikê– *VAI* do the milking
yîkinikêstamâso– *VAI* do the milking for oneself

MIND
mâmitonêyihcikan– *NI* mind; thought, worry

MISSED
kwîtawêyihcikâtê– *VII* be missed, be in short supply

MISTAKE
patinikê– *VAI* make a mistake, take a wrong step, transgress; [*Christian:*] sin

MITTEN
astis– *NA* mitten, glove

MOCCASIN
maskisin– *NI* moccasin, shoe
napakaskisin– *NI* flat moccasin
ocîhkwêhikan– *NI* pleated moccasin

MONEY
sôniyâhkât– *VTI* make money at s.t.
sôniyâhkê– *VAI* make money; earn wages
sôniyâw– *NA* money; wages
sôniyâwi *IPC* with respect to money, in financial matters

MONTH
tânitahto-pîsim *IPC* how many months; what month is it [*predicative*]; so many months

MOOSE
môso-pahkêkin– *NI* finished moose-hide
môso-wiyâs– *NI* moose-meat
môsw– *NA* moose [*e.g.,* môswa]

MORE
ayiwâk *IPC* more; [*in numeral phrases:*] plus
ayiwâkêyim– *VTA* think more of s.o., regard s.o. more highly
ayiwâkipayi– *VAI* have more than enough, have a surplus, have plenty
nawac *IPC* more, better, rather
nawac piko *IPC* sort of, kind of, approximately; more or less
tahk âyiwâk *IPC* increasingly, more and more

MORNING
kîkisêpâ *IPC* early in the morning

MOTHER
–kâwiy– *NDA* mother, mother's sister [*e.g.,* kikâwînawak]
okâwîmâw– *NA* mother

MOTHER-IN-LAW
–sikos– *NDA* father's sister, mother's brother's wife; mother-in-law, father-in-law's brother's wife, aunt [*e.g.,* nisikosak]

MOTIF
nêhiyaw-masinîwin– *NI* Cree design, Cree motif, Indian design, Indian motif [*sic:* -w-]

MOUNTED
têhtapi– *VAI* be mounted, be on horseback

MOUTH
–cônis– *NDI* mouth [*diminutive; e.g.,* ocônisiwâwa]
pîkokonêwêpayi– *VAI* have cracks in one's mouth, have one's mouth break out in blisters (*e.g.,* from thrush)

MOVE
âhc-âyâ– *VAI* move one's abode, move from one place to another
ispayi– *VAI* move thus, drive there
papâmipici– *VAI* move about, camp here and there
yîkatêpayin– *VII* move off to the side, move sideways (*e.g.,* braided strips of rabbitskin)

MUCH
iyikohk *IPC* so much, to such an extent
mihcêt *IPC* many, much
osâm *IPC* too much; because
ômayikohk *IPC* this much, to this degree, to this extent
pikoyikohk *IPC* no matter how much, to any extent

MUD
asiskîwikamikos– *NI* mud shack [*diminutive*]
sisoskiwakin– *VTI* mud s.t. (*e.g.,* log-house), plaster s.t.
sisoskiwakinamâso– *VAI* do the mudding for oneself
sisoskiwakinikâtê– *VII* be mudded
sisoskiwakinikê– *VAI* do the mudding

MUSKRAT
wacaskw– *NA* muskrat

MUST
piko *IPC* must, have to [*clause-initial predicative*]

NAME
isiyîhkâso– *VAI* be called thus, have such a name
isiyîhkât– *VTA* call s.o. thus, give s.o. such a name

isiyîhkât– *VTI* call s.t. thus, give s.t. such a name
isiyîhkâtê– *VII* be called thus, have such a name
nêhiyawi-wîhowin– *NI* Cree name, Indian name
nêhiyawiyîhkâso– *VAI* have a Cree name, have an Indian name
owîhowini– *VAI* have a name, have (it) as one's name
wîh– *VTA* name s.o., mention s.o. by name
wîhowin– *NI* name
wîht– *VTI* name s.t., mention s.t. by name

NATURALLY
cikêmâ *IPC* of course, naturally

NEARBY
kisiwâk *IPC* nearby

NECESSARILY
katâc *IPC* insistently; [*in negative clause:*] necessarily

NEVER
nama wîhkâc *IPC* never

NEVERTHELESS
âhci piko *IPC* still, nevertheless [*adversative*]

NEW
oski *IPN* young, fresh, new

NEXT
iyaskohc *IPC* next in sequence

NICE
miyonâkohcikê– *VAI* have one's property look nice, have things look prosperous
takahkêyim– *VTA* consider s.o. nice, like s.o.
takahkihtâkwan– *VII* sound nice
takahkisîhtâ– *VAI* make (it) nice

NIGHT
tipiskâ– *VII* be night
wani-tipiskâ– *VII* be dark night

NINETY
kêkâ-mitâtahtomitanaw *IPC* ninety

NO
namwâc *IPC* no, not [*]

NO LONGER HERE
ôyâ *PR* that one no longer here [*absentative, e.g.,* ôyâ]

NONEXISTENT
namatê– *VAI* be nonexistent, have disappeared

NON-INDIAN
môniyâw– *NA* non-Indian, Whiteman

NORTH
kîwêtinohk *IPC* in the north

NOT

êkamâ *IPC* it is not the case [*predicative*]

êkâ *IPC* not [*cf.* êkây, êkâya]

êkây *IPC* not [*cf.* êkâ, êkâya]

êkâya *IPC* not [*cf.* êkâ, êkây]

ma cî *IPC* is it not the case [*; predicative*]

môya *IPC* not [*cf.* namôya]

namôya *IPC* not [*cf.* môya]

namwâc *IPC* no, not [*]

NOTHING

ma kîkway *PR* nothing

nama kîkway *IPC* nothing

NOW

anohc *IPC* now, today

NUMEROUS

mihcêti– *VAI* be numerous, be plentiful

NUN

ayamihêwiskwêw– *NA* nun

NURSE

maskihkîwiskwêw– *NA* nurse

nôh– *VTA* suckle s.o., nurse s.o.

nôni– *VAI* suck at the breast, be nursed

OATS

asamastimwân– *NA* green-feed, oats [*sic: NA with reference to oats*]

OBEY

nanahiht– *VTI* listen well to s.t., obey s.t.

nanahihtaw– *VTA* listen well to s.o., obey s.o.

OBTAIN

ohtin– *VTI* take s.t. from there, obtain s.t. from there

ohtinikê– *VAI* take things from there, obtain things from there

OCCUR

ihkin– *VII* occur, take place

ispayin– *VII* occur thus, happen thus

OFF

aspin *IPC* off, away; the last I knew

kâskah– *VTI* scrape s.t. off

kîskicihcêpit– *VTA* tear s.o.'s hand off, tear s.o.'s finger off

paskin– *VTA* break s.o. off (*e.g.*, thread)

OH

â *IPC* ah, oh [*; exclamatory; cf.* âw]

âw *IPC* ah, oh [*exclamatory*]

kani *IPC* oh yes, I just remembered, I had forgotten [*cf.* kanihk]

OIL

pimiy– NI fat, oil; crude petroleum

OLD

kêhtê-ay– NA old person, elder [*e.g.,* kêhtê-ayak]

kêhtê-ayiwi– VAI be an old person, be an elder

kêhtêskwêw– NA old woman, old lady

kisêyiniw– NA old man, elder

nôcokwêsiw– NA old woman, old lady [*diminutive; also* nôtokwêsiw–]

nôtokwêsiw– NA old woman, old lady [*sic; cf.* nôcokwêsiw–]

OLD-PAN

kayâsiyâkan– NA [*man's name:*] Old-Pan

OLDER

–mis– NDA older sister [*e.g.,* omisa]

–stês– NDA older brother [*e.g.,* nistês]

omisi– VAI have an older sister, have (her) as older sister

OLDEST

omisimâw– NA oldest sister

ostêsimâw– NA oldest brother

OMASUM

omâw– NA "bible", manyplies, omasum (*i.e.,* third stomach of ruminant)

ONCE

âskaw IPC once in a while

pêyakwâw IPC once

ONE

pêyak IPC one; alone, single

ONION

wîhcêkaskosiy– NI onion

wîhcêkaskosîwi-sâkahikanihk INM [*place-name:*] Onion Lake, Saskatchewan [*locative; literally* at Onion Lake]

ONLY

nayêstaw IPC only

piko IPC only [*enclitic*]

OPEN

tawâ– VII be open, have room

yôhtên– VTI open s.t.

OR

ahpô IPC even, or

ORPHAN

kitimâk-ôhpikih– VTA raise s.o. in poverty; raise s.o. as an orphan

kîwâc-âwâsis– NA orphan

kîwâtisi– VAI be orphaned, be an orphan

OTHER
   kotak *PR* other, another [*e.g.,* kotakak, kotaka]

OUT
   kwâpah– *VTI* dip s.t. out
   manipit– *VTI* pull s.t. free, pull s.t. out
   pahpawiwêpin– *VTI* shake s.t. out
   pawin– *VTI* shake s.t. out
   payipis– *VTI* cut s.t. out, cut a hole in s.t.
   sîkiwêpin– *VTI* pour s.t. out
   sîn– *VTI* wring s.t. out
   sînâskwah– *VTI* wring s.t. out with a wooden tool
   têpwât– *VTA* call out to s.o., yell at s.o.

OUTHOUSE
   mîsîwikamikw– *NI* outhouse, toilet

OUTSIDE
   wayawî– *VAI* go outside; go to relieve oneself; leave school, leave hospital
   wayawîpahtâ– *VAI* run outside
   wayawîpakitin– *VTA* put s.o. (*e.g.,* diapers) down outside
   wayawîstamâso– *VAI* go outside for oneself, go to relieve oneself
   wayawîtimihk *IPC* outside
   wayawîwin– *NI* going outside, going to the toilet [*]

OVER
   awasitê *IPC* further over there
   êkotê *IPC* over there
   iskonikowisi– *VAI* be left over (*e.g.,* to survive) by the powers
   itê *IPC* there, over there
   misiwê *IPC* all over
   nêtê *IPC* over there
   ôtê *IPC* over there

OVERCAST
   titipikwanah– *VTI* sew s.t. in overcast stitch (*e.g.,* the spiral loops around the vamp of a moccasin)

OVERCOAT
   waskitasâkay– *NI* overcoat

OVERCOME
   sâkôcih– *VTA* overcome s.o., beat s.o.
   sâkôhtâ– *VAI* overcome (it), accomplish (it); be able to lift (it) up

OVERSEAS
   akâmaskîhk *IPC* across the water, overseas

OWN
   tipêyiht– *VTI* own s.t., control s.t.
   tipêyim– *VTA* own s.o., control s.o.

OX
ayêhkwêw– *NA* castrated bull; ox

PAIL
askihkos– *NA* little pail, little pot [*diminutive*]
askihkw– *NA* pail, pot

PAIR
pêyakw-ây– *NA* a single one (*e.g.,* stocking); one pair [*e.g.,* pêyakw-âyak]

PANTS
–tâs– *NDA* leggings, trousers, pants [*e.g.,* mitâsa]

PARENT
–nîkihikw– *NDA* parent [*e.g.,* ninîkihikonânak]
onîkihikomâw– *NA* parent

PARTICIPATE
wîcihiwê– *VAI* join in, participate, be part of something

PARTNER
–wîcêwâkan– *NDA* companion, partner [*e.g.,* kiwîcêwâkaniwâwak]
owîcêwâkani– *VAI* have a companion or partner, have (her/him) as companion or partner

PARTRIDGE
paspaskiw– *NA* partridge

PASS
âsawi *IPV* in passing something on
âsawinamaw– *VTA* pass (it/him) on to s.o. [*sic:* -awi-; *cf.* âsônamaw–]

PAST
nâway *IPC* behind; in the past

PATCHWORK
nanâtohkokwâso– *VAI* sew patchwork blankets

PATTERN
masinihtatâ– *VAI* trace (it), use (it) as pattern
wiyis– *VTI* cut s.t. out, cut s.t. to a pattern
wiyisamaw– *VTA* cut a pattern for s.o.
wiyisamâso– *VAI* cut a pattern for oneself, cut one's own pattern

PAUNCH
wînâstakay– *NI* "tripe", paunch (*i.e.,* largest stomach of ruminant)

PAY
tipahamaw– *VTA* pay s.o. for (it/him), repay a debt to s.o.; pay s.o. a pension

PEACE
wânaskêwin– *NI* being at peace with oneself

PENSION
tipahamaw– *VTA* pay s.o. for (it/him), repay a debt to s.o.; pay s.o. a pension

PEOPLE
　　–**ayisiyinîm**– NDA people, followers [*usually plural; e.g.,* kitayisiyinîmak]
　　–**iyinîm**– NDA people, followers [*usually plural; e.g.,* otiyinîma]
PERHAPS
　　mâskôc IPC perhaps, I suppose [*cf.* mâskôt]
PERMIT
　　pakitin– VTA let s.o. go, release s.o.; permit (it) to s.o.
　　pakitinikowisi– VAI be permitted by the powers
PERSEVERE
　　sîpihkêyiht– VTI endure s.t. by strength of mind; persevere
PERSIST
　　âhkamêyimo– VAI persist in one's will
　　âhkami IPV persistently, unceasingly, unwaveringly
PERSON
　　–**îcayisiyiniw**– NDA fellow person, fellow human [*sic:* -a-;
　　　　e.g., kîcayisiyinînaw]
　　ayisiyiniw– NA person, human being
　　ayisiyinîwi– VAI be a person, be a human being
　　kêhtê-ay– NA old person, elder [*e.g.,* kêhtê-ayak]
　　kêhtê-ayiwi– VAI be an old person, be an elder
　　osk-ây– NA young person [*e.g.,* osk-âyak]
　　oskayisiyiniw– NA young person [*sic:* -a-]
　　otâhkosiw– NA sick person
PERSONALLY
　　tipiyaw IPC personally, really
PETROLEUM
　　askîwi-pimiy– NI coal oil, petroleum
　　pimiy– NI fat, oil; crude petroleum
PHOTOGRAPH
　　masinipayiwin– NI picture, photograph
PICK
　　mawiso– VAI pick berries
PICTURE
　　masinipayiwin– NI picture, photograph
PIG
　　kôhkôs– NA pig
PITY
　　kitimâkêyihto– VAI feel pity towards one another, love one another
　　kitimâkêyihtowin– NI feeling pity towards one another, loving one
　　　　another
　　kitimâkêyim– VTA feel pity towards s.o., be kind to s.o., love s.o.
　　kitimâkinaw– VTA take pity upon s.o., lovingly tend s.o.

kitimâkinâso– *VAI* pity oneself, feel sorry for oneself

kitimâkisi– *VAI* be pitiable, be poor

PLACE

ah– *VTA* place s.o.

astamâso– *VAI* place (it/him) for oneself

astâ– *VAI* place (it)

astê– *VII* be placed

êkotowihk *IPC* in that place

ispastâ– *VAI* place (it) so high, pile (it) so high

itastâ– *VAI* place (it) thus

itastê– *VII* be placed thus; be written thus

itowihk *IPC* in this place

ômatowihk *IPC* in this place

pikw îta *IPC* in any place, everywhere

PLAN

mâmitonêyihtêstamâso– *VAI* think about (it/him) for oneself, plan for oneself

PLANT

kiscikêsi– *VAI* plant seeds; have a small garden [*diminutive*]

kistikê– *VAI* seed things, plant things

PLATTER

mistiyâkan– *NI* big dish, platter, large bowl

PLAY

mêtawê– *VAI* play; gamble

PLAYED OUT

nôhtêsin– *VAI* be played out

PLEASANT

miyohtwâ– *VAI* be good-natured, be of pleasant character

PLEASE

atamih– *VTA* make s.o. grateful, make s.o. indebted, please s.o.

kiyâm *IPC* let it be, let there be no further delay; please

mahti *IPC* let's see, please

PLEATED

ocîhkwêhikan– *NI* pleated moccasin

PLENTIFUL

mihcêti– *VAI* be numerous, be plentiful

PLENTY

ayiwâkipayi– *VAI* have more than enough, have a surplus, have plenty

PLOUGH

pîkopicikâtê– *VII* be ploughed soil, be cultivated

pîkopicikê– *VAI* plough, do the ploughing

pîkopicikêh– *VTA* make s.o. plough, use s.o. (*e.g.*, oxen) in ploughing

pîkopit– *VTI* break s.t. (*e.g.,* soil), plough s.t. (*e.g.,* field)

pîkopitamaw– *VTA* break (it) for s.o., plough (it) for s.o.

PLUS

ayiwâk *IPC* more; [*in numeral phrases:*] plus

POISON

piscipo– *VAI* be poisoned

piscipohtâ– *VAI* poison (it)

piscipôskaw– *VTA* poison s.o.

POLE

mistikw– *NI* pole, log, rail

POOR

kitimâkisi– *VAI* be pitiable, be poor

POT

askihkos– *NA* little pail, little pot [*diminutive*]

askihkw– *NA* pail, pot

POTATO

askipwâw– *NI* potato

POUR

sîkin– *VTI* pour s.t.

sîkiwêpin– *VTI* pour s.t. out

POVERTY

kitimâk-ôhpikih– *VTA* raise s.o. in poverty; raise s.o. as an orphan

POWDERY

pîwêyâwahkwâ– *VII* be powdery

POWER

pawâmiwin– *NI* spirit power; [*Christian:*] witchcraft

POWERS

iskonikowisi– *VAI* be left over (*e.g.,* to survive) by the powers

miyikowisi– *VAI* be given (it/him) by the powers

otinikowisi– *VAI* be taken by the powers

pakitinikowisi– *VAI* be permitted by the powers

sawêyimikowisi– *VAI* be blessed by the powers

wîcihikowisi– *VAI* be helped by the powers

PRACTISED

nakacihtâ– *VAI* be familiar with doing (it), be practised at (it)

PRAIRIE-CHICKEN

pihêw– *NA* prairie-chicken

PRAY

ayamihâ– *VAI* pray, say prayers; participate in a religious observance

ayamihâwin– *NI* prayer, saying prayers; religious observance; religion; the Roman Catholic Church

ayamihêstamaw– *VTA* say prayers for s.o.

mawimoscikê– *VAI* pray, wail

wîc-âyamihâm– *VTA* pray with s.o.

PREACH

kakêskihkêmo– *VAI* counsel people, preach at people

kakêskim– *VTA* counsel s.o., preach at s.o.

miyo-kakêskihkêmowin– *NI* good counselling, good preaching

PREFERABLY

iyâyaw *IPC* preferably, rather

PREOCCUPIED

otamiyo– *VAI* busy oneself, keep busy, be preoccupied

PREPARE

kwayâc *IPC* ready, prepared

kwayâci *IPV* in readiness, in preparation

osîh– *VTA* make s.o., prepare s.o. (*e.g.*, bread)

osîhcikâtê– *VII* be made, be prepared

osîhtâ– *VAI* make (it), prepare (it)

wawêyîst– *VTI* prepare s.t., be prepared

PRESERVE

kaskâpiskah– *VTI* can s.t., preserve s.t.

PRESUMABLY

êtokwê *IPC* presumably, I guess

PREVIOUSLY

kayâhtê *IPC* before, previously

PRIEST

ayamihêwiyiniw– *NA* priest

PRODUCT

osîhcikêwin– *NI* what is made, handiwork, product

PROGRESSIVELY

ati *IPV* progressively

PROJECT

sâkamon– *VII* stick out, project

sâkêkamon– *VII* stick out as cloth, project as cloth

PROMINENT

kîhkâtêyihtâkwan– *VII* be held in high esteem, be prominent

PROPERLY

kwayask *IPC* properly, right

kwayaski *IPV* properly

nahapi– *VAI* sit down in one's place, be properly seated

PROPERTY

miyonâkohcikê– *VAI* have one's property look nice, have things look
   prosperous

PROPHESY

kiskiwêh– *VTI* utter s.t. as a prophesy, utter prophesies

kiskiwêhw– *VTA* utter prophesies to s.o., utter prophesies
   about s.o.

PROSPEROUS
> **miyonâkohcikê**– *VAI* have one's property look nice, have things look prosperous
>
> **miyonâkwan**– *VII* look good, have a nice appearance, look prosperous

PROUD
> **mamihcisi**– *VAI* be proud

PROVISIONS
> **nîmâ**– *VAI* take provisions

PROVOKE
> **paciyawêh**– *VTA* wrong s.o. by one's utterance, provoke s.o.'s anger

PRY OFF
> **pahkwaciwêpah**– *VTI* knock s.t. off, pry s.t. off (*e.g.*, hide-scrapings)

PULL
> **kêcikopit**– *VTI* pull s.t. free, pull s.t. out
>
> **kipwahpit**– *VTI* pull s.t. close, tie s.t. close
>
> **manipit**– *VTI* pull s.t. free, pull s.t. out
>
> **nîhcipit**– *VTA* pull s.o. down, drag s.o. down

PURPOSELY
> **ohcitaw** *IPC* purposely; it has to be [*predicative*]

PURSUE
> **nawaswât**– *VTA* pursue s.o., chase after s.o.
>
> **nawaswât**– *VTI* pursue s.t., chase after s.t.
>
> **nôcih**– *VTA* pursue s.o., hunt s.o.
>
> **nôcihtâ**– *VAI* pursue (it), work at (it)

PUT
> **akohtitâ**– *VAI* put (it) in water, add (it) to water (*e.g.*, boric acid)
>
> **asiwatâ**– *VAI* put (it) inside
>
> **kikamohtâ**– *VAI* attach (it), put (it) on something
>
> **kikamôh**– *VTA* attach s.o., put s.o. (*e.g.*, yarn) on something
>
> **kikin**– *VTI* put s.t. on something, add s.t. in (*e.g.*, baking-powder)
>
> **kwayâtastamaw**– *VTA* put (it/him) aside in readiness for s.o.
>
> **kwayâtastamâso**– *VAI* put (it/him) aside in readiness for oneself
>
> **kwayâtastâ**– *VAI* place (it) in readiness, put (it) aside in readiness
>
> **nahastâ**– *VAI* put (it) in its place, put (it) away
>
> **pakitin**– *VTI* let s.t. go, release s.t., give s.t. up; put s.t. in (*e.g.*, seed potatoes)
>
> **sêkwâpiskin**– *VTI* put s.t. under the coals, into the oven
>
> **wayawîpakitin**– *VTA* put s.o. (*e.g.*, diapers) down outside

QUIET
> **wâskamisî**– *VAI* settle down; be of quiet disposition
>
> **wêtinahk** *IPC* quietly

QUIT
> **pôyo**– *VAI* cease, quit [*]

RABBIT
wâposw– NA rabbit
wâposwayân– NA rabbitskin
wâposwayânakohp– NI rabbitskin blanket

RACE-HORSE
kotiskâwêwatimw– NA race-horse [*sic:* -a-]

RAIL
mistikw– NI pole, log, rail

RAIN
kimiwan– VII rain, be rainy

RAISE
kitimâk-ôhpikih– VTA raise s.o. in poverty; raise s.o. as an orphan
ohpikih– VTA raise s.o.
wîc-ôhpikîm– VTA grow up with s.o., be raised together with s.o.

RASH
môskipayi– VAI break out in a rash, in sores (*e.g.,* with thrush)

RATHER
iyâyaw IPC preferably, rather
nawac IPC more, better, rather

RATION
asahkêwikamikw– NI ration house

RAW
askiti– VAI be raw, be uncooked (*e.g.,* flour)

REACH
otiht– VTI reach s.t.

READ
ayamihtâ– VAI read (it)
ayamihcikêwin– NI reading; [*Christian:*] bible verse

READY, READINESS
kwayâc IPC ready, prepared
kwayâci IPV in readiness, in preparation
kwayâtastamaw– VTA put (it/him) aside in readiness for s.o.
kwayâtastamâso– VAI put (it/him) aside in readiness for oneself
kwayâtastâ– VAI place (it) in readiness, put (it) aside in readiness

REALLY
mitoni IPC really [*cf.* mêtoni]
tipiyaw IPC personally, really

RECENTLY
âstamispî IPC more recently

RECOGNISE
nisitawêyihcikâtê– VII be recognised
nisitawêyim– VTA recognise s.o.

REFRIGERATOR
âhkwatihcikan– *NI* refrigerator; freezer

REFUGE
nâtâmototaw– *VTA* flee to s.o., seek refuge with s.o.

REGRET
mihtât– *VTI* regret s.t.
wiyakâc *IPC* it is regrettable [*predicative*]

REJECT
asên– *VTA* reject s.o.
asên– *VTI* reject s.t., turn s.t. back; shirk s.t., run away from s.t.
âtawêyiht– *VTI* reject s.t.

RELATED
itâhkôm– *VTA* be thus related to s.o., have s.o. as such a relative, use such a kin-term for s.o.
wâhkôm– *VTA* be related to s.o.
–wâhkômâkan– *NDA* relative [*e.g.*, niwâhkômâkanak]

RELEASE
mêki– *VAI* give (it/him) away, release (it/him); give (her) in marriage
pakitin– *VTA* let s.o. go, release s.o.; permit (it) to s.o.
pakitin– *VTI* let s.t. go, release s.t., give s.t. up; put s.t. in (*e.g.,* seed potatoes)

RELIANCE
mamisî– *VAI* place reliance

RELIEVE
wayawî– *VAI* go outside; go to relieve oneself; leave school, leave hospital
wayawîstamâso– *VAI* go outside for oneself, go to relieve oneself

RELIGION
ayamihâwin– *NI* prayer, saying prayers; religious observance; religion; the Roman Catholic Church

RELIGIOUS
ayamihêwâtisi– *VAI* be of religious disposition

RELY
mamisîtotaw– *VTA* rely on s.o.

REMEMBER
kiskisi– *VAI* remember
kiskisopayi– *VAI* think of something, suddenly remember
kiskisototaw– *VTA* remember s.o.

REMIND
kiskisôm– *VTA* remind s.o. [*also* -o-]
kiskisômito– *VAI* remind one another [*also* -o-]

RENT
awih– *VTA* lend (it/him) to s.o.; rent (it/him) out to s.o.
awihiwê– *VAI* lend (it/him) to people; rent (it/him) out to people

REPORTEDLY
  êsa *IPC* reportedly
RESERVE
  tipahaskân– *NI* reserve
RESIDENCE
  ihtâwin– *NI* abode, place of residence
  kihci-wîki– *VAI* live formally; [*Christian:*] live in residence
RESIST
  iyisâho– *VAI* resist, resist temptation, exercise restraint
  iyisâhowin– *NI* resistance, resisting temptation, restraint
RESPECT
  manâcih– *VTA* treat s.o. with respect
  manâcihtâ– *VAI* treat (it) with respect
  manâcim– *VTA* speak to s.o. with respect, speak of s.o. with respect
RESPOND
  naskomo– *VAI* respond, make a verbal response
REST
  ayiwêpi– *VAI* rest, take a rest
RESULT
  ohcipayin– *VII* come from there, result from that
RETURN
  kîwê– *VAI* return home
  kîwêtot– *VTI* return home to s.t.
  kîwêtotaw– *VTA* return home to s.o.
RIDE
  pôsih– *VTA* make s.o. board a conveyance, give s.o. a ride
RIDING
  têhtapîwitâs– *NA* riding breeches
RIGHT
  kwayask *IPC* properly, right
  sêmâk *IPC* right away, immediately
RING
  âhcanis– *NA* ring
  kihci-wîkihtowin-âhcanis– *NA* wedding ring
ROCK
  asiniy– *NA* rock, stone [*e.g.,* asiniy kâ-kîsisot 'quick-lime']
ROLL
  titipihtin– *VII* be rolled up, be twisted
  titipin– *VTI* roll s.t. up
ROOF
  apahkwât– *VTI* make a roof over s.t.
  apahkwâtê– *VII* have a roof, be roofed

ROOM
    apîwikamikw– *NI* sitting room, living room
    ascikêwikamikw– *NI* storage room, storage building
    tawâ– *VII* be open, have room

ROOT
    ocêpihk– *NI* root
    ocêpihkis– *NI* little root [*diminutive*]

ROUND
    wâwiyêyâ– *VAI* be round

RUIN
    misiwanâcihiso– *VAI* ruin oneself, destroy oneself; commit suicide
    misiwanâcihtâ– *VAI* ruin (it), destroy (it)
    misiwanâtan– *VII* be ruined, be destroyed

RUN
    ispahtâ– *VAI* run there or thus
    kisipipayin– *VII* come to an end, run out
    manêsi– *VAI* have run out of (it), lack (it)
    mâcipayin– *VII* begin to run (*e.g.,* tape-recorder) [*]
    nôhtêpayi– *VAI* run short, be in want
    sipwêpayin– *VII* start off to run (*e.g.,* tape-recorder) [*]
    wayawîpahtâ– *VAI* run outside

SACKING
    maskimotêkinw– *NI* sacking, cloth from flour-sacks

SADDLE LAKE
    onihcikiskwapiwinihk *INM* [*place-name:*] Saddle Lake, Alberta [*locative;*
    ?literally at the place of the indistinct dark figure]

SAME
    pêyakwan *IPC* the same

SARCI
    sasîwiskwêw– *NA* Sarci woman

SASKATOON
    misâskwatômin– *NI* saskatoon berry

SAUSAGE
    otakisîhkân– *NI* sausage

SAW THROUGH
    kîskipotâ– *VAI* saw (it) through

SAY
    it– *VTA* say thus to s.o., say thus of s.o.
    it– *VTI* say thus of s.t., say thus about s.t.
    itito– *VAI* say thus to one another, say thus about one another
    itwê– *VAI* say thus

SCATTER
    pîwêwêpin– *VTI* scatter s.t., sprinkle in a pinch of s.t.

SCHOOL
–**îci-kiskinohamawâkan**– *NDA* fellow student, school-mate
  [*e.g.,* nîci-kiskinohamawâkanak]
kiskinohamâkosiwin– *NI* being a student, going to school; schoolwork,
  homework
kiskinohamâtowikamikw– *NI* school, school-house
wîci-kiskinohamâkosîm– *VTA* be in school with s.o., have s.o. as a
  fellow-student

SCOLD
itâspinêm– *VTA* call s.o. thus in anger, angrily call s.o. such a name, thus
  scold s.o. in anger
kîhkâm– *VTA* scold s.o.

SCRAPE
kâskah– *VTI* scrape s.t. off
mihkit– *VTI* scrape s.t. (meat) off the hide
yôskipotâ– *VAI* soften (it) by scraping (*e.g.,* hide)

SCRATCHY
kâsisi– *VAI* be sharp, be scratchy (*e.g.,* wool)

SEAT
apiwinis– *NI* seat, chair

SECRETLY
kîmôc *IPC* secretly, stealthily

SEE
wâpaht– *VTI* see s.t.
wâpahtih– *VTA* make s.o. see (it), show (it) to s.o.
wâpam– *VTA* see s.o.

SEED
kiscikânis– *NA* grain, seed [*diminutive*]
kiscikêsi– *VAI* plant seeds; have a small garden [*diminutive*]
kistikân– *NA* grain, seed; sheaf of grain
kistikê– *VAI* seed things, plant things
pîwi-kiscikânis– *NA* garden seeds [*diminutive*]

SEEMINGLY
tâpiskôc *IPC* as if, seemingly, apparently

SELF-ESTEEM
pîwêyimo– *VAI* think little of oneself, have low self-esteem; [*Christian:*] be
  humble

SELL
atâwâkê– *VAI* sell things

SEND
itisahamaw– *VTA* send (it/him) to s.o. thus

SENSE
môsihtâ– *VAI* sense (it), feel (it)

SEPARATE
    paskêwihito– *VAI* leave one another; separate, divorce

SETTLE DOWN
    wâskamisî– *VAI* settle down; be of quiet disposition

SETTLEMENT
    ôtênaw– *NI* town, settlement

SEVEN
    têpakohp-askiy *IPC* seven years

SEVENTEEN
    têpakohposâp *IPC* seventeen

SEVERE
    âhkwâtisi– *VAI* be stern, be sharp, be of severe disposition

SEW
    âniskôkwât– *VTI* sew s.t. on as an extension
    kaskikwâso– *VAI* sew, do one's sewing
    kaskikwât– *VTI* sew s.t.
    kaskikwâtamaw– *VTA* sew (it/him) for s.o.
    kaskikwâtamâso– *VAI* sew (it/him) for oneself
    kaskikwâtiso– *VAI* sew for oneself
    kispakikwât– *VTI* sew s.t. thickly
    moscikwâso– *VAI* sew by hand
    moscikwât– *VTI* sew s.t. by hand
    nanâtohkokwâso– *VAI* sew patchwork blankets
    nihtâwiminakinikê– *VAI* be good at sewing on beads
    piskihcikwât– *VTI* sew an extension on s.t.
    pîhtawêkwât– *VTI* sew s.t. as lining into a garment; sew s.t. in between
        covers, sew covers on s.t.
    sakâpât– *VTI* attach s.t. by sewing, sew s.t. on
    titipikwanah– *VTI* sew s.t. in overcast stitch (*e.g.*, the spiral loops around
        the vamp of a moccasin)

SEWING MACHINE
    kaskikwâsopayihcikanis– *NI* sewing machine [*diminutive*]
    kaskikwâsopayihcikâkê– *VAI* do machine-sewing with (it), use (it) to
        machine-sew
    kaskikwâswâkan– *NI* sewing machine

SHACK
    asiskîwikamikos– *NI* mud shack [*diminutive*]

SHAKE
    pahpawiwêpin– *VTI* shake s.t. out
    pawin– *VTI* shake s.t. out

SHAME
    nêpêwih– *VTA* shame s.o., put s.o. to shame

SHARP
kâsisi– VAI be sharp, be scratchy (*e.g.,* wool)
misipocikê–, VAI run things (*e.g.,* hide) over a sharp edge
misipotâ– VAI run (it) (*e.g.,* hide) over a sharp edge

SHE
wiya PR he, she

SHEAF
kistikân– NA grain, seed; sheaf of grain

SHEEP
mâyatihkopîway– NI sheep's fleece; wool

SHIELDED
âkô IPV covered, shielded

SHIRT
papakiwayân– NI shirt

SHOCKED
sisikotêyiht– VTI be surprised, be shocked

SHOE
maskisin– NI moccasin, shoe

SHORT
kwîtawêyihcikâtê– VII be missed, be in short supply
kwîtâpacihtâ– VAI be short of (it) to use, lack tools
nôhtêpayi– VAI run short, be in want

SHOW
nôkohtâ– VAI let (it) appear, show (it)
wâpahtih– VTA make s.o. see (it), show (it) to s.o.

SHY
nêpêwisi– VAI be ashamed, be shy

SIBLING
–îtisân– NDA sibling [*e.g.,* nîtisânak]
–sîmis– NDA younger sibling [*e.g.,* nisîmis]
osîmimâw– NA youngest sibling
osîmimâwi– VAI be the youngest sibling
osîmisi– VAI have a younger sibling, have (him/her) as younger sibling
owîtisâni– VAI have a sibling, have (her/him) as sibling [*sic:* o-]

SICK
âhkosi– VAI be sick
mâyamahciho– VAI fare ill, be sick
otâhkosiw– NA sick person
paswêskôyo– VAI get sick from eating excessively fatty food

SIDE
âh–âyîtaw IPC on both sides [*reduplicated*]
ohpimê IPC off to the side, elsewhere
yîkatêhtê– VAI walk off to the side; [*Christian:*] walk away

yîkatêpayin– *VII* move off to the side, move sideways (*e.g.*, braided strips of rabbitskin)

yîkatêstaw– *VTA* go off to the side from s.o., go away from s.o.

SILLY

môhcowi– *VAI* be crazy, be silly

SIMPLY

nânitaw *IPC* simply; something, anything; something bad, anything bad

sôskwâc *IPC* simply, immediately, without further ado

SINEW

astinwân– *NI* sinew

SINGLE

môsâpêwi– *VAI* be a bachelor, be unmarried, be single

pêyak *IPC* one; alone, single

pêyakw-ây– *NA* a single one (*e.g.*, stocking); one pair [*e.g.*, pêyakw-âyak]

SISTER

–kâwiy– *NDA* mother, mother's sister [*e.g.*, kikâwînawak]

–kâwîs– *NDA* mother's sister; step-mother [*e.g.*, nikâwîs]

–mis– *NDA* older sister [*e.g.*, omisa]

–ôhkom– *NDA* grandmother, grandmother's sister, great-aunt [*e.g.*, nôhkom]

–sikos– *NDA* father's sister, mother's brother's wife; mother-in-law, father-in-law's brother's wife, aunt [*e.g.*, nisikosak]

omisi– *VAI* have an older sister, have (her) as older sister

omisimâw– *NA* oldest sister

SISTER-IN-LAW

–câhkos– *NDA* female cross-cousin; sister-in-law (woman speaking) [*e.g.*, nicâhkos]

SIT

api– *VAI* sit, be situated; stay

aspapi– *VAI* sit against something, sit on something (*e.g.*, blanket)

ay-api– *VAI* sit, be seated [*reduplicated*]

mâmawôpi– *VAI* sit together, hold a meeting

nahapi– *VAI* sit down in one's place, be properly seated

nîpêpi– *VAI* sit up with someone dead or dying; hold a wake

nîswapi– *VAI* sit as two, be situated as two, come together as two [*]

tâpapîstamaw– *VTA* sit in s.o.'s place, succeed s.o. in office

wîtapim– *VTA* sit with s.o.

SIX

nikotwâsik *IPC* six

SIXTY

nikotwâsomitanaw-askiy *IPC* sixty years

SIZE
ispîhcâ– *VII* extend thus, be of such size (*e.g.*, country)

SLEEP
katikoni– *VAI* sleep over, spend the night
nipâ– *VAI* sleep, be asleep

SLICE
tâsawisâwât– *VTI* cut into the middle of s.t., slice s.t. open
(*e.g.*, veal belly cordon-bleu)

SLIP
pîhtawêsâkân– *NI* slip, undergarment

SLOUGH
îhkatawâw– *NI* slough, marsh

SMALL
apisâsin– *VII* be small
apiscis– *VTI* cut s.t. into small pieces
apiscisasi– *VAI* cut (it) into very small pieces [*diminutive; cf.* apiscis–]
apisîsisi– *VAI* be small
pîkinis– *VTI* cut s.t. into small pieces
sikos– *VTI* chop s.t. small

SMOKE
kaskâpahtê– *VII* be smoked
kaskâpas– *VTI* smoke s.t.
kaskâpasw– *VTA* smoke s.o.
kaskitêwâpahtê– *VII* give off black smoke
osikwânâs– *VTI* smoke-dry s.t.
osikwânâstê– *VII* be smoke-dried
pîhtwâwin– *NI* smoking; [*Christian:*] cannabis abuse

SO
ihtasi– *VAI* be so many, be as many
isko *IPC* so far
isko *IPV* so far
iyikohk *IPC* so much, to such an extent
tahto *IPC* so many, as many
tahto-aya *IPC* so many [*sic:* -o-]
tahtw-âskiy *IPC* so many years, as many years
tahtwâw *IPC* so many times
tânitahto *IPC* how many; so many
tânitahto-pîsim *IPC* how many months; what month is it [*predicative*]; so
many months
tânitahtwâw *IPC* how many times; so many times

SOAP
kisêpêkinikan– *NI* soap

SOCK
  asikan– *NA* sock, stocking
  nâpêwasikan– *NA* men's socks
SOFT
  yôskâ– *VII* be soft
  yôskipotâ– *VAI* soften (it) by scraping (*e.g.,* hide)
SOIL
  asiskiy– *NI* earth, soil, dirt; clay
  asiskîwihkwê– *VAI* have soil on one's face, have dirt on one's face
  wiyipâ– *VII* be soiled, be dirty
SOLDIER
  simâkanisihkâniwi– *VAI* be a soldier; take part in war
      (*e.g.,* World War II)
SOME
  âtiht *IPC* some
SOMEONE
  awiyak *PR* someone, somebody; [*in negative clause:*] anyone, anybody;
      [*indefinite; e.g.,* awiyak, awiya]
SOMETHING
  kîkway *PR* something, thing; [*in negative clause:*] anything, any; [*indefinite*]
  nânitaw *IPC* simply; something, anything; something bad, anything bad
SON
  –kosis– *NDA* son [*e.g.,* okosisa]
SOON
  kiyipa *IPC* soon
  mayaw *IPC* as soon as
  wîpac *IPC* soon, early
SORES
  môskipayi– *VAI* break out in a rash, in sores (*e.g.,* with thrush)
SORRY
  kitimâkinâso– *VAI* pity oneself, feel sorry for oneself
SOUND
  miyoht– *VTI* like the sound of s.t.
  takahkihtâkwan– *VII* sound nice
SOUP
  mîcimâpoy– *NI* broth, soup
SPARE
  kayâcic *IPC* the spare, the surplus [*?sic; both record and gloss highly
      tentative*]
SPEAK
  âkayâsîmo– *VAI* speak English
  kisîkitot– *VTA* speak to s.o. in anger [*sic:* -î-]
  kitot– *VTA* speak to s.o., address s.o.

manâcim– *VTA* speak to s.o. with respect, speak of s.o. with respect

nêhiyawê– *VAI* speak Cree

nêhiyawêwin– *NI* speaking Cree, the Cree language

pîkiskwât– *VTA* speak to s.o.'

pîkiskwê– *VAI* speak

pîkiskwêh– *VTA* make s.o. speak, get s.o. to speak

pîkiskwêstamaw– *VTA* speak for s.o., speak on s.o.'s behalf

SPEECH

miyo-pîkiskwêwin– *NI* good speech; [*Christian:*] the good news

pîkiskwêwin– *NI* what is being said, speech; word; voice

SPILL

sîkipicikê– *VAI* spill things

SPIRIT

miyomahciho– *VAI* fare well, feel well, be in good health or spirit

pawâmiwin– *NI* spirit power; [*Christian:*] witchcraft

SPIRITUAL

kiskêyihtamâ– *VAI* have spiritual knowledge

SPOUSE

–wîkimâkan– *NDA* spouse, housemate [*e.g.,* niwîkimâkan]

SPREAD

anâskê– *VAI* spread a blanket

SPRING

miyoskamin– *VII* be early spring

SPRINKLE

pîwêwêpin– *VTI* scatter s.t., sprinkle in a pinch of s.t.

siswêwêpin– *VTI* sprinkle s.t. about (*e.g.,* ashes in cleaning)

STAND

cimatê– *VII* stand erect

itaskitê– *VII* stand thus (*e.g.,* lodges)

nîpawi– *VAI* stand, stand up, stand erect, stand fast

nîpawistamaw– *VTA* stand up for s.o., be a witness (*e.g.,* at wedding) for s.o.

START

mâcatoskê– *VAI* start to work [*sic:* -c-, -a-]

sipwê *IPV* departing, leaving, starting off

sipwêpayin– *VII* start off to run (*e.g.,* tape-recorder) [*]

STARTLE

koskoh– *VTA* startle s.o., surprise s.o.

STARVE

nipahâhkatoso– *VAI* starve to death, die from starvation

STAY

api– *VAI* sit, be situated; stay

kisât– *VTI* stay with s.t., hold fast to s.t.

STEAL
kimoti– *VAI* steal (it); be a thief
otin– *VTA* take s.o., steal s.o.
otin– *VTI* take s.t., steal s.t.

STEALTHILY
kîmôc *IPC* secretly, stealthily

STEEL
pîwâpiskw– *NI* metal, metal object; steel blade

STEER
ayêhkwêsis– *NA* young castrated bull; steer [*diminutive*]

STEP-FATHER
–ôhcâwîs– *NDA* father's brother; step-father [*e.g.,* ôhcâwîsa]

STEP-MOTHER
–kâwîs– *NDA* mother's sister; step-mother [*e.g.,* nikâwîs]

STERN
âhkwâtisi– *VAI* be stern, be sharp, be of severe disposition

STICK OUT
sâkamon– *VII* stick out, project
sâkêkamon– *VII* stick out as cloth, project as cloth

STIFF
sîtawâ– *VII* be stiff

STILL
âhci piko *IPC* still, nevertheless [*adversative*]
êyâpic *IPC* still [*also* kêyâpic]

STITCH
titipikwanah– *VTI* sew s.t. in overcast stitch (*e.g.,* the spiral loops around the vamp of a moccasin)

STOCKING
asikan– *NA* sock, stocking

STONE
asiniy– *NA* rock, stone [*e.g.,* asiniy kâ-kîsisot 'quick-lime']

STOP
kâh-kipîhci *IPC* stopping now and then [*reduplicated*]
nakî– *VAI* stop, come to a stop

STORAGE
ascikêwikamikw– *NI* storage room, storage building

STORE
atâwêwikamikw– *NI* store
otatâwêw– *NA* store-keeper, store-manager
otatâwêwi– *VAI* be the store-keeper, be the store-manager

STORY
âcimo– *VAI* tell things, tell a story
âcimostaw– *VTA* tell s.o. about (it), tell s.o. a story

âcimostâto– *vai* tell one another about (it), tell stories to one another
âcimowin– *ni* story, what is being told
âcimôh– *vta* make s.o. tell about (it), make s.o. tell a story
itâcimo– *vai* tell thus, tell a story thus
itâcimostaw– *vta* tell s.o. thus about (it), tell s.o. such a story

STOVE
kotawânâpiskw– *ni* stove [*sic:* NI]

STRAIGHTEN
mînom– *vta* straighten s.o. out, correct s.o. verbally

STRAIN
wîhkô– *vai* strain oneself, use all one's force

STRANGE
pîtos *ipc* strange, different

STRAWBERRY
otêhiminâni-cêpihk– *ni* strawberry root [*sic; cf.* ocêpihk–]

STRENGTH
maskawisîwin– *ni* strength

STRETCH
sêsâwipayi– *vai* stretch, become stretched
sîpah– *vti* stretch s.t.

STRIKE
pakamahw– *vta* strike s.o., hit s.o.

STRING
pîminahkwânis– *ni* string [*diminutive*]

STRONG
maskawâ– *vii* be hard, be strong
maskawâtisi– *vai* be strong, be of strong disposition
maskawisî– *vai* be strong

STUDENT
–îci-kiskinohamawâkan– *nda* fellow student, school-mate
  [*e.g.,* nîci-kiskinohamawâkanak]
kiskinohamawâkan– *na* student
kiskinohamâkosi– *vai* be a student, be in school
kiskinohamâkosiwin– *ni* being a student, going to school; schoolwork,
  homework

SUBSEQUENTLY
mwêstas *ipc* later, subsequently

SUCCEED
tâpapîstamaw– *vta* sit in s.o.'s place, succeed s.o. in office

SUCK
nôni– *vai* suck at the breast, be nursed

SUCKLE
nôh– *vta* suckle s.o., nurse s.o.

SUDDENLY
  kêtahtawê *IPC* suddenly; at one time

SUFFER
  kakwâtakihtâ– *VAI* suffer because of (it), have difficulties because of (it)
  kakwâtakî– *VAI* suffer, have difficulties

SUICIDE
  misiwanâcihiso– *VAI* ruin oneself, destroy oneself; commit suicide
  nipahiso– *VAI* kill oneself, commit suicide

SUMMER
  awasi-nîpinohk *IPC* the summer before last
  nîpin– *VII* be summer

SUNDAY
  ayamihêwi-kîsikâw– *NI* Sunday
  tahtw-âyamihêwi-kîsikâw *IPC* every Sunday

SUPPLY
  kwîtawêyihcikâtê– *VII* be missed, be in short supply

SURELY
  kêhcinâ *IPC* surely, for certain

SURFACE
  waskic *IPC* on top, on the surface

SURPLUS
  ayiwâkipayi– *VAI* have more than enough, have a surplus, have plenty
  kayâcic *IPC* the spare, the surplus [*?sic; both record and gloss highly tentative*]

SURPRISE
  koskoh– *VTA* startle s.o., surprise s.o.
  sisikotêyiht– *VTI* be surprised, be shocked

SUSTAIN
  pimâcih– *VTA* make s.o. live, give life to s.o.; make a living for s.o., sustain s.o.

SWAY
  wâhkêyêyiht– *VTI* be easily swayed; [*Christian:*] be too weak

SWEAT
  apwêsi– *VAI* sweat, perspire
  apwêsiwin– *NI* sweating, labouring

SWEEP
  wêpahikê– *VAI* sweep things, do the sweeping

TABLE
  mîcisowinâhtikw– *NI* dining table, table

TAIL-HAIR
  misatimwâyow– *NI* horse-tail; tail-hair of a horse

TAKE
  itohtah– *VTA* take s.o. there or thus

itohtatâ– *VAI* take (it) there or thus

kîwêhtah– *VTA* take s.o. home

kîwêhtatâ– *VAI* take (it) home

nîhtin– *VTI* take s.t. down, unload s.t.

ohtin– *VTI* take s.t. from there, obtain s.t. from there

ohtinikê– *VAI* take things from there, obtain things from there

otin– *VTA* take s.o., steal s.o.

otin– *VTI* take s.t., steal s.t.

otinikowisi– *VAI* be taken by the powers

otinito– *VAI* take one another; marry each other

pahkwatin– *VTI* take s.t. off by hand (*e.g.,* caked dirt from laundry)

papâmohtah– *VTA* take s.o. about, take s.o. here and there

papâmohtatâ– *VAI* take (it) about, take (it) here and there

pîhtokwah– *VTA* take s.o. inside

wîsâm– *VTA* ask s.o. along, take s.o. along

TALK

mâmiskôm– *VTA* talk about s.o., discuss s.o.

mâmiskôt– *VTI* talk about s.t., discuss s.t.

môskomo– *VAI* talk oneself into crying, cry while talking

TALL

iskosi– *VAI* be so tall, be of such height

kinosi– *VAI* be long, be tall

kinwâ– *VII* be long, be tall

TASTE

wîhkasin– *VII* taste good

wîhkist– *VTI* like the taste of s.t.

TEA

kisâkamisikê– *VAI* heat a liquid; make tea

TEACH

kiskinahamaw– *VTA* teach s.o., teach (it) to s.o. [*; *sic:* -a-; *cf.* kiskinohamaw–]

kiskinohamaw– *VTA* teach s.o., teach (it) to s.o.

kiskinohamâkê– *VAI* teach things

kiskinohamâso– *VAI* teach oneself

kiskinohamâto– *VAI* teach one another

kiskinohamâtowin– *NI* teaching, education

kiskinowâpahtih– *VTA* teach s.o. by example

kiskinowâpahtihiwê– *VAI* teach people by example

okiskinohamâkêw– *NA* teacher

TEAM

nîswahpiso– *VAI* be harnessed as two, be a team of two

TEAR

kîskicihcêpit– *VTA* tear s.o.'s hand off, tear s.o.'s finger off

yâyikâskocin– *VAI* tear one's clothes on wood (*e.g.,* in bush)

yîwêyâskocin– *VAI* tear one's clothes ragged on wood (*e.g.,* in bush)

TELL

âcim– *VTA* tell s.o., tell something to s.o.

âcimo– *VAI* tell things, tell a story

âcimostaw– *VTA* tell s.o. about (it), tell s.o. a story

âcimostâto– *VAI* tell one another about (it), tell stories to one another

âcimôh– *VTA* make s.o. tell about (it), make s.o. tell a story

âtot– *VTI* tell about s.t.

itâcimo– *VAI* tell thus, tell a story thus

itâcimostaw– *VTA* tell s.o. thus about (it), tell s.o. such a story

wîhtamaw– *VTA* tell s.o. about (it/him)

wîhtamâto– *VAI* tell one another about (it/him)

TEMPT

yêyih– *VTA* get s.o. excited by one's action, tempt s.o. by one's action

TEND

kitimâkinaw– *VTA* take pity upon s.o., lovingly tend s.o.

pamih– *VTA* tend to s.o., look after s.o.

pamihiso– *VAI* tend oneself, look after oneself

pamihtamaw– *VTA* tend to (it/him) for s.o., look after (it/him) for s.o.

pamihtamâso– *VAI* tend to (it/him) for or by oneself, look after (it/him) for or by oneself

pamin– *VTA* tend to s.o., look after s.o.

pamin– *VTI* tend to s.t., look after s.t.

paminiso– *VAI* tend to oneself, look after oneself

paminiwê– *VAI* tend to people, look after people

TENDER

kaskâciwahtê– *VII* be boiled until tender

kaskâciwas– *VTI* boil s.t. until tender

THANK

nanâskom– *VTA* thank s.o., speak words of thanks to s.o.

THAT

ana *PR* that [*demonstrative; e.g.,* ana, aniki, anihi; anima, anihi]

êkotowahk *IPC* of that kind

êkotowihk *IPC* in that place

êwako *PR* that one [*resumptive demonstrative; e.g.,* êwako, êkonik, êkoni; êwako, êkoni]

THEN

êkospî *IPC* then, at that time

êkwa *IPC* then; and

ispî *IPC* at such a time, then

pêci-nâway *IPC* from back then; down from the distant past

THENCE
ohci *IPC* thence, from there
ohci *IPV* thence, from there; [*in negative clause:*] past
THERE
anita *IPC* at that place, there
awasitê *IPC* further over there
êkota *IPC* there, at that place
êkotê *IPC* over there
ita *IPC* there
itê *IPC* there, over there
nêtê *IPC* over there
ôtê *IPC* over there
THEY
wiyawâw *PR* they
THICKLY
kispakikwât– *VTI* sew s.t. thickly
THIN
papakiwayânêkinw– *NI* thin cloth, cotton; canvas
THING
kîkway *PR* something, thing; [*in negative clause:*] anything, any; [*indefinite*]
THINK
ayiwâkêyim– *VTA* think more of s.o., regard s.o. more highly
itêyiht– *VTI* think thus of s.t.
itêyim– *VTA* think thus of s.o.
kihcêyiht– *VTI* think highly of s.t.
kihcêyihtamaw– *VTA* think highly of (it/him) for s.o.
kihcêyihtâkwan– *VII* be highly thought of
kihcêyim– *VTA* think highly of s.o.
mâmitonêyiht– *VTI* think about s.t., worry about s.t.
mâmitonêyihtêstamâso– *VAI* think about (it/him) for oneself, plan for oneself
mâmitonêyim– *VTA* think about s.o., worry about s.o.
pîwêyimo– *VAI* think little of oneself, have low self-esteem; [*Christian:*] be humble
THIRTEEN
nistosâp *IPC* thirteen
THIS
awa *PR* this [*demonstrative; e.g., awa, ôki, ôhi; ôma, ôhi*]
itowahk *IPC* this kind
itowihk *IPC* in this place
THOUGHT
itêyihtâkwan– *VII* be thus thought of
mâmitonêyihcikan– *NI* mind; thought, worry

THREAD
  sêstakw– NA yarn, thread
THREE
  nisti– VAI be three in number
  nisto IPC three
  nistopiponwê– VAI be three years old
  nistw-âskiy IPC three years
THROUGH
  kîskatah– VTI chop s.t. through
  kîskipotâ– VAI saw (it) through
THROW
  akociwêpin– VTA throw s.o. over top (*e.g.,* onto willow bushes)
  akociwêpin– VTI throw s.t. over top (*e.g.,* onto willow bushes)
  sôhkêhtatâ– VAI throw (it) hard, throw (it) forcefully
  wêpin– VTA throw s.o. away; abandon s.o. (*e.g.,* child)
  wêpin– VTI throw s.t. away
THUS
  êkos îsi IPC thus, in that way; that is how it is
  êkosi IPC thus, in this way
  isi IPC thus
  isi IPV thus
  ômisi IPC thus
THWARTED
  pwâtawihtâ– VAI be thwarted at (it), fail of (it)
TIE
  nîswahpit– VTI tie s.t. together as two (*e.g.,* bones)
  tahkopit– VTI tie s.t. fast
TIME
  êkwayâc IPC only now, for the first time [*]
  ispî IPC at such a time, then
  kinwês IPC for a long time
  nistam IPC first, at first, for the first time
TIMES
  tahtwâw IPC so many times
  tânitahtwâw IPC how many times; so many times
TIPI
  mîkiwâhp– NI lodge, tipi
TIRED
  kihtimêyiht– VTI be tired of s.t.
TODAY
  anohc IPC now, today
TOGETHER
  mâmawi IPN all together, all as a group [*e.g.,* mâmawi-ayisiyiniw–]

mâmawi-wîcihitowin– *NI* all helping together, general cooperation

mâmawôhkamâto– *VAI* work together at (it/him) as a group

mâmawôpi– *VAI* sit together, hold a meeting

nîsôhkamâto– *VAI* work together at (it/him) as two

TOILET

mîsîwikamikw– *NI* outhouse, toilet

wayawîwin– *NI* going outside, going to the toilet [*]

TOO

osâm *IPC* too much; because

TOOL

âpacihcikan– *NI* tool, appliance, machine

âpacihcikanis– *NI* small tool, small appliance [*diminutive*]

TOP

akociwêpin– *VTA* throw s.o. over top (*e.g.*, onto willow bushes)

akociwêpin– *VTI* throw s.t. over top (*e.g.*, onto willow bushes)

pâskac *IPC* to top it all

waskic *IPC* on top, on the surface

TORMENTED

kakwâtakêyiht– *VTI* be tormented, be tormented about s.t.

TOWEL

pâhkohkwêhon– *NI* towel

pâhkohkwêhonis– *NI* small towel [*diminutive*]

TOWN

ôtênaw– *NI* town, settlement

TRACE

masinihtatâ– *VAI* trace (it), use (it) as pattern

TRAIN

pôsiwin– *NA* train

takwâpôyo– *VAI* arrive by rail, arrive by train

TRANSGRESS

patinikê– *VAI* make a mistake, take a wrong step, transgress; [*Christian:*] sin

pâstâho– *VAI* breach the natural order, transgress; [*Christian:*] sin, be a sinner

TRAP

nôcihcikê– *VAI* trap things

nôcihcikêwaskiy– *NI* trapping territory, trapline

tasôh– *VTA* trap s.o. under something, catch s.o. in a trap

wanihikê– *VAI* set traps

TRAVEL

itâciho– *VAI* travel thus, lead one's life thus

itâcihowin– *NI* travelling thus, leading one's life thus

kiyôtê– *VAI* visit afar, travel to visit

pimohtatâ– *VAI* carry (it) along, travel with (it)

TREAT

manâcih– *VTA* treat s.o. with respect

manâcihtâ– *VAI* treat (it) with respect

tôtaw– *VTA* do (it) to s.o., treat s.o. so

TRIPE

wînâstakay– *NI* "tripe", paunch (*i.e.,* largest stomach of ruminant)

TROUBLE

nayêhtâwan– *VII* be difficult, be troublesome [*]

nayêhtâwêyim– *VTA* find s.o. difficult, find s.o. troublesome

nayêhtâwipayi– *VAI* run into difficulties, experience trouble

TROUSERS

–tâs– *NDA* leggings, trousers, pants [*e.g.,* mitâsa]

TRUE

tâpwê *IPC* truly, indeed

tâpwêwakêyiht– *VTI* hold s.t. to be true, believe in s.t.

TRUNK

mistikowat– *NI* wooden box, trunk

TRY

kakwê *IPV* try, attempt to

TUB

mahkahkw– *NI* barrel, tub

TURN

âpotah– *VTI* turn s.t. upside down, turn s.t. inside out

kwêskî– *VAI* turn around

wâskân– *VTI* make s.t. go around, turn s.t. (*e.g.,* treadle), crank s.t.

TWICE

nîswâw *IPC* twice [*]

TWISTED

titipihtin– *VII* be rolled up, be twisted

TWO

nîsi– *VAI* be two in number

nîso *IPC* two

nîsôhkamâto– *VAI* work together at (it/him) as two

nîsw-âskiy *IPC* two years

nîsw-âyamihêwi-kîsikâw *IPC* two weeks

nîswahpiso– *VAI* be harnessed as two, be a team of two

nîswahpit– *VTI* tie s.t. together as two (*e.g.,* bones)

nîswapi– *VAI* sit as two, be situated as two, come together as two [*]

UGLY

mâyâtan– *VII* be ugly, be bad

UNCEASINGLY
âhkami _IPV_ persistently, unceasingly, unwaveringly

UNCOOKED
askiti– _VAI_ be raw, be uncooked (_e.g._, flour)

UNDERCLOTHES
pîhtawêsâkân– _NI_ slip, undergarment
pîhtawêwayiwinis– _NI_ underclothes, underwear

UNDERNEATH
itâmihk _IPC_ inside (_e.g._, mouth); underneath (_e.g._, one's clothes)
sêkopayin– _VII_ run beneath, go underneath, get caught underneath
sîpâ _IPV_ beneath, underneath

UNDERSTAND
nisitoht– _VTI_ understand s.t.
nisitohtaw– _VTA_ understand s.o.

UNLOAD
nîhtin– _VTI_ take s.t. down, unload s.t.

UNMARRIED
môsâpêwi– _VAI_ be a bachelor, be unmarried, be single

UPRIGHT
simacî– _VAI_ stand upright; rear up (_e.g._, horse)

UPSIDE DOWN
âpotah– _VTI_ turn s.t. upside down, turn s.t. inside out

URGE
sîhkim– _VTA_ urge s.o. by speech
sîhkiskaw– _VTA_ urge s.o. bodily

USE
âpacih– _VTA_ use s.o., make use of s.o.
âpacihtâ– _VAI_ use (it), make use of (it)
âpatan– _VII_ be used, be useful
âpatisi– _VAI_ be used, be useful
itâpatan– _VII_ be thus used, be of such use
masinihtatâ– _VAI_ trace (it), use (it) as pattern
mêstinikê– _VAI_ use things up, exhaust things, spend it all

USUALLY
mâna _IPC_ usually, habitually

UTTER
kiskiwêh– _VTI_ utter s.t. as a prophesy, utter prophesies
kiskiwêhw– _VTA_ utter prophesies to s.o., utter prophesies about s.o.

UTTERANCE
paciyawêh– _VTA_ wrong s.o. by one's utterance, provoke s.o.'s anger

VAIN
konita _IPC_ in vain

VARIOUSLY
   nanâtohk *ipc* variously, various kinds

VEGETABLE
   pîwi-kiscikânis– *NI* vegetable garden [*diminutive*]

VENERABLE
   kihcihtwâwi *IPN* of exalted character; venerable, holy
      [*e.g.,* kihcihtwâwi-côsap 'Holy Joseph']

VESSEL
   wiyâkan– *NI* dish, vessel

VISIBLE
   kîhkânâkwan– *VII* be clearly visible
   nôkosi– *VAI* be visible; be born

VISIT
   kiyokaw– *VTA* visit s.o.
   kiyokâto– *VAI* visit one another
   kiyokê– *VAI* visit people, pay a visit
   kiyôtê– *VAI* visit afar, travel to visit
   nitawâpam– *VTA* go to see s.o., go to visit s.o.

VOICE
   pîkiskwêwin– *NI* what is being said, speech; word; voice

WAGES
   sôniyâhkê– *VAI* make money; earn wages
   sôniyâw– *NA* money; wages

WAGON
   otâpânâskw– *NA* wagon, automobile

WAIL
   mawimoscikê– *VAI* pray, wail

WAIT
   cêskwa *IPC* wait; [*in negative clauses:*] not yet
   pêho– *VAI* wait

WAKE
   koskon– *VTA* wake s.o. up
   nîpêpi– *VAI* sit up with someone dead or dying; hold a wake

WALK
   mostohtê– *VAI* walk (without conveyance)
   ohtohtê– *VAI* come walking from there
   pahkopê– *VAI* walk into water
   papâmohtê– *VAI* walk about, go here and there
   pimohtê– *VAI* go along, walk along
   yîkatêhtê– *VAI* walk off to the side; [*Christian:*] walk away

WALKING
   takohtê– *VAI* arrive walking

WALKS-LIKE-A-WOLF
kâ-mahihkani-pimohtêw *INM* [*man's name:*] Walks-like-a-Wolf

WALKS-TIL-DAWN
wâpanohtêw *INM* [*woman's name:*] Walks-til-Dawn [*?sic; gloss tentative, cf.* Walks-at-Dawn, Comes-Back-at-Dawn]

WANT
nitawêyiht– *VTI* want s.t.

nitawêyihtamaw– *VTA* want (it/him) for s.o., want (it/him) from s.o.

nitawêyim– *VTA* want s.o., want (it/him) of s.o.

nôhtê *IPV* want to, desire to

WARM
kisâkamicêwâpôs– *NI* warm water [*diminutive*]

kisis– *VTI* warm s.t. up, heat s.t. up

kisiso– *VAI* be warm, be hot

kîsowâ– *VII* be warm, provide warmth

kîsowihkaso– *VAI* warm oneself by fire, keep oneself warm by fire

WARMING-STOVE
awasowi-kotawanâpiskw– *NI* warming-stove, heater [*sic:*NI]

WASH
kanâtâpâwatâ– *VAI* wash (it) clean with water

kâsîhkwâkê– *VAI* wash one's face with (it), use (it) to wash one's face

kâsîyâkanê– *VAI* wash dishes, do the dishes

kisêpêkihtakinikê– *VAI* wash a wooden floor, wash floor-boards

kisêpêkin– *VTA* wash s.o.

kisêpêkin– *VTI* wash s.t.

kisêpêkinikê– *VAI* wash things, do the laundry

kisêpêkiniso– *VAI* wash oneself

WASH-BASIN
kâsîhkwêwiyâkan– *NI* wash-basin

WASH-BOARD
sinikohtakinikan– *NI* scrubber, brush; wash-board

WATCH
asawâpam– *VTA* watch out for s.o., lie in watch for s.o.

kiskinowâpam– *VTA* watch s.o.'s example

WATER
akâmaskîhk *IPC* across the water, overseas

akohtitâ– *VAI* put (it) in water, add (it) to water (*e.g.,* boric acid)

kisâkamicêwâpôs– *NI* warm water [*diminutive*]

kisâkamitêwâpoy– *NI* hot water

kwâpikê– *VAI* go for water, haul water

nipiy– *NI* water

tahkikamâpoy– *NI* cold water

WE

niyanân *PR* we (excl.)

nîstanân *PR* we (excl.), too; we (excl.) by contrast

WE-AND-YOU

kiyânaw *PR* we-and-you (incl.)

kîstanaw *PR* we-and-you (incl.), too; we-and-you (incl.) by contrast

WEAK

nêsowâtisi– *VAI* be weak, have a weak constitution

nêsowisi– *VAI* be weak, be near death

WEAR

kikisk– *VTI* wear s.t.

kikiskaw– *VTA* wear s.o. (*e.g.*, stocking, ring)

WEATHER

kisin– *VII* be very cold weather

kîsopwê– *VII* be hot weather

WEDDING

kihci-wîkihtowin-âhcanis– *NA* wedding ring

WEED

macikwanâs– *NI* weed

wîpâcikin– *VII* grow out of place, grow wild, grow as weeds

WEEKS

nîsw-âyamihêwi-kîsikâw *IPC* two weeks

WEIGHT

yâhkasin– *VII* be light in weight

WELL

aya *IPC* ah, well [*hesitatory; cf.* ayahk, ayi]

ayahk *IPC* ah, well [*hesitatory; cf.* aya, ayi]

ayi *IPC* ah, well [*hesitatory; cf.* aya, ayahk]

miyohtah– *VTA* guide s.o. well

miyomahciho– *VAI* fare well, feel well, be in good health or spirit

miyopayin– *VII* work well, run well

WET

sâpopatâ– *VAI* get (it) thoroughly wet

WHAT

kîkw-ây– *NA* which one; what kind [*e.g.*, kîkw-âyak]

kîkwây *PR* what [*interrogative*]

WHERE

tânitê *IPC* where over there

WHICH

kîkw-ây– *NA* which one; what kind [*e.g.*, kîkw-âyak]

tâni *PR* which one [*interrogative; e.g.*, tânihi; tânima]

tânimayikohk *IPC* to which extent

WHILE
> **kanak** *IPC* for a short while
> **mêkwâ** *IPV* while, during
> **mêkwâc** *IPC* while, during
> **pita** *IPC* first, for a while

WHIP
> **pasastêhw–** *VTA* whip s.o.

WHITE
> **wâpatonisk–** *NA* white clay [*?sic* NA]
> **wâpiskâ–** *VII* be white
> **wâpiskihtakâ–** *VII* be white boards, be white floor

WHITEMAN
> **môniyâw–** *NA* non-Indian, Whiteman

WHITEWASH
> **wâpiskah–** *VTI* whitewash s.t.
> **wâpiskahikê–** *VAI* do the whitewashing

WHO
> **awîna** *PR* who [*interrogative; e.g.,* awîna]

WHY
> **tânêhki** *IPC* why

WIFE
> **–îw–** *NDA* wife [*e.g.,* wîwiwâwa]

WILD
> **wîpâcikin–** *VII* grow out of place, grow wild, grow as weeds

WILL
> **masinahikan–** *NI* book; written document, will

WILLING
> **têpêyimo–** *VAI* be content, be willing

WILLOW
> **nîpisiy–** *NI* willow, willow bush
> **nîpisîhkopâw–** *NI* stand of willows, willow-patch
> **nîpisîhtakw–** *NI* willow piece, willow trunk
> **nîpisîs–** *NI* willow branch, willow switch; little willow [*diminutive*]

WIND
> **sâpoyowê–** *VII* have the wind blowing through

WINTER
> **pipon–** *VII* be winter

WIPE
> **kâsînamaw–** *VTA* wipe (it) off for s.o.; [*Christian:*] forgive s.o.
> **kâsînamâso–** *VAI* wipe (it) off for oneself; [*Christian:*] have one's sins forgiven, obtain forgivenness
> **kâsînamâto–** *VAI* wipe (it) off for one another; [*Christian:*] forgive one another

WITH
> **wîcêhto–** *VAI* live with one another
> **wîcêw–** *VTA* accompany s.o., live with s.o.

WITNESS
> **nîpawistamaw–** *VTA* stand up for s.o., be a witness (*e.g.,* at wedding) for s.o.

WOMAN
> **iskwêw–** *NA* woman, female adult
> **kêhtêskwêw–** *NA* old woman, old lady
> **nôcokwêsiw–** *NA* old woman, old lady [*diminutive; also* nôtokwêsiw–]
> **nôtokwêsiw–** *NA* old woman, old lady [*sic; cf.* nôcokwêsiw–]
> **oskinîkiskwêw–** *NA* young woman
> **oskinîkiskwêwi–** *VAI* be a young woman
> **sasîwiskwêw–** *NA* Sarci woman

WONDER
> **matwân cî** *IPC* I believe, I wonder

WOOD-CHIPS
> **pîwihtakahikan–** *NI* wood-chips

WOOD-COCK
> **sakâwi-pihêw–** *NA* wood-cock, wood-partridge, wood-chicken

WOODEN
> **mistikowat–** *NI* wooden box, trunk
> **wîhkwêhtakâw–** *NI* corner made by wooden walls

WOODLAND
> **sakâw–** *NI* bush, woodland

WOOL
> **mâyatihkopîway–** *NI* sheep's fleece; wool

WORD
> **pîkiskwêwin–** *NI* what is being said, speech; word; voice

WORK
> **atoskât–** *VTI* work at s.t.
> **atoskê–** *VAI* work
> **atoskêstamaw–** *VTA* work for s.o., do s.o.'s work for her/him
> **atoskêwin–** *NI* work
> **mâcatoskê–** *VAI* start to work [*sic:* -c-, -a-]
> **mâmawôhkamâto–** *VAI* work together at (it/him) as a group
> **miyopayin–** *VII* work well, run well
> **pimipayin–** *VII* work, function; go on
> **waskawîstamâso–** *VAI* work for oneself, be enterprising

WORRY
> **mâmitonêyihcikan–** *NI* mind; thought, worry
> **mâmitonêyiht–** *VTI* think about s.t., worry about s.t.

mâmitonêyim– _VTA_ think about s.o., worry about s.o.

wawânêyiht– _VTI_ worry about s.t., be worried

WRAPPED UP

wêwêkapi– _VAI_ sit wrapped up, sit bundled up

WRING OUT

sîn– _VTI_ wring s.t. out

sînâskwah– _VTI_ wring s.t. out with a wooden tool

WRITE

itastê– _VII_ be placed thus; be written thus

masinah– _VTI_ mark s.t., draw s.t.; write s.t.

masinahamâso– _VAI_ draw (it) for oneself; write (it) for oneself, write oneself

masinahikâtê– _VII_ have marks, have writing; be written

masinahikê– _VAI_ write things; write, be literate

masinahikêwin– _NI_ writing; letter, character

WRONG

mâyinikêwin– _NI_ wrong-doing, evil deed

paci _IPV_ wrongly, in error

paci-tôtaw– _VTA_ wrong s.o.

paciyawêh– _VTA_ wrong s.o. by one's utterance, provoke s.o.'s anger

patinikê– _VAI_ make a mistake, take a wrong step, transgress; [_Christian:_] sin

YARN

sêstakw– _NA_ yarn, thread

YEARS

ihtahtopiponwêwin– _NI_ having so many years, the number of one's years, one's age [_sic:_ iht-; _cf._ itahtopiponwê–]

itahtopiponê– _VAI_ be so many years old [*; _sic:_ -nê-; _cf._ itahtopiponwê–]

itahtopiponwê– _VAI_ be so many years old

nikotwâsomitanaw-askiy _IPC_ sixty years

nistopiponwê– _VAI_ be three years old

nistw-âskiy _IPC_ three years

nîsw-âskiy _IPC_ two years

tahtw-âskiy _IPC_ so many years, as many years

têpakohp-askiy _IPC_ seven years

YELL

têpwât– _VTA_ call out to s.o., yell at s.o.

YES

âha _IPC_ yes [*; _cf._ êha]

êha _IPC_ yes

YONDER

nâha _PR_ that one yonder [_demonstrative, e.g.,_ nâha, nêki; nêma]

YOU

kiya PR you (sg.) [*]

kiyawâw PR you (pl.)

YOUNG

osk-ây– NA young person [*e.g.*, osk-âyak]

osk-âyiwi– VAI be young

oskayisiyiniw– NA young person [*sic:* -a-]

oski IPN young, fresh, new

oskinîki– VAI be a young man

oskinîkiskwêw– NA young woman

oskinîkiskwêwi– VAI be a young woman

oskinîkiw– NA young man

oskinîkîwiyinîsiwi– VAI be a young man

YOUNGER

–sîmis– NDA younger sibling [*e.g.*, nisîmis]

osîmisi– VAI have a younger sibling, have (him/her) as younger sibling

YOUNGEST

osîmimâw– NA youngest sibling

osîmimâwi– VAI be the youngest sibling